Resources for Teaching

The Bedford Anthology
of American Literature

VOLUME ONE

Beginnings to 1865

Prepared by

Lisa Logan

University of Central Florida

VOLUME TWO

1865 to the Present

Prepared by

Michael Soto

Trinity University

BEDFORD / ST. MARTIN'S

Boston • New York

2   1   0   9   8
f   e   d   c   b

For *information, write:* Bedford/St. Martin's, 75 Arlington Street, Boston,
MA 02116 (617-399-4000)

ISBN-10: 0-312-44650-0
ISBN-13: 978-0-312-44650-5

Instructors who have adopted *The Bedford Anthology of American Literature*
as a textbook for a course are authorized to duplicate portions of this manual for their students.

Preface

Resources for Teaching is designed to provide suggestions and ideas for instructors using one or both volumes of *The Bedford Anthology of American Literature*. Lisa Logan, the author of the material to accompany Volume One, has written widely about early American literature. An accomplished teacher, she is the recipient of the College of Arts and Sciences Excellence in Undergraduate Teaching Award at the University of Central Florida. Michael Soto, the author of the material to accompany Volume Two, is the award-winning author of *The Modernist Nation: Generation, Renaissance, and Twentieth-Century American Literature* (2004) and editor of *Teaching the Harlem Renaissance: Course Design and Classroom Strategies* (2007). He is director of the McNair Scholars Program at Trinity University, where he teaches a wide range of courses on twentieth-century American literature and cultural history.

Their manual includes a wealth of information about new scholarship on American writers as well as discussions of individual writers and works, concrete suggestions for teaching, and practical advice about classroom activities. Whether you are an experienced instructor or teaching your first American literature course, we invite you to consult this manual as a part of your teaching process. In addition, we have provided suggestions and sample syllabi based on our own experiences and our many conversations with teachers of American literature.

Preparing to Teach

For most instructors of the survey course in American literature, the central challenge is deciding which texts to assign. As every instructor knows, the canon of American literature has grown dramatically. Not only are there now many more years to cover in the history of American literature, but the canon has also expanded and become more inclusive and diverse. At the same time, class meeting times and the length of the academic quarter and semester have not changed. In most college English departments, survey courses carry a heavy burden. They are designed to accomplish at least two goals: first, to introduce American literature to students in a general education program and second, to provide the basis for more advanced study in their majors and minors. Although some departments have established criteria for these courses in the form of aims and scopes statements or curriculum guides, many of the instructors we interviewed have wide latitude in deciding goals, texts, and methods. *The Bedford Anthology of American Literature* provides a broad representation rather than comprehensive coverage. It consequently offers a rich range of choices to instructors facing the daunting task of creating syllabi and reading assignments of representative works from every period of American literature. Still, even experienced instructors of American literature find some of the choices difficult. In order to help, we have provided some sample syllabi and assignments at the back of this manual. At the same time, we know that there are many ways to structure an effective course and create imaginative assignments. If you are willing to share your syllabus and assignments with other instructors, we would like to post it on our Web site: bedfordstmartins.com/americanlit. Send it directly to our editor by clicking on the link you find there.

Using Illustrations

Each volume in *The Bedford Anthology of American Literature* includes more than two hundred illustrations, ranging from engravings published in early travel narratives and examples of Native American arts to portraits of writers, paintings, or photographs of contemporary scenes. There is also a wide range of images illustrating the history of literary and print culture, including manuscript pages, broadsides, periodicals, and the covers, frontispieces, and title pages of books. Beginning with the artwork on the covers, instructors may want to use these illustrations as departure points, asking students to consider what the images indicate about the works themselves, the initial audience, and the historical context. Some illustrations will help instructors raise questions about identity; the roles of class, gender, race, and religion; and self-representation and the representation of reality, questions that we believe offer useful prompts for a discussion of the central concerns and broader contexts of the literary texts.

Using "American Contexts"

The Bedford Anthology of American Literature includes eleven clusters of related works gathered under the heading "American Contexts," a feature designed to extend the range of the anthology by introducing additional voices and other kinds of writing, from diaries, journals, and memoirs to editorials, critical essays, political speeches, and social criticism. Although individual selections within those clusters can be assigned separately, each "American Contexts" section is presented as a coherent unit and intended to be taught as either an introduction or a conclusion to a larger period or grouping in the anthology. Some clusters invite discussion of distinctive genres – such as the diary, journal, and memoir – while others allow an opportunity to explore contested ideological issues, critical controversies, cultural developments, and responses to events like the Civil War. We have included examples of various placements of "American Contexts" in the sample syllabi. In addition, readings in "American Contexts" might be used as the basis for writing assignments or for group presentations.

Using "Through a Modern Lens"

When we began to work on *The Bedford Anthology of American Literature*, many instructors urged us to find ways of helping students connect to early writers and their works. In order to bring later perspectives to bear upon some of the writers and texts in Volume One, we have included brief sections throughout the book called "Through a Modern Lens." In addition to revealing connections across time and space, the "Through a Modern Lens" feature offers rich opportunities for discussion of a number of connected issues: the imaginative effort required to understand the attitudes, conditions, and modes of expression in earlier periods; the sometimes tense relations between later readers and writers and earlier texts; and the ongoing influence of earlier authors on writers in the twentieth century, even as the works of those later writers reveal markedly different aesthetic values, literary practices, and philosophical or religious convictions. While most instructors will want to conclude discussion of a writer with a "Through a Modern Lens," it is also possible to begin a section with one. For example, several instructors have reported that they begin "Native American Origin and Creation Stories" with "The Becoming of the Native: Man in America before Columbus," by N. Scott Momaday, the "Modern Lens" with which this section concludes.

Using Novels in the Survey Course

Many of the instructors we surveyed during our work on *The Bedford Anthology of American Literature* told us that they teach novels as a part of the survey course. In order to assist those instructors (and to retain the comfortable size of the anthology itself), the Bedford College Editions were designed. These competitively priced reprints of five of the most frequently taught American novels are Nathaniel Hawthorne's *The Scarlet Letter*, edited by Susan S. Williams (Ohio State University); Harriet Beecher Stowe's *Uncle Tom's Cabin*, edited by Stephen Railton (University of

Virginia); Herman Melville's *Benito Cereno*, edited by Wyn Kelley (Massachusetts Institute of Technology); Mark Twain's *Adventures of Huckleberry Finn*, edited by Gregg Camfield (University of the Pacific); and Kate Chopin's *The Awakening*, edited by Sharon M. Harris (University of Connecticut). The text of each work is helpfully annotated and includes a chronology of the life of the author; an illustrated introduction to the contexts and major issues of the text in its time and ours; an annotated bibliography for further reading in backgrounds, criticism, and on the World Wide Web; and a concise glossary of literary terms. The text of the work is also accessible online at an accompanying Web site (visit bedfordst martins.com/americanlit), where it can be searched electronically. Many instructors may wish to adopt one or more of these works as a part of the course. The sample syllabi at the back of this manual provide examples of how instructors might integrate these novels, and the sample assignments within each syllabus give suggestions for using them as the basis for essays, class presentations, and other student work.

Using the Companion Web Site

A companion Web site, at **bedfordstmartins.com/americanlit**, provides resources for both students and instructors, including annotated research links (LitLinks) for almost every author in the anthology, as well as for broader topics in American literature; maps, including all of the maps in the book plus access to many more at Map Central; *This Year in History*, which offers snapshots of important literary, historical, and cultural moments; additional critical essays directly related to several selections in the anthology; the instructor's manual (downloadable); and additional sample syllabi as contributed by instructors using *The Bedford Anthology of American Literature*.

Using the Instructor DVD

Archive America is designed for instructors to use in classroom presentations to help contextualize literary works in a manner that captures students' attention. The focus is on major themes in American literary history, which are brought to life through a rich collection of material that includes art, contextual documents, maps, audio recordings, and video clips. The archival format allows for maximum use and flexibility. Using the DVD, instructors can design brief presentations for class meetings.

Additional Resources for Teaching

Background Readings for Teachers of American Literature, compiled by Venetria Patton of Purdue University, is a collection of critical essays designed to provide instructors with an overview of recent changes in the field of American literary studies and a survey of its popular themes. The twenty-three readings include important scholarship, newer critical approaches, and practical ideas from experienced teachers. Organized by various approaches — such as historical context, race and ethnicity, and gender and sexuality — this professional resource is relevant to a wide range of courses in American literature, from literature surveys to graduate seminars.

Sample Syllabi

Instructors have told us of a variety of ways in which they organize their syllabi for introductory courses in American literature. While the majority of instructors choose chronological surveys, some prefer to organize their courses according to themes or genres. While the possibilities of such approaches are too numerous to be illustrated here in separate sample syllabi, some themes that instructors use are conceptions of American identity; religion and spirituality; landscape and place; the individual and the community; domesticity and marriage; race and gender; home and displacement; and war and politics. A course organized on the basis of genres might be divided into historical narratives, indigenous tales and stories, poetry, travel literature, life-writing, the short story, journals and diaries, and the essay. We have included three sample syllabi, which can be found on pages 127, 132, and 000 of this manual, as examples of how instructors might use *The Bedford Anthology of American Literature* for a historical survey course and a course emphasizing specific American writers. The syllabi are designed as general guides and are intended to suggest outlines of schedules that instructors might use. Individual instructors will want to vary readings, emphasize particular writers or periods, and adapt their courses for their particular institutional context.

Susan Belasco
Linck Johnson

Contents

American Literature, 1750–1830   39

American Literature, 1830–1865   75

The Era of Reform   77

American Facts and American Fiction   98

American Literature, 1865–1914   139

American Literature since 1945   279

VOLUME ONE
Beginnings to 1865

Literature to 1750

T*HIS SECTION OF THE ANTHOLOGY* situates early American literary production in its historical context, a time of rapid growth in technologies of print, commerce, and empire. Literary production, colonization, religion, and cultural and economic exchange are so interwoven that one must understand the early literatures of America as implicated in and dependent on these processes. Even in the case of Puritan New England, economic and religious motives spurred colonization, and in the case of the Spanish, the clash of values led to bloodshed and brutality. In most modern anthologies of American literature there is a predominance of English literature from New England, but this section makes it clear that the Americas of 1492 sustained three hundred distinct cultural groups. Native American cultures were orally based, however, and so we have fewer records of their world in literature. As travel accounts to a destination filled with opportunity for riches and land were bestsellers in Europe, they spurred immigration and Western culture flourished in North America, even as natives were exterminated through disease, displacement, enslavement, and war.

The illustrations in this section portray European views of the landscape and inhabitants against modern maps and suggest how print culture was instrumental in the colonization of the Americas. For example, instructors might use the map of early European explorations (p. 16) and Waldseemüller's *Orbis Typus Universalis* (p. 60) to demonstrate the little that was known about America in 1507. *The American Colonies* (p. 1) depicts a man in European dress holding out his hand to an African slave as a Native American observes against the background of a European settlement. These images reinforce how European ideas about North America and its inhabitants were circulated in print culture. Students might consider these illustrations alongside the renderings of Niccolò and Maffeo Polo (p. 12), Bartolome de Las Casas's *Brief Relation* (p. 15), and the seal of the Massachusetts Bay Colony (p. 22) to discuss the impact on readers of such wide-ranging portrayals of the so-called New World in print. By comparing these early representations with modern images of ancient petroglyphs and maps, today's readers can observe the ways that print culture shaped the Americas of the popular imagination during this period. This contrast can help students to identify how modern print artifacts in the anthology shape a different view that stresses cultural diversity.

Native American Origin and Creation Stories

STORIES FROM THE IROQUOIS, CHEROKEE, AKIMEL O'ODHAM (PIMA), LAKOTA, AND HUPA (pp. 33–53)

Approaches to Teaching

Although challenging to teach, Native American oral literature enables an initial understanding of the many cultures and beliefs of America's first inhabitants. However, these texts offer us only a fragment of the tales as they occurred within the culture; the rest is lost in transcription. Instructors must begin any discussion of these texts by acknowledging that the record cannot begin to recover the following: the meanings of words, the narrative persona brought to bear on the tale by the teller, the cultural differences among tribes who shared the same or similar stories, the sounds of words and the language itself, the performative nature of the tales, and the historical and cultural contexts of the actual telling. That said, an examination of these tales affords a glimpse into the fundamental beliefs and values of America's indigenous peoples. Instructors might begin by looking at the Judeo-Christian creation story in Genesis and by discussing the cultural values transmitted by that text. One major difference between Native American and Judeo-Christian views is the hierarchical and human-centered perspective of the latter; that is, the world and its nonhuman inhabitants figure much more largely in Native American tales and stories. As well, instructors can ask students what assumptions and preconceived ideas they have about Native Americans and from where these ideas come. Students often have romanticized notions of nature-loving "Indians" derived from early schooling, movies, popular culture, and even specific traditions in certain geographic regions of the United States. These ideas are no less stereotypical than those of the "savage other" that pervaded much of America's earliest literature. While reading documents from another culture, it is often difficult to discern exactly what is happening, why events are important or not, and what motivates the characters. These exercises will help alert students to these difficulties.

Classroom Issues and Strategies

In each case, instructors can begin class with fundamental questions: What does this story explain? What does the nature of the explanation offered tell you about this particular culture and what is important to it? Why does the phenomenon bear an explanation? For example, "Origin of Folk Stories" (Seneca) conveys the importance of stories and their telling and establishes rules about how, when, and under what circumstances stories will be told and responded to. It establishes the importance of family, as Gaqka is a powerless orphan, and women, because his instruction in his own value and destiny comes from his wife and her family. Similarly, "*Wohpe* and the Gift of the Pipe" (Lakota) explains the origins of the pipe, its rituals, and sacredness, and "The Boy Who Grew Up at Ta'k'imiłding" (Hupa) elucidates ceremonial dances. "How the World Was Made" (Cherokee) and "The Story of the Creation" (Pima) can be compared to the Judeo-Christian creation myth. "A Tale of the Foundation of the Great Island, Now North America" (Tuscarora) exemplifies the processes of collaboration between European and Native American cultures in its resemblance to the Judeo-Christian myths of Noah and the flood, Eve's creation from Adam's rib, and Cain and Abel.

Connections to Other Authors and Texts

Knowledge of Native American tales and stories illuminates many of the conflicts that arose when Europeans arrived in North America; by reading these tales alongside those of the early explorers and settlers, one apprehends different and incompatible world views. This section provides excellent context for later Native American writers, including Samson Occom, Jane Johnston Schoolcraft, and William Apess.

Questions for Class Discussion

1. Origin tales both preserve and offer explanations of how something came into being. Choose two origin stories from this section and explain the cultural work that the story performs. What does it teach its audience about cultural values and habits, and why is this important?

2. Consider how at least two of the stories in this section deal with the
    role and importance of one of the following:

    women   a supernatural being
    family or parents   a particular animal

3. Genesis defines relationships of power, including those between God
    and humans, men and women, and humans and animals. Discuss the
    ways that two of the tales in this section establish relationships of
    power or some other structure of relationships in the world.

4. Compare two of the following: "How the World Was Made" (Cherokee)
    or "The Story of the Creation" (Pima) or "A Tale of the Foundation of
    the Great Island, Now North America" (Tuscarora) and Genesis. What
    fundamental similarities and differences do you find in the ways these
    stories assign value, power, order, and meaning?

5. Locate a confusing passage or moment in one of the tales or stories.
    What accounts for your confusion? Explain how your understanding of
    this moment is limited by your own cultural framework(s).

Brief Bibliography

Ruoff, A. LaVonne Brown. *American Indian Literatures: An Introduction.
Bibliographic Review and Selected Bibliography.* New York: MLA, 1990.

Wiget, Andrew. *Native American Literature.* Boston: Twayne, 1985.

———. "Reading Against the Grain: Origin Stories and American Literary
History." *American Literary History* 2 (1991): 209-31.

NATIVE AMERICAN STORIES
THROUGH A MODERN LENS   (p. 54)

Momaday's essay lays bare the persistence of words and story in Native
American cultures, a persistence that bears on the culture and spirit of civilizations ancient even at the time Europeans "discovered" them but alive
and struggling to be heard today. Speaking from the position of a Native
American (Kiowa) in the United States during the last decade of the twentieth century, Momaday explicates the vital role of storytelling against the
backdrop of European conquest and history.

"The Becoming of the Native: Man in America before Columbus" could
be taught either before or after the section "Native American Origin and
Creation Stories" and before students read Columbus. The essay synthesizes these tales and stories by focusing on the fundamental role of the
spoken word in Native American cultures. English, Spanish, and French
explorers recorded their narratives of America's landscape and inhabitants

in print, and these words have remained. Momaday's point is that Native Americans, too, possessed a "spiritual comprehension of the universe, a sense of the natural and supernatural, a sense of the sacred . . . [a] sense of morality, an irresistible craving for order, beauty, appropriate behavior" (pp. 57, 58). Just as Europeans told the story of exploration and conquest, so did Native Americans "tell stories in order to affirm our being and our place in the scheme of things." Although Momaday's ancestors lacked the technology of the printing press, he argues, they "conceive[d] of the spoken word as sacred" and possessed a "profound belief in the efficacy of language." To Native Americans, words have teeth and like arrows they penetrate the world and vanquish the speaker's enemies. Words are ceremonial, ritualistic, profound, sacred, and alive. Native Americans have always used words and continue to use them; to ignore them is to perpetuate the violence wrought by early European colonizers.

Explorations and Early Encounters

The exploration and colonization of early America is inextricably linked to print culture. Early explorers' travel accounts served multiple audiences and purposes. They assured monarchs of the economic prospects of colonization, demonstrated the credibility and ensured the continued good favor of their writers, helped to set government policies, encouraged Europeans to invest time and manpower in these ventures, characterized native inhabitants of the colonies for Western readers, and, finally, they reaffirmed the superiority of Western values, religion, and culture. At the same time, European explorers brought with them disease, brutal policies and practices toward native inhabitants, and, above all, technologies of print that shaped the future of the land and its people. By delineating new names, establishing geographical boundaries, and enumerating the resources of the lands they traversed in published maps and travel accounts, European explorers transmitted religious and cultural values.

Similar to maps, early explorers' accounts participate in staking claims on the American landscape for both their sponsors and themselves. In translating the "New World" to their audiences, explorers such as Christopher Columbus, Álvar Núñez Cabeza de Vaca, and Samuel de Champlain also laid claim to these territories. It is crucial that students view these works as political, social, cultural, and historical documents that shaped response to exploration. The first European accounts of the Americas established the ways that the colonies and their inhabitants would be viewed – and treated – by Europeans throughout the colonization process. That is, the Europeans' assurance of their own cultural superiority determined and even justified the relationship of the colonists to the Americas' human and nonhuman resources.

CHRISTOPHER COLUMBUS   (p. 66)

Approaches to Teaching

Teaching Columbus's letter raises the issues of reading works in translation, surmounting students' preconceived ideas about what Columbus did
for good or for ill, and the seeming transparency of travel accounts, which
students have difficulty understanding in a literary context. Instructors
can remind students that many modern literary scholars believe that the
novel evolved from travel literature. One strategy for introducing students
to this text is to design a "discovery" exercise: students pair up with someone they don't know and convey three things about themselves without
speaking or writing words. Since Columbus is often taught at the beginning of the semester, this works as a good icebreaker as well, and it demonstrates the difficulties of communication even between those who live in
the same culture. Also helpful is the biographical information about
Columbus included in the headnote; his class background combined with
his reading of *Marco Polo* and solicitation of several monarchs before securing support is helpful in analyzing how he views and reports the New World
to his audience.

Classroom Issues and Strategies

In reporting his "discoveries" of lands and people, Columbus also reveals a
self that is dependent upon an audience for credibility, continuation of the
mission, and even, one might argue, of the self that he constructs. The
illustration that accompanied this published letter in 1494 (p. 67) is consistent with Columbus's own portrayals, including the helpless, naked,
awed Indians; the stately ship bearing the Spanish flag; and the exchange
of gifts. On the surface, the letter describes the innumerable human and
agricultural resources of the land for Columbus's economic backers. A
closer look at the language reveals the writer's relationship to his audience,
systems of power, and cultural difference. Columbus's letter is never "value
neutral." That is, those aspects of the New World that Columbus notices
(resources, the apparent docility of the people) and those that he deems
unimportant (their "hamlets" and other evidence of complex culture),
reveal his attitude of cultural superiority and, to some degree, the apparent
value system of the natives he dismisses.

Connections to Other Authors and Texts

Columbus's letter works well with the accounts by Champlain and Cabeza
de Vaca as well as with texts included in the "Colonial Settlements" section.
Smith, Bradford, Winthrop, Bradstreet (perhaps to a lesser degree), and

Rowlandson are also engaged in constructing the New World. The suggestion that this new land resembles paradise (Columbus, Smith) is contra-
dicted by Cabeza de Vaca and, especially, Bradford; Bradford's and
Rowlandson's view of a "vast and desolate Wilderness" that yields little
sustenance contrasts with the land of abundant resources Smith and
Columbus advertise.

Questions for Class Discussion

1. Who are Columbus's audiences, and how can you tell? Explain how his
   letter reveals a specific self-characterization that is tailored for these
   audiences.

2. How does Columbus view the Native Americans? Discuss his interpretation of their culture, using his language. Is there any evidence in his
   account that another interpretation is possible?

3. Characterize Columbus's view of the landscape. Given his audience,
   what does he gain or lose by proposing such a view to readers?

4. Discuss the view of either religion or commerce that Columbus reveals
   in the letter and consider how those views inform the actions he
   recounts. Are there other possible readings?

Brief Bibliography

Axtell, James. *Beyond 1492: Encounters in Colonial North America.* New
York: Oxford, 1992.

Kolodny, Annette. "Fictions of American Pre-History: Indians, Archeology,
and National Origin Myths." *American Literature* 75.4 (2003): 693–721.

West, Delno. "Christopher Columbus and His Enterprise to the Indies:
Scholarship of the Last Quarter Century." *William and Mary Quarterly:
A Magazine of Early American History and Culture* 49.2 (1992): 254–77.

ÁLVAR NÚÑEZ CABEZA DE VACA   (p. 74)

Approaches to Teaching

Cabeza de Vaca's narrative provides an account of exploration that ends
not in conquest but in captivity. The text offers an alternative to
Columbus's heroic model of conquest by introducing students to Cabeza de
Vaca's indigenous captors' cultural and economic ways of life. The text
offers a rare view into the lives of Native Americans and the devastating
impact of the early stages of colonization, including the transmission of

European diseases. However, the narrative also explains how early contact transformed the Europeans. Students may have difficulty conducting a "literary" analysis of this travel account; instructors can emphasize Cabeza de Vaca's narrative strategies with regard to the events and objects he chooses to include, how he narrates his own role (and those of the other Spanish captives) in each exchange, his attitude toward his captors and their culture, and his negotiation of his captive role for his own benefit.

Classroom Issues and Strategies

As a failed colonizer, Cabeza de Vaca describes the New World as strange, diverse, and even threatening; nevertheless, he manages to accommodate himself to the culture of his captors and survive. Because of his position as a failed conquistador, and because of his apparent friendship with and empathy for Native Americans, Cabeza de Vaca faced challenges to his credibility that other successful explorers, including Columbus, avoided in their writing. Cabeza de Vaca emphasizes the roles of chance (Providence) and intentions (effort, duty, good will), but ultimately can offer only an incredible tale with exactness and truth, a record of the diverse customs of those he encountered, which he hopes "in some way . . . may avail your Highness" (p. 77).

Connections to Other Authors and Texts

Cabeza de Vaca's selection works effectively with other tales by explorers in this section, the literature of colonial settlement, especially those of Smith, Bradford, and Rowlandson, another captive. As well, Cabeza de Vaca provides an ethnographic description of Native American cultures that might be read alongside "Native American Origin and Creation Stories" at the beginning of this volume. Finally, the selection could be considered with other captivity and slave narratives throughout Volume One of this anthology.

Questions for Class Discussion

1. What is Cabeza de Vaca's attitude toward the New World? Compare his description of and relationship to the terrain to that of Columbus.
2. Cabeza de Vaca is in the disadvantaged position of having failed the emperor and now having to account for himself. How does this position influence the narrative itself? That is, when are you aware of the narrator's disadvantaged position, and how does he communicate this to his audience?
3. What is Cabeza de Vaca's attitude toward his captors and their culture?

4. What do you make of Cabeza de Vaca's roles as tradesman and medicine man while in captivity? By including this information, how does he attempt to affect his audience and, particularly, the emperor?

5. What qualities does Cabeza de Vaca possess that qualify him as an explorer before, during, and after his captivity? How might his adaptation to Native American culture be read?

Brief Bibliography

Adorno, Rolena. "The Negotiation of Fear in Cabeza de Vaca's *Naufragios*." *Representations* 33 (Winter 1991): 163–99.

Shields, E. Thomson, Jr., and Dana D. Nelson. "Colonial Spanish Writings." *Teaching the Literatures of Early America*. Ed. Carla J. Mulford. New York: MLA, 1999. 97–111.

Silva, Alan J. "Conquest, Conversion, and the Hybrid Self in Cabeza de Vaca's *Relación*." *Post Identity* 2.1 (Winter 1999): 123–46.

SAMUEL DE CHAMPLAIN   (p. 86)

Approaches to Teaching

Many modern students will not have heard of either Cabeza de Vaca or Champlain, and instructors might begin a discussion by asking students to speculate about the reasons. The study of American history and letters has tended to focus on New England, of course, and English-speaking settlements. Excellent starting points for such a discussion and comparison to other writers are Champlain's obvious ambition as a colonizer to claim the land and its inhabitants for France, his indisputable talents as a navigator, and his politically astute negotiations with Native Americans to achieve his ends. Like Columbus, Champlain addressed his account to his king, although he certainly understood the public interest in his unusual travels and experiences, and his accounts were published in France.

Classroom Issues and Strategies

The French colonization enterprise differs significantly from that of the Spanish. The French do not aim for conquest but rather for alliance and exchange with the Native Americans. The text operates in many of the same ways as other exploration and settlement narratives. Readers should attend to how the narrator constructs his character in relationship to his audience and his project, as well as how the narrator describes the Native Americans and the landscape. Whom does the narrator believe will read this text, and what is the narrator's relationship to that audience? What language is used to describe the indigenous people and their habits, appearance, and beliefs? What is the narrator's relationship to the landscape? What interests him and how does he imagine himself in that landscape? These questions, which can be applied to any of the accounts of exploration, reveal fundamental differences between the French, English, and Spanish attitudes toward North American exploration.

Connections to Other Authors and Texts

As stated above, Champlain's text works well with other accounts of early exploration and settlement, including those of Columbus, Bradford, Cabeza de Vaca, and Smith. As well, Champlain's relations with Native Americans might be read in the context of "Native American Origin and Creation Stories," which shed light on Iroquois culture.

Questions for Class Discussion

1. Characterize Champlain's attitude toward his job as leader of an expedition, and explain his qualifications, strengths, and weaknesses.

2. What accounts for Champlain's relationship with Native Americans? That is, unlike Columbus, Champlain forms alliances with those he meets and works alongside them. How do you explain this as a strategy of colonization?

3. What is Champlain's attitude toward the land and its resources? How and why does he convey this to his readers?

4. What is the significance of Champlain's dreams, and why does he share them with his allies and with his audience?

Brief Bibliography

Coles, John W. Rev. of *Explorations and Mapping of Samuel de Champlain, 1603-1632.* By C. E. Heidenreich. *Imago Mundi* 32 (1980): 106-07.

Delâge, Denys, and Mathieu d'Avignon. "We Shall Be One People: Quebec." Trans. Michel Lavoie. *Common-Place* 3.4 (2003). 1 Sept 2005 <http://www.common-place.org/vol-03/no-04/* >.

Stevens, John A., "Adventures of Champlain in the Eastern Lake Ontario Region, 1609-1629." *Inland Seas* 59 (Spring 2003): 20-32.

Colonial Settlements

This section documents early America in writers' imaginations and in reality. That is, each of these selections is informed by a degree of idealism, whether religious, political, or economic, about an experimental society in the so-called New World. The texts included reveal a range of approaches to government, religion, industry, and secular and religious culture in English-speaking North America, including New England, Virginia, and Pennsylvania. In addition to hope and opportunity, the writers included here also reveal hardships and sometimes devastating realities, from lost faith to the deaths of loved ones.

One approach to teaching these selections is to focus on the contrast between ideals and realities. Writers such as Captain John Smith, William Bradford, and Francis Daniel Pastorius convey this contrast in their descriptions of the process of settlement, while Mary Rowlandson and Anne Bradstreet divulge the extraordinary and ordinary realities of daily life in contrast to John Winthrop's "Citty upon a hill." With time and the success of both settlement and its public relations campaign, the diversity of populations and the creation of urban centers shift America even further from the ideals of the select few who settled there originally. The "Diaries and Journals" section along with Jonathan Edwards's work illustrate a few specifics of that shift.

CAPTAIN JOHN SMITH   (p. 106)

Approaches to Teaching

Because of its idiosyncratic spelling and syntax, Smith's *Generall Historie of Virginia, New-England, and the Summer Isles* proves difficult for students to comprehend at the sentence and plot levels. Best strategies for these difficulties include reading aloud and asking students to write modern paraphrases in the margins of each paragraph. These challenges provide an opportunity to talk about print culture and the fact that no standard spelling of English words existed at this time. While students may expect the conflict between English and Native American inhabitants of colonial Virginia, Smith's account also emphasizes the conflicts among the English, including the dissipation of chosen leaders, their willingness to abandon the enterprise and return to England, and their uneasiness with Smith's management. In publishing *The Generall Historie,* Smith, who had long since returned to England, delivered a compelling eyewitness defense of his role in the colony's success and generated a model of the heroic explorer that, as Disney's version demonstrates, persists even today.

Classroom Issues and Strategies

As with other early accounts of exploration in the Americas, Smith's text exemplifies the ways that colonization was intertwined with print culture, politics, economics, and power. Smith's decision to write *The Generall Historie* coincides with his fund-raising for a return trip and is, therefore, inseparable from his desire to promote and continue to be instrumental in Virginia's development and success. The text of "The Third Book" emphasizes English relations with Native Americans and casts Smith, originally appointed as a supply officer, as an important and heroic figure. Despite his use of a seemingly objective third-person narrative voice to characterize these events, Smith's rendition of the practices of dialogue, exchange, and war with his Native American captors should be considered as one person's eyewitness perspective. That is, instructors can ask students to analyze Smith's view of Virginia, himself, Native Americans, and the colonial enterprise itself. Smith's view of what transpired while in captivity misses a deep knowledge of Powhatan cultural practices, which he deemed "savage."

Connections to Other Authors and Texts

Smith's work should be compared to that of other early explorers, including Columbus, Champlain, and Cabeza de Vaca, who was also a captive. As well, *The Generall Historie* offers a vision of a colonial experiment much like Bradford's *Of Plimoth Plantation* or Winthrop's *A Modell of Christian Charity.* These sometimes idealized visions should be compared to realities expressed by Bradstreet, Rowlandson, and even Smith and Bradford.

Questions for Class Discussion

1. Choose one word that describes how Smith characterizes himself and discuss whether or not that self-characterization remains consistent or is complicated by the events he narrates.

2. Explain how the text advances certain values that are consistent with the project of colonization or the settlers themselves. What qualities or beliefs does Smith's text value, either implicitly or explicitly?

3. How does Smith view the Native Americans with whom he deals? Explain how this view influences his account of one or more events in the text.

4. How does Smith establish and maintain a relationship with his audience(s) in *The Generall Historie?* Give examples to support your viewpoint.

5. Smith includes the now legendary tale of his "rescue" by Pocahontas during captivity, which subsequent historians and scholars have cast into doubt. What purpose do you believe this story served for Smith and his audience(s)?

Brief Bibliography

Gura, Philip F. "John Who? Captain John Smith and Early American Literature." *Early American Literature* 21.3 (1986-87): 260-67.

Read, David. "Colonialism and Coherence: The Case of Captain John Smith's *Generall Historie of Virginia.*" *Modern Philology: A Journal Devoted to Research in Medieval and Modern Literature* 91.4 (1994): 428-48.

White, Ed. "Captaine Smith, Colonial Novelist." *American Literature: A Journal of Literary History, Criticism, and Bibliography* 75.3 (2003): 487-513.

JAMESTOWN THROUGH A MODERN LENS   (p. 120)

The subject of countless reenactments, plays, fiction, children's books, a Disney movie, and even the name of a town in Iowa, Pocahontas has long captured the Western imagination even as her image, like her body during her life, has been held captive by the West. As the headnote in the anthology explains, "Pocahontas to Her English Husband, John Rolfe" uses a Native American perspective to counter the Romantic image of the "Indian princess" generated in European mythologies. Allen's poem exposes the flaws in Western renderings of Pocahontas by playing on the idea of rescue, central to the legend of the Indian girl placing her head over John Smith's before her father's axe. In this poem, Allen takes the metaphor of rescue much further. The voice of Pocahontas speaks of the Englishman John Rolfe as a "foolish child," "cradled . . . in my arms" and "chattering nonsense about a God / you had not wit to name." Like a mother, Allen's Pocahontas "pluck[ed him] / from certain death in the wilderness," where he "stumbled / as though blind." The poem emphasizes Pocahontas's protection of her "fair husband," despite his cultural view of her and her people: "a simple wanton, a savage maid, / dusky daughter of heathen sires / who cartwheeled naked through the muddy towns." John Rolfe's "firm guidance" and "husbandly rule" are treated ironically by this Native American speaker who knows too well the "ploys" and "gaudy dreams" of her European captors, represented by Rolfe, "deceiver, whiteman, father of my son."

This poem should be used after reading Smith's account of Pocahontas and also in conjunction with the seal of the Massachusetts Bay Colony (p. 22), which features a woodcut of a savage-looking Native American below the caption, "Come Over and Help Us." Students can be asked to extrapolate from Smith's account those ideas and objects that Europeans seem to value before considering the contrasting values expressed in Allen's poem. Specifically, instructors can use Allen's poem to discuss a Native American view of European invaders, their cultural beliefs and practices, and, especially, their view of Native Americans. This poem provides an opportunity to discuss the literature of colonial settlement as the product of a particular group of eyewitnesses and to consider how the record might look with other perspectives. Allen's poem uses powerful and emotional language to depict European conquest built on "the wasting of [Native American] bones."

WILLIAM BRADFORD   (p. 124)

Approaches to Teaching

Students may be predisposed to dislike the Pilgrims and Puritans, whom they sometimes consider intolerant, life-denying, self-righteous, and drab. Despite Bradford's claims to a "plaine stile," students will find *Of Plimoth Plantation* rough going and may object that it is not really "literature." Depending on their backgrounds, students may also find the biblical references baffling. Bradford's account demonstrates the complexity of early New Englanders by showing their capacity for ambivalence, misery, and overall humanity. Perhaps the most important sentence in this regard is: "And that it cost them something this ensewing historie will declare" (p. 128). Because early American texts do not resemble familiar modern genres and because students are most comfortable with novels and stories, they should be coached about how to read. That is, this text is a history, but readers in literature courses are not reading for facts. Rather, literary scholars are interested in narrative strategies, or the how and why of narrative selections and the writer's negotiation of his position with relation to the facts and his audience. Students should focus on the text and elements of its production that may have had an impact on how it appears. The literary critic looks for patterns in language, style, narrative movement, and images. Literary critics ask, How does the text work, and *why?*

Classroom Issues and Strategies

Bradford's text has three aims. First, it serves as a model for the kind of theologically based government the Separatists tried. Second, it attempts to provide a coherent and accurate history of the founding of Plymouth at a time when thousands of Puritans (who were Congregationalists and not Separatists) were migrating to New England and imperiling the experiment and its role in the English Reformation. Finally, the text serves the Puritan purpose of glorifying God. Book 1 concerns the beginnings of the colony in Europe up to the moment of settlement, and book 2 recounts what happened in the New World in the context of Bradford's broader search for the spiritual meaning of these events. That is, Bradford is writing history in the service of God, and in some ways his account of the Plymouth experiment is a way for others to know God and his ways. This process is informed by: Bradford's insistence on the role of piety or faith even in the face of doubt; the concept of Providence, the belief that God's plan is present in all action, history, and events; and the reality that it is impossible for humans who live in the world to know God and understand his signs, no matter the extent of their faith.

Connections to Other Authors and Texts

Bradford's account of separation from the Church of England and settlement in New England stands with other narratives of the New World written by Columbus, Cabeza de Vaca, Champlain, and Smith. Bradford portrays a religious model of colonization that is nonetheless caught up in cultural, political, and economic processes. His views of the landscape and its inhabitants should also be compared to those of Rowlandson and Bradstreet, who experienced the "vast and desolate Wilderness" from the perspective of mothers and wives with household responsibilities. Of course, Bradford's view of Native Americans should be contrasted with accounts of their culture depicted in "Native American Origin and Creation Stories" and also in later literature by writers who straddled both cultures, such as Samson Occom, Tecumseh, Jane Johnston Schoolcraft, and William Apess.

Questions for Class Discussion

1. How did reading this text alter your preconceived views of the Pilgrims? For example, what surprised you or what insights did you gain about these people and their way of life?

1. What images of America and its inhabitants does Bradford's text present to the reader? That is, Columbus described America as a land of plenty and its inhabitants as docile and primitive. Consider the words

Bradford chooses, and explain how his writing characterizes what he finds there.

3. What aspects of daily life under the Plymouth experiment does Bradford believe are most important to his audience, and how can you tell?

4. What is the relationship of the individual to the community in Bradford's ideal? In Plymouth's reality?

5. To what extent does the reality of the New World in book 2 match Bradford's utopian vision expressed in book 1? What is the nature of the discrepancies, and how does he reconcile them with his world view?

Brief Bibliography

Anderson, Douglas. *William Bradford's Books:* Of Plimmoth Plantation *and the Printed Word.* Baltimore: Johns Hopkins UP, 2003.

Burnham, Michelle. "Merchants, Money, and the Economics of 'Plain Style' in William Bradford's *Of Plymouth Plantation.*" *American Literature: A Journal of Literary History, Criticism, and Bibliography* 72.4 (2000): 695-720.

Westbrook, Perry D. *William Bradford.* Boston: Twayne, 1978.

PLYMOUTH PLANTATION
THROUGH A MODERN LENS   (p. 147)

Like Pocahontas, the myth of a first Thanksgiving shared by peaceful Pilgrims and Native Americans persists largely because of the predominance of early American histories and literature written by Europeans. However, as even Bradford's account reveals, the history of English relations with the native inhabitants of New England is one of brutal and merciless conflict. Although Bradford initiated the first treaty with Massasoit, chief of the Wampanoag, the English also burned hundreds of Pequot women, children, and elderly in their beds in 1637. Wamsutta James's suppressed speech on the anniversary of the Pilgrims' landing at Plymouth Rock demonstrates the long history of political, cultural, and physical conflict unleashed by this momentous landing from the perspective of Native Americans. For Wamsutta, Thanksgiving is less a cause for celebration than it is a wake-up call to all Americans about the physical, social, political, and economic oppressions placed upon America's original inhabitants by a people who, even today, persist in celebrating these same actions with "anniversaries."

This section could be used after or during the study of Bradford's *Of Plimoth Plantation.* Wamsutta's speech can be read in dialogue with

Bradford's accounts of initial contact (book 1, chapter 10) and the first Thanksgiving (Anno: 1621). Wamsutta's suppressed speech protests the dominance of European American cultural myths over Native American experiences. Students could also be asked to read Wamsutta's text before Thanksgiving break and to comment on the status of Thanksgiving as a national holiday and/or a national day of mourning. Given Wamsutta's emphasis on Europeans' greed for land and goods, instructors could also encourage discussion of Thanksgiving as the official beginning of the holiday shopping season.

JOHN WINTHROP   (p. 153)

Approaches to Teaching

Winthrop's text presents many of the same challenges as other early writers in this section, including peculiar spelling and capitalization, syntax, and unusual word usage. Moreover, his "Modell" includes traits of Puritan sermons and legal arguments that are unfamiliar to today's readers. Finally, students may find it difficult to sympathize with the emotional toll immigration took on Puritans. Instructors might consider equating the decision to leave England to a decision to live on the moon, where there are no known sources of shelter, no assurance of sustenance, and no sense that one will ever see or speak again with those one leaves behind. Students should be reminded that Winthrop was a squire and that he left behind an estate and a comfortable life because of his and other Puritans' conviction that King Charles I was corrupting the Church of England and that pure and authentic worship was an act of treason in their homeland. Winthrop uses the difficult metaphor of Christ's body to explain God's relationship to his church (the Puritan people) and peppers his speech with biblical references that serve as "proof" for his arguments, a persuasive strategy that students typically fail to recognize. Since Winthrop's "Modell" advances values central to the Puritan experiment, instructors can assist students in parsing the argument, untangling its difficult metaphors, and reinforcing the importance to the Puritans of "a Citty upon a hill." Instructors may wish to untangle for students some of Winthrop's fundamental assumptions based in his Puritan world view: for example, the Covenant of Works, the Covenant of Grace, and the idea of election. Puritans believed that all humans were born into sin since Adam and Eve's fall from paradise, when God revoked the Covenant of Works (humans can be saved by deeds); later God sent his son to implement the Covenant of Grace (humans can be saved by faith alone). Finally, Winthrop believed that God had already chosen his select group of saved souls, and these few elect were most like God himself.

Classroom Issues and Strategies

Put simply, this text is a statement of the Puritan ideal and so is vital to an understanding of their vision of themselves and America. The document is religious, political, social, and economic in nature, advancing a model of human interaction and daily living in which God has determined that "some must be rich, some poore, some highe and eminent in power and dignitie; others meane and in subjection" (p. 155). As the headnote in the anthology observes, Winthrop draws on his training as a lawyer to establish a contractual model of government and society for New England. Under this contractual model, Christ and his church (the Society of the Elect) comprise one body knitted together by bonds (ligaments) of brotherly love. In this model, all parties are equally crucial to the survival of the whole, ensuring the solidarity and existence of the community as long as its members act for the common good. Winthrop uses legal language, such as "Commerce," "speciall commission," and even "Covenant" to underscore the contractual language of their enterprise. In making this special promise to God, the community undertakes to "rejoyce together, mourne together, labour and suffer together, allwayes haveing before our eyes our Commission and Community in the worke, our Community as members of the same body" (p. 166). By entering into this covenant, the Puritans undertook the burden of representing their faith to the rest of the world; that is, they became a City on a Hill, a society of the example whose rise or fall would demonstrate God's truth and dominion to all who looked on them. Winthrop's vision ties religion to civil authority and explains why, under such a government, the private is accountable to the public.

Connections to Other Authors and Texts

Winthrop presents a utopian vision of the New World that can inform our reading of the literature of early New England in the same way that Benjamin Franklin's *Autobiography* or Ralph Waldo Emerson's "The American Scholar" or *Nature* can be used as a touchstone for understanding texts in the eighteenth and early nineteenth centuries respectively. Winthrop's "Modell" can be read alongside other early visions of the New World by explorers, such as Columbus, Cabeza de Vaca, and Bradford. Winthrop's ideas about the fundamental organizing principles of society are crucial to Bradstreet's and Rowlandson's works, which evince a sense that women operate from and negotiate in their writing rather static social positions.

Questions for Class Discussion

1. Explain the political, social, or economic implications of Winthrop's text.

2. Winthrop invites listeners to compare themselves to the Israelites journeying out of Egypt and into the promised land. What is the nature of his listeners' bondage, and what will be the nature of their promised land, according to Winthrop?

3. We often think of America as a land of independence; however, Winthrop's text emphasizes the important role of interdependence for the Puritans. Explain the nature of humans' responsibility to one another in Winthrop's model.

4. Explain how Winthrop's model may have helped travelers to the New World as they faced particular hardships similar to those described in Bradford's *Of Plimoth Plantation*.

Brief Bibliography

Bremer, Francis J. *John Winthrop: America's Forgotten Founding Father.* New York: Oxford UP, 2003.

Jalalzai, Zubeda. "Race and the Puritan Body Politic." *MELUS: The Journal of the Society for the Study of the Multi-Ethnic Literature of the United States* 29.3-4 (2004): 259–72.

Schweninger, Lee. *John Winthrop.* Boston: Twayne, 1990.

ANNE BRADSTREET   (p. 167)

Approaches to Teaching

Students are generally charmed by Bradstreet and are surprised to find a Puritan woman's writing so accessible and interesting. While her religious or esoteric poetry, such as "The Flesh and the Spirit," "As Weary Pilgrim," and "The Prologue" may be off-putting or syntactically difficult for today's readers, Bradstreet's use of personal and everyday human experience invites and rewards even the reluctant. If the class has not yet discussed poetry, a brief overview is necessary on how to approach dense syntax, unpack tangled and sometimes unfamiliar metaphors, and paraphrase at the sentence level a poem's basic thought in prose. (Further strategies for approaching poetry at a basic level can be found in the Walt Whitman section of this manual on p. 118.) As well, students can benefit from knowledge of Renaissance poetic forms, including the sonnet, and conventions, such as expressions of humility about one's poetic talents. Bradstreet was quite well read in classical Greek literature as well as the English works of Edmund Spenser and Sir Philip Sidney. Instructors can introduce students to Bradstreet's poetry by analyzing a complex poem like "The Prologue" in class or by beginning with her more personal poems to her mother or grandchildren and then moving on to more challenging subjects.

Classroom Issues and Strategies

Instructors might begin discussion of Bradstreet's work with "An Epitaph on My Dear and Ever-Honoured Mother Mrs. Dorothy Dudley . . . ," which establishes the qualities of an ideal woman in New England Puritan culture. From there, move to "The Prologue," which deliberates the apparent discrepancy between the roles of poet and woman and can be read alongside the excerpt from John Woodbridge's preface included in the headnote in the anthology. The excerpt underscores the dominant cultural linkage between a woman's proper performance of her roles as Puritan wife and mother and her written work. That is, a woman writing – and any woman's writing – might very well be unseemly, impious, immodest, or, depending on the subject matter, criminal. The issues that underpin Bradstreet's work anthologized here concern how the poet works through the relationship between public and private, poet and woman, physical and spiritual, faith and loss or doubt. Bradstreet uses the language of her training in classical literature and her experiences as a woman, mother, and wife. Her poetry ranges widely in ancient Greek and classical European allusions and the daily hardships of keeping house and bearing and raising children. One might argue that this range of imagery is Bradstreet's poetic strategy; that is, the homeliness of some of her prose made her radical expressions of love beyond the grave and women muses more bearable to her audience.

Connections to Other Authors and Texts

Because she sailed to New England on the same ship as Winthrop, Bradstreet should be considered as a Puritan poet and read alongside other Puritan writers such as Winthrop, Bradford, Taylor, Sewall, Mather, and Rowlandson. Bradstreet also works well with other women writers, such as her contemporaries Rowlandson and Knight and later writers Hannah Griffitts, Judith Sargent Murray, Phillis Wheatley, and Catharine Maria Sedgwick, whose works also concern the role of the woman writer in the New World. Finally, America's first poet and first woman poet inaugurates a tradition carried on in the works of Wheatley and Emily Dickinson.

Questions for Class Discussion

1. Using either "The Prologue" or "The Author to Her Book," discuss Bradstreet's apparent relationship to the written word – her own and those of others. Does the language or imagery of this particular poem uphold, contradict, or complicate this relationship?

2. Using "Here Follows Some Verses upon the Burning of Our House . . ." or "To My Dear and Loving Husband," discuss what life in the New World seems to mean for Bradstreet. What does the poem suggest

about how a wife/mother/woman understands her relationship to daily life?

3. Compare the poems Bradstreet writes about her mother and father, "To Her Father with Some Verses" and "An Epitaph on My Dear and Ever-Honoured Mother Mrs. Dorothy Dudley. . . .". What do her language and choice of metaphors suggest about the different roles and expectations for men and women in Puritan culture?

4. Discuss "The Flesh and the Spirit" and "As Weary Pilgrim" in the context of Puritan spiritual views. What do these poems say about Bradstreet's views on life and salvation?

5. Discuss "In Honor of that High and Mighty Princess Queen Elizabeth of Happy Memory" in relation to what you have learned about Puritan women's roles from having read Winthrop, Rowlandson, and Bradstreet's epitaph on her mother. Is this poem consistent with or in contradiction to those roles?

Brief Bibliography

Cowell, Pattie, and Ann Stanford, eds. *Critical Essays on Anne Bradstreet.* Boston: Hall, 1983.

Harvey, Tamara. " 'Now Sisters . . . Impart Your Usefulness and Force': Anne Bradstreet's Feminist Functionalism in *The Tenth Muse* (1650)." *Early American Literature* 35.1 (2000): 5–28.

Martin, Wendy. *An American Triptych: Anne Bradstreet, Emily Dickinson, Adrienne Rich.* Chapel Hill: U of North Carolina P, 1984.

Rosenmeier, Rosamond. *Anne Bradstreet Revisited.* Boston: Twayne, 1991.

BRADSTREET THROUGH A MODERN LENS   (p. 187)

Written in 1971, "Puritan Woman" makes plain Bradstreet's continuing importance to modern readers. As the headnote in the anthology explains, Bradstreet's work has occupied an important place in American literature for three and a half centuries and appealed to poets and feminists alike, who have viewed her work in the context of American rebellion, feminist resistance, and women's traditions. Rose Murray's poem was written at the beginning of an important era in American literary scholarship, when researchers began the important work of recovering lost and lesser-known writers, especially women and people of color. Murray weaves all of these contexts into a tribute to Bradstreet's language, fortitude, and spirit.

Since Bradstreet is relatively accessible, this poem might work best as a capstone activity in the classroom, bringing together all that students have learned about Bradstreet's life and work. Instructors could begin by asking students to identify those aspects of the poem that remind them of Bradstreet's own work. For example, Rose Murray's use of homely images, including sewing and spinning, are reminiscent of Bradstreet's "The Author to Her Book," which compares her parallels – poetry and the poet – with an out-of-wedlock child and his mother. As well, the poem captures juxtapositions that Bradstreet frequently uses: public and private, poet and woman, physical and spiritual, faith and loss or doubt. These moments are portrayed with irony. The works of men, "city," the slashing and shaping of the land to "God's design / The stuff of law and state" are contrasted with the small and busy work of the woman/poet/mother. The poem gains force as the poet, alone in a "bare house" draws on "neat and airy couplets" that "[i]mposed design on savage vastness / And hemmed up the ragged edge of newness / With thread from across the seas." In her lone space with her small and busy hands, the poet gathers up the remnants of civilization lost beyond the Atlantic and shapes the world anew.

MARY ROWLANDSON   (p. 190)

Approaches to Teaching

English America's first poet was a woman, Anne Bradstreet; another woman, Mary Rowlandson, authored the first narrative published in the English colonies, *The Sovereignty and Goodness of God*. A runaway best-seller in both England and the New England colonies, Rowlandson's text demonstrates the centrality of representations of women and their voices to the formation of early American print culture. This very centrality also proves controversial, even today, for students, teachers, and scholars of the narrative. Given the oppressive social structures within which New England Puritan women lived and wrote, questions arise concerning the roles of Rowlandson and the writer of the preface, Increase Mather, in authoring the text. These questions can quickly derail a close analysis of the text, which is most usefully navigated through an understanding of the basic tenets of Puritanism (original sin, the Covenant of Grace, and the concepts of election and the providential universe explained more fully in the Winthrop and Edwards sections of this manual) and the well-defined roles of Puritan "goodwives," described extensively in Ulrich (and discussed in the Bradstreet section of this manual) and in the King James Bible (Proverbs 31:10-31). Rowlandson's captivity narrative became a touchstone for all such narratives that followed, establishing a set of conventions and practices that modeled a long literary tradition. Depending on time constraints and other texts selected, familiarity with the conventions of jeremiad (see the Edwards section of this manual), conversion narrative (a personal account by a church member of his or her conversion, also discussed

in the Edwards section of this manual), and the tendency of Puritan sermons to use scriptural passages as evidence or explication of the point at
hand will be invaluable. These stylistic conventions provide a helpful context for Rowlandson's extensive scriptural references, emphasis on spiritual well-being to the exclusion of personal details, and her sometimes
moralizing tone. As well, it is important to note that a relatively educated
woman in New England would be intimately familiar with scriptural passages in the same way that we are familiar with television shows or movies
that we watch repeatedly. Rowlandson would have learned to read using the
Bible, and she would have heard scripture read on a daily basis in the home
and then at church meetings. Students are probably unaware of the bloody
and tragic context of King Philip's War but can understand and even
empathize with Rowlandson's aggressive ethnocentrism if they perceive
the siege mentality of 1675-76.

Classroom Issues and Strategies

The title page from the 1682 Cambridge edition provides an excellent
access point for discussions of New England Puritan culture and women's
roles. Unlike the London edition, entitled *A True History of the Captivity
and Restoration of Mrs. Mary Rowlandson,* this title page visually emphasizes the word *God* as the subject matter of the text, with Rowlandson's captivity and restoration serving as an example of "His Promises." While the
word *narrative* could imply a less than godly genre, here it clearly serves a
pious purpose. The author is presented as "Mrs." Mary Rowlandson, and
New England readers would recognize her name from numerous newspaper accounts of the Lancaster attack and the published rumors about this
prominent minister's wife. The title page emphasizes Rowlandson's private
roles as wife, the mother of "dear Children," and a productive family and
community member, who comes forward only when invited by upstanding
friends to write her story "for the benefit of the Afflicted." The title page
also serves as a microcosm for the text's status in print culture, as it
includes the errors made by the Native American known as "James the
Printer" ("second Addition") and advances scripture as a strategy for appre-
hending its major purposes and theme. Because of the difficulty of the language, its use of scripture, which is off-putting to some students, and the
blatant hatred she expresses for her captors, students often miss the complexity of this narrative. Familiarity with Proverbs 31:10-31 and a careful
navigation of the title page and preface produce a clear list of the Puritan
community's apparent values. It might also be helpful to remind students
that New England newspapers published false information that
Rowlandson had been forced to marry the "one-eyed" Chief John Monoco.
Students can then be asked to compare those stated values with
Rowlandson's actual narration of events, especially in the scenes in which

she eats unusual foods, exchanges items and conversation with her captors, and remarks on her state of mind following her release.

Connections to Other Authors and Texts

Rowlandson's text can be effectively compared to Cabeza de Vaca's captivity narrative, which provides a different sort of ethnography, as well as the materials on Hannah Dustin. Her theological vision aligns with Winthrop's "A Modell of Christian Charity" and contrasts with "Native American Origin and Creation Stories." Rowlandson's view of life in the wilderness teaches well alongside those of Columbus, Cabeza de Vaca, Smith, and Bradford. Bradstreet's poem "Here Follows Some Verses upon the Burning of Our House . . ." emphasizes the difficulties of material loss and the tensions between the spiritual and the physical in the New World; other poems by Bradstreet offer significant insights into the daily life of a New England Puritan woman.

Questions for Class Discussion

1. The original editor's "Preface to the Reader" (probably written by Increase Mather, a Puritan minister) characterizes the Indians as "Barbarians" and "Heathens" motivated by "causless enmity." It characterizes Rowlandson as a modest, "worthy and precious gentlewoman" who only publishes her narrative because her friends "judge it worthy of publick view" for the "benefit of the Afflicted." Discuss the extent to which the narrative proper upholds, complicates, or negates these characterizations of either Rowlandson or her captors.

2. Rowlandson's narrative was a bestseller in New England and was entitled *The Sovereignty and Goodness of God*. Rowlandson herself was under some scrutiny because of her notoriety as a captive and rumors that she had been forced to marry a "one-eyed chief." Using evidence from the narrative, how would you characterize Rowlandson's audience, and how do you think they viewed her? What evidence leads you to this conclusion?

3. Consider the roles for Puritan women presented in Bradstreet's "An Epitaph on My Dear and Ever-Honoured Mother Mrs. Dorothy Dudley . . ." In what ways does Rowlandson respond to these roles as she narrates the events of her captivity? How can this poem deepen our understanding of what is included and excluded in the narration?

4. At what points in her narrative do you feel you have access to Rowlandson's emotions or inner self (inasmuch as we define *self* today)? What enables or prevents this access? To what extent do expressions of faith enable or disable these feelings?

5. What do the specific scriptural passages Rowlandson chooses have in common? What do these patterns suggest about how the narrator wants us to view her and the captivity experience?

6. What, if anything, do you make of Rowlandson's insomnia once rescued?

Brief Bibliography

Derounian-Stodola, Kathryn Zabelle, and James Levernier. *The Indian Captivity Narrative, 1550-1900.* New York: Twayne, 1993.

Logan, Lisa. "Mary Rowlandson's Captivity and the 'Place' of the Woman Subject." *Early American Literature* 28.3 (1993): 255-77.

Ulrich, Laurel Thatcher. *Good Wives: Image and Reality in the Lives of Women in Northern New England, 1650-1750.* New York: Vintage, 1980.

EDWARD TAYLOR   (p. 229)

Approaches to Teaching

Edward Taylor was Puritan New England's most prolific poet, producing an astounding range of work in a style somewhat akin to the Metaphysical poets such as John Donne, George Herbert, and Richard Crashaw. Rich with classical allusion and biblical inspiration, Taylor's poetry often relied on a literary device known as the metaphysical conceit, the use of an unusual, sometimes surprising, and even commonplace analogy that is extended with verbal dexterity almost to the point of absurdity. The effect of this "conceit," or the bringing together of such dissimilar subjects, is to invite the reader to view the subject of the poem in an entirely new light. This strategy is especially important because so much of Taylor's poetry was devotional and spiritual; his metaphors, therefore, enable a fresh and even shocking view of God in the everyday world by a man who believed in his strong personal relationship with God. Students should be familiarized with the Puritan ideas of the covenants of grace and works; Puritans believed that humans broke their covenant with God when Adam and Eve sinned in the garden and that God sent his son to initiate a new covenant based on Christ's love.

Classroom Issues and Strategies

The poetry anthologized here falls into three distinct types: *Preparatory Meditations, God's Determinations,* and *Miscellaneous Poems.* Although

Taylor's poems were not published in his lifetime, he certainly intended them to be preserved and was aware of an audience for his writing. According to Thomas M. Davis, who studied the manuscript evidence, Taylor copied his poems into final form and then gathered them into one collection in order of their composition, with the exception of *God's Determinations* and *Preparatory Meditations,* which he set off by placing apart and at the end of the collection (Davis 16–17). Taylor's work, therefore, comprises over fifty years of writing, from the time he was a divinity student at Harvard until he made his final revisions in an aged and often illegible hand. *Preparatory Meditations,* as the headnote in the anthology points out, were poems written as private acts of devotion to God as Taylor prepared himself for Communion. They offer readers a good sense of the relationships among emotion, intellect, and spirit in one Puritan minister's mind. *God's Determinations* traces a history of God's relationship to the world, including the Fall, the arrival and crucifixion of Christ, and the possibility of redemption and salvation for the elect. In these poems, Taylor considers the amazing powers of God in homely – and, therefore, memorable – images and reveals his elation in God's spirit. Taylor's *Miscellaneous Poems* examine the poet's relationship with the everyday world, in which, like those in his congregation, he faced grief, loss, joy, and wonder. Taylor's use of metaphors from the physical universe, including a spinning wheel, a spider, a bowling alley, as well as classical and biblical allusions from his study of Greek, Hebrew, and Latin, suggest his belief in humanity's connection to God.

Connections to Other Authors and Texts

Taylor works well with other poets in this anthology, from Bradstreet to Dickinson to other writers from the Puritan era, each of whom considered a sometimes tension-filled relationship between the material and spiritual worlds. Certainly, poets such as Bradstreet, Phillis Wheatley, William Cullen Bryant, Walt Whitman, and Emily Dickinson used their work to contemplate humanity's relationship to God and spirituality. One hears in Taylor's preface to *God's Determinations* a wonder similar to Whitman's in "Song of Myself." Just as Taylor asks who made all of this, so Whitman contemplates the grass as a "handkerchief of the Lord / designedly dropped." Finally, Taylor's worldview, in which God is present in all things and events, bears comparison to later writers, such as Franklin or Emerson, who posit a more human-centered perspective.

Questions for Class Discussion

1. Using a poem from *Preparatory Meditations,* consider Taylor's apparent relationship to God. That is, how does the poem characterize the relationship of nature or the body to God or the spirit?

2. Taylor uses some unusual and unexpected metaphors to convey his point about God, sin, man, and so on. Choose one of the following metaphors and explain exactly how the image works. Then discuss why the choice of such a metaphor is significant or effective:

crumb of dust	God's court of law
a pen	curious love-knot
bird of paradise	spider, wasp, fly
bread of life	spinning wheel

3. Compare Taylor's "Upon Wedlock, and Death of Children" to Bradstreet's "Here Follows Some Verses upon the Burning of Our House." Do Taylor and Bradstreet perceive their relationships to God similarly or differently? Do they reach similar or different conclusions? How do they deal with the tension between the spiritual and physical worlds?

4. While modern readers may have a tendency to view Puritans as dour and serious, Taylor seems to find hope, joy, and even comedy in the relationship between humans and God. Choose one of Taylor's poems and discuss his comic view of the universe.

Brief Bibliography

Davis, Thomas M. *A Reading of Edward Taylor*. Newark, DE: U of Delaware P, 1992.

Eberwein, Jane Donahue. " 'Art, Nature's Ape': The Challenge to the Puritan Poet." Ed. Dorothy Z. Baker. *Poetics in the Poem: Critical Essays on American Self-Reflexive Poetry*. New York: Lang, 1997. 24-45.

Shuldiner, Michael. *The Tayloring Shop: Essays on the Poetry of Edward Taylor in Honor of Thomas M. and Virginia L. Davis*. Newark, DE: U of Delaware P, 1997.

FRANCIS DANIEL PASTORIUS   (p. 244)

Approaches to Teaching

Because of the modern translation from the German, Pastorius's letter is accessible to today's students, and Pastorius has a likeable, straightforward, and even-toned voice, especially compared to the emotional heights and depths of the Puritans. Instructors may want to explain a bit about Pietism, which focused on the importance of the individual's relationship to God and so appealed to intellectuals like Pastorius.

Classroom Issues and Strategies

Pastorius's letter serves two purposes – to provide an honest account of life in early Pennsylvania and, specifically, Germantown, which Pastorius founded, and, like Smith's *Generall Historie* and *A Description of New England*, to encourage further immigration to the colony. In contrast to Bradford and Winthrop, Pastorius's letter depicts a secular civil government that assumes a basic trust of individuals to behave according to their consciences even as it reveals a reasonable awareness of human failings. While today's students will likely find Pennsylvania or Virginia the more appealing colonies, instructors might ask students to form three delegations, each of which must argue the benefits of living in one of the three regions represented here.

Connections to Other Authors and Texts

Like Columbus's letter and Smith's *Generall Historie*, Pastorius's letter served as an advertisement to an audience whom he hoped would settle in Pennsylvania. Like Bradford and Winthrop, Pastorius articulates structures of social organization and government. Pastorius's landscape includes much of the same area that Elizabeth Ashbridge wrote about in her autobiography.

Questions for Class Discussion

1. According to Pastorius, what are some benefits to life in Pennsylvania?
2. Compare Pastorius's account of religious or civil authority to that described by either Winthrop or Bradford.
3. Compare Pastorius's account of Native Americans to that of Bradford, Smith, or Knight. What is the reason for the differences and similarities, in your opinion?
4. What qualities, revealed in his letter, make Pastorius a good leader in the colony of Pennsylvania?

Brief Bibliography

Brophy, Alfred L. "The Intellectual World of a Seventeenth-Century Jurist: Francis Daniel Pastorius and the Reconstruction of Pietist Thought." *German? American? Literature? New Directions in German-American Studies.* Ed. Winfried Fluck and Werner Sollors. New York: Lang, 2002. 43–63.

Erben, Patrick M. " 'Honey-Combs' and 'Paper-Hives': Positioning Francis Daniel Pastorius's Manuscript in Early Pennsylvania." *Early American Literature* 37.2 (2002): 157–94.

Horle, Craig, ed., et al. *Lawmaking and Legislators in Pennsylvania: A*

Biographical Dictionary. 1682-1709. Vol. 1. Philadelphia: U of Pennsylvania P, 1991. 586-89.

Learned, Marion Dexter. *The Life of Francis Daniel Pastorius, the Founder of Germantown.* Philadelphia: Campbell, 1908.

AMERICAN CONTEXTS: Colonial Diaries and Journals (p. 252)

This section illustrates the wide range of experiences in early American daily life using the written evidence that remains. As well, this selection of diaries and journals demonstrates the importance of writing to early colonial settlers and shows us how our own views of this period are sometimes, mistakenly, tied to the literature of New England only. These private writings give us insight into the daily thoughts and concerns of specific early settlers in America and reveal their habits, foibles, foodways, important occasions, prejudices, business practices, sources of amusement, and emotional and spiritual struggles. By opening a door into the lives and homes of their writers, these diaries and journals make clear the impact of regional and class differences on the lives of early settlers.

The "Diaries and Journals" section could be used at any time after students are introduced to the initial settlers (Smith, Bradford, and Winthrop) of Virginia and New England. The selections are brief, readable, and even entertaining because they reveal their writers' personalities in sometimes unexpected ways. Sewall's seriousness about the witch trials is treated in much less detail than his concern over men's wearing of wigs; Mather wrings his hands over the artful young gentlewoman who besieges him; Knight is continuously in chagrin about the rural poor; and Byrd leads an astonishing life of privilege. These glimpses into daily domestic lives make a strong argument for the complexity of early America as it made the transition from the seventeenth to the eighteenth century. Students need to be taught how to approach diaries and journals, since they will not appear "literary" to them. Instructors might consider asking students to think about the relationship between personal writing and choices; that is, one cannot write down everything that one thinks or does during a day, and so one makes decisions about what is most important to include. By analyzing the patterns of events, language, and thoughts these writers recorded, students can learn a great deal about what that individual, and even the culture he or she lived in, valued. Although diaries and journals are not plotted in the same way that novels are, students can use the same tools of literary analysis that they bring to any text.

Questions for Class Discussion

1. Samuel Sewall includes a wide range of events in his diary, such as the developments in the Salem witch trials, social gatherings, the behavior

of his children, his thoughts on slavery, public executions, and Joseph Willard's wearing of a wig. Choose one word that characterizes Sewall's diary persona and explain how his retelling of a particular event reveals that persona.

2. What are the sources of anxiety for Cotton Mather with regard to the twenty-year-old amorous gentlewoman? How do Mather's response to her and his anguished discussion of the "courtship" in his diary compare with your understanding of the role of a Puritan minister?

3. Knight's travel journal was probably written to be shared in manuscript or aloud with her friends in Boston, most of whom would not have experienced this kind of travel along the early American frontier. Discuss Knight's persona as an authority on travel or business.

4. Byrd is the only Virginian besides Smith whom we have read so far. How are his concerns or values different from those expressed by the New England writers represented in the text?

5. At some point in each diary or journal included here, the writer considers a conflict that arises from difference, including differences in gender, class, race, or religion. Select one of these differences and compare how at least two writers treat the subject in their works.

JONATHAN EDWARDS   (p. 276)

Approaches to Teaching

Even though *Sinners in the Hands of an Angry God* is the exception rather than the rule for Jonathan Edwards, students will mistakenly believe the fire-and-brimstone approach typical of him and other Puritans. The selections reprinted in the anthology, including "On Sarah Pierpont" and the excerpts from his *Personal Narrative* and *Images or Shadows of Divine Things*, can help to offset this assumption and introduce this mystical and gifted writer who writes compellingly of the beauty of God, salvation, and the physical world. Central to an understanding of Edwards are the following concepts: the Covenant of Grace, the belief that faith in Christ's love is the only path to salvation; divine Providence, or God's plan, immanent in all things and events but perhaps not always apparent to humans; and election, the notion that God has predetermined both history and salvation. In order for students to fully grasp *Sinners*, instructors should introduce the jeremiad as a literary form. Taking its name from the biblical book of Jeremiah, which foretells the destruction of a group of people who have forsaken God, the Puritan jeremiad lamented the loss of spiritual courage and action of the early New England founders and exhorted listeners to reform and return to their lost faith, lest God's wrath break out again. Finally, students should know a bit about the Puritan conversion narrative, a form of spiritual autobiography that traces the writer's initial struggle from doubt, sin, and misunderstanding of spiritual matters, trials that lead to a change of heart, to the writer's joy and peace in newfound faith.

Classroom Issues and Strategies

The initial prose poem, "On Sarah Pierpont," is a good entry to Edwards, as it reveals the qualities he admired in his future wife and that he takes up in his *Personal Narrative*. The narrative downplays the emotional aspects of spirituality in favor of a mindful, reflective, and intelligent relationship with God, which nevertheless affords him delight and even elation. Edwards's conversion narrative reveals his capacity for rich and evocative language that relies on common imagery from the physical world, such as his comparison of the soul of a Christian to "a little white flower" (p. 284). In many ways, Edwards anticipates Ralph Waldo Emerson in his turn to nature; however, while Emerson focused on nature to know himself and God, Edwards finds confirmation of God's Providence and word in his glorious creations on earth. Edwards imagines a God-centered universe, but, like John Milton's *Paradise Lost* and as *Sinners* proves, he also depicts evil with vivid immediacy. His use of the word *you*, although delivered, according to the anthology headnote, in a calm and quiet manner, must have terrified his parishioners with a sense of their own sinfulness in the service of God's enemies. But Edwards's horrific portrayal of God's wrathful power is balanced by the conclusion, when the audience is reminded of its "extraordinary opportunity" for mercy and redemption. Most of Edwards's surviving sermons emphasize grace and salvation, which he recounts in gorgeous imagery in his *Personal Narrative* and *Images or Shadows of Divine Things*. As these extended analogies show, Edwards reasoned passionately for the clear relationship between the natural, physical world and the spiritual, divine realm. To him, nature itself was an argument for intelligent design.

Connections to Other Authors and Texts

Edwards works well with other Puritan writers in the "Colonial Settlements" section, especially Taylor and the diarists and journal writers. Like Taylor, Edwards viewed the physical world as a sign of God's marvelous powers and encouraged his parishioners to do the same. Edwards's work explains, in a way that is perhaps less abstract than other writings in this section, the capacity for an individual in Puritan culture to engage in a passionate and intellectual relationship with his God. Edwards should also be compared to Emerson, as both writers saw a clear correspondence between the physical and spiritual worlds, and both saw themselves as ushering in a new age and a new kind of individual. While Emerson viewed this correspondence between earthly and divine as the impetus for social and intellectual reform, Edwards considered the natural world as evidence of God's love and vastness. By drawing on the world in which his congregation lived, he encouraged the reform of individual souls.

Questions for Class Discussion

1. Using Edwards's piece on Sarah Pierpont and his *Personal Narrative,* describe his view of the individual's proper relationship to God. Explain the role that emotion or intellect plays in this relationship.

2. According to Edwards's works, what role does nature or the physical world play in understanding God? Explain your answer using specific passages.

3. *Sinners in the Hands of an Angry God* remains Edwards's most well-known sermon. What rhetorical techniques does he employ that must have galvanized his audience?

4. Explain the role of one of the following in Edwards's works: divine Providence, original sin, Covenant of Grace, election.

5. Choose one passage from Edwards of no more than one paragraph and explain its importance to understanding Edwards's work as a whole.

Brief Bibliography

Conforti, Joseph A. *Jonathan Edwards, Religious Tradition, and American Culture.* Chapel Hill: U of North Carolina P, 1995.

Gallagher, Edward J. " 'Sinners in the Hands of an Angry God': Some Unfinished Business." *New England Quarterly: A Historical Review of New England Life and Letters* 73.2 (June 2000): 202-21.

Knight, Janice. "Learning the Language of God: Jonathan Edwards and the Typology of Nature." *William and Mary Quarterly: A Magazine of Early American History and Culture* 48.4 (1991): 531-51.

Oberg, Barbara B., and Harry S. Stout, eds. *Benjamin Franklin, Jonathan Edwards, and the Representation of American Culture.* New York: Oxford UP, 1993.

EDWARDS THROUGH A MODERN LENS   (p. 306)

Despite a very large body of work, Edwards's *Sinners in the Hands of an Angry God* continues to be his most well-known production, a sermon that typifies that which modern readers find most abhorrent in Puritan history and culture, and Robert Lowell was no exception. A literal and literary descendant of Edwards, Lowell once began a biography on the Puritan minister; Paul Mariani's biography of Lowell bears the title *Lost Puritan*. As Lowell's poem shows, Edwards's vivid depictions of souls corrupted by sin on the brink of hellfire reverberate in the modern imagination. The poem reminds readers of Edwards's uncle, whose suicide was an apparent response to despair over the unremediated state of his soul.

Instructors may want to use this selection after completing a study of Edwards or even as an essay assignment on the Puritan minister's work. Lowell dwells on Edwards's depictions of sin and God's consequent wrath. Students could be asked to consider these images of punishment without abatement and life without hope of redemption; God seems brutally, bleakly absent. To what extent do students agree that this vision matches Edwards's work? Is Edwards really a purveyor of hopelessness? Of fire and brimstone only? In their opinion, is his focus on life or on death? What is Edwards's legacy to us?

American Literature
1750–1830

THIS SECTION DEMONSTRATES how the rise of an American national literature should be understood in the context of advances in print culture, rapid and diverse population growth, and Enlightenment thought and its concomitant political ramifications, including the American Revolution and the founding of the new republic. If universal laws were thought to structure nature, society, and the human capacity to think and act, then humans were essentially equal and deserving of fairness in government, law, and education. Books, newspapers, almanacs, and periodicals disseminated these ideas — and a sense of American identity despite the diversity of readers' origins — to an increasingly literate and politically astute reading public. Print culture encouraged American citizens to participate either publicly or privately in the moral life of the new nation. Using religion, reason, and precedent, writers waged arguments in periodicals, pamphlets, and newspapers about the propriety of, capacity for, and extent to which citizens were entitled to such participation, and these arguments spilled over into fiction, poetry, and drama. Once free of England's dominance, America emerged as a postcolonial nation in something of an identity crisis. America was not England nor Europe, but what was it? American writers hastened to provide answers in their works, which, taken together, offer rich and diverse answers to Crèvecoeur's famous question, "What is an American?"

The central issues underlying this section are the conflicting definitions of *America* and *Americans* present in the literature of this period. Beginning with the personal narratives in "Writing Colonial Lives," instructors can establish the range of definitions of the American self during the eighteenth century. Although the writers here may not have known one another's works, they were certainly engaged in a conversation about the nature of citizenship, rights, and identity. The portraits of the writers are particularly useful for demonstrating how self-construction is related to print. Instructors can ask students to talk about which definitions (and the sets of values or beliefs that underpin these definitions) continue to be in play today, which are more marginal, and why. From definitions of American selves, the anthology moves to definitions of America itself, presenting a wide range of views from writers and speakers of diverse ethnic, racial, cultural, and educational backgrounds. These definitions of America and Americans become the foundation for "Literature for a New Nation," both in theory and practice. One central concept that students should know for this section is John Locke's idea of *tabula rasa*, the notion that humans enter the world as a "blank slate" but possess natural reason that enables them to make moral decisions; therefore, some Enlightenment thinkers assumed moral educability of humans. Other important concepts for this section include the role of nature as a mirror for human life in Enlightenment thought, utilitarianism, Quakerism, spiritual autobiography, the difference between federalism and Jeffersonian agrarianism (or republicanism), and the functions of copyright law and authorship in print culture.

Writing Colonial Lives

While the Puritan propensity for examining individual lives for signs of God's grace manifested itself in early New England diaries and spiritual autobiographies, eighteenth-century Enlightenment thought stressed the role of reason, natural rights, and universal laws of nature as central to each human life. Thus, the examination of the individual life became one avenue through which Enlightenment ideas were disseminated to an increasingly diverse American reading public. If Thomas Paine's *Common Sense* illustrated the extent to which definitions of the new nation were caught up in print culture, then the autobiographies in this section demonstrate the inseparability of the written word from definitions of the American self. Like the portrait of Franklin that opens this section (p. 334), each text offers a representation of an American self that is constructed by its author for a specific purpose and audience. These texts might be viewed as portraits hanging in a gallery, where each image offers a snapshot of an individual life but is also enriched by its position among all of those hanging alongside it. The portraits in this literary gallery both speak for themselves and are immersed in a conversation about what it means to be an American, how the life of an American self is inflected differently, based on ethnicity, race, gender, class, and religion.

Because the texts in this section involve historical people and events, students often have difficulty reading them from a literary perspective. Moreover, readers today live in a culture in which people regularly reveal their innermost secrets on national TV, and so students will expect no less. The emphasis on self-construction in the headnotes encourages a strategy of analysis that can help overcome these difficulties. Just as students might prepare for an important photo shoot by choosing their clothing, expression, and surroundings based on the self-image they wish to convey, so eighteenth-century writers chose those aspects of themselves they wished readers to see. Their choices are best understood in their historical context, including eighteenth-century Enlightenment thought (John Locke's concept of *tabula rasa;* Hume's utilitarianism, which explained moral principles as that which promote the greatest utility), religious movements (Quakerism), and dominant cultural ideas about women and people of color. Students will recognize that Enlightenment thought persists in contemporary culture, as Benjamin Franklin is considered a national icon and mythological figure today.

BENJAMIN FRANKLIN   (p. 340)

Approaches to Teaching

Whether they love him or hate him, students have heard of Benjamin Franklin: Founding Father writ large; the inventor of electricity and bifocals, among other things; the subject of countless children's books; the cover story in a special issue of *Time* magazine (July 7, 2003; vol. 162.1); the face on the hundred-dollar bill; and even an action figure. Early Puritan spiritual autobiographies traced writers' trials from early trouble about spiritual matters to religious conversion; captivity narratives moved from affliction to redemption and captivity to freedom. Franklin's work, on the other hand, plots his path from the "Poverty & Obscurity in which [he] was born & bred, to a State of Affluence & some Degree of Reputation in the World" (p. 344). According to Franklin's own summary, therefore, this text is a record of his public life and rise from rags to riches. At the same time, he offers a manual, a veritable self-help book, for individual success in eighteenth-century America. A familiar story to readers today, the tale of Franklin's rise parallels that of the new nation.

Classroom Issues and Strategies

The challenge of teaching Franklin's text is the very familiarity of its subject. Students tend to take the text at face value and repeat Franklin's own thesis, that is, because he worked hard and used his own native wit, he became a successful American. An examination of George Dunlop Leslie's 1762 painting of Franklin (p. 334), which opens the section "Writing Colonial Lives," offers a useful starting point for analysis. Instructors might ask students to make a list of those things they notice in the picture, such as the storm outside the window, the bells, the manuscript and quill pen, Franklin's wig and clothing, and so on. Once the list is complete, students can discuss the overall impact this portrait has on the viewer and what kind of figure Franklin presents here. Such an exercise is a microcosm of what students must do when they read *The Autobiography.* According to R. Jackson Wilson, at least two Ben Franklins are present in the text: one, a boy escaping his past and embracing his future, and another, a wise and revered old man. Wilson contends that these two Franklins suggest two kinds of readers – those looking for lessons on morality and success and those who will appreciate the irony of that earnestness in the "wily old celebrity" (*Figures of Speech: American Writers and the Literary Marketplace, from Benjamin Franklin to Emily Dickinson* [New York: Knopf, 1989]). Using this theory of two very different and sometimes overlapping Franklin personae, students can consider the ways that Franklin's various anecdotes or vignettes – including his ancestry, youth in Boston, entry into Philadelphia, and design for achieving moral perfection – operate as strategies of self-construction in his *Autobiography.*

Connections to Other Authors and Texts

Franklin's *Autobiography* works effectively next to all of the personal narratives in this section as well as those from earlier sections. When teaching Franklin alongside other autobiographies from this period, instructors can ask students to consider his work as a touchstone against which we compare and contrast other writers. Students might consider the values and talents Franklin has in his toolbox and then discuss to what extent those values and talents enable success. Franklin's portrait of himself as a representative American works well with texts in " 'To Begin the World Over Again': The Emerging Idea of 'America'" (American Contexts, p. 427). *Autobiography* defines the inhabitant of this new land differently than does Crèvecoeur's American farmer, Absalom Jones, or Tecumseh. Franklin's humor might be taught with Augustus Baldwin Longstreet's *Georgia Scenes* (p. 556).

Questions for Class Discussion

1. Many critics have read this book as a statement about American national identity. Choose one stereotypically "American" ideal (e.g., hard work, individualism, self-education) that the book conveys, and consider how and why this ideal, according to Franklin, is worth pursuing. Include in your discussion a consideration of who may or may not access this ideal according to Franklin.

2. Make a shorthand list of the memorable anecdotes Franklin tells about himself (those that really stick in your mind, e.g., walking through Philadelphia with three large puffy rolls, building the wharf, teaching himself to read, etc.). Taken as a whole, what do these anecdotes have in common, and how do they convey a certain persona to the audience?

3. Other selections you have read in this text might be classified as spiritual autobiographies, which begin with doubt about one's religious
calling, trace personal afflictions, and end in salvation or conversion.
Does Franklin's text bear any relationship to that genre? Explain the
ways that Franklin's *Autobiography* complicates or modifies this tradition of autobiography.

4. Choose one value or idea that is central to eighteenth-century
Enlightenment thought and discuss how Franklin's text upholds or
makes use of that value (for example, Deism, *tabula rasa*, utilitarianism).

Brief Bibliography

Dauber, Kenneth. "Benjamin Franklin and the Idea of Authorship."
Criticism 28.3 (1986): 255-86.

Lemay, J. A. Leo, ed. *Reappraising Benjamin Franklin: A Bicentennial
Perspective.* Newark: U of Delaware P, 1993.

Morgan, Edmund S. *Benjamin Franklin.* New Haven: Yale UP, 2002.

FRANKLIN THROUGH A MODERN LENS   (p. 372)

Franklin's status as an American cultural icon originated during his own
time and persisted into the nineteenth, twentieth, and twenty-first centuries. Mark Twain's ironic sketch reveals the extent to which Franklin's
accomplishments and his moral and economic prescriptions pervaded the
consciousness of American readers from a very young age. Responding to
the lessons Franklin offers young boys and, more importantly, the parents
of those boys, who wish for their success, Twain offers a different perspective on Franklin's didacticism. The Franklin that emerges here uses max-
ims and aphorisms to rain on the parades of scores of American boys, who
desire only to sleep, play, and goof off. Franklin's inventions are tiresome
and his work overall has the effect of informing parents of the ways that
youth could be spent more usefully.

This sketch could be used at the end of the unit on Franklin or, with the
other Modern Lens inclusions in this section, as part of a broader retrospective on the unit "Writing Colonial Lives." Students might consider
which aspects of Franklin's narrative persona Twain emphasizes and how
that emphasis is similar to or different from their analysis in class. Twain's
piece offers a view of Franklin as an icon from a late-nineteenth-century
perspective, and students might be asked to write their own reflections on
Franklin from a twenty-first-century perspective. Which values and qualities of the legendary American forefather trouble them, and which do they
embrace?

ELIZABETH ASHBRIDGE   (p. 376)

Approaches to Teaching

Ashbridge's text is gripping in its own right and significant as one of the first personal narratives written by a woman and as an example of spiritual autobiography. However, most students will require some introduction to the Quaker belief system. Instructors will need to explain that Quakers (the Religious Society of Friends) believe that everyone possesses divinity; they demand freedom from civil and ecclesiastical authorities; they consider dreams and visions as visitations of divine truth; and they use the published word to convey the Inner Light (Quaker Truths) powerfully to those both within and outside of the Society of Friends (see Daniel Shea, "Elizabeth Ashbridge and the Voice Within" in *Journeys in New Worlds: Early American Women's Narratives*, ed. William L. Andrews [Madison: U of Wisconsin P, 1990]). Puritans disagreed with and persecuted the Quakers because the latter denied important Calvinist tenets, including the doctrine of election. Furthermore, Puritan thought emphasized the reading of scripture and the power of ministers and male church leaders to interpret that scripture with authority. However, for Quakers, Inner Light depends only on the self, not on the church, ministers, election, position, or patriarchy.

In addition to information about Quakerism, students will appreciate the following rubric for Quaker autobiographies, which they can add to their knowledge of spiritual autobiography from "Literature to 1750." In "Quest for Community: Spiritual Autobiographies of Eighteenth-Century Quaker and Puritan Women," Carol Edkins outlines the elements of a Quaker life story:

Early intimations of religious questioning
Attempt to find religious life in prevailing doctrines
A record of first knowledge of Quakers
Struggle against surrender to God and the Quaker community
Submission
Entry into and defense of the Religious Society of Friends

Classroom Issues and Strategies

Like Franklin's *Autobiography*, Ashbridge's account provides a record of her life for the instruction of others, in this case an audience of Quakers. For Ashbridge, religion works in at least two ways. First, it provides the pretext for the rare narration of an early American woman's personal experiences. Second, it affords an opportunity for a first-person account of domestic abuse, the role of marital authority, and the operations of gender in eighteenth-century America. It is worth noting that men play the role of adversaries in Ashbridge's text, from her father's early rejection and the master who sexually harasses her (not included in this excerpt) to the physically and emotionally abusive Sullivan. On the other hand, Ashbridge is saved from suicidal thoughts and encounters her first spiritual vision in the form of a woman, who bears a lamp (representing the Quaker Inner Light or divine truth). Ashbridge may be said to justify her defiance of her husband and eighteenth-century mores by dint of a higher spiritual authority. That is, in following her inner voice and resisting her husband's dictates, Ashbridge is also obeying God.

Connections to Other Authors and Texts

Both Ashbridge's and Woolman's texts provide narratives of Quaker spiritual life. Ashbridge's text works well with other selections in the "Writing Colonial Lives" section because it provides the viewpoint of a woman, also a former indentured servant, who travels throughout southeastern Pennsylvania and New Jersey with her husband in search of work. Ashbridge's account, therefore, offers an alternative perspective to Franklin's success story. Her negotiation of public space, both in life and writing, compares well to Bradstreet and Rowlandson in the "Literature to 1750" section and to Wheatley and Sedgwick in this section. Finally, Ashbridge's work, like Occom's and Wheatley's, is notable for its silences, or what it does not say. Perhaps because of the constraints of the genre or time period, Ashbridge avoids criticism of her husband except insofar as she disagrees with his religious practices.

Questions for Class Discussion

1. Discuss the difference between the roles that men and women play in Ashbridge's autobiography.

2. Characterize the relationship between Ashbridge's spiritual struggles and marital problems. How does each inform or influence the other?

3. What narrative strategies does Ashbridge use to win sympathy and support from readers? Why would such strategies work at the time? Would they be successful today?

4. Invent a dialogue between Ashbridge and either Mary Rowlandson or Anne Bradstreet about religious or gender issues. What advice would either of these Puritan women give to Ashbridge?

Brief Bibliography

Bacon, Margaret Hope. *Mothers of Feminism: The Story of Quaker Women in America.* New York: Harper, 1986.

Madden, Etta M. "Quaker Elizabeth Ashbridge as 'the Spectacle & Discourse of the Company': Metaphor, Synecdoche, and Synthesis. *Early American Literature* 34.2 (1999): 171-89.

Sievers, Julie. "Awakening the Inner Light: Elizabeth Ashbridge and the Transformation of Quaker Community." *Early American Literature* 36.2 (2001): 235-62.

JOHN WOOLMAN   (p. 390)

Approaches to Teaching

While Ashbridge's account includes a great deal of narrative about her private life, Woolman's journal defines private life somewhat differently. Woolman's text epitomizes Quaker spiritual autobiography in its unswerving focus on its author's spiritual condition. Woolman omits most of his personal life except insofar as it relates to his early spiritual awakenings and the persistent challenges of life in a public and secular world to the conscience of a "Friend." Such omissions might be difficult for students to understand because they often equate private life with emotional and relationship matters. Instructors might encourage students to view Woolman's earnest and conscientious struggle to live in accordance with his dearly held beliefs as both a highly personal and emotional one; in this sense, the journal serves as a record of his commitment to his convictions. Although the document was meant as a record of one Friend's spiritual journey, as the headnote and the accolades of centuries of readers attest, Woolman's journal is an inspiring account of a man who lived his beliefs ardently and unapologetically.

Classroom Issues and Strategies

Self-construction in Quaker spiritual autobiography is focused on the individual as an exemplar of Quaker beliefs. Therefore, this genre includes those events and details that demonstrate the trials and conversion of an individual as he comes to live his life according to the Inner Light. The selection included traces Woolman's early religious awareness and questioning and his spiritual comfort in the Quaker way, including the notion of the "pure opening," in which a Friend speaks the divine truth in "meeting," which is the Quaker religious service. This theme of speaking one's heart in a pure way that honors God is important in Woolman's work and life. He is instructed by his pious parents and, in the form of waking and dreaming visions, led by a loving and merciful God. Woolman's experiences as a child and young adult demonstrate to him that God, "whose tender mercies are over all his works[,] hath placed a principle in the human mind which incites to exercise goodness toward every living creature" (p. 392). Despite his love of "mirth" and "wanton company," which seem to be Woolman's chief weaknesses, he is convinced, converted, and thereafter struggles to love God "in all his manifestations in the visible world" (p. 395). Following his conversion, Woolman faces challenges from the daily world of commerce, in which he interacts with people bent on making money, living with more than they actually need (the Quakers believed in a plain style of speech, dress, and life), and especially troubling, the keeping of slaves. Woolman's journal documents his efforts to live according to his own sacred philosophy: "[I]t is the duty of everyone to be firm in that which they certainly know is right for them" (p. 398).

Connections to Other Authors and Texts

Woolman's journal exemplifies spiritual autobiography and the inner journey of a life lived in colonial America. The events of Equiano's *Interesting Narrative* (p. 415) and Occom's *Short Narrative* (p. 403) emphasize the difficulties in this time period of practicing Woolman's central value of loving all of God's creatures as God himself does. Woolman's introspectiveness and sense of conscience supply an interesting counterpoint to Franklin's *Autobiography* (p. 342), which celebrates the importance of commerce and public life and defines morality in utilitarian terms rather than specifically Christian terms. Woolman's work anticipates the nineteenth-century ideals of Ralph Waldo Emerson, Henry David Thoreau, and Frederick Douglass in the "Era of Reform" section, by asserting unequivocally that we must live according to our own ideals and consciences.

Questions for Class Discussion

1. What are the important events and details that shape the persona of John Woolman? How do these events and details form the self Woolman presents?

2. Woolman speaks often of the value of the private versus the public, both in speech and action. According to Woolman, when must one speak or act publicly and when is it best not to do so?

3. Choose one value, such as the integrity of individual conscience, that Woolman advances in his text. Explain how this value is consistent or inconsistent with what we normally think of as the values of American culture in the eighteenth century and in the twenty-first century.

4. Select an issue, such as slave ownership or the acquisition of wealth, and imagine a dialogue between Woolman and one of the following: Equiano, Occom, or Franklin. Using the tone and speech patterns of each author, present their conversation or argument.

5. Define and discuss Woolman's views on voluntary simplicity. Imagine making a case for such a lifestyle to your peers in this class. What arguments would you use? How are your assumptions different from or similar to Woolman's?

Brief Bibliography

Banes, Ruth A. "The Exemplary Self: Autobiography in Eighteenth-Century America." *Biography: An Interdisciplinary Quarterly* 5.3 (1982): 226–39.

Rosenblatt, Paul. *John Woolman.* New York: Twayne, 1969.

Shea, Daniel B. *Spiritual Autobiography in Early America.* 1968. Madison: U of Wisconsin P, 1988.

SAMSON OCCOM   (p. 402)

Approaches to Teaching

Students may find it difficult to understand why Native Americans converted to Christianity and then became practicing missionaries among their own people. It seems clear from the historical record that Occom, along with his mother, believed that Christianity offered Native Americans the possibility of equality under God. Education offered to Native Americans was sponsored and conducted by religious organizations for the purposes of converting them. Because of its straightforward and searing portrayal of the realities of his life as an "Indian" among Christians, students have a difficult time moving beyond the story line to an analysis of how the text works. One strategy is to use the two portraits included in the anthology, "An Indian Priest" (now identified as Samson Occom) by Nathaniel Smibert on page 402 and the portrait of the Reverend Samson Occom, the "first Indian Minister that ever was in Europe" on page 410. Specifically, the undressed hair, the blanket, and the plain shirt in the former and the stylized wig, formal coat, and knee breeches of the latter, in which Occom points to a large tome, presumably the Bible, are key starting points for this discussion. Occom's text exemplifies one way in which these very different cultural and self-constructions are negotiated in print culture. He adopts the reasoned tone and appeals to reader sympathy of Western rhetoric; he deploys the repetition and cadences of Native American storytelling; and, finally, he assumes an apparently subservient position of a man of color speaking to whites even as he subverts this power dynamic through his forthright critique of their treatment of him.

Classroom Issues and Strategies

Discussion of Native American traditions may enhance students' experience of Occom's work. In *For Those Who Come After: A Study of Native American Autobiography* (Berkeley: U of California P, 1985), Arnold Krupat argues that Native American autobiography is a bicultural composition, a "frontier" where the familiar meets the other. Native American autobiography, like most ethnic autobiography, is at once a chronicle of the individual life and the story of the community to which the individual belongs. The narrative is best approached as one that speaks with the voices of two radically different cultures. While European American influences are apparent in the narrative use of established literary conventions and Christian references, also present are elements of Native American oral storytelling, which rely on cadence, repetition, and powerful imagery to convey its emotional appeal. Finally, Occom's dual cultural awareness emerges most clearly in the final lines, in which he recounts the story of the "poor Indian boy" who was whipped by his English master "because [he was] an Indian."

Connections to Other Authors and Texts

In addition to the autobiographies in the "Writing Colonial Lives" section, this text compares well to that of Native American writer Jane Johnston Schoolcraft and the speech of Tecumseh. Occom is a Christian convert, like Equiano and Phillis Wheatley, whose letter to Occom is included in the "Literature for a New Nation" section. Occom's work contrasts effectively with the romanticized vision of vanished warriors that Philip Freneau presents in "The Indian Burying Ground" (p. 502).

Questions for Class Discussion

1. Imagine that Occom has read Crèvecoeur's and Franklin's texts and that he asks one or the other for some advice. First, consider what areas of common ground these writers have. Then, imagine the conversation that Occom might have with either one of these authors. You may use either a dialogue format or describe what would happen in this conversation. How does Occom's text uphold, complicate, or reject that of either Franklin or Crèvecoeur?

2. At the end of his Short Narrative, Occom describes in a matter-of-fact way the injustice of the compensation he received for a career of ministry, compared with the normal earnings of a white minister in a similar position. Discuss the rhetorical strategies Occom deploys to handle this inequity throughout the text while maintaining reader sympathy and authorial credibility. What do such strategies manage to establish about the writer whose life story we are reading?

3. Occom gives substantial space to descriptions of his "methods" for keeping a school at Montauk and for running religious services for his Native American congregation. What is gained and lost by describing these methods in such detail and by giving comparatively little space to his family and domestic life? What "self" are readers left with, and why is that significant to the text's apparent or implicit purpose?

4. Arnold Krupat argues that Native American autobiography is a bicultural composition that narrates the coming together of two radically different cultures. The two portraits included in this anthology offer snapshots of Occom from the perspective of native and English cultures. Identify passages in Occom's text that uphold, complicate, or negate Krupat's statement. That is, compare these snapshots and then examine the text for traces of each culture.

Brief Bibliography

Elliott, Michael. " 'This Indian Bait': Samson Occom and the Voice of Liminality." *Early American Literature* 29.3 (1994): 233-53.

Nelson, Dana D. " '(I Speak Like a Fool but I Am Constrained)': Samson Occom's Short Narrative and Economies of the Racial Self." Ed. and preface by Helen Jaskoski and foreword by A. LaVonne Brown Ruoff. *Early Native American Writing: New Critical Essays*. Cambridge Studies in American Literature and Culture. 102. New York: Cambridge UP, 1996. 42-65.

Peyer, Bernd. "Samson Occom: Mohegan Missionary and Writer of the Eighteenth Century." *American Indian Quarterly* 6.3-4 (Fall-Winter 1982): 208-17.

OCCOM THROUGH A MODERN LENS   (p. 410)

James Ottery's contemporary tribute, "The Diary of Samson Occum" (p. 411), attests to the continuing importance of this forefather of Native American writing. Since the 1970s, American literary scholars have addressed the problem of a largely white male "canon" of literature, and the work of feminist, Native American, and African American scholars has been instrumental in generating anthologies that resemble the diversity of early American culture and writers. A member of the Brothertown Indian Nation and a descendant of Occom, Ottery emphasizes the importance of reading *Short Narrative* from a Native American perspective.

This poem could be assigned after the unit on Occom or "Writing Colonial Lives," or it might be introduced during the initial discussions of *Short Narrative* in order to focus on the bicultural nature of the text. Using repetition that echoes the cadences of Native American speeches and storytelling, Ottery weaves Occom's language into his own, focusing on the silences in Occom's text. In addition to the absence of details about Occom's family and personal life, Ottery evokes the figure of Occom's mother, who would have taught him his first language, converted to Christianity with him, worked for Wheelock in order to make his education possible, and finally, as a woman, would have exercised an important role in the matriarchal culture of Occom's birth and upbringing. In recovering the figure of Occom's mother and, in the final stanza, listing those things that Occom does not include, Ottery compellingly advances his point that the white man's language is inadequate to express Native American experience.

OLAUDAH EQUIANO   (p. 414)

Approaches to Teaching

According to modern scholars, Equiano invented the slave narrative genre with *The Interesting Narrative*, which uses the Western genre of spiritual autobiography to record the narrator's journey from captivity to freedom. While historians have recently uncovered evidence that Equiano may have been born in South Carolina, his account tells a representative tale of a slave's early life in Africa, the horrors of capture and transportation via the Middle Passage aboard a slave ship, his experiences as a slave in Barbados, Virginia, and Great Britain, his self-education and industry, which eventually lead to his manumission, and his religious doubts and conversion to Christianity. The headnote to the narrative quotes Equiano's address to the English houses of Parliament, to whom he appealed for the abolition of slavery: "Permit me, with the greatest deference and respect, to lay at your feet the following genuine narrative; the chief design of which is to excite in your august assemblies a sense of compassion for the miseries which the Slave-Trade has entailed on my unfortunate countrymen" (p. 415). Equiano's evocation of his audience's "compassion" is apparent in the selection included here. Whether factually true or a literary construction, Equiano's compelling account of an African youth from a loving and respectable family includes excruciating details of the Atlantic slave trade that his contemporary audience and subsequent writers found representative of such a life. In addition to securing his audience's sympathies, Equiano faced the additional problem of credibility. That is, many late-eighteenth-century readers would have doubted that an African was capable of such erudition, morality, and intellectualism; in fact, the question of whether Africans were capable of reason was important and unresolved in eighteenth-century science and philosophy and the cornerstone of pro- and antislavery arguments. Readers would have been skeptical of Equiano's depiction of the Middle Passage and the cruelties of slavery. To counter such resistance, Equiano comported himself eloquently in his narrative and gathered a formidable subscription list of influential sponsors; his efforts seem to have worked, since the text was successful in England, Ireland, and the United States.

Classroom Issues and Strategies

The engraving of Equiano on p. 414, which appeared on the title page of the first edition of *The Interesting Narrative,* serves as an excellent entry point to the text. This image of Equiano conveys the dual nature of his identity as both Englishman and African. Dressed as a gentleman in coat, collared shirt, and ruffles at the neck and sleeves, Equiano holds a Bible, symbolic of his capacity to read, his English identity (the King James Version printed in English), and his Christianity. Yet this English gentleman is also clearly an African, as evinced by his features and his dark skin. Like the portrait, the text itself consistently reminds us of the ways that Equiano narrates himself as both African and English and challenges eighteenth-century readers' assumptions about Africa as a savage and uncivilized continent peopled with cannibals. Instead, the chapter selected demonstrates the marked contrast between slavery among Africans, a practice that existed among warring nations but that placed captives as well-treated servants with an opportunity to rise from their station, and the chattel slavery that characterized the mid-Atlantic trade. Equiano humanizes Africa for his white Western readers by detailing his loving relationships with his mother and sister, the systematic cultural practices of the tribes with which he lived, and his terror at his introduction to Europeans, who behave with far more savagery than he has experienced in his short ten years. Equiano's frank portrayal of the Middle Passage culminates in a series of rhetorical questions designed to appeal to his readers' Christian morality, sympathies, and universal laws of human nature.

Connections to Other Authors and Texts

The Interesting Narrative considers life in colonial America from the perspective of an African ex-slave and so is vital to an understanding of the range of lives and experiences in eighteenth-century America. Equiano's self-education, hard work, and intelligence invite comparisons with another self-starter Benjamin Franklin. Equiano's written negotiation of the dominant culture and the challenges that face writers of color (and women) suggest important parallels to Bradstreet, Rowlandson, Ashbridge, Occom, Phillis Wheatley, and Jane Johnston Schoolcraft and contrast dramatically with Crèvecoeur's description of the typical American in letter 3 of *Letters from an American Farmer.* Finally, Equiano's narrative should be compared to others in the genre, including those of

Frederick Douglass and Harriet Jacobs, which appear in the "Era of Reform" section of "American Literature, 1830-1865."

Questions for Class Discussion

1. What values does Equiano associate with his homeland in Africa?

2. How are the values discussed in question 1 contrasted with those of the Europeans during Equiano's first encounter with them? How are the manner and customs of the Europeans distinct from those of the Africans?

3. Besides the cruelties and inhumane conditions aboard ship, what elements does Equiano include in his narrative of the Middle Passage? Why do you think he includes these details?

4. Equiano concludes his chapter with appeals to his readers in the form of rhetorical questions. Discuss the ways that these questions work with the narrative to establish an argument against slavery.

Brief Bibliography

Marren, Susan M. "Between Slavery and Freedom: The Transgressive Self in Olaudah Equiano's Autobiography." *PMLA: Publications of the Modern Language Association of America* 108.1 (1993): 94-105.

Potkay, Adam, Srinivas Aravamudan, and Roxann Wheeler. "Forum: Teaching Equiano's *Interesting Narrative*." *Eighteenth-Century Studies* 34.4 (2001): 601-24.

AMERICAN CONTEXTS: "To Begin the World Over Again": The Emerging Idea of "America"   (p. 427)

This cluster includes a selection of documents from the Revolutionary era and the decades that follow. These documents, authored by a wide range of writers – from Thomas Paine to Tecumseh, Thomas Jefferson to Absalom Jones – demonstrate that in breaking from Great Britain and building a new republic, America and its inhabitants were engaged in a difficult and even heated process of self-definition. The building of America, as the title of this section suggests, amounted to beginning the world anew; all of those elements of a nation and its citizens had to be discussed, bargained, and put into action, including politics, religion, economy, culture, and social arrangements. As this cluster makes clear, even those engaged in the nation building disagreed about what constituted America and its citizens.

Because this group of readings establishes the issues that inform the selections included in the "Literature for a New Nation" section, issues which are no less present in the "Writing Colonial Lives" section, it can be used as a bridge between the two. That is, issues of individual and national identity, which are variously defined through religious, economic, racial, gender, ethnic, cultural, or even geographic identity in the autobiographical excerpts of "Writing Colonial Lives," take on urgency in the readings in this "American Contexts" section. The arguments made here resonate in the "Literature for a New Nation" as assumptions or definitions that underpin the new American literature. That is, when reading writers as different as Philip Freneau, Phillis Wheatley, Catharine Maria Sedgwick, or Jane Johnston Schoolcraft, there is a sense that Americans agree on certain things, such as that many different people share a continent and that these people possess, according to natural universal laws, the right to freedom, property, and opinion. What should be most clear is that the founding of the new nation was intimately linked to the founding of its literature, that this process took place not just on battlefields or in Congress but also in the pages of newspapers, periodicals, and books.

Questions for Class Discussion

1. Using the documents by Paine and Jefferson, explain two or three of the most fundamental rights that those who dwell in America are said to have. How are these rights reflected in the other documents in this section?

2. Choose one "American" characteristic as defined by Crèvecoeur. Discuss how another text in this section upholds, complicates, or negates that characteristic.

3. One thread that echoes through Paine, Jefferson, and Crèvecoeur is the importance of property to Americans. Explain how either Tecumseh or Absalom Jones deepens or makes more complex our understanding of the concept of property.

4. Consider the engraving on page 428, the frontispiece to the *Massachusetts Magazine* (1790). How does this engraving connect Hannah Griffitts's and Abigail Adams's work to the others in this section? What definitions of *America* or *Americans* do these writers add?

5. In defining the rights of Americans, the authors in this section also define the American people. In this effort at definition, what differences are erased or ignored?

Literature for a New Nation

This section documents the sustained efforts of post-Revolutionary War American writers to generate a uniquely American literature that reflects the political, cultural, social, and material conditions of the new nation. In the absence of international copyright laws, periodical editors and booksellers continued the practice of reprinting British texts, which dominated American tastes and markets. Nevertheless, with the support of the burgeoning periodical press, American writers of this era, the first generation to view themselves as professional writers, persisted in laying a foundation for what they saw as a distinct American culture. To do so, they focused on uniquely American places and subjects, including the wilderness, local landscapes, rural villages, the issue of slavery, and the cultural traditions co-opted from European and native peoples that made America different from Europe.

The illustrations in this section are particularly well suited as starting points for introducing and framing the larger issues raised by the texts themselves. Asher Durand's *Kindred Spirits* (p. 466) depicts painter Thomas Cole and poet William Cullen Bryant overlooking a gorge in the Catskill Mountains. The "kindred spirits" of the title are, of course, Cole and Bryant, artists who celebrated the American landscape in their works. The scene also demonstrates the eighteenth-century concept that nature and humanity are kindred spirits and advances the idea that universal natural laws underpin all life forms: two fundamental ideas that inform the literature in this section. Although the figures of the artists are tiny in comparison to the dramatic natural scene, the painting depicts nature and humans in consonance, and it seems as if Bryant doffs his hat both in reverence to nature and to usher in the scene before him. The composition of the painting suggests that nature opens (the sky and the gorge) to meet the human figures, who stand above the landscape. The tree stump in the foreground might be an image of the natural cycle of life and death, of which both humans and nature partake, as Bryant's poem "Thanatopsis" (p. 568) reminds us. Just as this painting brings together art, nature, and humanity, so the illustration from the *Columbian Magazine* (p. 469) allegorizes America's peace and prosperity: the horn of plenty, the book, and the lyre representing, respectively, America enjoying nature's bounty, the opportunities for education, and a thriving cultural arts. As these illustrations show, America's liberal laws, abundant pristine landscape, and democratic people reinforce eighteenth-century universal and natural laws about the sanctity of the individual and the sanctity of freedom that have come to fruition in the American ideal.

The literature in this section celebrates America as a physical, cultural, and political site and influenced later writers, such as Ralph Waldo Emerson, Nathaniel Hawthorne, and Emily Dickinson. Fiction writers such as Washington Irving, Catharine Maria Sedgwick, and Augustus Baldwin Longstreet focus on specific regions from which they generate mythologies and legends. Jane Johnston Schoolcraft extends this trend by committing Native American legends to the English language and to print and making these traditions available to both Native and Anglo-American readers. In nature, Philip Freneau and Bryant locate the spirit of a democratic and diverse America. Phillis Wheatley embraces the spirit of freedom and equality that resonates in post–Revolutionary War American literature and culture but challenges her readers to take this spirit further and apply the tenets of democracy to all Americans. Taken separately and together, the texts in this section comprise a body of literature that begins to answer the question of what America and its literary tradition will become.

AMERICAN CONTEXTS: "Who Reads an American Book?": Calls for a National Literature   (p. 476)

This cluster of brief essays conveys the urgency eighteenth-century writers and editors felt about the development of a national literature, which English essayist Sydney Smith claimed America lacked. The responses of these prominent men (and one woman) of letters, each of whom had much at stake in the formation and sustenance of an American national literature, offer today's students the chance to eavesdrop on the broad conversation taking place at this time about the subject matter, thematic concerns, and even the conditions of support necessary for such an enterprise. In tackling questions about what topics, characteristics, and strategies American writers might employ in their production of an American literature, these writers essentially take up the question, "What counts as American?"

This section is fundamental to an understanding of the readings included in the "Literature for a New Nation" section because it outlines the challenges of generating a completely new literary tradition based on the concept of nationality. That is, the argument for an American national literature assumes that America is different from everywhere else, especially Europe, and that this "exceptionalism," as literary scholars term it, drives the production of art as well as its consumption by a community of readers unified by their very "Americanness." The cluster could be used effectively at the beginning of the unit "Literature for a New Nation," anchoring discussions of works as apparently disparate as those written by Philip Freneau and Augustus Baldwin Longstreet or Phillis Wheatley and Washington Irving. From Irving's mythmaking to Wheatley's depictions of the plight of an African American slave to Catharine Maria Sedgwick's meditation on the woman writer, these texts share the common ground of defining what they view as centrally American concerns. The section demonstrates that American literature was not produced by artists living in ivory towers; rather, writers and the texts they generated were caught up in systems of cultural production that included booksellers, printers, and readers as well as newspapers, periodicals, and books.

Questions for Class Discussion

1. According to the texts included in this section, what are the particular problems facing American writers? How do these texts propose that these problems be solved? What are the responsibilities of the audience, the bookseller or printer, and the writer in reaching a solution?

2. According to the writers and editors included here, what constitutes an "American" book or subject? What are the characteristics of an American book or subject? Do these writers generally agree?

3. One might argue that in the process of defining an American literature, the texts included in this section also define an American national character and value system. Choose at least one text from this section and discuss the nature of this American national character and to what extent these ideas persist in today's culture.

4. Choose one characteristic of American literature offered in this section and demonstrate how a text from the chapter "Literature for a New Nation" upholds, complicates, or rejects this characteristic. For example, William Tudor discusses the importance of both the landscape and early American history to an American national literature. Demonstrate how one of the fiction writers or poets responds to Tudor's ideas.

PHILIP FRENEAU   (p. 495)

Approaches to Teaching

Freneau's work is straightforward in language, uses neoclassical forms, such as heroic couplets, and anticipates the love of nature and common humanity typical of the British Romantics. During the 1790s, when Freneau was writing, the concept of an American agrarian ideal, which is perhaps best epitomized in Crèvecoeur's letter 3 in *Letters from an American Farmer*, was widely circulated. This ideal of an egalitarian society peopled by reasonably educated gentlemen farmers became associated with Thomas Jefferson, whose "republican" views rested on the ideal of the original Roman Republic. To put it simply, Jeffersonian republicanism assumed that Americans were virtuous citizens who could and would act for the good of the whole; federalism, associated with John Adams and Alexander Hamilton, assumed that people could not be trusted to resist self-interest and so must be governed by a strong federal government. These conflicting politics would have been familiar to readers of the newspapers and periodicals in which Freneau's poetry appeared. Another option for introducing students to Freneau is to use the painting *Kindred Spirits* (p. 466) to remind students of eighteenth-century values, including the relationship of nature to the humans who cultivate it and universal natural laws, such as the human capacity for reason and virtue.

Classroom Issues and Strategies

Because of its investment in American themes, Freneau's work, including what students might view as rather apolitical nature poetry, can be viewed from a sociopolitical perspective. Instructors might begin with the frontispiece and title page of Freneau's 1809 *Poems* (p. 496), which offer clear guidelines for what readers of the time should expect: His work is associated with the American Revolution and the spirit of America itself, as symbolized by the "Indian Chief" figure. Beginning here encourages students to consider "To Sir Toby," which apparently treats a Jamaican sugar planter and uses British neoclassical forms, in the context of American slavery. "On the Emigration to America" takes up the themes presented in Durand's *Kindred Spirits* (p. 466), such as the harmonious relationship between nature and the humans who cultivate it and universal laws of reason and morality. The poem seems to usher in a new age, when the "genius" of America witnesses its reasoned democratic values overspreading the world. "The Wild Honey Suckle" uses the metaphor of this "fair," "hidden," and "untouched" flower to represent the common, transitory nature of life. Students can consider if the flower is also a metaphor for young America.

Finally, "The Indian Burying Ground" pays homage to the vanishing Native American, celebrating with Romantic nostalgia the warrior's primitiveness in contrast to Western reason.

Connections to Other Authors and Texts

Freneau is most obviously connected to William Cullen Bryant, another Romantic nature poet who tried to capture the spirit of the new nation in his work, and Phillis Wheatley, whose work also treats American politics and the issue of slavery. In theme, Freneau's poetry compares to Crèvecoeur's *Letters from an American Farmer* (p. 430), Paine's *Common Sense* (p. 438), and Jefferson's Declaration (p. 447) and *Notes on the State of Virginia* (p. 452). Freneau's romanticization of Native Americans contrasts with Schoolcraft's depiction of Native American culture and values in "Mishosha" (p. 578). Finally, Freneau's style, language, and subject matter offer one response to the "'Who Reads an American Book?': Calls for a National Literature" section (American Contexts, p. 476) by presenting new mythologies and subject matter typical of North America, including that of Native Americans and slaves.

Questions for Class Discussion

1. Choose one of the statements from "'Who Reads an American Book?'" and discuss the ways that Freneau's work responds to this call for a national literature.

2. Compare one of Freneau's poems to the work of one of the following authors in this anthology: Crèvecoeur, Jefferson, or Paine.

3. Connect the title page and frontispiece (p. 496) to one of the following poems: "To Sir Toby," "On the Emigration to America," or "The Indian Burying Ground." Explain how the poem upholds or develops one or more of the ideas presented on these initial pages.

4. Consider "The Wild Honey Suckle" as a poem about America. What aspects of the new nation does the flower represent, and what does the poet's view of it seem to be?

5. Explain how one of Freneau's poems conveys ideas similar to those of the Hudson River School and, specifically, Durand's *Kindred Spirits* (p. 466).

Brief Bibliography

Arner, Robert D. "Neoclassicism and Romanticism: A Reading of Freneau's 'The Wild Honey Suckle.'" *Early American Literature* 9 (1974): 53-61.

Bowden, Mary Weatherspoon. *Philip Freneau.* Boston: Twayne, 1976.

Marsh, Philip Merrill. *The Works of Philip Freneau: A Critical Study.*
Metuchen, NJ: Scarecrow, 1968.

PHILLIS WHEATLEY   (p. 503)

Approaches to Teaching

Because of the density and intensity of language and meaning, poetry is
often difficult for today's students. Wheatley's formulaic rhyme, meter, and
verse forms make her work even more challenging to teach. Students might
read over each of Wheatley's poems once and consider their assignment
done. Instructors can encourage interest in Wheatley by emphasizing her
position as the first African American and the second woman in America to
publish a book of poems in the colonies. Although she was captured and
brought to America when she was seven or eight, by the time she was fourteen she had mastered eighteenth-century poetic conventions and her work
began appearing in print. Although Wheatley's style of language resembles
Alexander Pope, her themes, which include religion, politics, and the problem of slavery, are often decidedly American in the sense that they address
the issues of her immediate time and place. Instructors might introduce
students to the poetic conventions of the eighteenth century, especially the
heroic couplet, as a way to demonstrate Wheatley's innovations, which
make her the founder of the African American and black women's literary
traditions.

Classroom Issues and Strategies

One of the difficulties of teaching Wheatley is her relationship to conventional eighteenth-century literary discourses, which at once enable and
disable certain kinds of written expression. The poetry of Wheatley's day
was highly stylized and used conventional meter and rhyme. Wheatley
wrote for an audience that may have viewed her intellectual and imaginative capabilities and even her humanity as inferior; for example, the headnote in the anthology includes Thomas Jefferson's statement, "Religion
indeed, has produced a Phyllis Whately [sic]; but it could not produce a
poet." Using statements such as this, instructors can encourage students
to consider how Wheatley negotiated issues of her own literacy, her position as author, and her readership in her works. Wheatley's position as a
black woman and a writer critical of slavery was not as anomalous as students might think. Wheatley had many friends among the free blacks in
New England, and her works were contemporaneous with that of ex-slave
Caesar Sarter, whose arguments against slavery appeared in a
Massachusetts newspaper in 1774. Wheatley wrote at the same time that

Massachusetts slaves circulated petitions against slavery. In her letter to Samson Occom, which was reprinted in newspapers throughout New England, Wheatley declares that "in every human Breast, God has implanted a Principle, which we call Love of Freedom; it is impatient of Oppression, and pants for Deliverance." Here Wheatley uses the eighteenth-century notion that each individual possesses certain inalienable, God-given rights to establish the validity of her position. She offers these sentiments again and again in her poetry and letters, which emphasize peace, liberty, and her own identity as an African American writer.

Connections to Other Authors and Texts

Wheatley's work should be compared to that of other poets in this section, including Philip Freneau, and also to earlier periods, specifically another woman who expressed through poetry subversive thoughts for her age Anne Bradstreet. Wheatley's poem "On Being Brought from Africa to America" might be read alongside Frances E. W. Harper's "Ethiopia" (p. 1230) and her thoughts on slavery and freedom compared to Harper's "The Slave Mother" (p. 1229). Because of their public navigations of dual cultural identities, Wheatley works well with Equiano as well as Occom, Schoolcraft, Harriet Jacobs, Frederick Douglass, and Sojourner Truth.

Questions for Class Discussion

1. Study Scipio Moorhead's engraving of Phillis Wheatley on page 504, which served as the frontispiece to her collection *Poems on Various Subjects* (1773). Consider the details of Wheatley's expression, dress, and physical position and characterize the impression the portrait would have made on an eighteenth-century reader. Select one of the poems included in this anthology and discuss the ways that the Phillis Wheatley of Moorhead's portrait is present or absent.

2. Read "On Being Brought from Africa to America" as an example of dual cultural identity. Poet and critic Naomi Long Madgett has argued that images of light and dark and the ambiguity of the last two lines suggest that this poem isn't as accepting of Western culture and the speaker's position in it as it seems on a first reading. Do you agree? Why or why not?

3. Using Wheatley's letter to Samson Occom and the poem "To S. M. a Young *African* Painter, on Seeing His Works," what argument do you think her poetry made to its eighteenth-century audience about African Americans?

4. Poems such as "To the Right Honourable William, Earl of Dartmouth," "To the University of Cambridge, in New England," and "To His

Excellency General Washington" use seemingly unusual subjects for a young African American woman. Choose one of these works and discuss how Wheatley provides a fresh perspective on her subject.

5. Discuss Wheatley's poem "A Farewell to America. To Mrs. S.W.," written on the occasion of the poet's voyage to England. Characterize Wheatley's treatment of her mistress and her adopted land throughout the poem.

Brief Bibliography

Balkun, Mary McAleer. "Phillis Wheatley's Construction of Otherness and the Rhetoric of Performed Ideology." *African American Review* 36.1 (2002): 121–35.

Desrochers, Robert, Jr. "On Her Own Footing: Phillis Wheatley in Freedom." *Genius in Bondage: Literature of the Early Black Atlantic.* Ed. Vincent Carretta and Philip Gould. Lexington: UP of Kentucky, 2001.

Robinson, William H. *Critical Essays on Phillis Wheatley.* Boston: Hall, 1982.

WHEATLEY THROUGH A MODERN LENS   (p. 517)

Although some eighteenth-century readers may have viewed her work more as a curiosity or as scientific evidence for or against their position on slavery, Wheatley stands as the foremother of African American literature. Her work continues to resonate for African American writers today, as shown by Kevin Young's choice to include his tribute to Wheatley in his anthology of new African American writers for the twenty-first century.

Young's poem evokes Wheatley's "A Farewell to America. To Mrs. S.W." (p. 510) and explores what might have transpired in the poet's mind as she embarked on the second sea journey of her life (the first being the Middle Passage). This "mild" trip to the "slight sun" of London among "polite and consumptive passengers" transpires in marked, if unspoken, contrast to Wheatley's initial entry into Western civilization. Young plays on Wheatley's recurring themes, including the democratic powers of Christianity and Death, "the dark mistress." Young takes up the silences of Wheatley's work, her homelessness ("Native / of nowhere"), anomalousness ("Who could resist a Negress who can recite Latin and speak the Queen's?"), and her "sadness too large to name." He deploys Wheatley's deferential addresses to powerful people in his own address to Wheatley, "My Most Excellence, my quill / and ink lady." Young captures the unspoken longing he imagines Wheatley must have had for her African home and loved ones lost. In Young's poem, the sea becomes a metaphor that expresses the breadth and freedom of her mind, which slavery and servitude could not contain.

WASHINGTON IRVING   (p. 520)

Approaches to Teaching

Many students will have read or heard of "Rip Van Winkle" or seen the movie *The Legend of Sleepy Hollow*, starring Johnny Depp, proof that Irving's fiction continues to appeal to American audiences. Because Irving is considered the first successful professional American writer, and because his works continue to be sold, used in classrooms, and made into Hollywood movies, his popularity with the American public makes an excellent entry point. The class will probably agree on some of the following elements as sources for Irving's persistent appeal: humor, supernatural elements, the short-story genre, which can be read in one sitting, memorable characterizations, and American landscapes and themes. Although he wrote and first published *The Sketch Book* in England, and the work was popular on both sides of the Atlantic, instructors may also engage students with the question of why Irving is an especially "American" writer. Such a discussion could include Irving's reinvention of American history and heritage in the setting of old New York and his response to the quintessentially American Franklin model of hard work as the way to wealth.

Classroom Issues and Strategies

The selections from *The Sketch Book* interweave the following themes and issues: American history, legend, tradition; American culture, manners, mores, and politics; the role and characterization of the artist or writer; and the role of art in the new nation.

In presenting readers with "Rip Van Winkle," Irving creates an American mythology that draws on truthful elements of its past. That is, Irving uses some historical facts: for example, the early Dutch settlement of New York, small-town life in the Catskill Mountains, and the American Revolution. In some respects, the story encourages a political or cultural critique. That is, Rip is the antithesis of Ben Franklin, possessing "an insuperable aversion to all kinds of profitable labour" so that "his patrimonial estate had dwindled away under his management, acre by acre" (pp. 532–33). Irving even includes a "junto" that parodies Franklin's assembly of erudite intellects; Rip's gang spends its time "talk[ing] listlessly over village gossip, or tell[ing] endless sleepy stories about nothing" (p. 534). The narrator professes to draw on the late "Diedrich Knickerbocker," a fictional researcher of the Dutch in New York, and Rip is visited by Dutchmen from another age, whose playing at ninepins in the mountains explains the phenomenon of thunder below. His return to civilization reveals signs of a new, postrevolutionary America. The nameless inn where he spent most days is now the Union Hotel. The image of King George on the signpost has been replaced by that of General Washington, and he is greeted by "a busy, bustling, disputatious tone" and a crowd of "tavern politicians" demanding to know if he is Federalist or Democrat (pp. 538-39). Irving seems to be romanticizing the simple days and ways of colonial times with the modern world, which seems to have passed Rip by. Finally, this story invites a discussion of the roles and stereotypes of women, who are presented in a less-than-positive light. Even the Native American mother of myth, once thought to be the source of thunder, is replaced by the bowling Dutchmen. Instructors should note that Irving's characterization of Dame Van Winkle follows immediately after "The Wife" in *The Sketch Book,* and so adds another layer of humor and complexity to the narrator, Geoffrey Crayon.

Irving's work also examines the role of the author and his art. In the prospectus to *The Sketch Book,* he presents the narrator, Geoffrey Crayon, as a humble and decidedly Riplike character, "unsettled," "subject to interruptions," and given to "the fluctuations of his own thoughts and feelings" (p. 522). In addition to a propensity for American subjects, "The Author's Account of Himself" presents the narrator as an amateur "get[ting] up a few" sketches on less-than-lofty subjects for the idle amusement of friends. That is, Irving's narrator makes no claims for the moral or historical value of art as earlier writers did. In fact, he seems to poke fun at art that masquerades as history, especially in his prefatory and appended notes and postscripts to "Rip Van Winkle." His use of fictional editorial apparatuses and dream sequences anticipates the work of Edgar Allan Poe and Nathaniel Hawthorne.

Connections to Other Authors and Texts

Irving's work counters Franklin's ideas of industry and self-improvement with idleness and art for art's sake. Like Freneau, Sedgwick, and Schoolcraft, Irving uses American landscapes and history as subjects. Irving's views of women seem to rely on common cultural stereotypes, and so comparisons of his depictions of women to those of Sedgwick, Lydia Maria Child, Harriet Beecher Stowe, and Fanny Fern might be in order. Finally, Irving's tendency to hoaxlike humor, the supernatural, and the "documentation" of pseudohistorical sources invites comparisons to Poe and Hawthorne.

Questions for Class Discussion

1. Using "The Author's Account of Himself," characterize Geoffrey Crayon as an artist and a character. What kinds of stories and perspectives does this sketch lead one to expect?

2. Using one of the essays in "'Who Reads an American Book?'" discuss how Irving invents American literature in "Rip Van Winkle."

3. Irving's depiction of Dame Van Winkle is less than positive, but the story appears immediately after "The Wife" in *The Sketch Book*. Choose one of the following prompts and discuss the story from a woman-centered approach:

   a. Explain how the placement of "The Wife" and "Rip Van Winkle" in the original publication generates an overall narrative view of women. That is, does "The Wife" help to soften your view of Irving's stereotype of Dame Van Winkle? Is "The Wife" some kind of joke?

   b. What would "Rip Van Winkle" be like as a story if it were told from the perspective of Dame Van Winkle? Choose one passage in the story and rewrite it from her perspective.

4. Compare Irving's view of the American dream to Benjamin Franklin's. Do their views share any common points? How do their views differ?

5. Consider "Rip Van Winkle" in the context of one or more of the texts from "'To Begin the World Over Again': The Emerging Idea of 'America'" (American Contexts, p. 427). How does Irving present America pre- and post-Revolution? How do these ideas about America relate to Irving's popular appeal?

Brief Bibliography

Aderman, Ralph M., ed. *Critical Essays on Washington Irving*. Boston: Hall, 1990.

Bowden, Mary Weatherspoon. *Washington Irving*. Boston: Twayne, 1981.

Fetterley, Judith. *The Resisting Reader: A Feminist Approach to American Fiction*. Bloomington: Indiana UP, 1978.

McLamore, Richard V. "The Dutchman in the Attic: Claiming an Inheritance in *The Sketch Book of Geoffrey Crayon*." *American Literature: A Journal of Literary History, Criticism, and Bibliography* 72.1 (2000): 31-57.

CATHARINE MARIA SEDGWICK   (p. 543)

Approaches to Teaching

Although Sedgwick was a well-respected and prolific writer in her time, very few of today's students will have heard of her. She takes on a subject, "Cacoethes Scribendi," literally the writing itch or disease, relevant to any student who has ever wished to be a writer or taken a creative-writing workshop. Moreover, Sedgwick's treatment of her subject concerns the relationships among writers, audiences, and the marketplace and the distinction between so-called high and low culture familiar to today's readers, who may be surprised to see that this discussion has such a long history. Finally, Sedgwick's satire is aimed specifically at women writers and readers and the Romantic subjects and conventions they seem to prefer, at least in her day. The gendered implications of Sedgwick's critique draw attention to one facet of American literature that the writers in "'Who Reads an American Book?': Calls for a National Literature" seem to have overlooked. Or is the absence of gender in that discussion precisely the point Sedgwick makes here?

Classroom Issues and Strategies

As the headnote states, Sedgwick "supported what was then the unconventional and even radical idea that not all women must be wives and mothers" (p. 544). Set in a village peopled predominantly by women, "Cacoethes Scribendi" explores women as creators of culture, literature, and community. Although the women evince "no great diminution of happiness in consequences of the absence of the nobler sex" (p. 545), the introduction of literature in the form of a gift annual disrupts the village and particularly Mrs. Courland, who, "like all New England women, had been taught to consider domestic duties as the first temporal duties of her sex" (p. 549). Once a "social, sympathetic, good hearted creature," Mrs. Courland forsakes her agreeable parlor, a hub of village exchange and community spirit, for a separate apartment, where she fashions into print the dearest secrets of her loved ones. As an author, "a sudden calamity, a death, a funeral, were fortunate events" to her (p. 551). Sedgwick's story concerns the power and right deployment of the written word in the lives of everyday people. Mrs. Courland's written work objectifies her subjects, including her beloved daughter Alice, replacing the convivial exchange of everyday news with the dramatic, the romantic, and the pathetic. Mrs. Courland fails to comprehend the fundamental value of the raw material of her own life but learns a powerful lesson from the "short and true story of [Ralph's] love for his sweet cousin Alice" (p. 555). Instructors should expect to moderate heated arguments about whether or not Sedgwick places the domestic role of wife and mother over that of author or if she is instead commenting more broadly on the nature of women's reading tastes and writing tendencies.

Connections to Other Authors and Texts

Sedgwick's story of an idyllic women's village contrasts with Irving's rather misogynistic views of women and domesticity and with Longstreet's images of the early American South. Her work looks forward to the ideas of Catherine E. Beecher, Fanny Fern, and even, to some extent, Margaret

Fuller, all of whom insist on the centrality of women's thought and action to American culture. Other tales that consider the writing life or the place of art in human society include Herman Melville's "Bartleby, the Scrivener" (p. 1074) and Rebecca Harding Davis's *Life in the Iron-Mills* (p. 1150). Nathaniel Hawthorne's "Young Goodman Brown" (p. 987), "The Minister's Black Veil" (p. 997), and "The Birth-Mark" (p. 1006) treat the dangers of allowing devotion to art, science, or belief to take over human sympathy and connection.

Questions for Class Discussion

1. Sedgwick's setting is the "secluded and quiet village of H.," peopled by "a community of women who lived like nuns." How does the dominant presence of women define the character of the community and the relationship women have to men?

2. Using one or more of the readings in "'Who Reads an American Book?': Calls for a National Literature" (American Contexts, p. 476), discuss the broader comment that Sedgwick's choice of setting or subject makes on what qualifies as American literature.

3. In satirizing Mrs. Courland, whose work tends to "pathos and sentiment," Sedgwick seems to make a statement about what literature is not. How does the story define what literature is or what it should be? (Note: "Cacoethes Scribendi" was published in a gift annual, *The Atlantic Souvenir*.)

4. According to the narrator, "Mrs. Courland did not know that in literature . . . the most exquisite productions are wrought from the smallest quantity of raw material." Discuss this observation, along with the rest of the story, as a call for American literary realism, or the adherence to the details, mores, and occurrences of everyday life.

5. Why, according to the narrator, is Ralph's "story" so much more successful than any Mrs. Courland writes? Is this success based on gender, and is this a story that dismisses women writers? Explain your answers using the language of the text.

Brief Bibliography

Damon-Bach, Lucinda, and Victoria Clements. *Catharine Maria Sedgwick: Critical Perspectives*. Boston: Northeastern UP, 2003.

Foster, Edward Halsey. *Catharine Maria Sedgwick*. Boston: Twayne, 1974.

Sanchez, Maria Carla. "'Prayers in the Market Place': Women and Low Culture in Catharine Sedgwick's 'Cacoethes Scribendi.'" *American Transcendental Quarterly* 16.2 (2002): 101–13.

AUGUSTUS BALDWIN LONGSTREET   (p. 556)

Approaches to Teaching

In keeping with the calls for a national literature in the " 'Who Reads an American Book?'" section (American Contexts, p. 476), Longstreet's nostalgic sketches about Georgia frontier life attempt to generate a specifically American literary culture and history. Students can review the excerpts, especially those by Tudor and Channing, in " 'Who Reads an American Book?'" and then consider Longstreet's importance as an author who brings the American South into the conversation about national literature. A brief review of the frontier sketch as a genre, which Longstreet pioneered, will be helpful to students, who may not understand its purpose. That is, the sketch presents a single scene, character, or an event in rather cursory detail in order to convey a sense of setting and place and, often, a bit of the writer's character. Although discussions of humor are almost always nonhumorous, students might be asked to locate the elements in the sketches that would lead to laughter: for example, incongruity, the narrator's self-deprecation, the recognition of familiar character types, or the difference between behavior in a past era and their own.

Classroom Issues and Strategies

The illustration accompanying "Georgia Theatrics" (p. 557) with its ironic caption, "A Lincoln Rehearsal," can elicit a discussion about frontier Georgia as a setting in Longstreet's work. From that, students can be asked to generate a list of character traits belonging to the narrators in these sketches and then to consider the setting itself as a character. These sketches use humor to convey the cultural mores and values of early Georgia, suggesting that the South is a legitimate site for exploring uniquely American culture in a uniquely American literature. Using the quotes from Poe's review (pp. 556, 558), students can discuss what Longstreet presents as typical of the South as well as why such sketches would have appealed to such a wide audience in the early nineteenth century.

Connections to Other Authors and Texts

Like Irving and Sedgwick, Longstreet participates in the building of a national mythology by emphasizing American subject matter and place. The sketches respond to the essays included in the " 'Who Reads an American Book?': Calls for a National Literature" section and anticipate the section titled " 'Countless Phenomena of the Times': The Role of the Periodical Press," especially James Ewell Heath's essay, "Southern Literature" (p. 947). Longstreet's rural sketches both invent and preserve a cultural history that Americans are in danger of losing to "progress," and so compare to Schoolcraft's recordings of Native American traditional tales, African American slave songs, and Hawthorne's Puritan and Revolutionary tales ("Young Goodman Brown," "My Kinsman, Major Molineux"). Of course, the narratives included by ex-slaves offer quite another view of the American South.

Questions for Class Discussion

1. Characterize the narrator in "Georgia Theatrics." How is this narrator's persona vital to the humorous effect of the story?

2. Using either "Georgia Theatrics" or "The Dance," identify those aspects of the sketch that convey a sense of typical culture on the early Georgia frontier. How does the narrator portray this culture? That is, does he respect it? identify with it? lampoon it? By adopting this perspective, what does the narrator wish to accomplish or with what view of Southern life does he wish to leave us?

3. Compare the narrators in "Georgia Theatrics" and "The Dance." How exactly are they different in their attitudes toward their subjects? toward themselves?

4. Choose one of the essays in the "'Who Reads an American Book?': Calls for a National Literature" section and discuss the ways that Longstreet's work responds to or complicates the idea of a national literature expressed in that essay.

Brief Bibliography

King, Kimball. *Augustus Baldwin Longstreet*. Boston: Twayne, 1984.

Rachels, David. "A Biographical Reading of A. B. Longstreet's *Georgia Scenes*." *The Humor of the Old South*. Lexington: UP of Kentucky, 2001. 113–29.

Wegmann, Jessica. "'Playing in the Dark' with Longstreet's *Georgia Scenes*: Critical Reception and Reader Response to Treatments of Race and Gender." *Southern Literary Journal* 30.1 (1997): 13–26.

WILLIAM CULLEN BRYANT   (p. 567)

Approaches to Teaching

Bryant's poetry is straightforward and concerns nature; students will either like it or hate it, but they will not find it difficult. His form and style draw on that of the British Romantic poets, for example, in his celebration of the common, emphasis on feeling and sentiment, and use of local land-scape to consider broader human problems in a moral context. The trick for instructors is to encourage students to view this work in its historical and cultural context. To that end, recourse to the "'Who Reads an American Book?': Calls for a National Literature" section and some visual aids from the Hudson River school will set the parameters for discussion. That is, nature is important here because it presents the unspoiled and panoramic landscapes that are the essence of America. Bryant's work appeared in newspapers, a strange phenomenon for today's students, and it might be helpful, for those who have electronic access, to show them a typical page or two from the *Hampshire Gazette,* in which his earliest poems appeared, or the *New York Evening Post,* where he was an editor for most of his life. Considering the ways that nineteenth-century newspapers brought together high and low culture for a general audience, the accessibility of Bryant's language, and his appeal to readers' sense of nationalism may illuminate discussion of why Bryant was America's most beloved poet at that time.

Classroom Issues and Strategies

As the headnote and the poem "To Cole, the Painter, Departing for Europe" assert, Bryant was a great admirer of the painter Thomas Cole, who founded the Hudson River school. Asher Durand's painting *Kindred Spirits* (p. 466) depicts Cole and Bryant overlooking a gorge in the Catskill Mountains, a typical Hudson River school scene. Like Cole, Bryant used nature to allego-rize moral ideas about the human condition. Instructors might offer stu-dents an online or face-to-face slide show of selected allegorical paintings by Cole, including scenes from the series *The Voyage of Life, The Course of Empire,* and *The Garden of Eden.* The class can then turn to Bryant's poem "To Cole" to determine exactly which aspects of the painter's vision the poet most admires. With these ideas in mind, students are then equipped to examine Bryant's work and consider how his poems use nature in similar ways. For example, "Thanatopsis" asks readers to view nature as at once the "glorious tomb of man" and humanity's teacher. "The Yellow Violet" pays homage to the first humble flower of spring and emphasizes the importance of context to interpretation. "To a Waterfowl" almost approaches a tran-scendental perspective; that is, in viewing nature (the waterfowl), the poet sees God and realizes that the same divine power guides all. Finally, "The Prairies" uses a fundamentally American setting to consider the rise and fall of civilizations and to celebrate the progress of American settlers. (Note: This poem works well with Cole's *The Course of Empire* series.)

Connections to Other Authors and Texts

Bryant obviously works quite well with Freneau, especially the poems "The Wild Honey Suckle" (p. 501) and "The Indian Burying Ground" (p. 502), which use American scenes to consider larger philosophical issues. Students can compare Bryant's use of conventional forms to that of Wheatley and Freneau and consider why Bryant alone was so successful and popular. Bryant's poetry in some ways anticipates Emerson and Thoreau in its argument that nature is a metaphor for divine truths, although instructors should be careful not to oversimplify this comparison. Finally, Bryant's treatment of nature using traditional poetic forms provides an interesting contrast to Whitman, a great admirer of Bryant.

Questions for Class Discussion

1. Bryant's poetry was influenced by the paintings of Thomas Cole, which often depicted the sublimity and power of nature. Examine one of Cole's paintings and then choose one of Bryant's poems to explore and discuss Cole's influence on Bryant's use of nature in his poetry.

2. Choose one of the essays in "'Who Reads an American Book?': Calls for a National Literature" and discuss the ways that one of Bryant's poems responds to the essayist's description of a uniquely American literature.

3. How is the poet's view of nature in "To a Waterfowl" and "The Yellow Violet" similar to or different from that depicted in "The Prairies?"

4. Compare the view of nature or death in "Thanatopsis" to Freneau's in "The Indian Burying Ground" (p. 502).

Brief Bibliography

Budick, Emily Miller. "'Visible' Images and the 'Still Voice': Transcendental Vision in Bryant's 'Thanatopsis.'" *ESQ: A Journal of the American Renaissance* 22 (1976): 71–77.

Krapf, Norbert, ed. *Under Open Sky: Poets on William Cullen Bryant.* New York: Fordham UP, 1986.

McLean, Albert F. *William Cullen Bryant.* Boston: Twayne, 1989.

JANE JOHNSTON SCHOOLCRAFT   (p. 577)

Approaches to Teaching

As her portrait in the anthology illustrates, Schoolcraft was bicultural by birth and education, and her literary work reflects the merging of European and Native American cultures. Brought up to appreciate European literary traditions by her Scotch-Irish father, she also learned the language and traditions of her mother, an Ojibwa chief's daughter.

Although Schoolcraft's work is relatively unknown to students today, she was admired by other writers of her time and nicknamed the "northern Pocahontas"; her work on the Ojibwa legends published in her husband Henry Rowe Schoolcraft's *Algic Researches* inspired Henry Wadsworth Longfellow's *The Song of Hiawatha*, probably the most renowned American poem in the nineteenth century. By Schoolcraft's time, Native Americans in the eastern United States had been removed to reservations and European Americans regarded them with romanticized nostalgia. Students might be asked to imagine themselves as members of a reading group in the frontier town of Sault Sainte Marie, eager to learn about the myths, poetry, history, and legends of the Ojibwa but accustomed to European literary conventions and traditions.

Classroom Issues and Strategies

Since Schoolcraft draws on Ojibwa culture, language, and lore, students are probably ill equipped to consider her work in its proper context. To address this challenge, instructors might remind students of a prominent story in European American culture, such as a familiar fairy tale, and discuss how such stories are used to convey cultural values before extrapolating them from Schoolcraft's "Mishosha, or the Magician and His Daughters." Certainly, the story transmits the value of family relationships and responsibilities and the importance of resourcefulness exhibited by both the young man and the magician's daughters. Because the daughters whom the young man rescues contrast wildly with the passive rescued heroines in Western traditions, the story models a different version of womanhood. In teaching these values through Native American tales that drew on European narrative traditions, Schoolcraft encouraged collaboration and understanding between the two cultures.

Connections to Other Authors and Texts

Schoolcraft's story provides an important contrast to other American and New England fictions included in this section, such as those by Irving, Sedgwick, and Longstreet. The use of oral traditions compares with Occom, Tecumseh, and the "Native American Origin and Creation Stories" in the "Literature to 1750" section of this volume.

Questions for Class Discussion

1. Consider that the purpose of this kind of story, passed down orally, was to transmit cultural values. What things, characteristics, and ideas seem culturally important in this story? Explain your answer with textual support.

2. In some characteristics oral tales in native cultures, there is no need to introduce and describe characters, since the audience is already familiar with the story, and often the teller relies on the audience to complete whatever is left unstated. Discuss the degree to which instances of these native qualities are present in Schoolcraft's text.

3. Schoolcraft's work and education are influenced by her participation in two distinct cultures, Ojibwa and European American. Locate a brief passage in the text in which both cultures seem present at once. That is, use a passage of no more than a paragraph to illustrate how Schoolcraft brings together two seemingly opposite cultures or sets of values. (Note: Use Sedgwick's "Cacoethes Scribendi" or Irving's tales as examples of conventional nineteenth-century literary style.)

4. Compare the roles of the hero and the heroines to those in fairy tales from Western traditions. How is the trickster brother like or unlike those heroes? How are the daughters like or unlike those heroines? Consider how these characteristics are related to dominant cultural ideas about masculinity or femininity in the West.

5. According to Suzanne Lundquist, "trickster" figures in Native American mythology "inadvertently create order out of chaos. Or Trickster's escapades mock foolish, obsessive behavior – gluttony, sexual avarice, gender arrogance, self-centeredness, ideological addiction. Through the adventures of Trickster, the contingent nature of human experience is established and invitations to appropriate behavior are made. However, because of the comic rather than tragic intention of Trickster discourse, survival in an often hostile world is made possible" (*Native American Literatures: An Introduction* [New York: Continuum, 2004]). Consider the brother/hero in Schoolcraft's story using this definition of *trickster.*

Brief Bibliography

Parins, James W. "Jane Johnston Schoolcraft." *Native American Writers of the United States.* Ed. Kenneth M. Roemer, Arlington, TX: Gale, 1997. 274–75.

Ruoff, A. LaVonne Brown. "Early Native American Women Authors: Jane Johnston Schoolcraft, Sarah Winnemucca, S. Alice Callahan, E. Pauline Johnson, and Zitkala-Sa." *Nineteenth-Century American Women Writers: A Critical Reader.* Ed. and intro. by Karen L. Kilcup. Malden, MA: Blackwell, 1998. 81–111.

———. "Jane Johnston Schoolcraft." *Dictionary of Native American Literature.* Ed. Andrew Wiget. New York: Garland, 1994. 295–97.

American Literature
1830-1865

AMERICAN HISTORY AND CULTURE during the antebellum period can be characterized by the word *expansion*. While readers immediately think of these decades in terms of westward expansion enabled by U.S. policies of Indian removal and the acquisition of lands west of the Mississippi by force, *expansion* typifies the whole context in which the literature of this period was produced. The rapid growth in population, especially in cities, brought about by immigration, the rise of industries, and mass agriculture; the developments in science and technology, including that of print production; the flourishing of the publishing trade, especially for mass-market books and periodicals; the proliferation of new religious denominations, reform societies, and movements; and the rising literacy rates of the general population all evince the pervasiveness of expansion throughout American culture. With growth came change, and from these shifts emerged calls for the expansion of the rights of individuals, including slaves, women, the laboring classes, and people of color.

American literature during this period reflects the expansions occurring in the broader culture in which it was produced and constitutes, literally, a period of renewal and rebirth in the arts and letters – a "renaissance." As Ralph Waldo Emerson exhorted in his so-called intellectual declaration of independence, "The American Scholar," the time had come for "the sluggard intellect of this continent [to] look from under its iron lids and fill the postponed expectation of the world with something better than the exertions of mechanical skill" (p. 671). Responding to Emerson and similar incitements in the nation's periodicals and universities for a uniquely American literature, writers assiduously attended to the business of the nation: its landscape, geography, people, dearly held beliefs, and, of course, its problems. The study of the literature of the American Renaissance demands that we ask how America and its citizens were being constructed. When considering the overarching ideas that inform much of the literature of this period, including self-reliance, domesticity, moral and social reform, and abolition, we need to ask how and to what purpose the relationships among America and its inhabitants were formulated. For example, instructors might ask students the following questions: What does self-reliance mean for an enslaved black man on a southern plantation? Judging from the illustrations in the anthology, which present a cross section of American life, what kinds of people were most concerned about building utopia? How was domesticity relevant to a woman of color or of the laboring classes? As the map on page 603 shows, this was a period of dramatic change for America, and its literature, although largely written by men (and sometimes women) from the eastern United States, was increasingly diverse. It is no surprise, then, that writers attempting to define an American people and landscape would deliver a wide range of hard-fought approaches.

The Era of Reform

While the Puritans imagined an immanent God at the center of a providential universe, eighteenth-century rationalists conceived of God as a kind of clock maker: Having produced humans, he looked on as they went about their business, guided by the moral machinery of his grand design. The American Renaissance placed even more faith in humans. Transcendentalists, abolitionists, purveyors of domestic advice manuals, advocates for the rights of women, Native Americans, and the laboring classes, and reformers of diet, drink, spending, and prostitution all held in common the notion that humans were powerful beings who could radically improve – or even perfect – themselves. The belief was that once humans had improved themselves society would have to follow suit. Reform proliferated as quickly as communication tools did, as churches, reform societies, and publishing houses generated tracts, newspapers, guidebooks, pamphlets, periodicals, and even novels spreading the gospel of reform.

The daguerreotype of the fugitive slave law convention (p. 606) that begins this section is a good starting point for discussion of the various interests in reform. Students can be asked about what general and specific shifts had to take place in order for this gathering to be possible. Discussion points could include the ways that innovations in transportation and communication had a broad impact. Students today, whose worlds are so shaped by the Internet, should grasp how technological improvements might enhance a sense of community and reinforce shared moral and religious beliefs. That same technology, however, brought with it a stronger sense of responsibility for the persistence of slavery, which became impossible to ignore with the availability of newspapers, traveling speakers, and tracts. While Emerson's work may seem a strikingly esoteric inclusion for a section on reform, students should be asked to make the connections between social action and the transcendentalist tenet of the divinity of nature and human beings. Similarly, Emerson's concept of self-reliance can be usefully applied to the political and economic positions of women and people of color. Emerson's and Thoreau's ethic of the individual is an interesting backdrop for discussing the responsibility of the individual to society in a democratic state.

AMERICAN CONTEXTS: "I Will be Heard": *The Rhetoric of Antebellum Reform*   (p. 617)

This short cluster of readings demonstrates a range of voices and rhetorical strategies on the central concerns of antebellum reform: abolition, labor and social reform, and women's rights and roles in the growing nation. This section could be assigned at the beginning of a unit on the American Renaissance so that students could begin thinking about how the readings in the section "The Era of Reform" are in dialogue with one another. Through this brief unit, students can be introduced to the central issues, arguments, and various rhetorical strategies of reform movements during this period. These rhetorical strategies include religious and emotional appeals as well as the deployment of the rhetoric of revolution and independence. Students can be referred to the daguerreotype that heads this subsection as a reminder of the diversity of voices and interests advancing reform. Attention to the sources of publication reinforces the expansions in print culture, especially the advent of newspaper and periodical literature. Finally, this brief section and the conversation it inspires can remind students of the intimate relationships among religion, democracy, individual rights, and social reform, which are still under contention today.

Questions for Class Discussion

1. The texts in this section are authored by people who have historically been denied access to print culture, including women and people of color. What strategies do these authors use to gain credibility with readers?

2. Make a list of characteristics that these writers use to demonstrate their expertise on their subjects. Note any variance across gender, race, and class.

3. What techniques of argumentation are used by these authors to convince readers of the rights and wrongs of certain groups of people? That is, to what extent do they use emotional appeals? logical appeals? faith-based appeals?

4. From the range of appeals discussed in question 3, consider what values and worldviews nineteenth-century readers held. That is, if an emotional appeal focuses on women, what might we deduce about dominant cultural views regarding women?

5. What is the relationship between the rhetoric of revolution and of independence as they broach reform issues in these texts? How do these writers exploit their readers' awareness of that relationship?

WILLIAM APESS   (p. 639)

Approaches to Teaching

Native American autobiography, like most ethnic autobiography, is at once a chronicle of the individual life and the story of the community to which the individual belongs. Arnold Krupat has argued compellingly that Native American autobiography is a bicultural composition; the narrative is best approached as one that speaks with the voices of two radically different cultures. While European American influences are present in the narrative use of established literary conventions and Christian references, Native American oral storytelling relies on cadence, repetition, and powerful imagery to convey its emotional appeal.

Classroom Issues and Strategies

To approach the issue of dual identity, begin with the engraved image of William Apess from the frontispiece of A Son of the Forest (1831). This portrait shows a beardless, brown-skinned man with decidedly Native American features wearing European American garb, including a plain neck cloth and fitted coat, that calls to mind other portraits such as those of Benjamin Franklin in Quaker dress (pp. 334, 372). The subject appears to be ensconced in a rather formal armchair, as shown by the rolled arm at the left side of the image. Using these visual anchors, students can then identify which aspects of the text seem emblematic of either (or both) identities. The importance of rhetorical strategy, including questions of narrative credibility, emotional and persuasive appeals, and the use of faith-based arguments, is central to the study of this text. That is, Apess is in the difficult position of arguing his personal case to the same audience (white Christians) that devalues him and native peoples, no matter their religion, and from whom he has received little monetary compensation for his work.

Connections to Other Authors and Texts

"An Indian's Looking Glass for the White Man" can be fruitfully compared to other Native American texts — including oral Native American tales and stories, which yield information about storytelling techniques and the importance of repetition and sound in spoken texts — and autobiographies such as Samson Occom's *A Short Narrative of My Life* (p. 403). The text uses some of the same rhetorical strategies as ex-slave narrators, including Olaudah Equiano and Frederick Douglass. Emerson's ideas about self-reliance and the transcendental ideal of the divinity of humans is a crucial backdrop for Apess's text, which critiques dominant cultural ideas about individualism and democracy. Nonconformity resonates differently for normative Americans, such as Franklin, Emerson, and Thoreau, than for those, such as Apess, who wear the signs of gendered or racialized "other" on their bodies.

Questions for Class Discussion

1. Using the image of Apess that appeared on the frontispiece of *A Son of the Forest* (p. 639), identify markers of European American and Native American identities. Explain how two or more of these visual markers are present in written form in the body of the text. For example, what aspects of Apess's writing draw on European American conventions? Native American conventions?

2. Arnold Krupat argues that Native American autobiography is a bicultural composition that narrates the coming together of two radically different cultures. Identify passages in the text that uphold, complicate, or negate Krupat's statement.

3. Apess consistently refers to "you" and "I" in the text. Who exactly are these entities as Apess defines them? What does the argument gain through use of these seemingly divisive pronouns?

4. Consider the ways that Apess uses Christian beliefs in his narrative. How would his decisions about the inclusion of scripture, admonition, and assumptions about shared Christian beliefs have affected nineteenth-century readers?

5. According to Apess, what is the relationship — or even the responsibility — of the individual to the community? Give examples from the selection to support your opinion.

Brief Bibliography

Krupat, Arnold. *For Those Who Come After: A Study of Native American Autobiography.* Berkeley: U of California P, 1985.

Ruoff, A. LaVonne Brown, "Three Nineteenth-Century American Indian Autobiographies." *Redefining American Literary History.* Ed. A. LaVonne Brown Ruoff and Jerry W. Ward Jr. New York: MLA, 1990. 251-69.

Tiro, Karim M. "Denominated 'SAVAGE': Methodism, Writing, and Identity in the Works of William Apess, A Pequot," *American Quarterly* 48 (December 1996): 653-79.

LYDIA MARIA CHILD   (p. 645)

Approaches to Teaching

Child's life, career, and works illustrate the intimate connections among the spiritual ideas of Unitarianism and transcendentalism and the social-reform movements on behalf of abolition and Native American and women's rights. This very interconnectedness is the key to understanding the impetus for reform in this era and the breadth and impact of Child's work. It might seem odd that the same woman who published the fantastically popular *The American Frugal Housewife* (1829), *The Mother's Book* (1831), and established the first magazine for children would write an essay in support of a woman accused of attempting to murder her seducer. For a woman whose writing earned her living, such a move constituted an enormous risk as well; in doing so, she allied herself with topics considered inappropriate for children and women. For this reason, Child's prolific work as a writer defines her as an important social activist (or reformist, in nineteenth-century terms) inspired by a faith-based vision of the divinity of all people, whatever their race, ethnicity, gender, or class. Even as establishment readers condemned her opinions, she was consistently able to mobilize the popular press to convey her agenda.

Classroom Issues and Strategies

In "Letter from New-York [The Trial of Amelia Norman]," Child considers the role that education, upbringing, and dominant cultural ideals for men and women played in the temporary insanity of Amelia Norman, accused of the attempted murder of her seducer, Henry S. Ballard. Child not only names Ballard prominently in her essay but also repeatedly prevents his skulking about on the edges of the story and demonstrates his central role in the plight of the accused. Just as she refuses to be silent on the subject of Ballard, so Child deals openly with the delicate subjects of female sexuality, prostitution, women's legal rights and education, prison reform, and the legal double standard for men and women. Child accomplishes this while maintaining her credibility as an upright woman writing on behalf of an "erring sister." Ultimately, Child indicts not only Ballard but also an entire society, which is "carrying on a great system of fraud and theft" not entirely dissimilar to that for which the "poor wretches" in prison were convicted. The difficulty of teaching this text to contemporary students lies in their inability to grasp exactly what seduction meant to nineteenth-century culture; students may see Amelia Norman as an extremist who simply needed to "get on with her life." One way to address this is to ask students to consider why men would bother to get married at all. It seems clear why women, who were denied most legal rights, including property ownership, and had very little access to desirable employment, would wish to attach themselves to men; students should be asked to consider what "assets" a woman of that time could bring to a relationship that would convince a man that she was worthy of marriage.

Connections to Other Authors and Texts

Like Fanny Fern (Sara Payson Willis Parton), Lydia Maria Child's skill and forthrightness earned her the respect of the popular audience. Child's work compares to Emerson's transcendentalism, Thoreau's ideas about individual responsibility for social reform, and Fuller's arguments about the role of women. In addition, Child's work should be considered next to Stowe's and Beecher's, both authors of which assume women's moral superiority even if they would direct it differently. Child's "Letter from New-York" uses an epistolary tradition employed by previous generations of women, including Abigail Adams, Judith Sargent Murray, Phillis Wheatley, and even Emily Dickinson in 441 / "This is my letter to the World" (p. 1327).

Questions for Class Discussion

1. Given the place of publication and the clues within the letter itself, who was Child's audience and what assumptions did they share about Amelia Norman and women in general?

2. According to Child, what are the social wrongs that led to the circumstances of Norman?

3. What strategies does Child use to discuss the delicate issues of sexuality without compromising her own authority and credibility?

4. What arguments does the selection make for women's roles, education, and position in the United States? In what sense are these arguments linked to other readings in this text regarding transcendentalism, domesticity, and individual rights?

Brief Bibliography

Karcher, Carolyn L. *The First Woman in the Republic: A Cultural Biography of Lydia Maria Child*. Durham: Duke UP, 1994.

Malone, Anne Righton. "Sugar Ladies and Strainers: Political Self-Fashioning in the Epistolary Journalism of Lydia Maria Child." *Women's Life-Writing: Finding Voice/Building Community.* Ed. Linda S. Coleman. Bowling Green, OH: Popular, 1997. 239-56.

Tingley, Stephanie A. "'Thumping against the Glittering Wall of Limitations': Lydia Maria Child's 'Letters from New York.'" *In Her Own Voice: Nineteenth-Century American Women Essayists.* Gender and Genre in Literature 9. Ed. Sherry Lee Linkon. New York: Garland, 1997. 41-59.

RALPH WALDO EMERSON   (p. 653)

Approaches to Teaching

David Leverenz writes that "having read Emerson once and come to him again, it is hard to remember having read him at all." At the same time, Emerson's work is rich with maxim and adage, and students often arrive in class having recognized some of them (or having underlined them in their books as at least memorable). This tension between the seemingly ephemeral nature of Emerson's ideas and the aphoristic quality of some of his prose affords a good opening for discussion of his work, much of which was delivered as lectures. While there is no denying the fundamental intellectualism of Emerson's *Nature* and other essays, his work is best contextualized not only within the tenets of transcendentalism and Unitarianism but also within the social and cultural moment of rapid growth, industrialization, and reform that characterized this period.

Classroom Issues and Strategies

Nature articulates many fundamental premises of transcendentalism even as it posits a way of being in and reading the world as a poet and an intellectual. The essay articulates Emerson's idealistic, philosophical views on the relationship of self to others, to the world, to language, and to God. Similarly, "The American Scholar" and "Self-Reliance" articulate a model for the poet-intellectual's daily participation in American society. These models might be understood in the following contexts: Emerson's relatively privileged socioeconomic position; the rapid growth, industrialization, and expansion of the United States; the issue of slavery; and the relative newness of the nation and its national literature. While heady intellectual transcendentalism and social reform may appear miles apart, one strategy for classroom discussion is to make a list of the tenets of transcendentalism and ask students to correlate each tenet with a social or a reform practice.

Connections to Other Authors and Texts

Emerson most obviously connects with other transcendentalist authors, including Fuller, Thoreau, and Whitman. His work articulates a vision of the universe that can be interestingly compared to Poe, Hawthorne, and Melville. While Emerson seems most explicitly to argue a theory that Thoreau and Whitman put into practice, students can also be asked to articulate the difference between Emerson's optimistic view of the correlations between nature, humans, and God and the human capacity to read those correlations and Poe's, Melville's, or Hawthorne's (especially in "The Birth-Mark" on p. 1006 and "Young Goodman Brown" on p. 987) more grim view of that same human capacity. Furthermore, Emerson's views on self-reliance and the role of the individual resonate quite differently when applied to Jacobs's *Incidents* (p. 768) or Douglass's *Narrative* (p. 857). Emerson's work is also effectively read next to other declarations of the American self, including those presented earlier in Captain John Smith's *Generall Historie* (p. 106), John Winthrop's *Modell* (p. 153), Benjamin Franklin's *Autobiography* (p. 340), and so on.

Questions for Class Discussion

1. Discuss the relationship of the self, or individual, and society in Emerson's essays. Include in your discussion Emerson's apparent view of his audience and readers.

2. Using the introductions to "American Literature, 1830-1865," and "The Era of Reform," make a list of the connections between Emerson's arguments and the historical context from which they emerged. Choose one item on your list to elaborate on with close analysis of one or more of Emerson's essays.

3. Emerson uses many metaphors of the body, especially in "The American Scholar" and "Self-Reliance." Make a list of those metaphors, and then explain why they are effective in works that posit transcendence.

4. According to Emerson, what is the function and purpose of art? How should it be read and used?

5. If we were to follow Emerson's advice in "The American Scholar" on how books are best used, how would Emerson's work be taught in the classroom? Develop a lesson plan for high school or college students based on your observations.

Brief Bibliography

Buell, Lawrence. *Literary Transcendentalism*. Ithaca: Cornell UP, 1973.

Porte, Joel, and Saundra Morris, eds. *The Cambridge Companion to Ralph Waldo Emerson*. New York: Cambridge UP, 1999.

Yanella, Donald. *Ralph Waldo Emerson*. Boston: Twayne, 1982.

MARGARET FULLER   (p. 725)

Approaches to Teaching

Fuller's work is that of a publicly and emphatically intellectual woman bent on reforming the role and status of women in the nineteenth century. Responding to a dominant culture that imagined women's roles as strictly tied to their physical bodies and reproductive functions, Fuller's work translates transcendentalist ideals and philosophy into social reform. Using a writing style that rivals Emerson in rhetoric and argumentation yet draws on her own educational series of "Conversations" for women in Boston, Fuller advances a program for the reform of women's education and women's "place" within and outside of the household, including the spheres of government and law. Because of Fuller's elevated use of language, her almost evangelical rhetoric, and her incorporation of a highly educated nineteenth-century conversational style, her work can be slow going for students. Instructors might invite students to consider the text as a response to "Self-Reliance" from a woman's perspective or to imagine themselves as Fuller's contemporaries listening as *Woman in the Nineteenth Century* is delivered from the podium of this inspiring and influential feminist teacher.

Classroom Issues and Strategies

In *Woman in the Nineteenth Century*, Fuller focuses on redefining the role of women as public, intellectual, and political rather than as private, domestic, and dependent. By dismantling the ideology of "separate spheres" for men and women, Fuller examines the possibility of woman not as a body but as an individual self, capable of learning, growing, and becoming. Students may not be aware of how radical a thought is her claim that a "house is no home unless it contain food and fire for the mind as well as for the body" (p. 732). Fuller rejects the premise that if a woman thinks, votes, and preaches, then "she cannot attend to those [affairs] of her own sphere" (p. 729). The European revolutions and the U.S. abolition movement revealed that dominant cultural and intellectual thought were at a tipping point. Students might be asked to consider the following claim: "Many women are considering within themselves, what they need that they have not, and what they can have, if they find they need it. Many men are considering whether women are capable of being and having more than they are and have, *and*, whether, if so, it will be best to consent to improvement in their condition" (p. 730). A pre-writing and pre-discussion exercise could ask students to consider the distinctions Fuller makes between men's and women's positions in these two sentences. According to Fuller, what is at stake for men and for women when they approach questions of what women need and have? How have these issues shifted or remained the same in our own culture? In a style reminiscent of Emerson's "Self-Reliance," Fuller proclaims, "Ascertain the true destiny of woman, give her legitimate hopes, and a standard within herself; marriage and all other relations would by degrees be harmonized with these" (p. 731). Students can be asked to make lists or free-write about exactly what Fuller believes is woman's "true destiny" and what she means by the phrase "standard within herself." Such an exercise opens up not only *Woman in the Nineteenth Century* but also Fuller's other essays on reform in this section.

Connections to Other Authors and Texts

Fuller's *Woman in the Nineteenth Century* might be said to respond directly to Emerson's "Self-Reliance" (p. 683) and to offer a critique of Emerson from a minority perspective in some ways similar to Douglass's *Narrative* (p. 855), Apess's "An Indian's Looking-Glass for the White Man" (p. 639), Jacobs's *Incidents* (p. 763), and Child's "Letter from New-York" (p. 645). Each of these writers is concerned with the limits and responsibilities of individual freedom under the law. Fuller's life and works might be compared as well to other women who earned a living through writing in the nineteenth century, including Fanny Fern and Harriet Beecher Stowe. Finally, "Things and Thoughts in Europe" contributes to the ongoing conversation among writers in this anthology about what constitutes America and its citizens; this and her other short essays might be compared to Emerson's "The American Scholar" (p. 670) and Thoreau's *Walden* (p. 809).

Questions for Class Discussion

1. List the specific reasons Fuller presents in defense of changing the role and position of women.

2. What strategies of argumentation does Fuller use to win over women to her point of view? Are these strategies the same as or different from her appeals to men?

3. Locate passages in which Fuller seems to respond directly to Emerson's "Self-Reliance" or other works by him. Consider whether Fuller is in agreement or disagreement with Emerson in these passages.

4. Consider "New Year's Day," "Our City Charities," and "Things and Thoughts in Europe." What fundamental values and themes underpin Fuller's opinions? How do these values and themes respond to the changes witnessed by and the concerns of readers during this period?

Brief Bibliography

Chevigny, Bell Gale. *The Woman and the Myth: Margaret Fuller's Life and Writing*. Rev. and expanded ed. Boston: Northeastern UP, 1994.

Kolodny, Annette. "Inventing a Feminist Discourse: Rhetoric and Resistance in Margaret Fuller's *Woman in the Nineteenth Century*." *New Literary History: A Journal of Theory and Interpretation* 25.2 (1994 Spring): 355-82.

Urbanski, Marie Mitchell Olesen. "'Woman in the Nineteenth Century': Genesis, Form, Tone, and Rhetorical Devices." *Margaret Fuller: Visionary of the New Age*. Ed. Marie Mitchell Olesen Urbanski. Orono: Northern Lights, 1994. 160-80.

HARRIET BEECHER STOWE   (p. 747)

Approaches to Teaching

Unlike Emerson or Fuller, Stowe made her living by writing for a popular audience in periodicals, newspapers, and, finally, in her novels and sketches. Stowe positioned herself as a "True Woman," a term coined by historian Barbara Welter to describe a nineteenth-century ideal circulated in print culture, including gift and guide books, periodicals, household manuals, and novels. According to Welter, the "Cult of True Womanhood" espoused the values of purity, Christian piety, submissiveness, and domesticity. This idealized value system assumed what historians have called separate spheres, the notion that women and men occupied different spaces in culture. That is, men operated in the public sphere of the world and market, while women were expected to exert their influence from the private sphere of the home. Stowe's work relies on readers who share these idealized values and on the use of sentiment, the evocation of feeling in the reader to elicit action and social reform. According to Jane Tompkins, Stowe's work can be viewed as feminist in the sense that Stowe used sentiment and the values of True Womanhood to revolutionize the world from a woman's point of view.

Classroom Issues and Strategies

Students might view Stowe's perspective on women's issues and roles as conservative, especially after having read Fuller. Yet both writers insist on the value of women's contributions to U.S. culture. One approach is to discuss what Stowe's use of True Womanhood and separate-sphere ideology enables or disables. That is, in what ways does Stowe's apparent conform-ity to middle-class ideals inspire readers to act on behalf of social change? Students should be encouraged to talk about the range and limits of women's capacity for reforming the public sphere through their actions in the private. By making use of the excerpt from Catherine E. Beecher's *Treatise on Domestic Economy* in the "American Contexts" section, instructors can ensure that students understand the sociopolitical thrust of Stowe's sentimental Christian reform agenda.

Connections to Other Authors and Texts

As a writer concerned with woman's domestic role as an important facet of social responsibility, Stowe's work invites comparison to Child, Jacobs, and Fern. Read as a cluster, these works raise questions about the social and political role of women and the home in the nineteenth-century imagination. Stowe and Fuller make an interesting study as influential women interested in education and reform who choose very different life paths and strategies for reaching their audiences. "The Freeman's Dream" and the preface to *Uncle Tom's Cabin* could be read next to Jacobs and Douglass to reveal differing rhetorical strategies based on gender and race.

Questions for Class Discussion

1. Both "Trials of a Housekeeper" and "The Seamstress" depict women working in service occupations but from different perspectives. What does Stowe wish readers to learn about their responsibility to servants?

2. How does Stowe address her readers? That is, what does she assume to be true about who they are, how they live, and what they believe? How do you know?

3. Stowe's sister, Catherine E. Beecher, wrote *A Treatise on Domestic Economy*, a section of which is included in the "American Contexts" section of this unit. The two collaborated on a revised version of this book, retitled *The American Woman's Home*, and this manual was given to girls and used in schools throughout the United States What values or ideas from *Treatise* do you find in Stowe's fiction?

4. Consider the role that one of the following plays in Stowe's work: emotion, Christianity, domesticity, democracy, class.

Brief Bibliography

Ammons, Elizabeth. *Critical Essays on Harriet Beecher Stowe*. Boston: Hall, 1980.

Hedrick, Joan D. *Harriet Beecher Stowe: A Life*. New York: Oxford UP, 1994.

Weinstein, Cindy. *The Cambridge Companion to Harriet Beecher Stowe.* New York: Cambridge UP, 2004.

HARRIET JACOBS   (p. 763)

Approaches to Teaching

Jacobs experienced a great deal of difficulty in getting her manuscript into print. For example, she initially sent her tale to Harriet Beecher Stowe, who, according to letters from the period documented by Jean Fagan Yellin, at first disbelieved her and approached her boss and benefactor Mrs. Willis to verify the story. Stowe finally offered to include Jacobs's story in her own sequel to *Uncle Tom's Cabin* rather than to assist Jacobs with publication, a slight that stung Jacobs for the rest of her life. Much of Jacobs's difficulty in securing a publisher can be traced to the problem of writing an ex-slave narrative from a woman's viewpoint. Not only did Jacobs's narrative raise issues of authorial credibility typical of responses to nonwhite and women authors, but she also made public the difficult subjects of rape and sexual harassment of slave women by white masters. Nevertheless, Jacobs insisted on writing her narrative herself and finally found Lydia Maria Child willing to take the risk and help her to bring it to print. Letters between Jacobs and her friend Amy Post indicate that Jacobs was not even present for the final negotiations with the publisher. A familiarity with the tenets of True Womanhood, or the nineteenth-century cult of domesticity, which idealized piety, purity, and submissiveness, is helpful in understanding Jacobs's approach to her audience.

Classroom Issues and Strategies

If Douglass's narrative focuses on the relationship of freedom to literacy, violence, and individualism, Jacobs's woman's viewpoint revises the genre and its definition of freedom. Jacobs offers us narratives of relationship, including the importance of her family, her grandmother, her white mistress, her free-black lover, and her home and children. Jacobs emphasizes the role of the community in the lives of slaves. The narrative continually insists on the dangers slavery poses to women and, for that matter, True Womanhood, suggesting to its audience the impossibility of upholding ideals of womanhood – for both slave woman and mistress – in a slave economy. The narrative plays on readers' expectations of stories about women by presenting and then aborting or fracturing stories of childhood innocence, love and romance, motherhood, marriage, and home. Students are sometimes insensitive to Jacobs's psychological experiences, especially if they have previously read Douglass, and they should be shown the radical potential of this work. Jacobs explicitly instructs her white readers how to read her, denies them permission to judge her, and asks whether any home in the country can be safe for women as long as slavery persists.

Connections to Other Authors and Texts

Incidents bears traces of the narrator's awareness of reader skepticism faced by all nonwhite and women authors during the nineteenth century and earlier periods. Like other slave narratives, the narrator assures readers of her credibility as a reasonable, moral, and Christian person with normal human feelings. These issues of credibility are exacerbated by Jacobs's gender. To what extent can her readers view a "fallen" woman as an authority on their own reform and that of their country and its laws? As well as other slave narratives and even captivity tales, the text is effectively compared to other abolition texts, including Stowe's *Uncle Tom's Cabin* (p. 761) and some of Wheatley's poetry. Both Fuller and Child deal with questions of women's work and roles. Furthermore, instructors might connect Jacobs's use of legal language (i.e., *loophole*) with the language of rights and independence during the formation of the new nation.

Questions for Class Discussion

1. According to the epigraphs listed on the title page, Jacobs intended that women should read her book. Discuss the narrator's strategies for appealing to this audience in the preface and the narrative proper. How do you think this intended audience influenced what was included or excluded?

2. How does Jacobs's text define *slavery* and *freedom?* What are the central metaphors and images that she uses to characterize them? How is Jacobs's definition of *freedom* similar to or different from that of other captives and slaves whose work we have read this semester?

3. Read chapter 10 of *Incidents* closely. What kind of language does the narrator use to describe her dilemma and her actions? Discuss why such language may have been chosen and how it may have worked on her intended audience.

4. Discuss the significance of Linda's hiding place (chapter 21) by considering either her use of the word *loophole* (a legal term) or the activities she performs there.

5. Discuss the last chapter, "Free at Last," and the extent to which readers are given a happy ending.

Brief Bibliography

Garfield, Deborah M., and Rafia Zafar, eds. *Harriet Jacobs and* Incidents in the Life of a Slave Girl: *New Critical Essays.* Cambridge and New York: Cambridge UP, 1996.

McKay, Nellie Y., and Frances Smith Foster, eds. Incidents in the Life of a Slave Girl: *Contexts, Criticisms.* New York: Norton, 2001.

Yellin, Jean Fagan. *Harriet Jacobs: A Life.* New York: Basic Civitas, 2004.

HENRY DAVID THOREAU   (p. 792)

Approaches to Teaching

Because his work taps contemporary readers' sense of rebelliousness and individualism, Thoreau can be fun to teach. Students often come to class feeling inspired by his idealistic actions and principled and good-humored erudition; they seem to enjoy thinking about how they might take a more Thoreauvian approach to their own lives. They are eager to consider how modern conveniences and gadgets influence our culture as well – although they are not necessarily eager to give them up – and how doing and thinking for themselves is made possible (or impeded) by modern educational and cultural institutions. (I sometimes remind them that, after all, Thoreau also accidentally burned 300 acres with a cooking fire.) It may be useful at the outset to discuss questions of genre with regard to *Walden,* since the work certainly blends nature writing, philosophy, social critique, and memoir and uses metaphor extensively.

Classroom Issues and Strategies

Both *Walden* and "Resistance to Civil Government" can be approached as applications of transcendental philosophy or as responses to the runaway train of nineteenth-century growth, industrialization, mass agriculture, and capitalist values. Certainly, nature is at the center of any study of *Walden,* in which Thoreau takes Emerson's notions about nature as a symbol for ideal and spiritual truths and applies them to humankind. If Emerson views nature as a cipher for the sacred, and if capitalists and industrialists view nature as raw material for profit and development, then Thoreau considers what it means for humans to be a part of nature. As he writes in the "Conclusion" to *Walden,* "there are continents and seas in the moral world, to which every man is an isthmus or an inlet, yet unexplored by him . . ." (p. 848). Thoreau has often been studied as an important voice in a long tradition of American environmentalist writers willing to consider nature for its own sake. Since Thoreau's text proceeds from the central metaphor of Walden Pond (in the same way that Whitman's "Song of Myself" on p. 1238 proceeds from a blade of grass), instructors might ask students to consider how each chapter of *Walden* defines some overlooked philosophical or metaphorical aspect of nature.

Connections to Other Authors and Texts

Walden and "Resistance to Civil Government" fall within a transcendental tradition of moral, social, and spiritual ideals applied to practical action and reform. Like Fuller, Douglass, and Stowe, Thoreau engages ideals as a way to promote real-world change. In addition to the transcendental thought of Emerson, Fuller, and Whitman, Thoreau's work draws on a long tradition of Americans writing about resistance (Paine, Jefferson, Franklin, Wheatley, Tecumseh, Murray, Stowe, Douglass, Jacobs). As well, *Walden* examines questions of the meaning of the American landscape that pervade the works of William Bradford, Mary Rowlandson, J. Hector St. John de Crèvecoeur, Philip Freneau, James Fenimore Cooper, and others.

Questions for Class Discussion

1. In both works, what is Thoreau's relationship to his audience and to society as a whole? How does he situate his narrative persona? That is, what kind of person is the "I" in these texts, and how do we know?

2. Locate passages in the text that seem directly comparable to one of the other authors we've read (Franklin or Emerson). How does Thoreau use one or more of the ideas of this author?

3. Discuss the way that *Walden* redefines a familiar word, such as *economy, travel,* or *shelter.*

4. Choose one tenet of transcendentalism and explain how Thoreau affirms, complicates, or rejects it in "Resistance to Civil Government" or a chapter in *Walden.*

5. Consider Thoreau's work as a reformist response to one of the following: industrial capitalism, manifest destiny, technological progress, or slavery.

Brief Bibliography

Myerson, Joel, ed. *The Cambridge Companion to Henry David Thoreau.* New York: Cambridge UP, 1995.

Schneider, Richard J. *Approaches to Teaching Thoreau's* Walden *and Other Works.* New York: MLA, 1996.

———. *Henry David Thoreau.* Boston: Twayne, 1987.

FREDERICK DOUGLASS   (p. 855)

Approaches to Teaching

Douglass's life story, which he revised three times, is a compelling example of the slave-narrative genre, an autobiography by an ex-slave that traces his or her journey to freedom. The genre is a vital part of African American literary history and doubly meaningful because of the difficulty for slaves of knowing anything about their lives and histories, including their fathers, who were often white overseers or masters, their birthdays, their families, and their own cultural traditions. According to William Andrews, author of *To Tell a Free Story: The First Century of African American Autobiography* (Urbana: U of Illinois P, 1986), by the 1830s, a network of abolitionist reformers, including clergy, printers, editors, politicians, and booksellers, used the genre in the cause of abolition. By the 1840s and 1850s, black narrators such as Douglass reclaimed the genre by telling their stories in their own voices and developing their own conventions. Ex-slave narrators typically depict the horrors of slavery to white readers, whom the narrators imply know very little of slaves' daily realities. Through appeals to the moral and emotional responses of their white audiences, ex-slave narrators challenged readers' ideas and assumptions about African Americans and slaves.

Classroom Issues and Strategies

Douglass's decision to revise his story throughout his life testifies to the importance of self-construction and its relationship to individual identity in this text. Instructors can begin such a discussion with the illustration on the cover of the sheet music for "The Fugitive's Song" (p. 855) and the daguerreotype of Douglass in his twenties (p. 923), which students should compare to the preface by William Lloyd Garrison (p. 857), the letter from Wendell Phillips (p. 863), and the narrative proper. In different ways, these portrayals of Douglass aim to position him as an archetypal American or a representative black man and ex-slave. These wide-ranging representations merit scrutiny, especially given Douglass's damning appendix, which seems to counter Garrison's and Phillips's efforts to portray him as humble and nonthreatening for a white audience that is perhaps moved to sympathy for a slave but less comfortable with an imposing and self-assured African American man. Much of the narrative hinges on Douglass's acquisition of literacy, but language is an important thread throughout the text, including the language of slavery, which mixes up truth and lies, silence and speech, and even the meaning of family. One might read the text as a narrative of Douglass's gradual "mastery" of the discourses of slavery and freedom.

Connections to Other Authors and Texts

Douglass's narrative can be compared with other autobiographies in the anthology, including the captivity narrative (Rowlandson), spiritual and secular autobiography (Edwards, Ashbridge, Franklin), and ex-slave narratives (Equiano, Jacobs). Douglass provides an important response to nine-

teenth-century transcendentalist ideals and to the possibilities and realities of self-reliance, civil disobedience, and the role of the individual in a
democratic society.

Questions for Class Discussion

1. What is the purpose of including the testimonial prefaces from
   William Lloyd Garrison and Wendell Phillips at the beginning of the
   narrative? How do these prefaces characterize Douglass?

2. Who was Douglass's audience and what relationship does he, as a
   narrator, assume toward his readers? To what extent does Douglass
   live up to, challenge, or complicate the characterizations of the prefaces?

3. How does the narrator's discussion of slave songs fit into or challenge
   his relationship with his readers?

4. Discuss the ways that Douglass defines *freedom* and *self* in relation to
   one of the following ideas: manhood or masculinity, violence, literacy.

5. Like Emerson, Douglass learns the value of self-reliance. What is at
   stake for Douglass in this lesson? What must he give up in order to
   gain self-reliance? (Note: You might consider his relationship to the
   community and to other African Americans.)

Brief Bibliography

Hall, James C. *Approaches to Teaching* Narrative of the Life of Frederick
    Douglass. New York: MLA, 1999.

McFeeley, William S. *Frederick Douglass.* New York: Norton, 1995.

Sundquist, Eric J., ed. *Frederick Douglass: New Literary and Historical
    Essays.* Cambridge: Cambridge UP, 1991.

DOUGLASS THROUGH A MODERN LENS   (p. 923)

As the headnote explains, Douglass's life and work have been inspirational
to many American writers, one of whom is the African American poet
Robert Hayden. His poem, "Frederick Douglass," published just before the
passage of the Civil Rights Act of 1964, reveals Douglass's importance to
the ongoing struggle for equal rights in the United States.

    This poem can be aptly used at the end of the unit on Douglass to recall
initial conversations about how Garrison, nineteenth-century illustrators,
and Douglass himself generated representations of their subject. Students
could be asked first how this sonnet summarizes what they have learned

about Douglass through reading his *Narrative*. Students might consider how Hayden's representation revises or reshapes those earlier images. The words *diastole* and *systole* may be unfamiliar to students but are crucial to Hayden's meaning – the choice of language from physiological discourse emphasizes the centrality of Douglass to the African American struggle for freedom. The poem seems to say that Douglass, like air, like freedom, is the root from which African American lives grow.

AFRICAN AMERICAN SLAVE SONGS   (p. 925)

Approaches to Teaching

Remembering the slave songs of his boyhood in *Narrative,* Frederick Douglass writes, "The mere recurrence to those songs, even now, afflicts me; and while I am writing these lines, an expression of feeling has already found its way down my cheek" (p. 871). As the headnote suggests and as Douglass's narrative acknowledges, slave songs were the subject of controversy because they were used by proslavery forces as evidence that the slaves were happy. Douglass, however, puts such arguments to rest, stating, "I have sometimes thought that the mere hearing of those songs would do more to impress some minds with the horrible character of slavery, than the reading of whole volumes of philosophy on the subject could do" (p. 871) Douglass's belief in the emotional power of these songs provides a helpful introduction to, as well as a reminder of, the fact that these songs should be heard as well as read in the classroom. Students today may have a difficult time seeing songs as literature. However, as scholars of African American literature have observed, these are perhaps the earliest form of expression we have of African Americans in this country. If we do not accept the expressions of oral cultures, including Native Americans and African Americans, then American literary history fails to reflect the diversity of people who gave voice to the questions, What is America? and Who are Americans?

Classroom Issues and Strategies

Because slaves were denied access to literacy, slave songs are an especially important element of African American literary history. Slave songs probably developed through a process of intersecting oral traditions – including sermons, hymns, biblical stories, traditional African chants and praise songs – and the experiences of those who sang them. Douglass alludes to the contradictory nature of the songs, writing that "[t]hey would sometimes sing the most pathetic sentiment in the most rapturous tone, and the most rapturous sentiment in the most pathetic tone" (p. 870). This seeming contradiction is symptomatic of what W. E. B. Du Bois in *The Souls of Black Folk* termed "double consciousness," the sense that African Americans have of "always looking at one's self through the eyes of others." Slave songs functioned on a number of levels. Because of their performative nature, they enabled individuals and groups to shape their experiences into song, to voice their physical and emotional experiences, to express their faith, resignation, and resistance, and even to communicate in coded fashion in ways that eluded their oppressors. The lyrics to the songs often operated doubly; for example, the *Jordan River* served as a metaphor for the Ohio River, *heaven* or *home* for the North and freedom, and *Egypt* for the captivity of both the Israelites and African Americans.

Connections to Other Authors and Texts

Slave songs are an important component of Frederick Douglass's experience of slavery and so might be taught in conjunction with his narrative, especially chapter 2, which concerns plantation life. These songs are also a vital, yet often overlooked, part of American literary history similar to Native American tales, stories, and even speeches that were finally recorded in print. Like Thoreau's "Resistance to Civil Government" (p. 793), they comprise a type of protest literature in the nineteenth-century United States.

Questions for Class Discussion

1. Identify and explain the biblical story behind one of the slave songs. How does the song transform the story through language, repetition, and metaphor?

2. Slave songs used African American dialect and West African traditions of meter, improvisation, and call-and-response, when the leader of the song would call to the group to respond and, through this ritual, deepen the group's sense of communal identity. Choose one slave song and demonstrate how these elements work to create either double consciousness or resistance to oppression.

3. After listening to these songs in class, discuss the difference between reading them on the page and experiencing them as oral performances.

4. *Signifying*, a term used by Henry Louis Gates Jr. in African American literary criticism, is a practice of verbal play that — through improvisation, repetition, copying, and revising the elements of a certain text — criticizes or extends the meaning of its source. (One example that you might recognize is the use of sampling in contemporary music, the act of taking part of a sound recording and reusing it as part of

another sound recording.) Consider one or more of the slave songs as signifying practices.

Brief Bibliography

Epstein, Dena J. *Sinful Tunes and Spirituals: Black Folk Music to the Civil War*. American Life Music. Urbana: U of Illinois P, 1977.

Johnson, James Weldon. "From Preface to *The Books of American Negro Spirituals*." *Signifyin(g), Sanctifyin', & Slam Dunking: A Reader in African American Expressive Culture*. Ed. Gena Dagel Caponi. Amherst: U of Massachusetts P, 1999. 45-71.

Radano, Ronald. "Denoting Difference: The Writing of the Slave Spirituals." *Critical Inquiry* 22.3 (1996): 506-44.

The Songs Are Free. Dir. Gail Pelletto. With Bernice Johnson Reagon and Bill Moyers. Videocassette. Mystic Fire Video, 1991.

White, John. "Veiled Testimony: Negro Spirituals and the Slave Experience." *Journal of American Studies* 17.2 (1983): 251-63.

SLAVE SONGS THROUGH A MODERN LENS   (p. 931)

Poet and fiction writer James Weldon Johnson used slave songs and spirituals extensively in his work. His *Book of American Negro Spirituals*, a two-volume work that he coedited with his brother, J. Rosamond, demonstrates that slave songs originated in African chants and offers an extensive argument about the collaborative process of their composition by individuals and the community. Johnson's poem emphasizes the extraordinary development of these powerful songs and the remarkable survival of both the songs and those who sang them.

In some ways Johnson's poem "signifies" the slave songs themselves, incorporating the language of the original texts into his modern celebration. Once students understand how these songs were used and interpreted in the cultural context in which they were sung, instructors might turn to this poem as a way to talk about the persistence of the genre in American literary history. Specifically, Johnson employs quite elevated poetic language to apostrophize the singers of these songs: *bards, minstrel's lyre, mighty trumpet, valorous deeds, music empyrean*. His poem enables us to consider the ways that literary history and poetic conventions have operated to exclude African American traditions and voices and to reconsider the role of this genre and its anonymous authors.

American Facts and American Fiction

As the illustrations from periodicals and the satirical watercolor in this section show, by the third decade of the nineteenth century reading had become a national pastime. The increased availability and affordability of books and magazines, rising literacy rates among working classes, the emergence of leisure time among the middle class, especially women, and the stress on women's education and abolition contributed to the centrality of the printed word during this time. The absence of international copyright law meant that the works of U.S. writers competed for attention with cheap reprints of British writers, such as books by Sir Walter Scott and Charles Dickens; nevertheless, an important number of American fiction writers established themselves through periodicals and newspapers.

Although secular and religious leaders acknowledged the entertainment value of reading, publishers, editors, and even writers themselves focused on its usefulness for personal and social instruction and reform. Even as Ralph Waldo Emerson and John O'Sullivan pronounced the nation eager to found and sustain its own national literature, readers remained uncertain of the role of fiction for individuals in a democracy.

The selections in "American Facts and American Fiction" demonstrate that the foundation of an American national literature in the nineteenth century was laid by a diversity of voices representing a range of beliefs. As with the founding of the colonies themselves, the development of an American literature is inseparable from the political, social, and philosophical concerns of the age, including slavery, women's education, domesticity, moral reform, rapid industrialization and urbanization, the exploration of the American West, and so on. Just as there is no single ideal American citizen, so this literature shows, there is no single American voice. Rather, American literature grew out of the varying histories, experiences, geographical regions, and daily realities of its myriad inhabitants. While readers today have heard of Nathaniel Hawthorne's and Edgar Allan Poe's fiction, and perhaps even Fanny Fern's, they may be unaware of the context in which these works were produced; such awareness sheds light on the ways these writers imagined America, its inhabitants, and its literature, and the central questions of the age.

AMERICAN CONTEXTS: "Countless Phenomena of the Times": The Role of the Periodical Press   (p. 944)

This section is composed of editorial statements from a range of nineteenth-century periodicals, demonstrating the diversity of magazines and their audiences during this time. The selections are drawn from periodicals geared toward southern, women, and African American readers, as well as those for a more general, if erudite, audience. Some magazines were quite short-lived, perhaps lasting only a year, while others were published for decades. By considering the wide range of audiences and writers engaged in periodical literature, readers today begin to sense the breadth and diversity involved in composing a national literature.

Since the selections in this section are brief and exemplify the reading habits of several different magazine consumers, instructors might begin a conversation about the values, politics, and concerns of the idealized readers represented here. That is, by eliciting profiles of the imagined readers of these periodicals, students arrive at a cross section of America and are better able to consider the ways that the writers in "American Facts and American Fiction" went about appealing to those readers. Since today's readers are more likely familiar with novels and their writers, the section reminds us that, unlike nowadays, in the nineteenth century most American authors first made names for themselves in the periodical press before embarking on careers as novelists. The editorial statements included here demonstrate diverse possibilities for defining a national literature; they also suggest that readers used print culture to construct identities for themselves that were at once individual and yet associated with a community of imagined readers.

Questions for Class Discussion

1. The statements by periodical editors discuss in some detail the values, assumptions, and concerns of their presumed audiences. Choose one of these statements and make a list of the characteristics, beliefs, and concerns — both explicit and implicit — of the periodical's implied readers.

2. Given what you know about the implied readers of each periodical, what reform issues treated in the previous section of this anthology do you expect to appear in the pages of each?

3. Nearly all of the editorial statements make reference to women readers. Compare the statements – implied and explicit – about women
across this section. How are these imagined women readers similar or
different?

4. Each of these periodicals attempts to define democracy for its readers
as it participates in the building of an American national literature.
What definitions of *democracy* do you find? What are the characteristics of the American literature each wishes to build? How do you
account for the similarities and differences among definitions?

5. What do the editors hope will prompt readers to purchase or subscribe
to their periodicals? As you read the fiction that follows in this chapter,
consider the extent to which individual writers deliver what editors
promise. Can you uncover other unstated reasons for purchasing, sub-
scribing to, or reading these magazines?

NATHANIEL HAWTHORNE   (p. 966)

Approaches to Teaching

Many students may think of him as merely the author of *The Scarlet Letter,*
which they struggled through in high school, but the selections included in
the anthology highlight the ways Hawthorne's work addresses the call in
American periodicals for American themes, landscapes, and stories.
Students are most familiar with *The Scarlet Letter* and "Young Goodman
Brown" and often make the initial mistake of assuming that Hawthorne is
a "Puritan" writer. They might be interested to know that Stephen King, in
the afterword to his story "The Man in the Black Suit," wrote, "My favorite
Nathaniel Hawthorne story is 'Young Goodman Brown,' I think it's one of
the ten best stories ever written by an American." Students are also quick
to search for and attach defined meanings to "symbols" in Hawthorne's literature, a tendency instructors can mitigate by introducing him as a playful American writer whose work is best characterized by ambiguity. In an
essay called "How Ambiguous Is Hawthorne?" (*Hawthorne: A Collection of
Critical Essays,* ed. A. N. Kaul [Saddle River: Prentice, 1966]), H. J. Lang
argues that Hawthorne's work operates on three different levels of ambiguity: (1) language, especially poetic language, (2) human conduct and motivation, and (3) external action. That is, these three levels of ambiguity operate in tandem so that what happens in Hawthorne's fiction complicates our
ideas about what is real or imagined, fact or fiction, conscious or unconscious. By complicating our ideas about what is real, true, or factual,
Hawthorne raises questions that are central to mid-nineteenth-century
American writers. Emerson looks at nature and sees divinity; Hawthorne is
not as certain, either about what one sees or about one's capacity to see
clearly at all.

Classroom Issues and Strategies

The anthology includes selections from *The Token*, an illustrated gift annual, and from American periodicals (*New-England Magazine* and the *Pioneer*) whose editors appreciated American writers and subjects. Hawthorne's stories retell American history from at least a century and sometimes two centuries' distance. This distance enables him to consider the concerns of his own day in the retelling of the history that helped to shape nineteenth-century America. One might say that in doing so Hawthorne revises or remakes history. The selections here participate in the creation of American myths and legends about its history even as they question the usefulness of those very myths. That is, "Young Goodman Brown" and "My Kinsman, Major Molineux" seem to ask readers to consider what stories they tell themselves about American history and the degree to which those stories reflect their consciousness, perceptions, and fictions. How do their beliefs influence what they are able to see? These questions are relevant not only to the shaping of American history but also to the American national consciousness in which Hawthorne's texts were produced and are read. If individual and national consciousnesses shape perceptions, beliefs, and what counts as truth or fact, imagination or fiction, then how is it possible to act in responsible ways to fellow human beings? How should Americans negotiate their pursuit of morality or science ("Young Goodman Brown," "The Birth-Mark") in the world? In "The Doctrine of Colors," an essay published in the *American Magazine of Useful and Entertaining Knowledge*, Hawthorne writes, "The gay coloring in which the Almighty has decked the pale marble of nature, is not the result of any quality inherent in the colored body, or in the particles by which it may be tinged, but is merely a property of the light in which they happen to be placed." For Hawthorne, all knowledge seems to derive from the knower rather than the object the knower regards. Hawthorne demonstrates the danger of erring on the side of self-reliance or the mob ("My Kinsman, Major Molineux") and emphasizes the importance of sympathy, community, and a wisdom tempered by the knowledge of the world's ambiguities ("The Wives of the Dead").

Connections to Other Authors and Texts

Hawthorne's short stories compare and contrast effectively with Emerson's essays, especially *Nature* (p. 655), "Self-Reliance" (p. 683), and "The American Scholar" (p. 670). While Emerson sees a clear correspondence among nature, humankind, and the divine, Hawthorne, like Melville and Poe, tends to complicate Emerson's optimistic views of these relationships. While Emerson emphasizes the inherent divinity of nature and humans, Hawthorne focuses on the differences among human perceptions and the uncertainty these differences reveal about us. While Whitman and

Emerson see these differences as cause for celebration and the source of creativity, Hawthorne's short stories dwell on the difficulties, misunderstandings, and cruelties to which differences in perception give rise in human history. Finally, Hawthorne's evocation of women – including the widows in "The Wives of the Dead," Faith in "Young Goodman Brown," and Georgiana in "The Birth-Mark" – invites comparison to Melville's "The Tartarus of Maids" (p. 1101) and Poe's "Ligeia" (p. 1020) and "The Fall of the House of Usher" (p. 1030) and raises questions about nineteenth-century women's roles and powerlessness that Fern, Stoddard, and Fuller address.

Questions for Class Discussion

1. Explain the final lines of "The Wives of the Dead": "Before retiring, she set down the lamp, and endeavored to arrange the bedclothes so that the chill air might not do harm to the feverish slumberer. But her hand trembled against Margaret's neck, a tear also fell upon her cheek, and she suddenly awoke." Who is the "she" that awakes? Which aspects of the tale are a dream and which are reality? Do these distinctions matter to Hawthorne or to this story?

2. "My Kinsman, Major Molineux" seems to be a parable of America's Revolutionary period. In what ways does Robin represent young America? What lessons can readers draw from the story about America's Revolutionary past?

3. "Young Goodman Brown" operates as a parable of sin and faith set in Puritan America. What conclusions does the parable make? How is Brown changed by his encounter in the forest, and what does that reveal about him and those with whom he will spend his life?

4. "The Birth-Mark" presents a scientist who pursues truth relentlessly at the expense of the woman he loves. How does the story comment on our ability to know or to act on truth?

5. Hawthorne is known for his ambiguity, or the uncertainty that operates within his stories on the levels of language, human conduct, and plot. Choose one short story from this section and explain how such ambiguity asks readers to rethink their assumptions about a particular character, mindset, historical moment, and so on.

Brief Bibliography

Bunge, Nancy L. *Hawthorne: A Study of the Short Fiction.* New York: Twayne, 1993.

Friedlander, Benjamin. "Hawthorne's 'Waking Reality'." *American Transcendental Quarterly* 13.1 (1999): 51–68.

Reynolds, Larry, ed. *A Historical Guide to Nathaniel Hawthorne*. New York: Oxford UP, 2001.

Turner, Arlin. *Nathaniel Hawthorne: A Biography*. Oxford: Oxford UP, 1980.

EDGAR ALLAN POE   (p. 1018)

Approaches to Teaching

Many students confuse Poe's life and works; they rely on myths of Poe as a drug addict or an alcoholic and assume that his admittedly gothic, macabre, and fantastic fiction is the result of a mind under the influence of sub-stances or mental illness. The tightly controlled, highly stylized, and effec-tive short stories here demonstrate that Poe was in fact a master craftsman of the genre and, in many ways, can be said to have originated the detective and speculative fiction we still read today. Instructors might begin by debunking some of these Poe myths and offering a brief review of Poe leg-ends and facts: that is, he did at times drink; he was familiar with death and the rituals of mourning from a young age, as were most nineteenth-century readers, because the culture had not yet relinquished caring for the chroni-cally ill to hospitals nor preparing the dead for burial to funeral homes, and so on. Students should be introduced to the genre of the symbolic fantasy, the detective story, the arabesque (an intricately stylized tale of wonder or the supernatural, often deploying themes from the Far East), and the grotesque (a tale in which one aspect of human behavior is take to the extreme or shown as bizarre, unnatural, incongruous, or abnormal).

Classroom Issues and Strategies

The difficulty of approaching Poe in the classroom, aside from the myths surrounding his biography, derives from our critical inability to make him fit literary-historical paradigms of the American Renaissance. That is, although Poe is certainly a Southern American writer and an editor of sev-eral nineteenth-century magazines, his works seem not to concern American landscapes or the central issues facing Americans of his time (i.e., slavery, the oppression of women and people of color, industrializa-tion, immigration, etc.). His fiction reveals the precision and craft of a skilled writer who understands the literary marketplace, a forum he sati-rized in "How to Write a Blackwood Article" (1850). Because we read Poe recursively, through the very traditions he helped to create, we are in dan-ger of overlooking the original contributions of his work to the building of an American literature that was able to cross the Atlantic and influence European writers and artists, especially Sir Arthur Conan Doyle's Sherlock Holmes and the French Symbolist poets. One strategy for overcoming this

challenge and for unifying apparently disparate works in wide-ranging fictional subgenres is to consider the selections as fictional meditations on
art, the imagination, or the subconscious.

Connections to Other Authors and Texts

Poe's short fiction is most clearly related to that of Hawthorne; both use
romantic images and address questions of human perfectibility, including
the operations of reason and imagination, the conscious and subconscious
mind, and the cost of knowledge. Both writers use figures of male artists
and somewhat objectified women to work out these questions. While Poe's
work at times seems to share Emerson's idealism regarding human potential, his fiction nevertheless registers the underside of the intellect and
imagination in ways that Emerson overlooks. Poe's craftsmanship in the
genre is ably compared to the other short-story writers in the "American
Facts and American Fiction" section.

Questions for Class Discussion

1. Characterize the narrator of "Ligeia" and his relationship to the title
   character. What is her source of power in the story, and what does that
   suggest about the narrator?

2. Note the number of times the narrator of "The Fall of the House of
   Usher" uses the words *I perceived* or *it seemed*. Aside from making him
   a somewhat unreliable narrator, what does this use of language convey
   about the relationship between thought and action or imagination and
   reality?

3. Characterize the narrator of "The Tell-Tale Heart" and his relationship
   to the old man. To what extent are these characters opposites? similar?

4. What enables Dupin to solve the mystery of "The Purloined Letter"?
   Extend your answer beyond what happens in the plot to consider how
   and why the mystery is solved and what this might say about the
   human imagination.

Brief Bibliography

Hayes, Kevin J., ed. *The Cambridge Companion to Edgar Allan Poe*. New
York: Cambridge UP, 2002.

Quinn, Arthur Hobson, and Shawn Rosenheim. *Edgar Allan Poe: A Critical
Biography*. Baltimore: Johns Hopkins UP, 1998.

Silverman, Kenneth, ed. *New Essays on Poe's Major Tales*. Cambridge:
Cambridge UP, 1993.

FANNY FERN
(SARA PAYSON WILLIS PARTON)　　(p. 1062)

Approaches to Teaching

When Hawthorne complained that "America is now wholly given over to a d–d mob of scribbling women," he no doubt referred to the likes of Fanny Fern, the beloved popular columnist in the Boston *Olive Branch,* the *New York Musical World and Times,* the Philadelphia *Saturday Evening Post,* and, finally, the *New York Ledger.* Fern's popularity provides a good starting point for reading the sketches in this section, which take on subjects that would have been controversial in her time, such as the role of a wife, responsibility to the poor, prostitution, the treatment of the mentally ill, and prison reform. Instructors and students might discuss how cultural figures introduce difficult subjects today and consider to what extent those techniques are apparent in Fern's work. Such techniques emerge most readily when students read Fern's work aloud, the way it was often read by families in the evenings before the age of television.

Classroom Issues and Strategies

Fern's direct style includes both sympathy and satire to call attention to social inequities and demand that her audience question their views and act on their feelings and principles. Combining acerbic wit with genuine sympathy, Fern's life and work challenged the ideal of True Woman even as she lived up to it in many ways. For example, Fern is a public figure who nonetheless writes from home for those who read in the home. Her work criticizes social ills and demands reform regarding topics considered unseemly for women, including prostitution, mental illness, and criminality, yet her outspoken approach to what readers might find inappropriate is tempered with so-called feminine sympathetic feeling. Fern's message seems to be that Americans have a moral responsibility to their fellow creatures; more often than not, the problems she uncovers are caused by the unthinking and unsympathetic powerful few, often men, whose entitlement and persistence in a double standard of behavior flies in the face of what is truly democratic. Instructors might ask students to make two lists: the first containing the qualities of Fern's writing or narrative persona that conform to the then-dominant cultural ideas about women and the second delineating the ways that her writing seems to refute those same dominant cultural ideas. From there, instructors might talk about how Fern negotiates a relationship with her audience based on these two lists.

Connections to Other Authors and Texts

Fern's opinions and method of delivery are aptly compared to the writers in "The Era of Reform" section of this anthology, including Child, Fuller, and Jacobs, all of whom focus on women. Fern's able and competent voice evokes comparisons to Emerson's charge to Americans to be self-reliant. Her command of narrative and the short sketch invite comparison to each of the fiction writers in this section as well. Most apparent is the affinity of her work with Stoddard, Alcott, and Davis, each of whom addresses the disparity between men and women, rich and poor. Such comparisons then give way to Melville's unromantic depictions of men and women as well as Mitchell's bachelor's satire on marriage. Finally, Fern's discussions of the role of women are in marked contrast to those of Hawthorne, whose women bear the burden of men's mistakes, and Poe, whose women serve as idealized creatures against which his powerful and misguided narrators construct or unravel their senses of self.

Questions for Class Discussion

1. Identify one or more rhetorical strategies that Fern uses to connect with her audience and to encourage them to adopt her viewpoint.

2. Discuss the ways that Fern's narrative voice upholds, challenges, or complicates the ideal of True Woman. (See section on Stowe on p. 87 of this manual for a definition of the term.)

3. Certainly, many of Fern's readers were men. Explain how she addresses that audience as she calls for reform of women's roles and treatment.

4. Margaret Fuller writes in *Woman in the Nineteenth Century*, "A house is no home unless it contain food and fire for the mind as well as for the body." How do Fern's sketches respond to this statement?

5. Fern was one of the first women to praise Walt Whitman's *Leaves of Grass*, which scandalized much of the country. What values does her work espouse that you find in Whitman?

Brief Bibliography

Pettengill, Claire C. "Against Novels: Fanny Fern's Newspaper Fictions and the Reform of Print Culture." *American Periodicals* 6 (1996): 61–91.

Walker, Nancy A. *Fanny Fern*. Twayne's United States Authors Ser. 616. New York: Twayne, 1993.

Warren, Joyce W. *Fanny Fern: An Independent Woman*. New Brunswick: Rutgers UP, 1992.

HERMAN MELVILLE   (p. 1072)

Approaches to Teaching

Both of the Melville tales in the anthology recall Emerson's characterization of the masculine, self-reliant scholar persevering in his convictions
from positions both above and amid a people too busy for literature and
thought. In "Self-Reliance," Emerson states that the self-reliant individual
must be as a "boy who is sure of his dinner." Melville's short fiction offers
a range of responses to Emerson's statement. Certainly, "The Paradise of
Bachelors" offers readers a comfortable window into the rarefied lives of
privileged English gentlemen, taking their ease among nine-course meals
and cigar smoke. By contrast, the sexually charged "The Tartarus of Maids"
offers a grim view of women factory workers at the mercy of male domina-
tion. In some ways "Bartleby" mirrors the failures of Melville's own literary
career; as the headnote reminds us, Melville's popular and critical success
following his seafaring novels was replaced by critical misunderstanding
and even hostility when he experimented with the novel form, and he
turned to magazine writing to pay the bills. Bartleby, who refuses to work,
speak, and write, manifests a form of passive resistance – civil disobedience – to the Wall Street milieu and the faceless monotony of labor behind
walls. The extermination of the artist/resistant individual in this story
echoes Thoreau's statement in *Walden* that "most men lead lives of quiet
desperation."

Classroom Issues and Strategies

Most students are familiar with Melville as the author of that weighty tome
Moby-Dick, although some may have encountered "Bartleby" in high
school. His magazine fiction included here suggests a Melville both thoroughly of his time and remarkably relevant for today's audiences.
Instructors might stress the ways that Melville's themes regarding the
relationships among poverty, work, and gender or the dehumanization of
the workplace continue to resonate, especially because Melville's nineteenth-century prose style and syntax will prove slow going for some of
today's students.

Connections to Other Authors and Texts

The short fiction included here works effectively with the texts included in
"The Era of Reform," including the transcendental beliefs expressed by
Emerson and Thoreau and the calls to action on behalf of women and the
oppressed. Melville undertakes themes addressed by several writers in
"American Facts and American Fiction," including Fern, Stoddard, and

Alcott (women's lives); Mitchell (the life of a bachelor); Davis (labor); and Hawthorne and Poe (the role of the artist/scientist/intellectual).

Questions for Class Discussion

1. How do the narrator's self-revelations prepare us to understand Bartleby and the narrator's reaction to him?

2. What does Melville gain by telling the story through the narrator's point of view? How reliable is this narrator? Provide evidence in support of your answer.

3. What ethic does Melville provide as an alternative to the ethic of Wall Street?

4. Characterize the reasons for the differences between the sexes in "The Paradise of Bachelors and the Tartarus of Maids." How does this characterization respond to American transcendentalist beliefs, including self-reliance?

5. Comment on the use of sexualized imagery in "The Paradise of Bachelors and the Tartarus of Maids." To what end does Melville's narrator use such imagery; what is its effect on the reader?

Brief Bibliography

Levine, Robert S., ed. *The Cambridge Companion to Herman Melville*. New York: Cambridge UP, 1998.

Newman, Lea Bertani Vozar. *A Reader's Guide to the Short Stories of Herman Melville*. Boston: Hall, 1986.

Parker, Hershel. *Herman Melville: A Biography: II, 1851–1891*. Baltimore: Johns Hopkins UP, 2002.

Wiegman, Robyn. "Melville's Geography of Gender." *American Literary History*, 1.4 (1989): 735–53.

DONALD GRANT MITCHELL
(IK MARVEL)   (p. 1119)

Approaches to Teaching

Readers may wish to return to James Ewell Heath's editorial statement published in the first issue of the *Southern Literary Messenger*, included in the section "'Countless Phenomena of the Times': The Role of the Periodical Press" (American Contexts, p. 944), to review a Southern perspective on an American national literature. While considering that statement, readers might also attend to the depiction of Southern gender roles and consider how those relate to Mitchell's New England bachelor's visions of his future life. At the time this work appeared, marriage was viewed by many as a microcosm of American democracy, a union in which men and women performed the vital labor of producing, rearing, and educating young citizens. Mitchell ably combines wit, feeling, and scholarly erudition in his extraordinarily popular text. Readers might be reminded of the importance of sentiment – the evocation of feeling through style, tone, or subject matter – to nineteenth-century readers.

Classroom Issues and Strategies

Mitchell's amusing work concerns the roles of men and women and the function of marriage in America. For this reason, readers are best recalled to those works they have read so far that describe or critique these concerns. Catherine E. Beecher's *Treatise on Domestic Economy* (p. 627) offers an excellent, if idealized, statement about the importance, as well as the gendered division, of labor in marriage in the new American nation. Students might be asked to develop profiles of the ideal roles of men and women as well as an image of the home within marriage, according to Beecher. Then they can turn to Mitchell and explore those same issues from the bachelor's perspective. What things, ideas, or people does Mitchell's bachelor choose as targets for his satire? What things, ideas, or people does he seem to value or even place on a pedestal?

Connections to Other Authors and Texts

Mitchell's "Reverie" seems to respond directly to Stowe's "Trials of a Housekeeper" (p. 749), Fern's "The Tear of a Wife" (p. 1064) and "The 'Coming' Woman" (p. 1071), and Fuller's *Woman in the Nineteenth Century* (p. 727). The sketch parallels the concerns raised by Melville in "The Paradise of Bachelors" (p. 1101). In his sense of wood-paneled privilege, the bachelor is in marked contrast to the characters in Davis's *Life in the Iron-Mills* (p. 1150) and many of the women characters portrayed by women writers throughout this chapter. Melville's work, Thoreau's *Walden* (p. 809), and Emerson's "The American Scholar" (p. 670) provide other comparisons for representations of masculinity in the nineteenth century.

Questions for Class Discussion

1. What kind of man is the narrator? What does he value and how can you tell?

2. What effect does the physical location of the narrator's reverie have on his thoughts?

3. What does the narrator think of women? According to him, what do women think, do, and offer in life?

4. What kind of audience does the narrator imagine, and what strategies does he use to appeal to it? List especially telling passages that support your point.

5. Write a two-paragraph contemporary reverie of a bachelor or bache-lorette or an imagined response by Fanny Fern to Mitchell's "Reverie." Share your work in class.

Brief Bibliography

Pancost, David W. "Donald Grant Mitchell's 'Reveries of a Bachelor' and Herman Melville's 'I and My Chimney.'" *American Transcendental Quarterly: A Journal of New England Writers* 42 (1979): 129-36.

Spiro, Lisa. "Reading with a Tender Rapture: Reveries of a Bachelor and the Rhetoric of Detached Intimacy." *Book History* 6 (2003): 57-93.

Tew, Arnold G., and Allan Peskin "The Disappearance of Ik Marvel." *American Studies* 33.2 (1992): 5-20.

ELIZABETH BARSTOW STODDARD   (p. 1134)

Approaches to Teaching

As the headnote explains, Stoddard came from a small New England coastal community, a milieu that influenced much of her work and may account for critical depictions of her as a regional writer. In *American Women Regionalists, 1850-1910* (New York: Norton, 1995), literary critics Marjorie Pryse and Judith Fetterley argue that regional literature upholds woman-centered values of domesticity, affection, and community. The attention to the character of the locale and its inhabitants, including local speech, manner-isms, beliefs, customs, and landscape reinforce this critical understanding. The headnote also points to Stoddard's use of Cinderella stories, a popular plot in the first half of the nineteenth century that traced the trials and tri-umphs of a young girl coming of age, according to Nina Baym's *Woman's Fiction*. Stoddard's story exhibits both threads by focusing on two very strong women attempting to exert power and independence in the public world. However, Stoddard's ending gives the Cinderella plot that readers might expect an edgy twist, suggesting that all is not as well as it seems at home.

Classroom Issues and Strategies

Students might be asked to outline the plot of a Cinderella tale, emphasiz-ing the heroine's situation, the reasons behind and her responses to her sit-

uation, and the typical resolution. Then invite students to discuss the similarities and differences between that plot and "Lemorne *versus* Huell," in
particular the comparisons between the narrator and Cinderella (especially discrepancies between active and passive heroines), Aunt Eliza and
the wicked stepmother, and the so-called happy endings. Such discussion
might elicit emphasis on Stoddard's rather wry and straightforward heroine, readers' assumptions about the role and value of marriage and
courtship, and the economic underpinnings of gendered lives in the nineteenth century.

Connections to Other Authors and Texts

Stoddard's work invites immediate comparison to Fern, Fuller, and Stowe,
and some of the writers in the section "'I Will Be Heard': The Rhetoric of
Antebellum Reform" (American Contexts, p. 617) whose works share an
attention to and a critique of the roles of women in domestic and economic
contexts. In addition, Stoddard's refutation of the sunny side of life,
whether in her frank and unromanticized characters or her apparent views
of courtship and marriage, suggests comparisons to what some critics
have characterized as Hawthorne's, Melville's, and Poe's interests in the
underside of human behavior and motivation. Finally, Stoddard's use of
realist techniques places her work alongside that of Davis and Alcott.

Questions for Class Discussion

1. Characterize Aunt Eliza and the narrator's relationship to her. What
   behaviors do you expect from Aunt Eliza, and how does the story reinforce or unsettle those expectations?

2. What kind of person is the narrator? What is her attitude toward her
   position, her future, and the role of courtship and marriage in her life?
   Does this change over the course of the story?

3. How does Margaret characterize the gentlemen in the story? How do
   you account for that characterization?

4. Explain the meaning of the ending: "As it struck I said, '*My husband is
   a scoundrel*,' and woke with a start." Be careful in your answer to go
   beyond the plot to examine the thematic and cultural implications of
   such a statement.

Brief Bibliography

Humma, John B. "Realism and Beyond: The Imagery of Sex and Sexual
Oppression in Elizabeth Stoddard's 'Lemorne *versus* Huell.'" *South
Atlantic Review* 58.1 (1993): 33–47.

Smith, Robert McClure, and Ellen Weinauer, eds. *American Culture, Canons, and the Case of Elizabeth Stoddard.* Tuscaloosa: U of Alabama P, 2003.

Zagarell, Sandra A. "Legacy: Profile: Elizabeth Drew Barstow Stoddard (1823-1902)." *Legacy: A Journal of Nineteenth-Century American Women Writers* 8.1 (1991): 39-49

REBECCA HARDING DAVIS   (p. 1149)

Approaches to Teaching

Although Davis grew up with affluence and culture, she used her education and erudition to call attention to the plight of immigrants laboring thanklessly in America's industries. Far from the myth of the American dream depicted in John Smith's *Generall Historie* (p. 106) or Benjamin Franklin's *Autobiography* (p. 340), *Life in the Iron-Mills* invites readers to consider the relationships among work, well-being, respect, fulfillment, social position, and individual and social responsibility. Written and published at the outset of the Civil War, the story draws on the domestic themes that Stowe raises in *Uncle Tom's Cabin* to consider another form of oppression facing the already divided nation. Like Stowe, Davis relies on emotional appeals and direct reader address to deliver her critique. Davis's work is an early example of realism, a literary movement that emphasizes faithfulness to everyday situations, characters, and language; her focus on the impact of industrial capitalism on individuals became an important facet of this movement.

Classroom Issues and Strategies

The "American Facts and American Fiction" section includes a variety of images of nineteenth-century readers. Students might be asked to contrast those images with the characters in *Life in the Iron-Mills*. For example, students should consider how the surroundings, dress, and apparent lifestyles of the figures in the images contrast with those in the story. Once these discrepancies are acknowledged, instructors can discuss how Davis uses literary and rhetorical strategies to bridge this gap between reader and subject matter. The narrator's concern is to "make [the secret of these lives] a real thing" (p. 1152) to her readers. One such technique is her use of careful, even painterly, detail to evoke the opening scene, which students may not at first realize is that of a home. The images of smoke, dirt, and the canary contrast with idealized images of home and convey an overall feeling of oppression. By introducing the romantic artist Hugh into this scene, Davis asks questions about the relationships among art, sensibility or feeling, and socioeconomic position. Students in the United States often resist talking about social class because of the very American myth the story seeks to debunk. That is, *Life in the Iron-Mills* contests America's dearly held national belief that hard work leads to success. Against this story, axioms from Franklin's *Poor Richard's Almanack*, which are also illustrated in *Autobiography* and have found their way into our national consciousness, no longer hold true: "He that hath a Trade hath an Estate," "If we are industrious, we shall never starve," and "God gives all Things to Industry." In the eighteenth century, a man with a trade owned the "means of production." With the rise of industrialization, however, capitalists took over these means and a worker no longer profited in the same way.

Connections to Other Authors and Texts

Davis's text works well with those from "The Era of Reform" by extending the problem of oppression to working-class immigrants. While her characters may look different from Child's Amelia Norman, Stowe's seamstress, Jacobs, Alcott's Robert, or even Fern's inhabitants of Blackwell's Island, Davis argues that immigrants, too, are American citizens who share American hopes and dreams. Although, like Hawthorne, Poe, and Melville, Davis considers the position of the artist in America, her work concerns the artist living in a culture that values only "the exertions of mechanical skill." Even as her protagonist suggests a romantic artist, the story represents an important development in American magazine fiction in the 1860s toward more realistic plots and characters than those of Poe and Hawthorne.

Questions for Class Discussion

1. How does the introduction, or "frame" story, work? What is the purpose of conveying the narrator's perspective in this way?

2. Who is the narrator talking to? How can you tell? Why would this particular audience find such a story important or interesting?

3. Characterize each of the following and his role in the story: Kirby, Dr. May, "Captain," and Mitchell.

4. What is the function of Hugh Wolfe? In what ways is his character specifically designed to address the audience Davis addresses?

5. Describe and explain the function and meaning of the korl-woman statue.

Brief Bibliography

Harris, Sharon M. *Rebecca Harding Davis and American Realism.* Philadelphia: U of Pennsylvania P, 1991.

Pfaelzer, Jean. *"Parlor Radical": Rebecca Harding Davis and the Origins of American Social Realism.* Pittsburgh: U of Pittsburgh P, 1996.

LOUISA MAY ALCOTT   (p. 1178)

Approaches to Teaching

Many readers may be familiar with Alcott's *Little Women* and its tomboy heroine, Jo March, but few students today are familiar with Alcott as an impressive literary figure, whose first success was *Hospital Sketches* (1863). Although remembered often as the writer of children's literature, Alcott published a wide range of fiction that included romance, sensational thrillers, and realistic novels. "The Brothers," like *Hospital Sketches,* is based on Alcott's six-week stint as a volunteer nurse in the Georgetown, Washington, D.C., Union Hotel Hospital during the Civil War. It was published in the *Atlantic Monthly* in 1863 and reprinted as "My Contraband" in the collection *Hospital Sketches and Camp and Fireside Stories* (1869). "The Brothers" establishes Alcott's narrative voice – realistic, intelligent, and tinged with a note of satire or wit – and anticipates a theme that pervades Alcott's writing: the importance of women's self-sufficiency and work outside of marriage. The story is based on the July 18, 1863, attack on Fort Wagner, near Charleston, by the black Fifty-fourth Massachusetts Regiment, which was led by Robert Gould Shaw, a white man, and which resulted in the deaths of half of the black soldiers. Published just a few months after the attack, "The Brothers" daringly takes on complex and controversial issues for its time, including war, the working conditions at the Union Hotel Hospital, and the female narrator's relationship with a sympathetic and sexually compelling man of mixed race.

Classroom Issues and Strategies

The image of the Civil War nurse sitting beside the beds of wounded soldiers emphasizes the emergence of new roles for women in the latter half of the nineteenth century. No longer at home, the nurse carries her nurturing, womanly role into the public space of a hospital, where she ministers to and works alongside doctors and, as the story observes, freed black men. The use of the word *contraband* evokes both the literal term for escaped slaves working for the Union cause and the possibility of the illicit or illegal. Certainly, the term plays on Nurse Dane's attraction to the "strong-limbed and manly" Robert, the twenty-five-year-old mulatto whose "passionate melancholy" elicits in her a desire to "know and comfort him." In addition to the unspoken desire of the protagonist, the story concerns the nature of black masculinity, which is compromised by Robert's characterization, like all black men, as a "boy," his servitude as a slave and a hospital worker, his powerlessness to stop his white half-brother's rape of his wife, and, finally, his obedience to Nurse Dane, after whom he names himself and abides by her request to spare the life of his tormentor. This story asks hard questions about the work, sexuality, gender roles, and power of white women and black men. Students may initially state that these questions are more relevant for "the old days when race relations were a problem." One way to examine these issues more analytically is to consider the extent to which today's readers are comfortable with Nurse Dane's response to Robert. That is, how closely tied to race are her responses to his physical appearance, his presence as an assistant, and her advice to him on how to handle his rage against his half-brother?

Connections to Other Authors and Texts

"The Brothers" works exceptionally well next to Douglass's *Narrative* (p. 855) because of the focus on black masculinity and the relationships among freedom, violence, and manhood. The passage about Douglass's battle with Covey, in which he tells readers that they shall see how a slave was made a man, can be compared with the representation of Robert as a would-be murderer and then a fearless soldier. The story could be taught in connection with other Civil War literature in this section, including Stowe's "The Freeman's Dream: A Parable" (p. 760) and the preface to *Uncle Tom's Cabin* (p. 761) and Whitman's poetry in *Drum-Taps*, especially "The Wound-Dresser" (p. 1298).

Questions for Class Discussion

1. *Contraband* is a term used to describe escaped slaves brought behind Union lines during the Civil War. The term also conjures the notion of something illegal or illicit. When the story was republished in 1869, Alcott gave it the name "My Contraband." What reasons does the story offer for focusing on this term?

2. How does Nurse Dane conform to, complicate, or challenge the typical roles women were expected to play in the mid-nineteenth century?

3. Classic abolitionist literature often deployed the figure of the "tragic mulatto," a light-skinned person of mixed race whose physical attractiveness invites sympathy from white readers and assures his/her demise, either in death or suicide, as a tragic victim of slavery. To what extent does Robert fulfill, challenge, or complicate this characterization?

4. Because of his race, Robert is referred to as a "boy." As the story progresses, he heeds Nurse Dane's plea not to avenge the rape and suicide

of his wife, Lucy, on his half-brother and then adopts Nurse Dane's last name. How do these events characterize Robert in relation to her? Is she his friend or his "mistress"?

5. What social or spiritual issues does the story critique? Explain the nature of and arguments behind this critique.

Brief Bibliography

MacDonald, Ruth K. *Louisa May Alcott*. Twayne's United States Authors Ser. 457. Boston: Twayne, 1983.

Patterson, Mark. "Racial Sacrifice and Citizenship: The Construction of Masculinity in Louisa May Alcott's 'The Brothers'." *Studies in American Fiction* 25 (Autumn 1997): 147-66.

Stern, Madeleine B. *Louisa May Alcott: A Biography*. Rev. ed. New York: Random, 1996.

New Poetic Voices

This section is designed to demonstrate the range of poetic voices in the nineteenth century, all of which responded to the call for an American national literature by using its most exalted form. The ornately formal illustration on the title page to Lydia Sigourney's *Select Poems* (p. 1194) contrasts effectively with the title page of Whitman's *Leaves of Grass* (p. 1237), implying a diverse range of patriotic voices in this new and culturally independent country. The strong presence of women in this section indicates the growing availability of books of poetry but it is also an indication that the work of women writers was becoming increasingly popular among Americans.

American poets expressed their nationalism in a variety of ways, and a good leading question for students reading this brief but comprehensive section is What do these poets take as their subject matter? Some poets interpret the call for a national literature as an invitation to write about American history and legend while others take up the crucial issues of the day, including slavery and abolition. For this section, students can be asked to consider what each author's work claims, perhaps implicitly, is the purpose of poetry (or language) and of the poet. As well, students might compare how the poets in this section use nature in their work and how they characterize the relationship between humans and nature.

AMERICAN CONTEXTS: *The American Muse: Poetry at Midcentury* (p. 1202)

This cluster of poems enables students to understand the works of Walt Whitman and Emily Dickinson in the context of nineteenth-century poetry, which they may not realize was a thriving and popular form. The poems included here represent a range of poetic voices that nineteenth-century readers may have encountered in newspapers and periodicals as well as in single, bound volumes of poetry. As the headnote to this section states, this poetry, for the most part, observed conventional forms but addressed particularly American subject matter and attempted to develop an American audience.

This section provides a useful backdrop for a discussion of the development of a uniquely American poetry at midcentury. As these selections demonstrate, the writing of poetry may be, for some, an explicitly patriotic act, but definitions of *patriotism* vary, from immersion in America's natural landscapes to demands for American citizens' accountability for injustice. These poems address questions about the purpose and role of poetry and the poet from many different perspectives, including those of the Harvard educated and the self-taught, of abolitionists and university lecturers, of the well-to-do and the struggling writers, whose publications were meant to earn a living. The diversity of subject matter reflects that of the writers included and points to the broad range of voices involved in developing a national literature. Instructors and students might use these selections to consider the role of nature, the relationship of humans to nature, as well as the importance of language, themes that emerge again and again during this period. These responses will provide a backdrop for the more detailed discussions of Whitman and Dickinson that follow.

Questions for Class Discussion

1. What do the poets in this section take as their subject matter? Develop a list of two or three important themes in the poems you read.

2. Given the list compiled for question 1, what is particularly American about these subjects or the way they are handled by these poets?

3. Consider the poetic voice in each poem. Do the poets in this section seem to be in agreement about the purpose of poetry and the role of the poet in America?

4. How do the poems represent nature? What is the relationship of nature to humans, and how does that vary across the selections?

WALT WHITMAN   (p. 1236)

Approaches to Teaching

Since most students today are unfamiliar with and intimidated by poetry, instructors might start a unit on Whitman by discussing the challenges of reading poems. One of the best resources for instructors is Molly Peacock's *How to Read a Poem . . .: And Start a Poetry Circle* (New York: Riverhead, 1999). Her chapter "The Main Systems of a Poem" is both brief and easily disseminated; she explains that poems should be approached on three levels – line, sentence, and image. These three levels are practical and straightforward and in their simplicity manage to explain why poems look and sound the way they do. When approaching Whitman's poetry in particular, students should be encouraged to simply read and not worry about the things they have learned about poetry, such as finding symbols and hidden meanings. They should read each poem once to the end without stopping to get a sense of its movement. In class, instructors can ask students to read aloud and see how it feels to utter Whitman's expansive words. Students should be familiarized with the definitions of *epic, free verse,* and *elegy.*

In many ways, Whitman's story parallels the American dream: a middle-class newspaper man who began as a typesetter and sold perhaps only three dozen copies of his self-published first book, *Leaves of Grass,* became one of America's most iconic and canonized poets. Students who have read the selections in the section "The American Muse: Poetry at Midcentury" will note the innovations he brought to the genre from the appearance of Whitman's sprawling lines on the page. Upon publishing *Leaves of Grass,* Whitman sent a copy to Ralph Waldo Emerson, who responded with a letter of effusive praise, mentioned in the headnote in the anthology: "I greet you at the beginning of a great career." A glance at the daguerreotype on the title page and a reading of the "Inscription," both included as illustrations in the anthology, give credence to Emerson's praise in that letter of Whitman's "free and brave thought" and "courage of treatment." Today's students, inundated with images of bodies and sexuality, might at first overlook the revolutionary nature of Whitman's work, which treats the body as sacred and sex as a union of body and soul. His careful construction of himself as "one of the roughs," facing his audience with a frank openness in plain shirt, slouch hat, and beard, prepares readers for his unapologetic treatment of work, race, sex, death, prostitution, crime, suicide, urban areas, and many other realities of antebellum America.

Classroom Issues and Strategies

In the 1855 preface to *Leaves of Grass,* Whitman writes that the "United States themselves are essentially the greatest poem." As a poet, Whitman viewed his prophetic, redeeming, and unifying role as crucial to an increasingly conflicted nation. How were Americans to balance or even reconcile individualism and equality, country and city, labor and capital, market and home, body and spirit, black and white, male and female, North and South? Whitman invites his American readers into a conversation about the nation and challenges them to think through the questions and contro-versies facing a democratic union. Asserting new definitions of poetry and religion, the spiritual aspects of sexuality, the value of each individ-ual whether high or low, the sacredness of work of all kinds and the American landscape in all its diversity, Whitman "sings" what amounts to an epic, complete with exhaustive catalogs and a range of treatment as yet unseen in American poetry. Students should be asked to consider how Whitman treats race, gender, and the eroding ideals of America after the Civil War.

Connections to Other Authors and Texts

Whitman connects most readily to Emerson, whose "The American Scholar" (p. 670) calls for a national literature by authors who will tell America's stories in its own language. Whitman's practice echoes Emerson's call for "Self-Reliance" (p. 683) in thought and action. His asser-tion of the universal and divine meaning of a blade of grass ("a uniform hieroglyphic") responds to Emerson's belief in *Nature* (p. 655), especially the section on language, that nature is transparent in meaning and a metaphor for both human and divine realms. Whitman's concern for com-mon humanity allies him with many of the writers in the "American Facts and American Fiction" section, including Fern, Melville, Stoddard, Davis, and Alcott. The social conscience of his work recalls Douglass, Jacobs, Stowe, Child, Apess, and Fuller.

Questions for Class Discussion

1. Consider the importance of the metaphor in the title *Leaves of Grass.* Using stanza 6 in "Song of Myself," discuss the title of Whitman's book of poems within the context of his definitions of *grass.*

2. Emerson wrote to Whitman to congratulate him on his "free and brave thought" and "courage of treatment." Using Emerson's views about lit-erature expressed in "The American Scholar" (p. 670) and Whitman's poems, explain the reasons for this response.

3. Choose one of Whitman's shorter poems or a stanza or two from a longer poem and discuss its structure and order. That is, to what extent does Whitman use, modify, or reject traditional forms of poetry? What defines the organization for the poem you have chosen?

4. Whitman claimed that there was a close relationship between his self-expression and that of the American national spirit. Choose a shorter poem or a stanza in a longer poem and discuss the parallels between the speaker and the characteristics of America in the nineteenth cen-tury.

5. Explain how either the picture of Whitman in the headnote (p. 1237) or the "Inscriptions" to *Leaves of Grass* (see "One's-Self I Sing" on p. 1240) prepare readers for a particular aspect of his work. Use one poem or a stanza or two from a longer poem to support your answer.

Brief Bibliography

Kummings, Donald D. *Approaches to Teaching* Leaves of Grass. New York: MLA, 1990.

Morris, Roy. *The Better Angel: Walt Whitman and the Civil War.* New York: Oxford UP, 2000.

Reynolds, David S. *Walt Whitman's America: A Cultural Biography.* New York: Knopf, 1995.

Selby, Nick. *The Poetry of Walt Whitman: A Reader's Guide to Essential Criticism.* New York: Palgrave, 2004.

WHITMAN THROUGH A MODERN LENS   (p. 1311)

Published nearly a century after the first edition of *Leaves of Grass*, these poems by Langston Hughes, perhaps the greatest African American poet, and Beat-generation poet Allen Ginsberg attest to Whitman's centrality to later U.S. poets. Whitman became a muse of sorts to Hughes, who, according to Arnold Rampersad's biography, threw all of his books overboard on his trip to Africa, saving only *Leaves of Grass*. Ginsberg, whose very lines and form echo the cadences of Whitman, approaches the occasion of the poem's centennial celebration as a State of the Union address, examining America one hundred years later from the perspective of another gay poet looking on what America has become – suburbia.

This section could be used effectively at the end of the unit on Whitman to reassert his pervasive influence on American culture and poetry and also to observe that the issues that concerned Whitman are still vital today. Hughes's poem, "Old Walt," reiterates Whitman's focus on process, his continual throwing out of a line to reach, connect, and catch another human in the vast universe. Students might be asked to note in "Song of Myself" the consistent use of words ending in -ing to emphasize the point Hughes makes. Ginsberg's poem echoes Whitman's joy in the mundane, his celebration of the common, "wives in the avocados, babies in the tomatoes." Just as Whitman invites readers to "look for me under your bootsoles," so Ginsberg finds himself following Whitman down the grocery aisles in the spirit of discovery: "Where are we going, Walt Whitman? . . . Which way does your beard point tonight?" Both Hughes and Ginsberg honor the old, rumpled, sage-like Walt Whitman as depicted in the portrait by Thomas Eakins (p. 1311). Ginsberg's address, "dear father, graybeard, lonely old courage-teacher," reaches across the century, indeed the history of literature itself, to ask what has become of America.

EMILY DICKINSON   (p. 1314)

Approaches to Teaching

Since students find poetry more difficult than prose and comprehend idea and mood less readily than narration, the study of Dickinson will prove challenging for them. The poet's strange syntax and grammar, unfamiliar language, baffling punctuation, and use of metaphor in such compressed textual units conspire to put students off. In addition, some students might hold stereotypes about Dickinson herself; they may have heard of her as a weird girl who wore white all the time or an eccentric old lady who never left the house, and her frequent theme of death only adds to students' misconceptions. Instructors should also keep in mind students' reading habits; used to narrative, students who are not coached may read the poems once through and consider their assignment complete. Close and careful study of Dickinson yields a better understanding of the written word and helps students to comprehend that ambiguity, uncertainty, and tension are vital elements of literature in general and Dickinson in particular. Patient instructors will assign and discuss a few poems at a time, work through the process of paraphrasing or "translating" Dickinson in class, and demand that students "textualize" their own readings by writing about those poems they interpret and by connecting their readings to specific language in the text.

Classroom Issues and Strategies

Discussing her approach to teaching Wallace Stevens, Helen Vendler once wrote that she copied his poems onto the board and deliberately left off certain adjectives; she then asked students to fill in adjectives that they believed fit in those spaces, which led to a rich discussion of why Stevens used certain words (*Teaching Wallace Stevens*, ed. John N. Serio and B. J. Leggett [Knoxville: U of Tennessee P, 1994]). The inclusion of 130 / "These are the days when Birds come back – ", provides the opportunity to consider how readers (including those who have edited Dickinson's poetry) understand her work and deal with her word choice (*resume* versus *put on*) and seemingly odd punctuation. Poem 216 / "Safe in their Alabaster Chambers," provided here in the 1859 and 1861 versions, yields a similarly rich discussion, in this case through the revision of the second stanza, which the poet writes about in her letter to Susan Gilbert Dickinson, included in this anthology. In addition to working through syntax, image, and meaning together, instructors can guide students by reading poems about certain themes together or by using information about Dickinson's own groupings derived from her "fascicles," handtied packets of around twenty poems that Dickinson prepared herself. That is, students could be asked to read the poems included in the anthology by subject or theme, such as the natural world, death, loss, love and human relationships, the tension between religious faith and doubt, or innocence and experience, women's roles, creativity, and the power and responsibility of the poet. To facilitate discussion and to discourage the notion that Dickinson's poems can mean anything at all, instructors might encourage students to work in groups or to explain their readings of particular stanzas in writing, tying their interpretation to Dickinson's language.

Some instructors teach Whitman and Dickinson together in a unit on American poetry. The anthology includes two poems that work well together in the classroom, Whitman's "A Noiseless Patient Spider" (p. 1308) and Dickinson's 605 / "The Spider holds a Silver Ball" (p. 1335). On the surface, of course, both poems concern the same subject, a spider; however, in each case, the speaker seems to compare the work of the spider to that of an artist or poet, and the depiction of the spider in each poem matches that poet's view of the role of poetry and the poet. For example, Whitman's spider is isolated and, from his perch on a "promontory" in the vast universe, it spins filament after filament in an effort to reach out and connect with something or someone outside of itself. In the second half of the poem, the spider is compared to the soul, also engaged in the unending process of connection. Dickinson's spider, on the other hand, exists in the microuniverse of the household, seemingly unnoticed and unassuming. Dickinson's spider "rear[s] supreme" only briefly, but in that hour "supplants" human work with "Continents of Light." While Whitman's poem ends with a vision of connection, Dickinson's ends with the spider's web being swept away by a mere "Housewife's Broom." Side by side, the poems afford an opportunity to talk about the role of poetry and the poet in the world, the process of generating art, and the relationship between the seemingly mundane world of the home and the cosmic universe.

Connections to Other Authors and Texts

In addition to Whitman's poems, Dickinson's work should be compared to that of the poets in "The American Muse: Poetry at Midcentury" (American Contexts, p. 1202). As well, instructors can link individual poems to other authors depending on thematic similarities. For example, Dickinson's poetry about the role of the poet and creativity in general – poems 441, 448, 605, 657, 675, 709, 1129, and 1651 – might be read next to Emerson's "Self-Reliance" (p. 683) and "The American Scholar" (p. 670) as well as Whitman's "Song of Myself" (p. 1240). Dickinson's poetry about the natural world – poems 258, 328, 986, for example – might be compared to Emerson's and Thoreau's views of nature, and certainly Dickinson's views of God – poems 49, 303, 338, 357, 508, and 1545 – merit comparison to the transcendentalists'. Finally, Dickinson's views of women and gender bear consideration, as she definitely challenges the cult of True Womanhood in poems 271, 508, 754, 1072, 1129, and 1737.

Questions for Class Discussion

1. Compare Dickinson's poetic persona in either 441 / "This is my letter to the World" or 1129 / "Tell all the Truth but tell it slant – " to Whitman's in "Song of Myself" (p. 1240). What characterizes the poet's relationship to his or her audience and the rest of the world?

2. Consider one of Dickinson's poems about the natural world. Discuss the tension in that poem between celebration or safety and danger.

3. Compare the endings from the 1859 and 1861 versions of 216, "Safe in their Alabaster Chambers." How would you characterize the difference between these two stanzas? What words achieve this effect?

4. Discuss either 280 / "I felt a Funeral, in my Brain," or 754 / "My Life had stood – a Loaded Gun –" as depictions of a state of mind. Explain how the metaphor of the house or the gun operates to inform the reader about the mind's perceptions.

5. Select one of Dickinson's poems about women or gender and discuss the ways that her work upholds, complicates, or rejects nineteenth-century ideals. Poems 271, 508, 754, 1072, 1129, and 1737 should work well for this assignment.

Brief Bibliography

Fast, Robin Riley, and Christine Mack Gordon. *Approaches to Teaching Dickinson's Poetry*. New York: MLA, 1989.

Habegger, Alfred. *My Wars Are Laid Away in Books: The Life of Emily Dickinson*. New York: Modern Library, 2002.

Martin, Wendy. *The Cambridge Companion to Emily Dickinson*. Cambridge, UK and New York: Cambridge UP, 2002.

DICKINSON THROUGH A MODERN LENS   (p. 1350)

In addition to her status as one of the most important American poets, Dickinson has been central to a tradition of women's literature and is an important figure for feminist critics. As these poems by Adrienne Rich and Cathy Song attest, Dickinson's work and voice continue to fascinate and inspire women poets today. Rich was one of the first feminist critics to emphasize the recovery and reevaluation of women writers and has written a compelling essay on Dickinson's work ("Vesuvius at Home: The Power of Emily Dickinson," *On Lies, Secrets, and Silence* [New York: Norton, 1979]). Both Rich and Song are concerned with the situation of the woman poet and the seeming contradiction between Dickinson's roles as woman and artist.

These poems might be taught at the end of the unit, after stereotypes about Dickinson's life and work have been addressed. On the other hand, these poems might assist in debunking gender-based stereotypes of Dickinson as an eccentric old maid by acknowledging the role that gender played in her life and work and by helping students to become self-aware about how gender informs their readings of Dickinson's work. By examining the portrayal of Dickinson as a woman and an artist, these poems reveal the contrast between the life of the mind and a life immersed in a daily domestic world. Such a contrast enables a discussion about our gender-based assumptions about the nature of poetry and poets. Students might discuss how each contemporary poet seems to feel about Dickinson and on which points they agree, or disagree, with the writers. Both poets find in Dickinson a powerful muse and a persistent enigma. Students might be asked to talk about a person who inspires or influences them and to consider what they would include were they to write a poem based on that person.

AMERICAN CONTEXTS: "Mine Eyes Have Seen the Glory": The Meanings of the Civil War   (p. 1354)

Although students may have studied the impact of the Civil War on American economic, political, and even cultural history, this section provides an opportunity to consider its relationship to American literary history. The texts in this section represent a broad range of voices and interests, including North and South, African American and Anglo-American, religious and political leaders and a wife who kept a diary, poets and insurrectionists, and even the anonymous Union and Confederate citizens, who sang the songs that expressed their anguish and anger as well as their hope and solidarity.

This unit comprises what might be viewed as a capstone to the American Renaissance in that it considers the issues endemic to the period, including growth, change, and reform, in the context of the event that might be said to have closed the era. The American Renaissance was characterized by the birth and expansion of an American literature and by the exploration of what this new nation might mean to the range of people inhabiting its diverse landscape. This section examines the political, religious, economic, and cultural fallout of a war that was in many ways fought in the press as well as on the battlefield and shaped not only the nation but also its literature. Just as the American Renaissance was characterized by a struggle over the meaning of the terms *America* and *American,* so writers and orators struggled to shape the meaning of the Civil War, which would decide the fate of the nation. The literature of the American Renaissance was produced at a moment of geographic, demographic, industrial, agricultural, economic, political, and cultural expansionism that also gave rise to the problems of oppression, imperialism, and inequity. These difficulties culminated in the Civil War, the writings of which are defined by each side's dearly held definition of national identity. These definitions were circulated in the periodical press through powerful images and rhetoric attesting to the passionate complexity of the struggle over the meaning of the Civil War and the fate of the nation.

Questions for Class Discussion

1. Discuss how at least three writers from various perspectives (such as geographic, ethnic, or gender) use rhetorical appeals to explain the causes for and justification of the Civil War.

2. Both sides used emotional appeals to narrate the meaning of the Civil War. Using the songs and poetry included in this section, discuss the nature of these appeals. How do writers draw on similar or different emotions of their audiences?

3. How does the Civil War enable the construction of a black national identity as depicted in this section? Use the writings by Garnet, Douglass, and Harper to make your case.

4. How do the writers in this section attempt to make meaning out of the war after it is over? Choose a common theme that appears in Chesnut, Piatt, Bryant, Harper, and Whitman and consider how these writers respond to it from different perspectives.

5. Choose an image from this section and discuss how it informs two or more of the texts included. Begin by looking closely at the image and its caption and noting the details. Then shift your focus to scenes and passages in the texts and demonstrate how the image helps you to understand them.

Sample Syllabus 1: Historical Survey Course

INTRODUCTION TO EARLY AMERICAN LITERATURE: FROM THE BEGINNINGS TO THE CIVIL WAR

(15-WEEK COURSE, ADAPTABLE TO A 12-WEEK COURSE)

NOTE TO INSTRUCTORS: *According to instructors, the chronological historical survey is the most commonly taught course in American literature. The challenges of this course include the decision about how much material to cover and how much students will be able to read and absorb. We have provided a sample syllabus below that includes most of the options in* The Bedford Anthology of American Literature. *Naturally, instructors will want to alter the length and number of readings and, of course, omit writers and works, according to their own priorities and interests. In the sample assignments included here, we have indicated ways in which instructors might use materials that are not included on the syllabus.*

Course Description

This course is a chronological survey of American literature that begins with Native American origin and creation stories and concludes with some of the poetry of Walt Whitman and Emily Dickinson. The intention is to provide a broad overview of what constitutes American literature from its origins to the end of the Civil War. We will read and study works of poetry, fiction, and nonfiction prose, including autobiography, by men and women of diverse backgrounds and interests. Our object will be to study the many voices that constitute what we call American literature, addressing questions such as How do the gender, race, and class of writers and readers affect the creation and reception of a literary text? What constitutes a literary canon? What does *American* mean? What role has literature played in the cultural and historical story of what came to be the United States?

Required Texts

The Bedford Anthology of American Literature, Volume One

NOTE TO INSTRUCTORS: *Instructors who wish to use one of the Bedford College Editions designed for the first half of the American literature survey,* Benito Cereno *or* The Scarlet Letter *or* Uncle Tom's Cabin, *might substitute one or more of these texts for other works given on the syllabus below.*

Calendar

Literature to 1750

WEEK 1: Native American Origin and Creation Stories (Iroquois Confederacy, Cherokee, Akimel O'odham/Pima, Lakota, Hupa, and "Through a Modern Lens," Momaday)
Explorations and Early Encounters (Columbus, Cabeza de Vaca, Champlain)

WEEK 2: Colonial Settlements (Smith, Bradford, Winthrop, Bradstreet)

WEEK 3: Colonial Settlements (Rowlandson, Taylor, Pastorius, Edwards)
American Contexts: Colonial Diaries and Journals (Sewall, Mather, Knight, Byrd, Edwards)

American Literature, 1750-1830

WEEK 4: Writing Colonial Lives (Franklin, Ashbridge)

WEEK 5: Writing Colonial Lives (Woolman, Occom, Equiano)
American Contexts: "To Begin the World Over Again": The Emerging Idea of "America"

WEEK 6: American Contexts: "Who Reads an American Book?": Calls for a National Literature
Literature for a New Nation (Freneau, Wheatley, Irving)

WEEK 7: Literature for a New Nation (Sedgwick, Longstreet, Bryant, Schoolcraft)

American Literature, 1830-1865

WEEK 8: American Contexts: "I Will Be Heard": The Rhetoric of Antebellum Reform
The Era of Reform (Apess, Child, Emerson, Fuller)

WEEK 9:   The Era of Reform (Stowe, Jacobs, Thoreau)

WEEK 10:   The Era of Reform (Douglass, African American Slave Songs);

WEEK 11:   American Contexts: "Countless Phenomena of the Times": The Role of the Periodical Press
American Facts and American Fiction (Poe, Fern)

WEEK 12:   American Facts and American Fiction (Stowe, Mitchell, Stoddard, Davis, Alcott)

WEEK 13:   American Facts and American Fiction (Hawthorne, Melville)

NOTE TO INSTRUCTORS: Benito Cereno *or* The Scarlet Letter *or* Uncle Tom's Cabin *could be used in Weeks 12 and 13 of the syllabus.*

WEEK 14:   New Poetic Voices (Whitman)
American Contexts: The American Muse: Poetry at Midcentury

WEEK 15:   New Poetic Voices (Dickinson)
American Contexts: "Mine Eyes Have Seen the Glory": The Meanings of the Civil War

Course Requirements

NOTE TO INSTRUCTORS: *The requirements listed below are examples of a variety of activities for use in courses and may be readily adapted to particular institutional contexts.*

Periodic Response Papers, Quizzes, and Class Participation

Several times during the semester, students will write brief responses in class to questions about topics in the course or a response to a short reading quiz of several questions. These will be unannounced. All students are expected to come to class meetings prepared to discuss reading assignments and to interact with members of the class. Learning how to speak on one's feet is an important aspect of education, and students will be asked to give opinions, respond to questions, and make assessments of what they are reading and learning.

Writing Assignment(s)

NOTE TO INSTRUCTORS: *The following assignments could be adapted for use in courses requiring either one or multiple writing assignments.*

EXAMPLE ASSIGNMENT USING WORKS NOT INCLUDED ON THE SYLLABUS

1. Choose a work that is NOT on the syllabus for this course. Read the selections carefully and write an essay in which you argue for the inclu-

sion of this work on a syllabus that surveys American literature. Some questions to consider are: What is the nature of the work? What strikes you as important about this work? this writer? How is the work different from or similar to others we have read? How would this work relate to others we have read in the class?

EXAMPLE ASSIGNMENT USING "AMERICAN CONTEXTS"

2. Using the texts in "American Contexts: Colonial Diaries and Journals," write an essay in which you explore the topics and themes of the works you've read. What are some of the similarities in these informal writings? the differences? What conclusions can you draw about life in the colonies from reading these "private" works?

EXAMPLE ASSIGNMENT USING A LONGER WORK IN COMPARISON WITH OTHERS

3. Frederick Douglass's slave narrative is often considered a subgenre of autobiography. What are the special problems involved in representing the experience of someone who, by law, was not a person and who had such limited knowledge of his ancestry and background? How does Douglass deal with these problems? Are his solutions effective? How is this narrative a "genre within a genre"? Compare the audience for whom this autobiography was written with those of Rowlandson and Franklin. Douglass's autobiography has the unique characteristic of being the result of speeches he gave for the abolitionist movement. How has this development from oral tradition to written form affected the result? How does this compare with the works of Rowlandson, Equiano, Franklin, or Jacobs? Develop an essay in which you analyze Douglass's slave narrative as autobiography and compare it with other examples of life-writing we have read in this course.

OTHER EXAMPLE ASSIGNMENTS

4. A frequent theme in Native American literature is the close association between human beings and nature. Select one or more of the Native American origin or creation stories you read and compare it with a Euro-American text on the syllabus that also has such an association. What are the similarities and differences?

5. Elegies about untimely death and the death of specific loved ones represent an important category of poetry in the nineteenth century. A number of poets on the syllabus wrote such poems: Bradstreet, Taylor, Bryant, Whitman, and Dickinson. What is an elegy? What are the conventions of elegiac poetry? Select poems by at least two of these writers and compare and contrast their use of death as a topic for their work.

6. It has been said that Thoreau's "Resistance to Civil Government" (now better known as "Civil Disobedience" is Emerson's doctrine of self-

reliance carried to its logical political conclusion. How or why is this statement true? Be sure to describe Emerson's notion of *self-reliance* and the ways Thoreau depends on these ideas in his essay. What other writers use variations of Emersonian "self-reliance" in their work?

7. What are the main themes of Bradstreet's poems? Some readers have said that she is a prefeminist, in that she gives women and women's experience particular prominence in her work. How would you construct a feminist reading of these works? What are the issues that are involved in such a reading? How are her works different from those of Phillis Wheatley?

Group Presentation

INTRODUCTION TO A WRITER, WORK, OR GROUP OF WORKS

Each student will be assigned to a small group to work on a twenty-minute introductory presentation on one of the works from the syllabus. In addition to the historical, social, or cultural context, groups are encouraged to consider a variety of topics concerning the work, for example its initial reception, including any controversies it generated. Multimedia presentations are strongly encouraged if the classroom is fully equipped to handle a variety of presentation formats. The first task of each group will be to select a chairperson, who will be responsible for coordinating the group's activities and for communicating with the instructor. The second task will be to read the work well in advance and to decide on the major topic(s) of the presentation, in consultation with the instructor. Groups will be responsible for notifying the class in advance about any additional works they are to read (and how to find them), making the presentation, and leading a discussion based on questions that the group will distribute to the class.

Midterm Exam

Comprehensive Final Exam

Sample Syllabus 2:
Major Authors Course

EARLY AMERICAN WRITERS
(15-WEEK COURSE, ADAPTABLE TO A 12-WEEK COURSE)

NOTE TO INSTRUCTORS: *Many instructors have reported that courses such as Major American Writers, Introduction to American Writers, or Early American Writers are a part of the curriculum at their institutions. The difficulty of preparing such courses is determining how to choose the "major" writers, especially in the presence of such a greatly expanded canon, one that often includes Native American works that were originally oral and not the work of a single "writer." One solution to this problem is to take the notion of "major American writers" as an investigative inquiry for the class and ask students to consider throughout the semester what it means to be* major *or* American *or even* a *writer. The syllabus below is one example of how instructors might approach such a course.*

Course Description

This course on American writers focuses on the changing notions of authorship in America, with attention paid to writers who were viewed as important in their own time or those who have emerged as important at a later time. We will read and study works of poetry, fiction, nonfiction prose, and autobiography by men and women of diverse backgrounds and interests.

Required Texts

The Bedford Anthology of American Literature, Volume One
Uncle Tom's Cabin, Bedford College Edition
Benito Cereno, Bedford College Edition

NOTE TO INSTRUCTORS: Uncle Tom's Cabin *and* Benito Cereno *are used as examples here.*

Calendar

WEEK 1:   Native American Origin and Creation Stories; Momaday, "The Becoming of the Native: Man in America before Columbus"; Columbus; de Vaca; Champlain

WEEK 2:   Smith, Bradford, Winthrop

WEEK 3:   Bradstreet, Rowlandson

WEEK 4:   Franklin, Ashbridge

WEEK 5:   Woolman, Occom, Equiano

WEEK 6:   American Contexts: "Who Reads an American Book?": Calls for a National Literature; Wheatley; Irving; Bryant; Schoolcraft

WEEK 7:   Apess, Emerson, Fuller, Jacobs

WEEK 8:   Thoreau, Douglass

WEEK 9:   American Contexts: "Countless Phenomena of the Times": The Role of the Periodical Press; Hawthorne; Poe

WEEK 10:   *Uncle Tom's Cabin*

WEEK 11:   *Uncle Tom's Cabin*

WEEK 12:   Melville; *Benito Cereno*

WEEK 13:   American Contexts: The American Muse: Poetry at Midcentury

WEEK 14:   Whitman

WEEK 15:   Dickinson

Course Requirements

NOTE TO INSTRUCTORS: *The requirements listed below are examples of a variety of activities for use in courses and may be readily adapted to particular institutional contexts.*

Periodic Response Papers, Quizzes, and Class Participation

Several times during the semester, students will write brief responses in class to questions about topics in the course or a response to a short reading quiz of several questions. These will be unannounced. All students are expected to come to class meetings prepared to discuss reading assignments and to interact with members of the class. Learning how to speak on one's feet is an important aspect of education, and students will be asked to give opinions, respond to questions, and make assessments of what they are reading and learning.

Writing Assignment(s)

NOTE TO INSTRUCTORS: *Listed below are a variety of examples of writing assignments that focus on a writer and ask students to incorporate the works of others. These could be easily adapted for courses requiring one or multiple writing assignments.*

1. Many critics have commented that Harriet Beecher Stowe participated in one of the central political debates of her time by writing *Uncle Tom's Cabin?* What specific historical and political events prompted Stowe to begin *Uncle Tom's Cabin?* Choose one and discuss the ways the event is treated in the novel.

2. In what ways does *Benito Cereno* contribute to the antislavery argument raging in the United States in the 1850s? What different techniques does Melville use? How do his techniques compare with those of other writers we have read in this course?

3. Consider carefully the comments that Hawthorne made in "The Custom House" about the characteristics of a romance. Investigate the distinction that is made between romance and novel in American literature and discuss *The Scarlet Letter* in that context. Is it a romance or a novel? How important is such a distinction? How important was it to Hawthorne? Some early reviewers commented that the novel did not have a "proper mixture of romance and reality." Do you support this view? Why or why not?

4. *The Scarlet Letter* draws on early American history and Puritan sources for its settings. Based on what you've learned from reading the early Puritan writers, how would you assess Hawthorne's use of these materials? In what ways does Hawthorne strive to make his work authentic? How does he succeed? How does he fail?

5. Relate *Narrative of the Life of Frederick Douglass* to Emerson's "Self-Reliance." You may focus on any aspect of the works, but you might consider how each author defines *self-reliant individualism* or *manhood*, how each depicts the obstacles confronting the individual, and how each suggests the means by which those obstacles may be overcome. More broadly, you might consider how each author views human nature, especially in relation to various social forces and institutions.

6. How do Olaudah Equiano and Phillis Wheatley portray themselves as part of the American experience? What difference does race play in the conception of an "American writer," to use part of the title of this course? Write an essay in which you explore the "American-ness" of these two writers. Why is this a pertinent issue?

7. How does either Whitman or Dickinson differ from the poets in "American Contexts: The American Muse: Poetry at Midcentury"? Select one or two major ways in which this poet was writing unconventional poetry and discuss those innovations.

Group Presentation

NOTE TO INSTRUCTORS: *This assignment could be easily adapted by making up a list of terms for another long work, such as* Benito Cereno, The Scarlet Letter, *or* Narrative of the Life of Frederick Douglass.

TERMS AND TOPICS FOR INVESTIGATION INTO THE CONTEXT OF UNCLE TOM'S CABIN

Students will be divided into small groups, where they will choose a topic and prepare a ten-minute presentation for the class. During that presentation, the group provides the following information about the term, person, place, or event: a definition, description, or an explanation; examples; visual or audio illustrations; and an assessment of relevance to understanding *Uncle Tom's Cabin.*

Fugitive Slave Law
Calvin Stowe
Lyman Beecher
Daniel Webster
Gamaliel Bailey
the *National Era*
John P. Jewett
colonization
Dred Scott
women's antislavery societies
Godey's Lady's Book
European revolutions of 1848
The Key to Uncle Tom's Cabin
Quakers and slavery
Dr. Joel Parker

Catherine E. Beecher
slave rebellions
Manifest Destiny
Missouri Compromise
serialization
sentimental novel
domestic novel
cult of domesticity
James Baldwin, "Everybody's Protest Novel"
Frederick Douglass's response to *Uncle Tom's Cabin*
facts and figures about slavery in 1850-52

Midterm Exam

Comprehensive Final Exam

VOLUME TWO
1865 to the Present

American Literature
1865–1914

THE FIRST SECTION in Volume Two of *The Bedford Anthology of American Literature* spans the five decades between the Civil War and 1914, the dawn of literary modernism. (Virginia Woolf had famously remarked that human character changed "on or about December 1910"). During this brief but pivotal time in U.S. history, the range of associations built into the terms *America* and *American* transformed in unforeseen and striking ways. Westward expansion, sectional conflict, and subsequent attempts to repair the nation's wounds illustrated the malleability of the American social contract and strained the premise that the government affords its citizens basic human and legal rights. If official measures (including the Fourteenth and Fifteenth Amendments, the Compromise of 1877, and *Plessy v. Ferguson*) could offer no stable version of membership in "American" society for large numbers of persons residing within U.S. borders, it is hardly astounding that creative writers imagined American identity in myriad and often conflicting ways. Never mind unreconstructed racists such as Thomas Dixon; even Booker T. Washington and W. E. B. Du Bois, intelligent and articulate spokespersons for African American uplift, found little on which to agree. When we also consider the various positions of Mexican Americans dislocated by the Mexican War, and Native Americans displaced by the "winning" of the American West, and Chinese Americans excluded by an act of Congress, and European immigrants struggling to carve out a life in the Midwest or in urban ghettos, then Tocqueville's deceptively simple question – What then is the American? – presents intriguing problems and wonderful teaching possibilities. Beginning with John Gast's *American Progress,* a visual allegory of late-nineteenth-century modernization, you might ask, What stories of American social and technological change does this painting depict? – and just as important, What stories does it leave out?

The best approach to sweeping cultural historical questions obviously depends upon each specific classroom setting. Most students on America's relatively sheltered college campuses will find it somewhat difficult to grasp the profound social changes that took shape in the latter nineteenth century. They will more likely be able to appreciate concurrent (and not unrelated) forms of modernization: industrialization and urbanization. All brands of modernization – social, technological, even literary – might be understood in terms of generational evolution, a frame of reference easily available to most students. The invention of the linotype machine, which revolutionized literary publishing just over a century ago, for example, might be compared to our own revolution in the digital transmittal of all cultural forms (including, to some extent, literary forms). *The Bedford Anthology of American Literature* offers sufficient variety to address virtually all kinds of modernization, whether social or technological or cultural; the anthology provides a sweeping overview of American cultural history, and it offers a vast reservoir of aesthetic pleasure.

Realism, Regionalism, and Naturalism

In the second half of the nineteenth century, one of the surefire ways a writer could signal innovation was to take up the banner of "realism." Dozens if not hundreds of European and American writers challenged literary convention as self-conscious (and sometimes self-proclaimed) realists, and in so doing they helped shape a new and influential set of conventions for literary expression that eventually found a large and loyal readership. The works of America's most important realists – including William Dean Howells, Henry James, and Mark Twain – are quick and convincing evidence of realism's multiple aims and literary ends. If we also consider local colorists from the four corners of the country – Sarah Orne Jewett in New England, Charles W. Chesnutt in the South, Kate Chopin on the Gulf Coast, Willa Cather in the Midwest, and Mary Austin in California – then realism spans wide expanses of American geography, society, and literary style.

Depending on the course level, students will require more or less guidance when it comes to arriving at working definitions of *realism, regionalism,* and *naturalism.* Lower-level undergraduates and high-school students will be well served by the definitions supplied by the editors of *The Bedford Anthology of American Literature* and by the critical statements collected in this section. Advanced undergraduates and graduate students should be encouraged to view straightforward definitions more critically; Donald Pizer's discussion of realism and naturalism ("Realism and Naturalism: The Problem of Definition," which is reprinted in the companion volume, *Background Readings for Teachers of American Literature*) offers perhaps the best survey of the conflicted terrain. Students might even debate the utility of the category "realism" (and its literary historical predecessor, "romanticism") itself. At all levels, though, students should be asked to view realism and its literary theoretical cousins as a set of historically and culturally determined conventions designed to capture reality in literary form. These conventions include, but are hardly limited to, chronological location in the present time or the recent past; the representation of recognizable character types and places, especially within middle- and lower-class society; the use of limited omniscience, either from a first- or third-person narrator; and the exploration of likely (in other words, unhappy) plot outcomes. Many writers explore reality by means of reference to analogs from the visual arts (sculpture, painting, photography, and eventually film and virtual reality); such art forms provide a useful backdrop against which the conventions of literary realism stand in sharp relief.

AMERICAN CONTEXTS: "The America of the Mind": Critics, Writers, and the Representation of Reality   (p. 40)

The American Civil War (1861-65) had an impact on every man, woman, and child in the United States. The armed conflict cost well over half a million lives and uprooted untold numbers of families. The end to hostilities only lessened, but did not quell entirely, the bitter rivalry between the states, and peace scarcely concluded the debate over the present and future shape of U.S. society. American writers in the aftermath of the Civil War grappled with how to depict the war's heroic deeds and unprecedented brutality, and they considered how individuals and social groups would find a place in the reunited national fabric. Quite often, the transatlantic debate over "realism" – a loose set of literary conventions associated with the depiction of "real life" – informed how American writers approached their craft during this unsettled time. This short cluster of readings presents a sampling of the discussion. The section might be assigned at the start of a historically organized syllabus to inform students that much of what was new (even modern) about late-nineteenth-century literature depended on the rise of literary realism as a goal of literary expression. It quickly becomes clear to most students that reality and realism are in the eye of the beholder. Henry James's blurry line between "experience" and "imagination," for example, locates the vast territory of human psychology within the confines of the "real." Because the question of U.S. literary nationalism was crucial throughout the nineteenth century – and well into the twentieth century – writers repeatedly asked, "Do we have a national literature, and what should it look like?" The idea functions as a leitmotif in *The Bedford Anthology of American Literature*. (Even a cosmopolitan such as Julian Hawthorne seems mildly obsessed with the question.) The American Civil

War and the rise of realism shaped the debate over literary nationalism for decades.

Questions for Class Discussion

1. Some of the writers in this section (James, Howells, Norris) are also represented in the anthology's selection of prose fiction. How does their fiction measure up against the ideas set forth in their nonfiction prose?

2. According to the writers in this section, what seems to be wrong with American literature in the late nineteenth century? What seems right about American literature? What can be salvaged, and what must be jettisoned altogether?

3. According to the writers in this section, what counts as "real"? Are particular subjects better suited to the representation of reality? Does realism seem to favor or marginalize particular social groups (for example, upper-class versus working-class society)? Do writers favor specific geographic references? How are the various indexes of the real aligned with American nationalism?

4. This section consists almost entirely of the work of white men, in large part because women writers and nonwhite writers (including recently arrived immigrants from non-English-speaking European countries) tended not to address directly issues of realism and literary nationalism. How might a woman writer approach differently the issues dealt with here? How might a recently freed slave approach them? How might an immigrant from (for example) China or Turkey approach them?

5. In what ways do theories of American literature seem to depend on European ideas and sources for inspiration? Are there subjects that are more American than others? Are there forms (genres, cadences, etc.) that seem inherently American? Is there an American language?

MARK TWAIN (SAMUEL L. CLEMENS)   (p. 61)

Approaches to Teaching

By the end of the nineteenth century, Mark Twain was much more than the range of associations suggested by the often-assigned anachronism "celebrity writer"; Twain was easily the most famous American writer living or dead, and his celebrity reached well beyond the rarified circles of the literary marketplace. This fame, including Twain's carefully cultivated visual image, extends to the present era, and virtually all students in the

United States (and many overseas) will have encountered him at some point in their primary or secondary education. For this reason, Twain's celebrity status provides a useful point of entry into his work. The selections included in *The Bedford Anthology of American Literature* either contributed directly to Twain's popularity, or they were made possible only because Twain was a world-famous writer whose opinions on nonliterary matters meant more than those of just about anyone else. Investigating how and why specific titles might contribute to a writer's fame, and how and why fame might contribute to writing, merits early attention when it comes to Twain. A related, obvious, and important – but exceedingly difficult – approach to Twain requires attending to the role of humor in his work. Finally, some mention of his enduring influence (writers as different as Ernest Hemingway and Toni Morrison grappled with Twain's effect on their thinking and writing) and institutional presence (Twain as academic icon, Twain as popular icon) should be made.

Classroom Issues and Strategies

"What makes writing humorous?" is too important a question to ignore when it comes to the study of Twain. Even so, it can be a tricky question to pull off in the classroom, particularly if students are not familiar with the intricacies of irony and tone. Many students may have encountered "Jim Smiley and His Jumping Frog" at a young age and can consider why the story might not be funny in an early first encounter and also why it is funny to an adult readership. (They may have read the story with its alternate title, "The Celebrated Jumping Frog of Calaveras County.") A young reader won't necessarily realize that being beside the point *is* the point of the story. Similarly, it usually takes an adult to see the absurdity of a dog named *Andrew Jackson* or to know that Andrew Jackson (the dog) likely didn't shoot Smiley a reproachful look before willing itself to death. In general, asking students what skills ironic or satiric language demands of a reader – the term *implied reader* is useful but not necessary – allows students to pinpoint how irony and tone work.

Old Times on the Mississippi, among the many volumes of autobiographical writing produced by Twain, lends itself to an examination of Twain's careful cultivation of regional identification, a tack chosen by generation after generation of Twain scholars. Although he spent the bulk of his career in Hartford, no other writer is as closely identified with the grand Mississippi River as is Twain. "A True Story" further complicates the issue by superimposing racial identity over regional identity. Whether or not *Old Times* is assigned along with the *Adventures of Huckleberry Finn,* the autobiographical narrative simultaneously personifies the river as a larger-than-life, inscrutably complex character and introduces a wide variety of memorable, highly individuated characters who make a life (if not a living) on the river. The book also gives us a clear and humorous picture of why Twain chose a career not as a steamboat pilot but as a writer. "A True Story" allows us to consider even more pointedly how language reinforces and subverts traditional racial boundaries and hierarchies. Aunt Rachel carefully deploys language to assert her authority (and, by extension, Twain's authority) with other characters and with readers, even as she undercuts her authority with an "aw-shucks" attitude.

"The War Prayer" exemplifies the deadly serious verbal irony that did not necessarily make Twain famous but that added an important dimension to his career. When "God's messenger" delivers the "unspoken part" of the minister's war prayer, the strange old man instructs the congregation (and thus the reader) on the double meaning of "pregnant words." An interesting contrast is "The Private History of a Campaign That Failed." Because Twain sets things up by introducing a hapless cast of ne'er-do-wells, led by a fellow who was "young, ignorant, good-natured, well-meaning, trivial, full of romance, and given to reading chivalric novels and singing forlorn love-ditties" – in other words, someone ridiculously ill suited to lead a company into battle – the narrative offers a clear example of situational irony that governs longer, better-known titles such as *Huck Finn* or *Connecticut Yankee.* The cynical narrator and his readers recognize pitfalls that the green soldiers simply cannot see for their actual worth.

Connections to Other Authors and Texts

Twain worked in a wide range of genres, and as such his work compares well with narratives of exploration and immigration (by, for example, Columbus in Volume One and Antin in Volume Two), humor (Irving in Volume One and Cummings in Volume Two), and nature writing (Thoreau in Volume One and Frost in Volume Two). The comparisons – really, the contrasts – suggest that Twain is remarkably successful wearing many different hats and that his sometimes jaded understanding of the known universe, of human foibles, and of the natural landscape forms an important bridge between the nineteenth and twentieth centuries. Twain's thoughts about and literary approach to the sectional conflict over slavery and the resulting legacy of racial animosity, however, are his greatest contribution to American literary history. As such, Twain compares profitably with the many slave narratives and the genre's descendants and with the many rich discussions of racial identity, printed in both volumes of *The Bedford Anthology of American Literature.* For example, Twain's use of dialect might be set alongside Harlem Renaissance writers such as Brown and Hurston (or, for that matter, alongside his contemporary, Rebecca Harding Davis in Volume One). More abstractly, Twain's voice has been called consummately "American," which suggests comparison with any writer interested in forging a national language and literature.

Questions for Class Discussion

1. Explain the difference between what Twain *says* and what he *means* (verbal irony). Explain how a narrator's or a character's limited perspective creates a situation in which language means one thing to the narrator or character and another thing to the reader (situational irony).

2. Describe the logic (or illogic) that determines the shape of individual paragraphs and transitions between paragraphs in "Jim Smiley and His Jumping Frog."

3. *Old Times on the Mississippi* describes Twain's abortive apprenticeship as a steamboatman. How does this line of work resemble the craft of writing? How does it differ?

4. How does dialect inform the experience of reading "A True Story"? Is Aunt Rachel a more or less sympathetic character because of her language and speech patterns? When she uses the racial epithet "nigger," is she being a racist? Is the narrator? Is Twain?

5. Devise a print advertisement (for your school newspaper, perhaps) that makes the same point as "The War Prayer." How does your advertisement differ from Twain's narrative version?

Brief Bibliography

Leonard, James S., ed. *Making Mark Twain Work in the Classroom.* Durham: Duke UP, 1999.

Robinson, Forrest G., ed. *The Cambridge Companion to Mark Twain.* Cambridge: Cambridge UP, 1995.

Sundquist, Eric J., ed. *Mark Twain: A Collection of Critical Essays.* Englewood Cliffs, NJ: Prentice Hall, 1994.

Ziff, Larzer. *Mark Twain.* Oxford: Oxford UP, 2004.

WILLIAM DEAN HOWELLS   (p. 109)

Approaches to Teaching

References to Howells as the "dean of American literature" abound, and rightly (if too punnily) so. No other nineteenth-century literary figure – writer, editor, publisher, or critic – left an imprint on American literary culture as clear or as lasting as Howells, and for that reason it is too easy to stress his role as editor and critic and literary go-between at the expense of his gifts as a writer of lively fiction. (The best in recent Howells criticism provides insufficient help in this regard.) Fortunately, "Editha" is a short story rich in timeless themes (romantic love, patriotism, honor and duty, transcendent humanism) and careful craft work. The short story's fairly obvious politics, a bitter indictment of American imperialism at the end of the nineteenth century, yields a subtle approach to narrative focus and tone. How the narrator treats the title character – what he (presuming without much evidence a male narrator) allows Editha to notice and think and say and do, what he reflects on in turn – might well emerge as the central focus of an entire class period.

Classroom Issues and Strategies

The short story's closing phrase – "she rose from grovelling in shame and self-pity, and began to live again in the ideal" – signals a profound concern with the distinction between (pacifist) realism and (bellicose) idealism. Take care that students do not arrive at overly simplified bases for the real-ideal distinction. Editha's idealism defies gendered explanations (her father, after all, seems no less naive than Editha), it defies literary sourcing (patriotic clichés stem from Shakespeare and yellow journalism and much in between), and it defies religious explanation (we see little more than a cartoon version of religious sentiment in the story). Instead, "Editha" presents a complex range of associations and explanations for the hapless, idealistic rush to war.

At an early point in the short story, Editha "hardly knew whether [George] was mocking or not, in the ironical way he always had with her plainer mind." From beginning to end, Editha never fully comprehends either George or the larger implications of their fateful situation. Put another way, the story brims with irony. Indeed, the narrator's understanding so clearly exceeds Editha's that the narrator emerges almost as a full-fledged character in the short story. Asking students to describe the narrator in those terms – as a living, breathing person with a gender, a social class, a geographic and racial identity, an education – allows them to investigate the short story's approach to narrative tone and irony.

Connections to Other Authors and Texts

Because Howells so profoundly influenced late-nineteenth- and early twentieth-century literary culture, connections to dozens of writers represented in *The Bedford Anthology of American Literature*, Volume Two, can be made on the basis of biographical or literary historical evidence. Still, a few merit special attention. The short story's interest in a divide between realism and idealism warrants reference to Howells's romantic forerunners (particularly Emerson and the other transcendentalists). Mark Twain's and Ambrose Bierce's wide-ranging use of irony to support antiwar positions bears useful comparison. And the relationship between Daisy Miller and her narrator in Henry James's novella provides interesting parallels to the narrator-character dynamic in "Editha."

Questions for Class Discussion

1. When George describes Editha's "red hair," "blue eyes," and "face with the color painted out by the white moonshine," he's obviously drawing a comparison between his fiancée and the Stars and Stripes (and, by extension, the United States of America). If the short story makes an allegorical connection between Editha and America, what does her characterization say about the nation?

2. How would you describe the short story's third-person narrator? Is it a man or a woman? Old or young? Rich or poor or in-between? What is the narrator's racial or ethnic identity? How do we know the answers to these questions?

3. Does Editha learn a significant life lesson as the story evolves? Does she miss an obvious chance to grow emotionally, ethically, or otherwise?

Brief Bibliography

Goodman, Susan, and Carl Dawson. *William Dean Howells: A Writer's Life*. Berkeley: U of California P, 2005.

Howard, June. *Publishing the Family*. Durham: Duke UP, 2001.

Piacentino, Edward J. "Arms in Love and War in Howells's 'Editha.'" *Studies in Short Fiction* 24 (1987): 425-32.

AMBROSE BIERCE   (p. 122)

Approaches to Teaching

Today's media-saturated students, it is often said, do not shock easily. If you ask them to describe the most shocking thing that they've ever seen on television, usually several will try to outdistance their peers with displays of media violence ennui. "What does it take for film or television violence to shock you?" you might ask. The question is relevant because by the 1880s, most Americans had had their fill of shocking tales and photographs from the "late war." The place name *Chickamauga* was by then synonymous with horrific violence. The more disturbing elements of Ambrose Bierce's short story – a soldier whose jaw was blown off, men too weak to lift their thirsty heads out of the river, a woman with brains spilling from her skull – are all the more unsettling because the narrative's focus is a naive little boy, one who projects romantic fantasy onto grim reality. Bierce's narrative device adds to the shock and suspense of the short story, furthering its antiwar ends.

Classroom Issues and Strategies

On a handful of occasions, the narrator of "Chickamauga" calls attention to the situational irony driving the narrative's uncanny style: "Not all of this did the child note; it is what would have been noted by an older observer"; "[a]n observer of better experience in the use of his eyes would have noticed that these footprints pointed in both directions." The defamiliarization born of a narrative focused around a six-year-old boy sometimes produces endearing results (the child is startled by a rabbit but he "vaguely wished to meet" a bear, for example). More often, Bierce deploys defamiliarization to escape heroic clichés and instead to emphasize the shocking brutality of war. A soldier's bloody face, for instance, reminds the boy of a "painted clown"; rather than see butchered men crawling in retreat, he instead imagines himself the leader of a march into battle.

Although "Chickamauga" derives its title from an infamously bloody Civil War battle — one experienced firsthand by the young Ambrose Bierce — the horrifying description of wartime violence is sadly universal. Questions of innate violence, imperialism, racial ambiguity, and the ghastly horrors of war do not begin with (and certainly don't end with) the Civil War. One critic, Susan Kalter, has even made a suggestive case that issues raised by the short story resonate within the Native American experience. (The Chickamauga River takes its name from the Cherokee people.)

Connections to Other Authors and Texts

Comparing "Chickamauga" to roughly contemporaneous antiwar literature by, for example, Twain and Howells, dramatically underscores the novelty of Bierce's approach. His use of a six-year-old boy as the narrative's focus anticipates the more experimental versions of the device found in the work of William Faulkner and Richard Wright.

Questions for Class Discussion

1. Nowhere does "Chickamauga" explicitly announce its antiwar aims. How do we know that it is an antiwar short story?

2. As the short story progresses, track the emotional states of the following individuals: the six-year-old boy, the narrator, and the reader.

3. Because the narrator follows the pseudoheroic exploits of a six-year-old boy, the short story offers a unique and startlingly naive perspec-

tive of war. Locate and describe a few instances in which the boy's perspective fails to grasp the horror that surrounds him. How would an adult describe and respond to the same situations?

Brief Bibliography

Davidson, Cathy N. *The Experimental Fictions of Ambrose Bierce: Structuring the Ineffable.* Lincoln: U of Nebraska P, 1984.

Kalter, Susan. "'Chickamauga' as an Indian-Wars Narrative: The Relevance of Ambrose Bierce for a First-Nations-Centered Study of the Nineteenth Century." *Arizona Quarterly* 56.4 (2000): 57–82.

Morris, Roy, Jr. *Ambrose Bierce: Alone in Bad Company.* New York: Crown, 1995.

HENRY JAMES   (p. 130)

Approaches to Teaching

Whether or not Henry James belongs in a course about or in an anthology of American literature deserves some attention, and this question often provides useful ways of casting his accomplishments in relief against the accomplishments of those whose Americanness never comes into question. That F. R. Leavis would include James among his examples of *The Great Tradition* of British novelists says much not only about James's citizenship at his death (a year after becoming a British subject) but also about the fastidiousness of his prose and prose theories (a sharp contrast from the blurry romanticism of his American forebears). Biographically, James bears little resemblance to most of his counterparts in the American canon: the child of privilege, he grew up in the finest homes in New York, Cambridge, and Newport and studied at a number of Swiss and German schools. James spent much of his adult life among the European cultural elite, and many of his best-known works, including *Daisy Miller* (which made him famous) and "The Real Thing," are set overseas. American publishers originally shied away from *Daisy Miller* – they thought it performed an injustice against the reputation of American maidenhood – but its instant success in England also meant that American pirated editions sold briskly. Readers then, as now, recognized the novella and *Daisy Miller*, the tale's title character, as unmistakably American creations.

Classroom Issues and Strategies

Daisy Miller offers an excellent example of the Jamesian self-revealing narrator, whose distinct point of view emerges as the narrator distances himself from the "hero" of the tale, Winterbourne. "I hardly know . . ." the narrator confesses at the start of the second paragraph, and the unnamed narrating "I" appears a full four times in this paragraph. The novella's "I" emerges as a distinct character in his own right, although one whose presence in the storytelling exerts no apparent consequence on the plot. James's self-revealing narrator highlights the "art" of character and plot development, and the device signals the "play" of storytelling. The narrator regularly corrects himself – as when he offers, "When his enemies spoke of him they said – but, after all, he had no enemies" – all of which suggests omniscience and doubt at the same time.

Randolph and Winterbourne represent polar versions of American manhood, an unstable form of personal identity in the so-called Gilded Age, an era of rapid social transformation and unprecedented social mobility. Winterbourne, like James, is the stereotypically effete bachelor type who disdains American boorishness and gladly finds a place among an outmoded (by American standards at least) European aristocracy. Randolph's precocious assertiveness might be seen as a version of the new, vulgar American manhood; he's clearly on his way to being a stereotypical, ugly American tourist, whose economic capital easily trumps all forms of cultural capital. The narrative's ambivalence toward the two characters does not obscure the fact that the narrator holds Randolph in higher esteem than Winterbourne and that the novella's plot rewards the lad more than his elder.

Ironically, "The Real Thing" might be described as a reflection on realism that approaches the antirealist shape of allegory. The character names – which include the patrician Monarchs, Miss Churm (perhaps a mangled version of "charm"), and Oronte (the name of a failed poet and failed suitor in Molière's *The Misanthrope*) – deserve some attention in this regard. But if the short story provides an object lesson about the nature of the "real," about realism, then what should we learn from it? Literary critic Sam Whitsitt, who views the short story as a kind of metaparable (reflecting on mimetic narratives *about* mimesis), offers useful guidance, but the question is perhaps best asked directly of students.

Connections to Other Authors and Texts

The phrase *psychological realism,* often used in association with James's fiction, invites comparisons with other writers in Volume Two also associated with the phrase, including those whom James influenced directly (William Dean Howells) and indirectly (Kate Chopin, Eugene O'Neill, Nella Larsen). While psychological realism is a somewhat vague category, it nevertheless draws our attention to the connection between a narrative's style and a character's interiority. *Daisy Miller* might also be compared with other narratives taking up the "Americans abroad" theme, such as

Hemingway's "Hills Like White Elephants," and more provocatively with other narratives about European immigrants finding their way in an unfamiliar United States, such as Mary Antin's *The Promised Land*. A final element for comparison in *Daisy Miller* would be its strong-willed and misunderstood title character; specifically, Daisy warrants comparison with other strong female characters – I hesitate to generate a list, but no list would be complete without Mary E. Wilkins Freeman's Louisa or Katherine Anne Porter's Laura – whether these are narrators, protagonists, or (like Daisy) objects for a narrative to "study."

Questions for Class Discussion

1. What does it mean that James subtitled the novella "A Study"?

2. Describe the narrator of *Daisy Miller* as if he were a real person. How old is he (assuming it is a "he")? How well educated is he? What social class does he belong to? How can we infer the answers to these questions?

3. Explain the significance of these character names: Daisy, Winterbourne, Walker.

4. How does *Daisy Miller* (the novella) reveal information about Daisy Miller (the character)? How are Daisy's words, actions, and inner thoughts mediated by the narrator or by other characters?

5. Provide an inventory of representational media (such as photography and novels) in "The Real Thing." Rank your list in terms of "cultural capital," that is, in terms of each medium's relative importance to culture.

6. In what ways do *Daisy Miller* and "The Real Thing" develop a distinctive style or reveal any obvious writing tics? In other words, what makes each work "Jamesian"?

Brief Bibliography

Graham, Kenneth. *Henry James, A Literary Life*. New York: St. Martin's, 1995.

Johnson, Lisa. "Daisy Miller: Cowboy Feminist." *Henry James Review* 22 (2001): 41–58.

Pollack, Vivian R., ed. *New Essays on* Daisy Miller *and* The Turn of the Screw. Cambridge: Cambridge UP, 1993.

Whitsitt, Sam. "A Lesson in Reading: Henry James's 'The Real Thing.'" *Henry James Review* 16 (1995): 304-14.

SARAH ORNE JEWETT   (p. 193)

Approaches to Teaching

Students often identify closely with the precocious Sylvia, the protagonist of Jewett's "A White Heron." In Sylvia's keen sense of the natural landscape, and in her seemingly related self-awareness of her burgeoning womanhood, Jewett has rolled together two regular facets of the *Bildungs* plot into a singular fictional consciousness. (The name *Sylvia* means "of the woods.") The challenge, but hardly a difficult one, is to allow students to see beyond Sylvia's tenuous search for identity, or beyond the story's obvious explorations of inter- and intragenerational communication (including budding romance), so that they can appreciate Jewett's playful shifts in narrative focus. Indeed, recent Jewett criticism has been tending toward ecocritical approaches to her work, and "A White Heron" deserves similar attention for its interest in interspecies communication and transcendence.

Classroom Issues and Strategies

An important early step in interpreting "A White Heron" is coming to terms with the third-person narrator's shifting focus. At the short story's beginning, Jewett appears to be having fun with point of view and narrative focus by introducing Sylvia and her cow Mistress Moolly, only to vacillate back and forth between the two perspectives and to unsettle the reader even further with vague references to the pronoun "her."

Jewett's narrative strategy takes a more serious turn (one suggested by recent ecocritical approaches) when the narrative subsequently shifts focus among Sylvia, Mrs. Tilley, the young man, the old pine-tree, and various birds. Jewett extends the playful boundary crossing when she describes the birdlike features of Sylvia's body: "There was the huge tree asleep yet in the paling moonlight, and small and silly Sylvia began with utmost bravery to mount to the top of it, with tingling, eager blood coursing the channels of her whole frame, with her bare feet and fingers, that pinched and held like bird's claws to the monstrous ladder reaching up, up, almost to the sky itself." The narrative strategy underscores Sylvia's distance from and rejection of the young man, who wishes to study the heron by killing and stuffing it.

Finally, you may wish to explore how the story connects interpretation of the natural landscape with literary interpretation, perhaps by isolating similarities between birding and reading; both, Jewett reminds us, are acts of verbal expression and interpretation.

Connections to Other Authors and Texts

Jewett has traditionally been featured with other realists strongly connected with a particular regional identity, and students can easily piece together a mental geography of regional expressions and styles when they consider her coastal Maine alongside Twain's West and Midwest, Austin's West, and subsequently Chopin's Louisiana, Faulkner's South, and Hurston's South. An interesting adjunct to the traditional approach would be to consider Jewett alongside so-called mainstream writers from centers of literary production such as Boston and New York. The cultural logic of the "region," as a number of critics have shown, insists on a particular kind of nostalgia for relatively transient economies and related cultural traditions (such as whaling, cotton plantations, and gold mining). When students encounter Jewett with Howells or Fitzgerald, to offer just two examples, they often gain a sharper sense of coastal Maine's idiosyncrasies, as well as an appreciation of what the mainstream literary marketplace valued (and still values) in her work.

Questions for Class Discussion

1. Starting with Mrs. Tilley's home and the "great pine-tree" half a mile away, draw a map of the terrain described in "A White Heron." Which details are easy to place on the map, and which details require speculation?

2. List the specific ways in which the narrator describes Sylvia as one might describe a bird. Which traits from this list seem to transcend the limits of human physical ability and human consciousness?

3. What value does Mrs. Tilley seem to derive from nature? What value does the young man derive? What value does Sylvia derive?

4. What might be the lost "treasures" and revealed "gifts," "graces," and "secrets" mentioned in the short story's concluding lines?

Brief Bibliography

Blanchard, Paula. *Sarah Orne Jewett: Her World and Her Work.* Reading, MA: Addison-Wesley, 1994.

Church, Joseph. "Romantic Flight in Jewett's 'White Heron.'" *Studies in American Fiction* 30 (2002): 21-44.

Renza, Louis A. *"A White Heron" and the Question of Minor Literature.* Madison: U of Wisconsin P, 1984.

MARY E. WILKINS FREEMAN   (p. 202)

Approaches to Teaching

Mary E. Wilkins Freeman's place in American literary history has for some time been largely bounded by two overlapping categories within literary discourse: local color and humor. "A New England Nun" fits most comfortably into the former category, although it should not be reduced to a simple formula for local-color expression. Indeed, the short story redefines the very category of New England identity by superimposing the familiar figure of the spinster onto the larger problem of gendered self-reliance. Louisa Ellis's strictly ordered life is symptomatic of an era in which female self-possession and self-determination occupy the closely guarded margins of American society, in which spinsterhood might be seen as the only acceptable way to resist the cultural imperative to marry. That Freeman would take up Louisa's life story – and her cause – says much about the concerns of local-color fiction during this same time. Louisa is no Emersonian free-thinking individualist – but at least she's not trapped in an unhappy marriage. At the same time, Freeman's short story offers a subtle commentary about the avenues of artistic self-reliance open to women writers.

Classroom Issues and Strategies

Students typically react quite negatively to Louisa; they have said she's too "uptight," too "obsessive-compulsive" for their easy liking (quoting directly from class discussion). What's more, the way she treats her dog is alarming. You may wish to remind your students that Louisa's dog, Caesar, happens to be an object of literary imagination, and one with an especially symbolic name at that. "Why would Freeman name the dog Caesar and then chain him up?" you might ask. More important, be sure to address the limited options available to "respectable" young women such as Louisa in late-nineteenth-century American society: marriage not so much for love as for practicality on the one hand, spinsterhood on the other hand. "Would you want to marry Joe Dagget?" you might also ask. Most students quickly reevaluate their opinion.

The short story's opening description of Louisa's every last preparation for a simple, home-cooked meal for one speaks volumes not only about the character but also about Freeman's literary artistry. Ask your students to examine carefully the third and fourth paragraphs (in which Louisa gathers currants and makes tea). The passage reveals a meticulous attention to detail, a mastery over Louisa's rather limited domain, somewhat akin to the prose efforts of women local colorists in nineteenth-century American literary culture. Freeman's readers, from her time to our own, can take pleasure in the domestic details, much as Louisa obviously takes pleasure in them.

Connections to Other Authors and Texts

Freeman ranks among the great masters of tone in American literary history, and she arguably equals such greats as Hawthorne and Twain (and later Zora Neale Hurston and Kurt Vonnegut) when it comes to tonal subtlety. Her careful positioning of the reader in relation to individual characters allows for comparison to virtually any fiction writer in *The Bedford Anthology of American Literature*; consider, for example, the opening description of Louisa in relation to Twain's opening description of a character. The very title of the short story almost demands comparison to other narratives (and perhaps poetry) that explore the place of New England in the American cultural imagination. The frustrated romance also warrants consideration alongside other versions of the marriage plot or, more broadly, other narratives addressing the role of women in society. Hawthorne's work certainly fits the bill, as does Chopin's, Gilman's, Wharton's, and Glaspell's.

Questions for Class Discussion

1. In what ways is homemaking an art form? Is it an art form? What are some of the similarities between Louisa's homemaking and Freeman's prose?

2. Louisa and Joe are decent people who were at one point romantically interested in one another. Why can't the two be happily married? Why do they almost marry in spite of their unhappiness together?

3. How do male characters (Joe and Caesar) fare in "A New England Nun"?

4. Explain the significance of the caged bird and the chained dog in the larger context of the short story.

Brief Bibliography

Glasser, Leah Blatt. *In a Closet Hidden: The Life and Work of Mary E. Wilkins Freeman.* Amherst: U of Massachusetts P, 1996.

Marchalonis, Shirley. *Critical Essays on Mary Wilkins Freeman.* Boston: Hall, 1991.

Reichardt, Mary R. *Mary Wilkins Freeman: A Study of the Short Fiction.* New York: Twayne, 1997.

KATE CHOPIN   (p. 213)

Approaches to Teaching

Kate Chopin's academic stock rose over the last three decades as much as any nineteenth-century American writer thanks largely to the revisionist work of feminist scholars. (This work has been so successful, in fact, that it would be almost unthinkable not to account for Chopin in a general study of turn-of-the-century American fiction.) A useful way to introduce key issues in the study of Chopin is to ask students why they think her writing has risen from relative obscurity to a central place in the American canon – in other words, ask, don't tell. Their answers may well depend on whether or not you have assigned *The Awakening* (1899), a novel that tends to elicit a wider range of responses than "At the 'Cadian Ball" and "The Storm." (Bedford/St. Martin's publishes a reprint edition of Chopin's novel, which can be packaged with the anthology.) If students tend to focus on the short stories' more melodramatic or unreconstructed elements, some guidance on irony and historical contextualization (on issues pertaining to the place of women and ethnic and racial minorities in nineteenth-century U.S. society) may be called for. Many students, however, will quickly see the stories' unconventional, and even revolutionary, perspectives on gender relations and social class.

Classroom Issues and Strategies

That "At the 'Cadian Ball" would need a "sequel," as Chopin subtitled "The Storm," provides a unique and potentially fascinating avenue for investigation. "At the 'Cadian Ball" arrives at a neat and tidy conclusion judging by the standards of comedy; after all, the two sets of lovers end up engaged in one case and virtually engaged in the other. Even so, students will readily admit that the narrative leaves the romantic situation awkwardly unsettled. A key issue, then, is asking them to arrive at a satisfactory explanation of why and how the narrative produces such an unsettling effect, why a sequel makes sense.

The discrepancy between what happens in "At the 'Cadian Ball" and how it's allowed to unfold requires close attention to tone and to dramatic irony. (Bobinôt, for example, seems not to appreciate that he's setting himself up for a woefully unhappy marriage.) "The Storm" offers an evolved version of this irony; the characters either accept unflinchingly or obliviously fail to register that happy domestic routine masks profound disconnection between husbands and wives.

Both short stories, more obviously in "At the 'Cadian Ball," also offer ample opportunity to explore the social (and linguistic) construction of class, ethnic, and racial hierarchies; more advanced students might even be introduced to social analysis along the lines suggested by, for example, Pierre Bourdieu. His notion of a cultured *habitus* informs a sense of why characters act as they do, and why they are rewarded (or punished) for their performances. Careful analysis reveals Chopin's attentive and sometimes critical view of Creole social life.

Finally, one note of caution: Some students might feel squeamish discussing erotically charged literature; Chopin's work might appear tame by twenty-first-century standards, but students should be made to feel that their discussion environment is a safe place to address (or demur from) issues of sexuality.

Connections to Other Authors and Texts

Whitman's influence on Chopin has long occupied literary scholars, and rightly so. Students in a year-long literature survey might be asked to consider thematic and even formal continuities between the two writers. The same students might also be asked to contrast the unapologetic sensuality of Chopin's characters with writers and characters more connected to the Puritan tradition. As with many writers in this section of Volume Two of *The Bedford Anthology of American Literature* (Twain, Jewett, Freeman, and so on), Chopin deserves consideration as a local colorist; in fact, many recent definitions (or deconstructions) of *local color* rely on careful consideration of Chopin's work. An important and ongoing controversy surrounding Chopin, one that deserves special attention in "At the 'Cadian Ball" and "The Storm," is her status as a proto-New Woman or protofeminist writer; in this respect, her work looks forward to such deft handlers of gendered language as Mina Loy, Dorothy Parker, and Nella Larsen.

Questions for Class Discussion

1. If you were to cast film versions of the short stories using contemporary actors, who would play the roles of Bobinôt, Calixta, Alcée, and Clarisse? What necessary qualities and skills would the actors bring to the roles?

2. Classify and divide the short stories' characters according to their standing within Creole society. What details (of speech, of visual appearance, of manner) reveal each character's position?

3. Both short stories deploy fairly obvious symbols from the human world and from the natural landscape. How do symbols (storms, for example) work in expected and unexpected ways?

4. Chopin wrote "The Storm" as a sequel to "At the 'Cadian Ball," but she chose not to submit the sequel for publication, even though "At the 'Cadian Ball" was fairly well received. What does her self-censorship

reveal about Chopin's view of the late-nineteenth-century literary marketplace?

Brief Bibliography

Evans, Robert C. *Kate Chopin's Short Fiction: A Critical Companion.* West Cornwall, CT: Locust Hill, 2001.

Petry, Alice Hall. *Critical Essays on Kate Chopin.* New York: Hall, 1996.

Toth, Emily. *Unveiling Kate Chopin.* Jackson: UP of Mississippi, 1999.

CHARLES W. CHESNUTT   (p. 228)

Approaches to Teaching

Of the 3.2 million slaves in the United States in 1850, around the time "The Passing of Grandison" is set, only a very tiny percentage escaped bondage to find freedom in the North. The journey was particularly difficult because, as Charles W. Chesnutt points out in his short story, "the constant drain of fugitive slaves into the North [before 1850] had so alarmed the slaveholders of the border States as to lead to the passage of the Fugitive Slave Law," which made harboring or otherwise assisting escaped slaves a federal offense. "The Passing of Grandison" is suspenseful on its own terms; providing students a brief historical primer about the rise of sectional tensions in the wake of the Fugitive Slave Law, and about the difficulties facing African American authors in the late nineteenth century, further amplifies the suspense. At one point in the short story, Chesnutt alludes to the laws prohibiting slaves from learning how to read; as a fiction writer born five years before the Emancipation Proclamation, Chesnutt faced literary hardships well beyond those faced by most of his contemporaries. The mere attempt to make a living as an African American writer should be understood for the bold act that it was.

Classroom Issues and Strategies

"The Passing of Grandison," first published in 1899, is set roughly fifty years earlier, during the period "befo' de war" (to borrow a phrase from, among others, Thomas Nelson Page). The short story dispels the myth, propagated by Page and many more, of a romantic Old South, in which distinguished gentlemen acted with chivalry toward women and kindheartedness toward slaves. The myth very much animated American culture at the turn of the century; the understated critical language that the narrator deploys against the Owens family – Colonel Owens, for instance, displays a "feudal heart," and Dick naively assumes that Grandison possesses "the native gregariousness and garrulousness of his race" – fully informed late-nineteenth-century debates about post-Reconstruction economy and culture.

Grandison's behavior during his encounters with Colonel Owens and Dick Owens might well be understood as a virtuoso performance. Significantly, we see part of this performance directly, in the form of direct discourse (marked off by the typical quotation marks), but we see the remainder of the performance through the distorting lens of the Owenses' responses to Grandison. As a result, the short story is thick with situational irony.

Connections to Other Authors and Texts

"The Passing of Grandison" offers a belated example of a fugitive slave narrative, although one primarily seen from the perspective of oblivious slave owners. For this reason, the short story provides an interesting counterpoint to the slave narratives (by Douglass and Jacobs) found in *The Bedford Anthology of American Literature*, Volume One. Chesnutt's career ambitions, which surface as a concern only indirectly in his short story, find an interesting place in relation to the debate between Booker T. Washington and W. E. B. Du Bois about the future place of African Americans in U.S. society.

Questions for Class Discussion

1. The term *passing* ordinarily refers to a light-skinned African American pretending to be white. In what ways does Grandison "pass"? How does he deceive Colonel Owens and Dick Owens?

2. The first words we hear Grandison utter are "Yas, marster" and "Y-a-s, marster." How do these phrases mean different things? What does each phrase mean?

3. What racial stereotypes (for both blacks and whites) does Chesnutt explore in the short story? Which does he undermine? Which remain in place?

Brief Bibliography

Keller, Frances Richardson. *An American Crusade: The Life of Charles Waddell Chesnutt.* Provo: Brigham Young UP, 1978.

McWilliams, Dean. *Charles W. Chesnutt and the Fictions of Race.* Athens: U of Georgia P, 2002.

Wonham, Henry B. *Charles W. Chesnutt: A Study of the Short Fiction.* New York: Twayne, 1998.

PAULINE E. HOPKINS   (p. 242)

Approaches to Teaching

Thanks largely to the recovery work of feminist scholars, Pauline E. Hopkins has since the 1980s emerged as an important figure in African American and American literary history. We now know much about her life, career, and work, especially her once again in-print novels. Literary scholars have given Hopkins's long fiction (especially *Contending Forces*) and journalism much attention; less has been given her work as a short-story writer. "As the Lord Lives, He Is One of Our Mother's Children" presents an invigorating challenge, then; because of the author's wonderfully interesting life, and because of the short story's wealth of engaging detail, students might be asked (singly or in small groups) to approach the work as an object for in-depth literary critical or literary historical research. Surprisingly little has been written about "As the Lord Lives"; with a little prodding, today's students might soon fill in the literary critical gap.

Classroom Issues and Strategies

Hopkins has been cast as a trailblazing writer, which is certainly true. What is becoming clear only very slowly, however, are the precise trails she blazed just about a century ago. Was she a radical when it came to advancing the cause of African Americans? of women? As Jill Bergman argues, the evidence can be contradictory at times. The politics of "As the Lord Lives" defies any simple description.

   "As the Lord Lives" arranges a broad network of discursive references. In some respects, the short story is entirely traditional, with numerous references to the Bible, to American cultural stereotypes (about New Englanders and mining towns, for instance), and to natural philosophy (specifically, the idea that one might encounter the divine in the study of nature). In other respects, the short story evokes the thoroughly modern science of crowd psychology (the angry mob and the repentant congregation stand in sharp contrast even though they're comprised of the same people) and the timeless presence of the supernatural (after all, for no perceptible reason, George Stone knows that Stevens and his son are on the doomed train).

   "As the Lord Lives" is not without its melodrama and heavy-handedness. George Stone inexplicably escapes the angry, vicious lynch mob; he improbably winds up at the right bend on the railroad tracks at just the right time; and he miraculously knows that his friends are on a train about to plow into a fallen tree. Stone says of his initial escape: "Somehow I did it – you know the rest." And when Stevens refuses to turn in the fugitive, Stone remarks, "I can't thank you, Mr. Stevens, but if I ever get the chance you'll find me grateful." The short story thus calls attention to its implausible design so that readers might focus on its larger ethical significance.

Connections to Other Authors and Texts

Literary scholar Claudia Tate once described Pauline E. Hopkins as the "literary foremother" of the many important African American women writers of the twentieth (and now the twenty-first) century. A complex interweaving of religious and political rhetoric contributes to the antebellum discourse concerning slavery, and so many of the abolitionist statements found in *The Bedford Anthology of American Literature,* Volume One, help bring Hopkins's short story into focus. The same is true of Twain's "The War Prayer." Even though she was ten years his senior, Hopkins's work is often said to reflect Du Boisian political and social ideals. James Baldwin's "Going to Meet the Man" provides a more recent investigation into the disturbing culture of lynching.

Questions for Class Discussion

1. If available at your library, examine a few copies of the *Colored American Magazine.* What seem to be the editorial aims of the magazine? Which of these aims does Hopkins's short story embody?

2. Which elements of the plot seem far-fetched? What is their larger purpose in Hopkins's narrative? (Why is it acceptable for the short story to include some far-fetched details?)

3. What do the narrator's descriptions of the natural landscape add to the short story's tone and plot development?

Brief Bibliography

Bergman, Jill. "'Everything We Hoped She'd Be': Contending Forces in Hopkins Scholarship." *African American Review* 38 (2004): 181-99.

Tate, Claudia. "Pauline Hopkins: Our Literary Foremother." *Conjuring: Black Women, Fiction, and Literary Tradition.* Eds. Marjorie Pryse and Hortense J. Spillers. Bloomington: Indiana UP, 1985. 53-66.

Wallinger, Hanna. *Pauline E. Hopkins: A Literary Biography.* Athens: U of Georgia P, 2005.

CHARLOTTE PERKINS GILMAN   (p. 251)

Approaches to Teaching

Rarely do authors announce their literary intentions as clearly and directly as Charlotte Perkins Gilman in "Why I Wrote 'The Yellow Wall-Paper.'" For this reason, Gilman's short story presents a distinct opening to challenge students to venture beyond a writer's "intention" and to think instead about the text's adaptability to playful readerly interpretation. The drama of Gilman's life and career, though, makes strictly textual analysis difficult to stick to. Because it is also tremendously rewarding to address autobiographical elements within the text, and to discuss Gilman's subsequent career as a major voice in American feminism, I recommend saving time for biographical discussion, but only after encouraging strictly textual exploration and even speculation. A simple, open-ended question such as, "What associations do you bring to the color yellow?" is often all it takes to spark lively student discussion. The short story's sometimes baffling descent into madness invites a wide range of approaches from beginning and advanced students of all academic backgrounds. A first-year student with an interest in psychology may illuminate the prose in a manner that rivals the insights of an advanced English major with an interest in avant-garde narrative. Let your students wander; when it comes to "The Yellow Wall-Paper," overpreparation can be a greater risk than underpreparation.

Classroom Issues and Strategies

The realism of "The Yellow Wall-Paper" – the narrative's commitment to the logic of a narrator who descends into madness – reveals itself textually in fairly obvious ways: the one sentence paragraphs, the regular shifts in attention, the sudden section endings, the repeated exclamations. I often ask students to re-create the text even more "realistically," by mimicking the narrator's handwriting at the story's beginning, middle, and end. The results usually speak for themselves.

Although I have not screened any of them, "The Yellow Wall-Paper" has inspired a number of film adaptations. The narrative's highly individuated, first-person perspective defies filmic re-creation, but if asked to imagine their own film version of "The Yellow Wall-Paper," students will often arrive at intriguing visual analogs for the story's formal features (such as jerky camera movements in lieu of choppy paragraphs, suggestively blurred camera focus in lieu of visual hallucinations).

As the narrator's mental condition draws her closer and closer to the woman trapped in the wallpaper, it alienates her from the rest of the household and, presumably, the reader. Even so, she remains a remarkably sympathetic figure. A close look at the story's last page or so allows for an interesting discussion of the narrator's simultaneously estranging and endearing qualities.

Connections to Other Authors and Texts

"The Yellow Wall-Paper" might be discussed alongside Jewett's "A White Heron" as a text in which a female protagonist faces a controlling male

authority figure; because each story dramatizes a unique set of circumstances and deploys a unique set of characters, steer clear of identifying
patterns at the expense of individuality. "The Yellow Wall-Paper" anticipates subsequent literature about mental instability, including the confessional poetry of Berryman and Plath.

Questions for Class Discussion

1. Why do you think Gilman cast the narrator's husband and brother as
   physicians? How might the short story differ if these characters followed Gilman's advice in "Why I Wrote 'The Yellow Wall-Paper'"?

2. Which details in the short story support the fiction of its narration;
   that is, how does the short story appear to be written by a mentally
   unhinged narrator?

3. Select a passage from the short story in which the narrator describes
   the yellow wallpaper. How does her interpretation of its significance
   resemble the act of reading the short story? How do the two activities
   (reading the wallpaper versus reading the short story) differ?

4. Rewrite the ending to "The Yellow Wall-Paper" from a mentally stable
   perspective. How does your version differ from Gilman's?

Brief Bibliography

Erskine, Thomas L., and Connie L. Richards, eds. *The Yellow
    Wallpaper/Charlotte Perkins Gilman.* New Brunswick: Rutgers UP,
    1993.

Lane, Ann J. *To Herland and Beyond: The Life and Work of Charlotte Perkins
    Gilman.* New York: Pantheon, 1990.

Weinstock, Jeffrey Andrew. *The Pedagogical Wallpaper: Teaching Charlotte
    Perkins Gilman's "The Yellow Wallpaper."* New York: P. Lang, 2003.

ABRAHAM CAHAN   (p. 266)

Approaches to Teaching

In his autobiography, *The Education of Abraham Cahan* (1969) [trans. of
Bleter fun mayn leben (1926-31)], the first among many world-famous
Jewish American writers marvels that a prominent American editor does
not know the meaning of the term *ghetto.* Today's students, in sharp contrast, will likely have a very concrete, and perhaps a very narrow, understanding of the term. (The *OED* has yet to capture the contemporary, colloquial sense of *ghetto,* which also signifies "jury-rigged," "impoverished,"

"déclassé," and in rare cases "stylish.") A discussion of the short story's title, including what it suggests to present-day students, warrants some attention, particularly since "A Ghetto Wedding" first appeared (in 1898) in the *Atlantic Monthly,* a magazine whose readership certainly had little direct experience of ghettos. That a literary magazine so often associated with the cultural elite, and with a uniquely American variety of realism, would publish the short story says much about Cahan and about turn-of-the-century American literary taste.

Classroom Issues and Strategies

Goldy's transformation during the few pages of the short story is nothing less than radical (in multiple senses of the word). Midway through the tale, the narrator tracks her foremost thoughts: "For hours together [Goldy] would go on talking nothing but rooms, rent, and furniture; . . . in her imagination, humanity was divided into those who were interested in the question of rooms, rent, and furniture and those who were not — the former, of whom she was one, constituting the superior category; and whenever her eye fell upon a bill announcing rooms to let, she would experience something akin to the feeling with which an artist, in passing, views some accessory of his art." By the short story's end, we encounter a chastened, more enlightened Goldy. The contrast could hardly be sharper.

Turn-of-the-century American ethnic literature often resembles the newly emergent science of anthropology. Cahan explores in much detail some of the more obscure (to a mainstream American audience) aspects of Jewish wedding rituals; like a social scientist, he linguistically establishes his credentials and asserts his authority: "[i]t is customary to send the bulkier wedding presents to a young couple's apartments a few days before they become man and wife"; "[a]ccording to the orthodox custom"; "[t]he song or address to the bride usually partakes of the qualities of prayer and harangue." Such details, which filled the pages of the *Atlantic Monthly,* offered much valued entertainment for that magazine's socially and culturally elite readership.

Connections to Other Authors and Texts

Abraham Cahan shaped the Jewish American cultural experience more profoundly than anyone before or since; he should certainly be regarded as a (if not *the*) founding father of Jewish American literature in both Yiddish and English. Cahan's socialist naturalism invites specific comparison with such figures as Frank Norris and Jack London and (later) John Dos Passos and Langston Hughes. Cahan also contributed importantly to the literature of the urban ghetto; his New York is fascinating to consider alongside Dreiser's or Wharton's New York and Sandburg's Chicago.

Questions for Class Discussion

1. What significant life lessons does Goldy learn as the short story evolves? How does she grow emotionally, ethically, or otherwise? How do we know the answers to these questions; that is, what textual cues do we have to recognize her growth as a character?

2. How does setting (the narrator's description of the urban landscape, including natural and artificial environs) establish the short story's tone at its beginning and its ending?

3. What details from the "ghetto wedding" does the narrator assume the reader doesn't yet know; in other words, what aspects of Jewish tradition does the narrator take pains to elucidate?

Brief Bibliography

Cahan, Abraham. *The Education of Abraham Cahan.* Trans. Leon Stein, Abraham P. Conan, and Lynn Davison. Philadelphia: Jewish Publication Society of America, 1969.

Chametzky, Jules. *From the Ghetto: The Fiction of Abraham Cahan.* Amherst: U of Massachusetts P, 1977.

Marovitz, Sanford E. *Abraham Cahan.* New York: Twayne, 1996.

EDITH WHARTON   (p. 279)

Approaches to Teaching

Edith Wharton's "The Other Two" ends with its protagonist, Waythorn, laughing at his wife's apparent social ease when faced with her present and former husbands. With little or no prompting, students will often arrive at very strong and wildly divergent opinions about Alice, the principle female character in the short story. Some will find her a misunderstood and maligned woman; others will find her a manipulative gold digger; still others will find her a horrible or desperately preoccupied mother; many will find her a combination of the above. The short story supplies intriguing and sometimes overlapping evidence in support of each of these opinions; a full-fledged debate over the question – What is the narrator's (or Wharton's) view of Alice? – readily surpasses impressionistic views and encourages discussion of the intricate detail and precise prose that brought Wharton popular and critical fame. No detail, from the description of characters' clothing to their tone of voice to architectural symbolism, is too small.

Classroom Issues and Strategies

If nothing else, "The Other Two" yields memorable figures of speech to describe marriage and divorce. The narrator informs us, for example, that Waythorn imagines a wife's primary role, "to make a man happy," as an art, "[f]or it *was* an art, and made up, like all others, of concessions, eliminations and embellishments, of lights judiciously thrown and shadows skillfully softened." Elsewhere he compares Alice's successive marriages to a "syndicate"; at first he relishes the "joy of possession" of his wife, only to describe her later as "a shoe that too many feet had worn." Divorce is pictured as an instrumental legal procedure, but one that requires delicate "adaptation" and "social justification," especially of women.

Significantly, "The Other Two" relies on a tricky (and perhaps ironic) gender coding of more and less successful social behavior. The vexing contingencies of modern urban life require "mannish" composure, the short story suggests: Waythorn "hated the womanish sensibility which made him suffer so acutely from the grotesque chances of life. He had known when he married that his wife's former husbands were both living, and that amid the multiplied contacts of modern existence there were a thousand chances to one that he would run against one or the other." Judging by the evidence, however, Alice seems the best suited, perhaps too well suited, to the poised handling of chance encounters with former spouses.

Connections to Other Authors and Texts

For biographical and stylistic reasons, Wharton's work is compared most often with that of Henry James; in spite of their dramatically different fates, Daisy Miller and Alice Waythorn share important traits in common. The rarefied New York society depicted in "The Other Two" comes into clearer view when considered against the backdrop of the working-class New York portrayed by Cahan and Dreiser. Finally, Wharton's short story places the institution of marriage under a looking glass, as does the fiction of Chopin and Freeman (among others).

Questions for Class Discussion

1. As the short story progresses, how does Alice change in Waythorn's eyes? How do we recognize such a change even though the short story utilizes a third-person narrator? What language does the narrator borrow from Waythorn's thoughts to describe Alice? What language belongs strictly to the narrator?

2. According to the short story, what social skills does Alice acquire in each of her three marriages? How does she take advantage of her newly acquired skills?

3. Which details reveal a character's social status in "The Other Two"?

Brief Bibliography

Benstock, Shari. *No Gifts from Chance: A Biography of Edith Wharton.* New York: Scribner's, 1994.

Inverso, Mary Beth. "Performing Women: Semiotic Promiscuity in 'The Other Two.'" *Edith Wharton Review* 10 (1993): 3-6.

Singley, Carol J., ed. *A Historical Guide to Edith Wharton.* Oxford: Oxford UP, 2003.

White, Barbara A. *Edith Wharton: A Study of the Short Fiction.* New York: Twayne, 1991.

SUI SIN FAR
(EDITH MAUD EATON)   (p. 296)

Approaches to Teaching

A growing number of literary critics claim that the Asian American literary canon begins with the long-ignored work of Sui Sin Far, the pen name of Edith Maud Eaton. The first Chinese American to publish English-language fiction in the United States, Sui Sin Far clearly deserves the mantle from our privileged position of hindsight. But what does it mean to be the first in a tradition that doesn't yet exist? "In the Land of the Free" presents a unique opportunity to address the theoretically vexing and, in American literary studies, surprisingly ubiquitous question. Did Phillis Wheatley see herself as the progenitor of an African American literary tradition? Did Charles Brockden Brown see himself as the first American novelist (as have many literary historians)? In her autobiographical essay, "Leaves from the Mental Portfolio of an Eurasian," Sui Sin Far recalls, "I am only ten years old. And all the while the question of nationality perplexes my little brain. Why are we what we are?" The short story gives narrative form to the existential dilemma posed here. Issues of nationality and childhood existence furnish the short story a moral indignation and a poignancy commonly found in Sui Sin Far's work.

Classroom Issues and Strategies

"In the Land of the Free" extends the sentimental tradition by crafting an analogy of gendered morality: Women are to men as the spirit of the law (justice) is to the letter of the law (bureaucracy). At one point, the aggrieved mother, Lae Choo, upbraids her husband, "You do not know − man − what it is to miss the feel of the little fingers and the little toes and the soft round limbs of your little one." The appropriate response to a heartrending situation like Lae Choo's, tears, functions as an emotional (and physiological) primer for the reader; by transforming the thoughts (and bodies) of enough readers, the short story might bring about social change.

As in much of Sui Sin Far's work, "In the Land of the Free" spotlights the blurry line between cultural Other and universal humanity. Chinese American characters speak and dress and behave outside the American mainstream; at the same time, the short story reverses the usual white-above-Chinese hierarchy by exposing the callousness of American immigration law and the acquisitiveness of the white lawyer, James Clancy. Lae Choo may speak a broken English dialect, but the devoted mother is the short story's clear moral center.

Connections to Other Authors and Texts

As the editors of *The Bedford Anthology of American Literature* suggest, pairing Sui Sin Far with Du Bois reveals their shared concern with "double-consciousness" as well as their similar narrative strategies for exploring the "color line." A writer more readily connected with straightforward assimilation (such as Mary Antin) provides an interesting counterpoint. If we take up the influence of turn-of-the-century ethnography on Sui Sin Far's work (as does Lori Jirousek), considering a fellow literary ethnographer such as Mary Austin helps bring Sui Sin Far's aesthetic choices to light.

Questions for Class Discussion

1. How do patterns of light and darkness (or day and night) sustain the emotional trajectory of the short story?

2. How does "In the Land of the Free" represent Chinese in English? How does it represent Chinese American English? How does it represent the toddler's Chinese and English? How do these forms of direct discourse (directly quoted speech) compare to the short story's standard English?

3. Locate the most emotionally gripping parts of the short story. How does the prose tug at our emotions?

Brief Bibliography

Jirousek, Lori. "Spectacle Ethnography and Immigrant Resistance: Sui Sin Far and Anzia Yezierska." *MELUS* 27 (2002): 25–52.

Song, Min Hyoung. "Sentimentalism and Sui Sin Far." *Legacy* 20 (2003): 134–52.

White-Parks, Annette. "A Reversal of American Concepts of 'Other-ness' in the Fiction of Sui Sin Far." *MELUS* 20 (1995): 17–34.

———. *Sui Sin Far/Edith Maud Eaton: A Literary Biography.* Urbana: U of
   Illinois P, 1995.

MARY AUSTIN   (p. 305)

Approaches to Teaching

Although "The Basket Maker" appeared over one hundred years ago, much
about the sketch, and about Mary Austin, remains urgently up-to-date. The
themes Austin explores in "The Basket Maker" include feminist identity,
the coding of racial difference, environmental awareness, and aesthetic
theory. And yet something feels dated about Austin's prose. Austin speaks
with confidence and authority about both Paiute and mainstream U.S. society in a manner that reflects the reigning ethnographic assumption of her
day: that keenly observant writers can know and represent in language not
just an individual life (in this case, the Indian woman Seyavi) but also the
larger tribal culture from which it emerges. It helps to remind students that
they are reading a single, gifted writer's account of a single, though perhaps extraordinary, Paiute woman. Nevertheless, students should also feel
encouraged to enjoy and interpret the sketch as a remarkable work of literary art.

Classroom Issues and Strategies

Austin interprets Paiute culture primarily for the mainstream U.S. readership of the *Atlantic Monthly.* Doing so compels some intriguing figures of
speech, as when she draws an analogy between American women's hair
fashion and Indian basket design. Both art forms, Austin suggests, depend
on a woman's "crisis" of "experience"; that is, women are likely to change
hairstyles or basket designs until they settle into a comfortable maturity.
Similarly, Austin elsewhere indicates that "[e]very Indian woman is an
artist – sees, feels, creates, but does not philosophize about her
processes." Austin's language repeatedly vacillates between a sense of collective womanhood and a sense of ethnic difference; her figures of speech
might be understood as a part of this movement between the universal and
the particular.

Women's self-sufficiency – among the many qualities that Seyavi represents – has as its major component a profound understanding of the natural landscape and the cycles of nature. Austin's acute attention to nature's
detail represents the smallest fraction of the ecological knowledge possessed by Seyavi and other Paiutes like her. As Austin reveals her naturalist credentials, she also demonstrates her knowledge of the Paiute way of
life.

Connections to Other Authors and Texts

If your course covers the antebellum period, Thoreau's environmental understanding, at once rooted in and critical of mainstream American traditions, offers an interesting counterpoint to Austin's work. Certainly those writers whose local color depends on a rich description of the natural landscape (Jewett and Cather, for example) might also merit some consideration next to Austin. Finally, Sarah Winnemucca Hopkins's *Life among the Piutes* (1883) represents a direct antecedent to Austin's sketch.

Questions for Class Discussion

1. According to Austin's sketch, what does it mean to be a woman? What does it mean to be Paiute? Where do these categories diverge, and where do they overlap?

2. Based on your understanding of "The Basket Maker," describe the Paiute sense of time and the Paiute sense of place. What details does Austin provide for your description?

3. How does "The Basket Maker" compare with other westerns (fiction, nonfiction, and film) that you have encountered?

Brief Bibliography

Fink, Augusta. *I-Mary: A Biography of Mary Austin.* Tucson: U of Arizona P, 1983.

Graulich, Melody, and Elizabeth Klimasmith, eds. *Exploring Lost Borders: Critical Essays on Mary Austin.* Reno: U of Nevada P, 1999.

Schaefer, Heike. *Mary Austin's Regionalism: Reflections on Gender, Genre, and Geography.* Charlottesville: U of Virginia P, 2004.

EDWIN ARLINGTON ROBINSON   (p. 313)

Approaches to Teaching

Among the topics in Robinson criticism, his thematization of failure and his steadfast commitment to traditional verse recur about as often as any others. These two facets of the Robinsonian aesthetic often prove high hurdles to cross for today's students. The difficulty is best understood as an opportunity: Because Robinson's poetry can be off-putting to student readers, opening up a single poem reveals the value of close, careful attention to language. And because Robinson's poems are often mysteriously oblique, they are fertile territory for fanciful speculation. "Miniver Cheevy" is a good place to start. The title figure's very modern psychological problems update the seemingly old-fashioned verse form. To give students ample room to speculate about the connection between form and content, you might ask, "Which contemporary musician or music group would do the best job setting the poem to fitting music? What would the result sound like?"

Classroom Issues and Strategies

Although Robinson is closely connected with small-town life in Maine, much of his work takes on an aspect that Donald Justice aptly describes as "benign obscurity," that is, an aspect that sparks the imagination in spite of (and partly because of) poetic difficulty. (Robinson and Hopkins are Justice's primary examples, but his essay applies to a much larger number of difficult poets.) Take the examples of "Luke Havergal" and "Eros Turannos": The two poems are extraordinarily difficult because superbly oblique. Even the most attentive reader can arrive at little more than a skeletal understanding of the details behind the disastrous love stories. But the poems' tone and rhythm interact in such a way to reveal their deeper, unforgettable meaning. If students can take away from the poems a sense of their emotional burden, they will have been successful readers.

It would be a shame, though, to take away nothing besides emotional burden (even if Robinson is a notoriously depressing poet). The ironic (if predictable) twist in "Richard Cory," or the cutting satire of "Miniver Cheevy" (who "thought, and thought, and thought / And thought about" the gold he both seeks and scorns), or the brilliant framing of "The House on the Hill" in a taciturn villanelle (because "[t]here is nothing more to say") – clever and idiosyncratic verse such as this should be celebrated as a playful take on heavy emotions.

Connections to Other Authors and Texts

Robinson's consistent use of traditional verse forms often suggests glancing backward into literary history, but his idiosyncratic regional types, plagued by neuroses revealed by modern psychology, recommend glancing forward. For reasons of diction and regional identification, a number of critics have drawn connections between Robinson and Whitman and Frost. The quirky, regionally inflected characters of Twain, Freeman, and Anderson also help bring Robinson's poems into focus.

Questions for Class Discussion

1. Track the emotional trajectories of "Richard Cory," "Miniver Cheevy," and "Mr. Flood's Party." (The latter two poems are about problem

drinkers.) Where do sharp emotional turns take place? What specific language suggests each turn?

2. In "The House on the Hill," the poet announces in the first stanza that "[t]here is nothing more to say." Even so, the poem (a villanelle) continues for five more stanzas. What does the poem go on "to say"?

3. What makes Robinson's poetry "Robinsonian"? In other words, what persons, places, themes, and styles does Robinson consistently return to?

Brief Bibliography

Barnard, Ellsworth, ed. *Edwin Arlington Robinson: Centenary Essays.* Athens: U of Georgia P, 1969.

Bloom, Harold, ed. *Edwin Arlington Robinson.* New York: Chelsea, 1988.

Coxe, Louis. *Edwin Arlington Robinson: The Life of Poetry.* New York: Pegasus, 1969.

Justice, Donald. "Benign Obscurity." *Sewanee Writers on Writing.* Ed. Wyatt Prunty. Baton Rouge: Louisiana State UP, 2000. 105-16.

FRANK NORRIS   (p. 323)

Approaches to Teaching

Those of us who pursue a career teaching American literature tend not to pay close attention to the goings-on of commodity futures markets, and we certainly don't find much drama in the day-to-day trading of wheat. Fortunately for us and for our students, Frank Norris, in "A Deal in Wheat," manages to inject suspense into commodity trading, and perhaps more importantly he humanizes the seemingly abstract process of getting a grain to market. The intricate, half-hidden rules of futures trading emerge slowly but clearly enough to gain our interest; we acknowledge but perhaps do not fully recognize that the Chicago Board of Trade is but one spoke in the global wheel of commerce and that a family farm in Kansas, the locus of local color, represents a pale extension of the spoke. Such is Norris's gift as a naturalist writer: He seamlessly and significantly shifts attention from the "laws" of commerce to their sinister effects upon individuals; he reveals connections between the local and the global, suggesting that no deed, good or bad, goes unfelt. The careful, many-faceted unfolding of the short story's plot raises the scientistic approach of naturalism to the level of literary art.

Classroom Issues and Strategies

Most of the commercial details recorded in "A Deal in Wheat" are provisional; their full significance can be obscure until the arrival of further information. The short story's third section, "The Pit," is suspenseful seemingly against the odds because Norris discloses relevant information (market prices, the available supply of wheat, the source of funds and grain) in real time, as though readers occupied a space on the pit's margins.

The hidden forces driving the market are so mysterious, in fact, that Norris inserts a private detective (Cyrus Ryder) so that the underhanded machinations of wheat brokers might come to light. These machinations, the narrator later tells us, ultimately find their way into the pages of the local newspapers. Ironically, the dovetailed discourses (private detection, journalism, fiction) reveal a modern, late-capitalist American economy in which the control and exchange of information exerts more influence than the hard labor of someone like Sam Lewiston.

Connections to Other Authors and Texts

Norris inhabits literary conventions that at first glance seem to be at odds with each other. On the one hand, Norris describes the details of regional geography and character with the attention (if not the sympathy) of writers connected with the local-color movement: Jewett, Freeman, and Cather, for example. On the other hand, Norris helped popularize and advance literary naturalism, and so Crane and Dreiser might enter into the picture. "A Deal in Wheat" provides evidence that the two approaches to narrative form overlap in important ways.

Questions for Class Discussion

1. Chart the progress of the short story from section to section in terms of characters (i.e., Who inhabits each section?) and in terms of geography (i.e., What is the setting of each section?). Why might Norris unfold the short story as he does?

2. Why does section two, "The Bull," begin with an excerpt from a wheat futures contract?

3. What information does Norris reveal about the trade in wheat futures? Which characters' perspective most closely mirrors our understanding of the trade? Which characters know more about the trade than we do?

4. What are the politics of "A Deal in Wheat"? What, if anything, does Norris suggest changing in American (or global) society and economics?

Brief Bibliography

Davison, Richard Allan. "Frank Norris and the Arts of Social Criticism." *American Literary Realism* 14 (1981): 77–89.

McElrath, Joseph R., Jr. *Frank Norris: A Life.* Urbana: U of Illinois P, 2006.

———. *Frank Norris Revisited.* New York: Twayne, 1992.

STEPHEN CRANE   (p. 334)

Approaches to Teaching

The post-Romantic cliché holds that writers live more fully (for better or for worse) than most persons, and few writers, American or otherwise, led as adventuresome a young life as Stephen Crane. While it's often a good idea to give students an impression of a writer's life and career, doing so in this case proves particularly useful, given Crane's uniquely interesting background and the factual basis for the fictional "The Open Boat." Indeed, the question, "What makes this fiction?" offers a good point of entry into Crane's macronarrative strategies and microesthetic choices, particularly when the short story is compared to his nonfiction account of the ordeal in "Stephen Crane's Own Story." (A large body of Crane criticism addresses the comparison.) Any discussion of Crane's life should speak to his view of the influence of religion and social forces on individual lives. And if naturalism receives systematic treatment in a syllabus, Crane's efforts – including his philosophical poems – could easily be central to an analysis of the movement.

Classroom Issues and Strategies

Discussions of American naturalism very often take the following quotation from "The Open Boat" as emblematic of the movement's philosophy: "When it occurs to a man that nature does not regard him as important, and that she feels she would not maim the universe by disposing of him, he at first wishes to throw bricks at the temple, and he hates deeply the fact that there are no bricks and no temples." (Crane's poem "XXI [A man said to the universe]" often performs a similar duty in studies of naturalism.) In addition to explaining the movement's basic tenets and its narrative strategies, a useful question to address is, Why would a writer who possesses such a belief bother to record his thoughts at all, and why would he provide an added, artistic flourish to his thoughts? (Note, for instance, the female personification of nature, and the figurative dimension of the bricks and temple.) In other words, how does fiction provide a sense of (to quote the short story again) "a human, living thing"? Discussions of naturalism can often seem prescriptive, and an open-ended question such as this encourages discussion to progress beyond the narrower (but obviously crucial) questions concerning "What is naturalism?" and "How is naturalism carried out?"

The short story's plot offers moments of obvious drama and suspense – particularly in the final section – but the majority of "The Open Boat" concerns itself with relatively abstract considerations of the characters' plight, the interior thoughts of individual characters, and dialogue; put another way, the plot consists of elements we might expect from a short story about four men set adrift at sea (rather than, say, the shipwreck itself). Less-experienced students (such as non-English majors) will require extra guidance in discovering the intricacies of the short story's narrative structure, particularly in understanding the significance of the shifting narrative focus. Tracking how the narrative remains solidly within the correspondent's consciousness, and how it also slips free, gives students an appreciation of the short story's real drama.

Connections to Other Authors and Texts

Crane's connection to the naturalist movement brings him squarely in a tradition also populated by Norris, Dreiser, and London, and the narrative strategies of "The Open Boat" come to life when seen against their fiction (and, in the case of Norris, nonfiction) reprinted in *The Bedford Anthology of American Literature*, Volume Two. The comparison especially yields results when the writers' various approaches to narrative focus are contrasted. If naturalism can be considered an exploration of the effects of biological and social pressures on human consciousness, then Crane's work might also be compared to James or Gilman. Finally, although shipwreck narratives are hardly central to American literary history – indeed, the genre questions the very possibility of a stable home – students may bring up without prompting comparisons to other well-known depictions of shipwrecks in literature and film (such as *Robinson Crusoe*, *Life on the Mississippi*, *Vandover the Brute*, *Titanic*, and the TV series *Lost*). The theme's connection to naturalism is one among many avenues for discussion.

Questions for Class Discussion

1. Compare and contrast "The Open Boat" with Crane's journalistic response to the ordeal, "Stephen Crane's Own Story" (available online at http://www.ponceinlet.org/open-boat-newspaper.pdf and elsewhere). Pay particular attention to narrative focus and tone.

2. Narratives set on a ship in the open sea often suggest a part-for-whole connection between the crew onboard and the wider society that they represent. What does "The Open Boat" say about American society?

3. Why is the short story broken up into seven sections? Explain why each section begins and ends where it does.

4. Where is "God" (or where are "gods") in "The Open Boat"? What does the short story suggest about the characters' attitudes toward religion? about the narrator's attitude toward religion? Whose voice utters the refrain, " 'If I am going to be drowned . . .' "?

5. The characters onboard the boat have great difficulty seeing the shore clearly and often have difficulty interpreting (or misinterpret) what they see. Why might Crane embed such difficulties in the narrative? What do their misinterpretations say about the characters?

6. Describe the occasion of individual Crane poems; in other words, what prompts the lyric voice to utter each poem's lines?

Brief Bibliography

Brown, Bill. *The Material Unconscious: American Amusement, Stephen Crane, and the Economies of Play.* Cambridge: Harvard UP, 1996.

Davis, Linda H. *Badge of Courage: The Life of Stephen Crane.* Boston: Houghton Mifflin, 1998.

Nelson, Harland S. "Stephen Crane's Achievement as a Poet." *Texas Studies in Literature and Language* 4 (1963): 564–82.

Szumski, Bonnie, ed. *Readings on Stephen Crane.* San Diego: Greenhaven, 1998.

THEODORE DREISER   (p. 359)

Approaches to Teaching

Theodore Dreiser's continuing legacy – his sharp eye in furtherance of an unflinching American naturalism – is perhaps best understood in relation to his ambitious, and quite lengthy, novels, especially *Sister Carrie* (1900) and *An American Tragedy* (1925). All the same, it is possible to offer a sense of Dreiser's place in American cultural history using the example of his more thoughtful short fiction, and "Butcher Rogaum's Door" certainly fits the bill. The short story, which is in some respects more subtle than his more obviously naturalist work – Theresa fares better in the wilds of urban America than Carrie, for example – still presents its subject with noteworthy detachment and suggests the influence of strong, animalistic drives behind individual behavior. (Theresa is of an age when "thoughtless, sensory life holds its greatest charm"; her would-be amour Almerting is described at one point as a "natural animal.") Although Theresa and Rogaum seem to transcend mere animal inclinations, the characters' observable actions and speech patterns clearly mark their stifling social positions, particularly their class (predominantly urban working class) and ethnic (predominantly German American and Irish American) backgrounds. Dreiser even prevents the story's outwardly sentimental ending, which reunites father and daughter, from arriving at a comfortable moral. Neither father nor daughter seems to have learned an appropriate lesson.

Classroom Issues and Strategies

Key elements in "Butcher Rogaum's Door" seem too contrived to be real, let alone realist: the symbolic significance of doorways (portals between vastly different social spheres); the equally symbolic clothing (color-coded to reveal a character's social standing); the mirror-image characters, Theresa and Emily; chance encounters on otherwise dark and deserted city streets; and chance utterances in the course of a conversation. It is worth stressing that naturalism does not depend on the likelihood of an occurrence, just its possibility. Naturalism might be productively compared to a science experiment: Just as a scientist contrives a well-ordered set of conditions in a self-contained laboratory and lets nature run its course, so too does a naturalist writer create discrete settings and scenarios and let characters go about their lives.

The theme of generational identity formation and intergenerational conflict holds a prominent place in American letters; this is especially the case in immigrant fiction, in which first-, second-, and third-generation characters follow predictable patterns of accommodation or resistance to an American way of life. As in much immigrant literature, the older generation (Rogaum and his wife) represents Old World beliefs and traditions, whereas the younger generation (Theresa and her cohorts) represents the promise and peril of New World existence. As is often the case, "Butcher Rogaum's Door" explores generational identity formation in terms of Old World romantic constraint and New World romantic freedom.

Connections to Other Authors and Texts

"Butcher Rogaum's Door" is one of the great narratives of turn-of-the-century New York City, a metropolis teeming with the energy and bustle of commerce, inter- and intraethnic encounters, and sheer urban density. There is something almost inevitably naturalistic about such fiction, and Dreiser's short story might be paired with the work of Abraham Cahan or (for greater contrast) Edith Wharton. Beyond the ethnic enclaves of New York City, the fiction of Crane, Norris, and London stand alongside Dreiser's as definitively naturalist.

Questions for Class Discussion

1. What elements of "Butcher Rogaum's Door" seem too contrived to be plausible? In other words, what happens that wouldn't likely happen in real life? What details (visual or otherwise) does Dreiser appear to stress to the point of exaggeration?

2. Describe the speech patterns of the following characters: Rogaum, Theresa, Almerting, Delehanty, and Maguire. What does a character's speech tell us about her or his social identity? Does a character's speech make her or him more or less likeable?

3. What lessons should Rogaum and Theresa learn from their experiences? What lessons (if any) do they learn?

Brief Bibliography

Cassuto, Leonard, and Clare Virginia Eby, eds. *The Cambridge Companion to Theodore Dreiser.* Cambridge: Cambridge UP, 2004.

Loving, Jerome. *Last Titan: A Life of Theodore Dreiser.* Berkeley: U of California P, 2005.

Newlin, Keith, ed. *A Theodore Dreiser Encyclopedia.* Westport, CT: Greenwood, 2003.

PAUL LAURENCE DUNBAR   (p. 372)

Approaches to Teaching

Writers' lives often abound in irony, and there's perhaps no career in American literary history more ironic than that of Paul Laurence Dunbar. The precocious son of a former slave who wanted nothing more than to express himself in the traditional forms of English poetry, Dunbar was best known during his lifetime as a writer of dialect verse. William Dean Howells went so far as to claim (in his preface to Dunbar's *Lyrics of Lowly Life*) that Dunbar's "poems in literary English" might have been written by just about anyone but that Howells did not "know any one else at present [besides Dunbar] who could quite have written the dialect pieces." Perhaps more ironically, Dunbar's most often referenced and anthologized work, the standard English poem "We Wear the Mask" (which appeared in the pages of *Lyrics of Lowly Life*), is usually interpreted as the bitter refrain of a serious poet forced to "wear the mask" of dialect for a mainstream American audience. This is not to say that such an interpretation rings false; rather, the interpretation is but one of many ways to approach Dunbar's life and work. The "We" of the poem is obviously racialized — it is the "we" of an African American collectivity, a "we" misunderstood by the "world" – but nothing in the poem prohibits inventive interpretation and speculation. "Why might Dunbar, or anyone else for that matter, wear a figurative 'mask'?" is a simple but useful way to start.

Classroom Issues and Strategies

As with all good poetry, Dunbar's work rewards efforts to draw connections between the form and content of the verse. "Sympathy" develops a visual metaphor for pent-up ambition that's matched by the forceful iambic pentameter straining within the limits of a strict *abaabcc* rhyme scheme. (The poem's stanza form derives from rhyme royal, long associated with Chaucer.) Similarly, "We Wear the Mask" utilizes just two rhyme sounds (-*ize* and -*ile*) to suggest a vast range of hidden emotions.

In "An Ante-bellum Sermon," Dunbar transports the reader back to a time when biblical interpretation both justified and repudiated the institution of slavery. His use of dialect is faithful to the poem's persona – "An Ante-bellum Sermon" is voiced by an African American slave-preacher – and the device partly deflects attention from the preacher's critical logic. (According to his self-effacing reasoning, the preacher considers slavery and freedom "[i]n a Bibleistic way.") Understood as a formal logical proposition, the poem critiques slavery in two key ways: First, it suggests the relative importance of freedom over humble servitude in popular Christian thought. Second, the poem represents the voice of God in a dialect widely identified with the black South: " 'Look hyeah, Moses, go tell Pher'oh / Fu' to let dem chillun go.' " In other words, the poem critiques slavery rhetorically, by reading the Bible as a radical political document, and dramatically, by forcing readers to imagine God as an African American.

Connections to Other Authors and Texts

Dunbar's dialect work has its antecedents, including Mark Twain's dialect prose. By the 1920s, Dunbar was consistently held up by Harlem Renaissance intellectuals as an example of what is possible or what should be avoided in African American poetry. He influenced (negatively or positively) such figures as Sterling Brown, Countee Cullen, Langston Hughes, and James Weldon Johnson (whose *God's Trombones* takes up the device of an African American preacherly persona).

Questions for Class Discussion

1. Who is the "we" in "We Wear the Mask"? Who is the "world"? What textual evidence from the poem supports your answer?

2. Rewrite "An Ante-bellum Sermon" in standard English. How does your version differ from Dunbar's?

3. How does the verse form of Dunbar's poems reinforce the ideas expressed in each?

Brief Bibliography

Blount, Marcellus. "The Preacherly Text: African American Poetry and Vernacular Performance." *PMLA* 107 (1992): 582-93.

Mvuyekure, Pierre-Damien. "Paul Laurence Dunbar (1872-1906)." *African American Authors, 1745-1945: A Bio-Bibliographical Critical Sourcebook.* Ed. Emanuel Nelson. Westport, CT: Greenwood, 2000. 132-38.

Revell, Peter. *Paul Laurence Dunbar.* New York: Twayne, 1979.

WILLA CATHER   (p. 378)

Approaches to Teaching

During the early part of her long and prolific writing career, Willa Cather was known as a leading figure among what was sometimes called the "Cornbelt Renaissance," a sudden outburst of literary creativity from such famous midwesterners as Sinclair Lewis and Theodore Dreiser. Unlike these forerunners, though, Cather subsequently found a very comfortable home in academic studies of literary modernism. Among all the Great Plains writers of the early twentieth century, Cather is most frequently paired with quintessential high modernists such as Gertrude Stein and Virginia Woolf. (Cather's informal apprenticeship via the works of Henry James has inspired another frequent and ongoing partnership in academic literary studies.) Even before the rise of queer theory breathed fresh life into an already robust Cather scholarship, her obvious devotion to the intricacies of literary craft, and her openness to experimenting with narrative time and point of view, animated scholars and influenced writers willing to venture beyond the confines of regional expression. "A Wagner Matinée" provides a short, precise, and wonderfully accessible entrée into Cather's experimental modernism.

Classroom Issues and Strategies

The modernist short story emerged partly as a concession to the newly emergent mass-market journal and partly as statement of artistic integrity and independence. At least since Poe, short-story writers have striven for narrative self-containment, for the completion of a consistent and self-referential whole (a feature that dovetailed nicely with the more pecuniary needs of magazine publishers). "A Wagner Matinée," which first appeared in the mass circulation *Everybody's Magazine*, presents a clear case of narrative self-containment: The storytelling is framed by two devices that call attention to their narrative function (the arrival of a letter and the ending of the symphony performance); in addition, the narrative spans a short and clearly defined time span.

Point of view in "A Wagner Matinée" presents an intriguing opportunity to consider Cather's modernism, and not simply because the choice of Clark as narrator posed a transgender, transgenerational challenge for Cather. Throughout the symphony's performance, Clark's mission as narrator is to represent the unknowable, to express Aunt Georgiana's deeply hidden thoughts and emotions. At one point he muses, "The overture closed. My aunt released my coat-sleeve, but she said nothing. She sat staring at the orchestra through a dullness of thirty years, through the films made, little by little, by each of the three hundred and sixty-five days in every one of them. What, I wondered, did she get from it?" Throughout the matinée, he continues to wonder; the only understanding we ever arrive at is limited, clouded in Clark's recurrent doubt. In effect, the short story takes advantage of a limited point of view to evoke the theme of the ultimate contingency of all knowledge.

A hallmark of literary modernism is its inspiration by (and aspiration to) the so-called sister arts. In the case of Cather's short stories, music obviously represents a problem of and challenge to representation, although each story takes up the challenge in a unique way. In "A Wagner Matinée," Clark looks for language capable of representing music primarily in water metaphors; as his aunt's tears stream down her face, Wagner's work takes shape as a "deluge of sound [that] poured on and on"; Clark "never knew what she found in the shining current of it; [he] never knew how far it bore her, or past what happy islands." Significantly, as Aunt Georgiana finds herself transported into a sea of music, Clark finds himself carted off to the plains of his Nebraska memories.

Connections to Other Authors and Texts

Henry James, an important early influence on Cather, and Sarah Orne Jewett, an important later influence on and correspondent with Cather, might be considered part of the same literary historical family tree. The literary resemblance appears closest between Cather and her fellow local-color writers, many of whom approach local cultures with a similar mix of nostalgia and dread. And numerous contemporaneous writers – from Ezra Pound to Langston Hughes to Mina Loy – were inspired by musical forms as they sought out literary structures.

Questions for Class Discussion

1. What details does Clark, the narrator of "A Wagner Matinée," recall about his childhood in the Nebraska plains? What details can you discern about his adult life in Boston?

2. What figures of speech does the narrator deploy to represent the experience of listening to music in "A Wagner Matinée"? What figures of speech does he deploy to represent the Nebraska landscape?

3. Track the flow of time in "A Wagner Matinée." Where does the narrative quickly summarize events? Where does the narrative depict events in roughly the amount of time that it takes them to transpire? Where does the narrative seem to bring time to a standstill?

Brief Bibliography

Lindemann, Marilee, ed. *The Cambridge Companion to Willa Cather.* Cambridge: Cambridge UP, 2005.

Meyering, Sheryl L. *A Reader's Guide to the Short Stories of Willa Cather.* New York: G. K. Hall, 1994.

Stout, Janis P. *Willa Cather: The Writer and Her World.* Charlottesville: UP of Virginia, 2000.

Wasserman, Loretta. *Willa Cather: A Study of the Short Fiction.* Boston: Twayne, 1991.

JACK LONDON   (p. 388)

Approaches to Teaching

Many students will have encountered Jack London at a relatively early point in their reading lives, some as young as ten or twelve years old. If so, they likely did not learn about his rather severe outlook on life, and they surely did not consider his work representative of literary naturalism. Because London led such an interesting life, it helps to introduce students to these important matters by way of his biography, beginning with his early privation and progressing through his flirtations with socialism, social Darwinism, and scientific racism. Often these ideologies existed simultaneously, in concert and in conflict, as they do in "The Law of Life." The short story delivers an uncompromising message about the survival of the fittest in the animal and human worlds, and it will surely elicit interesting discussion about the representation of a culture (the Inuit people of the Arctic region) that London viewed as unavoidably fading in the face of white incursions.

Classroom Issues and Strategies

"The Law of Life" dramatizes an enduring principle of London's naturalism – that nature follows its course without heeding morality or sympathy – but not before it addresses the laws of nature more abstractly and, arguably, less interestingly. London's narrative strategy allows the side-by-side unfolding of drama and abstraction. The third-person narrator shows us how human society (in this case, an Inuit tribe) and the animals of the Arctic grow or die, eat or are eaten. But the focus of the narrative, the dying, old Koskoosh, reflects back on life's lessons and ponders his coming death. The narrator even calls our attention to the discrepancy between action and thought: "He did not complain. It was the way of life, and it was just. . . . Nature was not kindly to the flesh. She had no concern for that concrete thing called the individual. Her interest lay in the species, the race. This was the deepest abstraction old Koskoosh's barbaric mind was capable of, but he grasped it firmly." The short story wears naturalist messages on its sleeve, but we can be sure that London wants to explore even deeper abstractions than these.

Connections to Other Authors and Texts

"The Law of Life" draws a conclusion about the relation between humanity and nature similar to Crane's "The Open Boat"; both short stories, in spite of their vastly different strategies, agree that nature is sometimes cruel and always indifferent. It is also interesting to consider the representation of Native American cultures from an insider or outsider perspective; the works of Mary Austin (London's close friend), Sarah Winnemucca Hopkins, and Zitkala-Ša are useful points of reference.

Questions for Class Discussion

1. Jack London was an immensely successful author in his day, and "The Law of Life" was first published in *McClure's*, one of the most popular magazines in the late nineteenth and early twentieth centuries. What about the short story might have attracted a large audience?

2. The narrator shares with readers some of the life lessons – the "law" – that old Koskoosh draws from his experiences. Do readers draw different (or broader) lessons from the short story? If so, what are some of these lessons?

3. Is old Koskoosh a sympathetic character? Why or why not? How do you feel about the short story's conclusion?

Brief Bibliography

Blyth, Hal, and Charlie Sweet. "Course Writing Objectives and London's 'Law of Life.'" *Eureka Studies in Teaching Short Fiction* 5 (2004): 16-19.

Kershaw, Alex. *Jack London: A Life*. New York: St. Martin's, 1999.

Reeseman, Jeanne Campbell. *Jack London: A Study of the Short Fiction*. New York: Twayne, 1999.

Writing "American" Lives

Immigration historians often point out that American society at the present moment is the most ethnically diverse in our nation's history – with the exception of American society a century ago. Today, one in nine Americans (11 percent) were born outside U.S. borders; similar numbers have not been seen since the period between 1860 and 1930. (The percentage of foreign-born Americans peaked between 1890 and 1900 at nearly 15 percent.) Unlike today, however, the national debate a century ago over the role of immigrants and other racial and ethnic minorities in American society took on a much more heated, and sometimes disturbing, tone. Several prominent Americans took up the cause of "100 percent Americanism": They espoused the view that only "native Americans," that is, white Anglo-Saxon Protestants born in the United States, deserved a place in American society. Many urged strict eugenic measures (including forced sterilization) and the repatriation of newly arrived immigrants. Some went so far as to endorse the "repatriation" to Africa of U.S.-born African Americans.

Today's students sometimes find it difficult to believe that such intolerant views occupied a position in mainstream American political and cultural thought. Students find it much easier to comprehend the positions of African American, immigrant, and other writers who suggested more inclusive alternatives to xenophobia. This section of Volume Two of *The Bedford Anthology of American Literature* introduces students to a range of opinions informing the period's social policies and literary expression, including many opinions that still resonate today. The thought-provoking illustrations offer radically different approaches to human form, primarily in the service of the humanist belief in the innate value of the individual. Similarly, the writers anthologized here extend Crèvecoeur's lingering question – "What is an American?" – into an age marked by unprecedented social mobility and technological change; in other words, they explore the convergence of nationality and modernity.

Questions for Class Discussion

1. In what ways do the writers in this section appeal to America's foundational texts (such as the Declaration of Independence and the Constitution), myths of origin (such as notions of Puritan or pioneer foundations), or democratic ideals? Do they feel that America has lived up to its original promise as a nation?

2. How do individual writers advocating a specific cause (such as honoring treaties with Indian tribes or providing humane conditions for workers) invoke comparisons to other similar causes (such as civil rights for African Americans)?

3. Which writers are willing to compromise with their political opponents, and which are steadfast in their positions? How does their political flexibility (or inflexibility) influence the tone or figurative language of their work?

4. Which political causes among those represented here have been realized, and which remain a part of ongoing discussions about the shape of American society?

JOSÉ MARTÍ   (p. 404)

Approaches to Teaching

American literary scholars long ago dispensed with the question of whether or not Cuban expatriate José Martí warrants attention in discussions of U.S. literature. As Martí's inclusion in *The Bedford Anthology of American Literature* suggests, the almost universal answer to such a question is "yes." How to discuss Martí is a less clear proposition. Is it best to emphasize his role as Cuban revolutionary? his role as one of the founding figures of *modernismo*? his role as Latin American popularizer of such U.S. writers as Emerson and Whitman? his role as architect of Pan-American identity? his role as staunch critic of European and U.S. imperialism? his role as astute social commentator and cultural critic? Martí's "Impressions of America" very obviously recommend the latter approach, but it also helps to point out that the essays' ambivalence toward the United States animates the full range of his political and cultural writing. Even in prose, Martí writes with the suggestiveness of a poet, and he typically views culture and politics and society as inextricably bound together. The essays thus anticipate the academic discipline that we now call "cultural studies."

Classroom Issues and Strategies

One of the most striking features of "Impressions of America" are their alternately pained and humorous ambivalence about all things American. Martí's claim that the United States is "a country where every one looks like his own master," where individuals "can breathe freely, freedom being here the foundation, the shield, the essence of life," departs substantially from the views expressed in Martí's more famous and more sharply critical "Nuestra América" [Our America]. At the same time, Martí looks askance at the Franklinesque business ethic that drives American social and cultural life; he bemoans a slavish devotion to material wealth at the expense of more lasting cultural expression.

Although he criticizes America's neocolonial devotion to European fashion and acknowledges the "vulgar storm of immigration" falling upon U.S. shores, Martí frequently references a single, easily recognized "American" (elsewhere he would call it "North American") national identity. This "American" is the "you" to whom the essays are addressed. While the I/you relationship remains fairly stable, the essays' tonal shifts require a more subtle understanding of the European/American dichotomy implied by the subtitle "By a Very Fresh Spaniard." The essays' tonal instability perhaps reflects a United States on the verge of emerging as a military and industrial giant (while at the same time retaining the stereotype of cultural backwater).

Connections to Other Authors and Texts

Martí helped to popularize in Latin America many of the key figures represented in Volume One of *The Bedford Anthology of American Literature* (including Emerson, Whitman, and Longfellow). But "Impressions of America" is closer in spirit to works by writers of the late nineteenth century (including Howells and Henry Adams) who were critical of America's Gilded Age pretensions and its failure to live up to its democratic ideals.

Questions for Class Discussion

1. Which aspects of American political, social, and cultural life does Martí value most? Which does he explicitly criticize? Why? On balance, does Martí express a more positive or a more negative view of the United States?

2. "Impressions of America" is a work of nonfiction, but it deploys many elements common in fictional prose (including characterization and narrative). Describe the rhetorical effects of specific "fictional" elements in the essays.

3. According to Martí, what is the typical American man like? What is the typical American woman like?

Brief Bibliography

Fountain, Anne. *José Martí and U.S. Writers.* Gainesville: UP of Florida, 2003.

Giles, Paul. "The Parallel Worlds of José Martí." *Radical History Review* 89 (2004): 185–90.

Hames-García, Michael. "Which America Is Ours?: Martí's 'Truth' and the Foundations of 'American Literature.'" *Modern Fiction Studies* 49 (2003): 19–53.

Montero, Oscar. *José Martí: An Introduction.* Basingstoke, Hampshire: Palgrave Macmillan, 2004.

SARAH WINNEMUCCA HOPKINS　　(p. 412)

Approaches to Teaching

The old cliché about an anthropologist from Mars is quite serviceable as a means of introducing students not so much to Sarah Winnemucca Hopkins as to the challenges she faced in capturing the wonder and the terror she felt encountering whites for the first time in her young life. Hopkins's language strains to accommodate the fear and the shock that she experienced as a young girl. Rather than shy away from the difficulties of representing the first encounters between Paiutes and white immigrants, she instead adopts a unique mix of firsthand autobiography and secondhand memoir. The book's first paragraph, for example, opens with the quintessentially autobiographical statement, "I was born," but quickly moves on to record her grandfather's initial reaction: "When the news was brought to my grandfather, he asked what they looked like? When told that they had hair on their faces, and were white, he jumped up and clasped his hands together. . . ." Hopkins's subsequent account of cultural contact relies on her understanding of her community's varied reactions to cooperation and conflict with the whites; her informants, who emerge as distinct characters in the narrative, include her mother, her father, and especially her grandfather, whose great joy at discovering his long lost "white brothers" evolves into a cagey pragmatism.

Classroom Issues and Strategies

The formalist notion of "defamiliarization" very nicely describes Hopkins's foremost literary device. She routinely introduces readers to the familiar by way of the strange, as when she reconceives "two negroes wearing red shirts" as a men on fire with charred heads. This early example indicates that contact with previously unknown cultures demands a recalibration of everyday language. Elsewhere, Hopkins describes covered wagons as "houses that move"; she portrays ocean vessels as "the big houses that go on the mighty ocean, and travel faster than any horse"; and she remarks that white people are "more like owls than any thing else. They had hair on their faces, and had white eyes, and looked beautiful."

This latter example suggests literary expression's role in ethnic boundary formation and maintenance (in spite of the Paiute creation myth of common ancestry and universal brotherhood). Hopkins upends the traditionally negative stereotypes applied to Native American cultures in nineteenth-century travel narratives by exploiting figurative, dehumanizing language in her description of white immigrants (who are compared to lions as well as owls). In *Life among the Piutes*, whites are largely indistinguishable from each other; what's more, Hopkins deploys verbal irony as she characterizes her "downtrodden people" as "savages" and continually suggests that whites are cannibals.

Connections to Other Authors and Texts

Perhaps the closest analog to *Life among the Piutes* can be found among the accounts of voyages of "discovery" located in *The Bedford Anthology of American Literature*, Volume One. Hopkins, like Columbus or Cabeza de Vaca before her, must create a whole new language to depict unprecedented cultural contact. Mary Austin's fiction, in contrast, approaches Paiute life with a greater degree of familiarity and even comfort.

Questions for Class Discussion

1. How does Hopkins establish her authority to speak on behalf of the Paiute people?

2. As the editors of *The Bedford Anthology of American Literature* point out, Hopkins addresses her book to white readers. What textual cues indicate that the implied reader of *Life among the Piutes* is white?

3. What are some traits of white persons that Hopkins finds strange? How does she express her estrangement in language?

Brief Bibliography

Carpenter, Cari M. "Tiresias Speaks: Sarah Winnemucca's Hybrid Selves and Genres." *Legacy* 19 (2002): 71-80.

Tisinger, Danielle. "Textual Performance and the Western Frontier: Sarah Winnemucca Hopkins's *Life among the Piutes: Their Wrongs and Claims*." *Western American Literature* 37 (2002): 171-94.

Zanjani, Sally. *Sarah Winnemucca*. Lincoln: U of Nebraska P, 2001.

ZITKALA-ŠA
(GERTRUDE SIMMONS BONNIN)   (p. 426)

Approaches to Teaching

Most students experience discomfort, embarrassment, or sheer terror at some routine point during their primary school education. Childhood memories, one hopes, grow less troubling with time, and our adult selves would likely relate such moments differently than would our child selves. Investigating the discrepancy between voiceless childhood experience and subsequent adult storytelling informs any reading of Zitkala-Ša's autobiographical essay. Her evocative language recalls the anguish of growing up Indian in an alien world: "The melancholy of those black days has left so long a shadow that it darkens the path of years that have since gone by. These sad memories rise above those of smoothly grinding school days. Perhaps my Indian nature is the moaning wind which stirs them now for their present record." On an unrelated matter: Be sure to inform students not to separate the compound name Zitkala-Ša into a first and last name.

Classroom Issues and Strategies

In this era of government-mandated standardized testing, it is too easy to understand education as little more than the three Rs. Even so, we see nothing of the formal curriculum implicit in "The School Days of an Indian Girl." This is not to say that Zitkala-Ša learns nothing from the experiences that she describes; indeed, she gains a wealth of knowledge about socially accepted behavior and dress, religious devotion and hypocrisy, discipline at school and at home, and more.

Although scholars of immigration and ethnicity in Zitkala-Ša's own day would likely evaluate and discuss her experience in terms of acculturation to American customs, cultural theorists today often refer to cultural contact in terms of transculturation, an expression that implies that both majority cultures and minority individuals (immigrant or not) are mutually changed by ethnic conflict and cooperation. Transculturation also has some bearing on the act of reading: As we grow, so too does a text's meaning; as a text informs our understanding, we evolve as readers. We might measure Zitkala-Ša's contribution to our understanding of childhood learning in terms of linguistic invention; she re-creates schoolgirl naivete as a series of clever or cliché phrasings for familiar things: "iron horse" (train), "upward incline of wooden boxes" (staircase), "indolent chieftain" (devil), "Great Spirit" (the Christian God), "paleface" (white person), and "civilizing machine" (school).

Connections to Other Authors and Texts

Because "The School Days of an Indian Girl" marks the (partial) entrance of a young Dakota Sioux into a mainstream American existence, the memoir overlaps thematically and formally with narratives of the immigrant experience (such as Antin's *The Promised Land*), with coming-of-age stories (such as Jewett's "A White Heron"), and with accounts of racialized identity formation (such as Hopkins's *Life among the Piutes* and Du Bois's *The Souls of Black Folk*). Whether based on the facts of a life or not, all of these genres develop the autobiographical mode, which traces a narrative arc from innocence to experience.

Questions for Class Discussion

1. List a few autobiographies with which you are familiar. What are some common themes and approaches to expression found in multiple autobiographies? How does Zitkala-Ša's essay compare with expectations for a traditional autobiography?

2. What does Zitkala-Ša give up of her Dakota Sioux identity as she receives an American education? What does her life experience seem to provide the educational institution? What have you learned about Dakota Sioux life that you did not know before; in other words, how has the essay transformed you as a reader?

3. How does Zitkala-Ša perform her "Indian-ness"? How does the narrative mark her as different from the white persons she encounters (and, by extension, her original white reading audience)? What does the young Dakota Sioux schoolgirl think, do, and say that a white schoolgirl would not?

Brief Bibliography

Cutter, Martha J. "Zitkala-Ša's Autobiographical Writings: The Problems of a Canonical Search for Language and Identity." *MELUS* 19 (1994): 31-44.

Enoch, Jessica. "Resisting the Script of Indian Education: Zitkala-Ša and the Carlisle Indian School." *College English* 65 (2002): 117-41.

Six, Beverly G. "Zitkala-Ša (Gertrude Simmons Bonnin) (1876-1938)." *American Women Writers, 1900-1945: A Bio-Bibliographical Critical Sourcebook*. Westport, CT: Greenwood, 2000. 383-87.

BOOKER T. WASHINGTON   (p. 438)

Approaches to Teaching

Almost all students will initially express a negative reaction to Booker T.
Washington's views recorded in "The Atlanta Exposition Address." The students are, of course, joined by the overwhelming majority of today's scholars who deal with *Up from Slavery*. Even scholars who defend Washington's
politics concede that he was the product of his time or that he lacked the
eloquence of his rival, W. E. B. Du Bois. Providing historical context is crucial to an appreciation of Washington's important autobiography – Mark
Bauerlein's excellent overview of Washington's strategic political career
comes in quite handy – but instructors should feel entirely comfortable
when students continue not to appreciate Washington's views or his prose.
The obligations born of the text's and the author's historical significance
outweigh any compulsions to like the man or his work. For these reasons,
Washington's autobiography must be seen as important if not "great" (or
even "good"). Allowing students to debate the aesthetic value of the work,
while still acknowledging its importance, frees students from the perceived need to approach literary texts with veneration and instead forces
students to achieve critical distance from literature.

Classroom Issues and Strategies

"The Atlanta Exposition Address" might function as a primer on the art of
blunt rhetoric. In the opening three paragraphs, Washington weaves into
the speech first hyperbole (the Atlanta Exposition "is a recognition that
will do more to cement the friendship of the two races than any occurrence
since the dawn of our freedom," he argues, as if Reconstruction were but a
trifle); then paradox ("Ignorant and inexperienced, it is not strange that in
the first years of our new life we began at the top instead of at the bottom;
that a seat in Congress or the state legislature was more sought than real
estate or industrial skill"); and finally analogy, in which blacks are to
whites as a "distressed" ship is to a "friendly" ship (and, by extension, U.S.
society is to the Atlantic Ocean at the mouth of the Amazon).

Importantly, though, the chapter is not without its reformist politics,
either stated or implicit. Washington specifically calls for equal access to
the ballot box for black men as for white men, and he urges qualified
African Americans to vote. (Women, of course, did not achieve universal
suffrage for two more decades.) He also insists on the rule of law in the Jim
Crow South. Implicitly, Washington dispels negative stereotypes about
African American workers, and he issues a thinly veiled warning about the
chaos and violence that might ensue if African Americans are continually
disenfranchised.

Connections to Other Authors and Texts

Up from Slavery is, as the title suggests, a slave narrative, although a strikingly turn-of-the-century one, and so comparison with the slave narratives found in Volume One of *The Bedford Anthology of American Literature* will only go so far. As the consistent foil of W. E. B. Du Bois, it is difficult to imagine assigning one author without assigning the other. Perhaps just as interestingly, the artistic social program of James Weldon Johnson and the "back to Africa" program of Marcus Garvey seem partly spurred by Washington's repudiation of poetry in favor of industrial labor and by Washington's famous injunction to "cast down your bucket where you are."

Questions for Class Discussion

1. What are the advantages and disadvantages to Washington's famous "distressed vessel" analogy for U.S. race relations? In other words, does the analogy work?

2. What textual cues indicate that "The Atlanta Exposition Address" was delivered for a primarily white audience? What cues suggest the possibility of a subsequent African American readership?

3. Look at W. E. B. Du Bois's response in *The Souls of Black Folk* (reprinted in the anthology) to Washington's speech. Which aspects of Washington's thought does Du Bois criticize? On what do the two men agree?

Brief Bibliography

Bauerlein, Mark. "The Tactical Life of Booker T. Washington." *Chronicle of Higher Education* 50 (28 Nov. 2003): B12–B13.

Carroll, Rebecca, ed. *Uncle Tom or New Negro?: African Americans Reflect on Booker T. Washington and* Up from Slavery *One Hundred Years Later.* New York: Broadway, 2006.

Harlan, Louis R. *Booker T. Washington: The Wizard of Tuskegee, 1901–1915.* New York: Oxford UP, 1983.

West, Michael Rudolph. *The Education of Booker T. Washington: American Democracy and the Idea of Race Relations.* New York: Columbia UP, 2006.

W. E. B. DU BOIS   (p. 450)

Approaches to Teaching

Scholars of American literature and culture have long regarded W. E. B. Du Bois as the single most important African American intellectual in U.S.

history. Even so, students will know far less about Du Bois than about more strictly political activists such as Frederick Douglass, Martin Luther King Jr., and Malcolm X, and perhaps less about Du Bois than contemporaneous creative writers such as James Weldon Johnson and Nella Larsen. This is hardly a surprise; for every "W. E. B. Du Bois Street" there are hundreds of "Martin Luther King Jr. Boulevards." Instructors may wish to consider what a person's fame within and beyond the academy says not just about our broader culture's intricate system of social rewards (no small feat) but also about an individual writer's style. Why, in other words, is a foundational text such as *The Souls of Black Folk* not more widely read and appreciated? Students must above all arrive at an understanding of *Souls* as a foundational text: It is a book that looks at America's past self-consciously and critically to interpret the present and to shape the future. We may debate whether or not "the problem of the Twentieth Century [was] the problem of the color-line"; many of the debate's key terms, though, were undoubtedly put in place by Du Bois.

Classroom Issues and Strategies

The title of the book invites a wide range of associations. You might consider possible alternatives that would shift the reader's focus in telling ways: *lives, fortunes,* and *authentic selves* instead of *Souls; Negro, colored,* and *Afro-American* (all in use during the early twentieth century) instead of *Black;* and *people, masses,* and *men* instead of *Folk.* What does the book's title indicate about its focus? its methodology? its politics?

Although it is difficult to gain a sense of the larger arc of *The Souls of Black Folk* from two short excerpts, it nevertheless makes sense to sketch out the book for beginning students by suggesting how "Of Our Spiritual Strivings" anticipates later chapters, including the critique of Booker T. Washington. (Both chapters were first published as discrete essays, so they merit special attention as units of independent expression as well.) "Of Our Spiritual Strivings" develops many of the themes (alienation, racial misunderstanding, and animosity), symbols (significant numbers, light and dark, shadows), and structural patterns (folk wisdom intermixed with autobiography, history, and sociology; poetic and musical epigraphs; rhetorical questions; sweeping geographic, historical, and religious references) found elsewhere in the collection.

Students in high school and lower-level undergraduate courses will likely need some guidance when it comes to appreciating *The Souls of Black Folk's* relation to history. On the one hand, they will need specific historical and intertextual references (such as references to Reconstruction and to the Bible) glossed for them. On the other hand, they will need to appreciate Du Bois's words in the context of more reactionary and more radical responses to widespread racism in U.S. society. It helps to refer to (and even to assign alongside *Souls*) counterexamples such as the works of Booker T. Washington and Marcus Garvey.

Connections to Other Authors and Texts

It would be difficult to find texts in the African American literary tradition that did not directly influence Du Bois or that were not directly influenced by him. More than perhaps any other writer in any literary tradition, Du Bois stands at the epicenter of African American letters. *The Souls of Black Folk* very obviously incorporates elements from slave narrative and from folklore; less obviously, the book owes a debt to American pragmatism and to investigations of the Puritan influence on American life. Looking forward, *Souls* anticipates the folk modernism of Harlem Renaissance writers such as Sterling Brown and Zora Neale Hurston. And although Du Bois was a dyed-in-the-wool Yankee, the earliest readers of *Souls* considered it a contribution to the southern literary tradition that also includes Jean Toomer and William Faulkner.

Questions for Class Discussion

1. How does the famous metaphor of the veil work? What associations does it suggest literally and figuratively?

2. Du Bois makes the case that American democracy, music, and folklore owe a great debt to African Americans. How does Du Bois incorporate these facets of American culture into *Souls*? How might we extend his list to account for the last century of American cultural evolution?

3. In "Of Mr. Booker T. Washington and Others," Du Bois repudiates efforts to limit African American educational opportunities to strictly industrial training and advances the idea that gifted African Americans deserve an education in the liberal arts tradition. How does your educational institution embody or deviate from Du Bois's vision of higher education? How does *The Souls of Black Folk* put liberal arts ideals into practice?

4. In what ways do individuals feel their "two-ness" other than racially?

Brief Bibliography

Andrews, William L. *Critical Essays on W. E. B. Du Bois.* Boston: G.K. Hall, 1985.

Hubbard, Dolan, ed. *The Souls of Black Folk: One Hundred Years Later.* Columbia: U of Missouri P, 2003.

Lewis, David Levering. *W. E. B. Du Bois: Biography of a Race, 1868-1919.* New York: H. Holt, 1993.

Rampersad, Arnold. *Art and Imagination of W. E. B. Du Bois.* Cambridge: Harvard UP, 1976.

HENRY ADAMS   (p. 470)

Approaches to Teaching

Given the symbolic importance of dynamos and Gothic cathedrals in *The Education of Henry Adams*, you may wish to share illustrations of these places and things that will be unfamiliar to a great many students. (Few students these days will have ever seen firsthand a dynamo larger than a few inches in height and length.) And because Volume Two of *The Bedford Anthology of American Literature* includes excerpts from the longer book, it helps to provide some context that's supplied by the earlier chapters. Important elements to share include the following: Henry Adams was one of the most privileged persons in nineteenth-century American society; the unusual, third-person narrative defies some of the conventions of autobiography, reference to Jean Jacques Rousseau notwithstanding (it's missing the first-person pronoun, it ignores his married life, it generally lacks confessional sincerity); and the life story takes as its theme alienation and failure, in effect revaluing failure as an opportunity to shed light on important truths about the individual and about the nation. You might also point out that we continue to read Henry Adams in the twenty-first century, but we no longer read the more official and time-bound work of his president ancestors.

Classroom Issues and Strategies

The Education of Henry Adams is a wonderfully allusive text, with references in "The Dynamo and the Virgin" chapter alone to modern and premodern science, to modern and premodern art and literature, and to all manner of historical events and personages. The sheer number of footnotes can throw off student readers, so be prepared to demonstrate how an understanding of a particular reference increases the range of textual meaning. Showing illustrations of a few St. Gaudens statues alongside illustrations of the cathedral at Amiens, for example, might help students appreciate what Adams means when he writes, "St. Gaudens's art was starved from birth, and Adams's instinct was blighted from babyhood. Each had but half of a nature, and when they came together before the Virgin of Amiens they ought both to have felt in her the force that made them one; but it was not so. To Adams she became more than ever a channel of force; to St. Gaudens she remained as before a channel of taste." At any rate, be prepared to spend some time answering student questions about the text's numerous historical references.

More important than glossing historical references, though, is imparting a sense of the cultural critique at work in *The Education*. Adams finds much to fault in America precisely for its modernity. The nation's worship of technology requires a surrender of the mysterious power of religion and sexuality: "The true American knew something of the facts, but nothing of the feelings; he read the letter, but he never felt the law. . . . On one side, at the Louvre and at Chartres, as he knew by the record of work actually done and still before his eyes, was the highest energy ever known to man, the creator of four-fifths of his noblest art, exercising vastly more attraction over the human mind than all the steam-engines and dynamos ever dreamed of; and yet this energy was unknown to the American mind." As you point out the heavy-handed analogies in the chapter – dynamo is to Virgin as technology is to religion as America is to Europe as Puritanism is to sexuality – invite your students to consider the practical implications (for education, for art, for politics) of Adams's critique.

Connections to Other Authors and Texts

The Education of Henry Adams is a far cry from the up-by-the-bootstraps narratives that are common in the American autobiographical tradition; for this reason, the autobiographies of Benjamin Franklin (from Volume One) and Booker T. Washington and Mary Antin (from Volume Two) supply useful counterpoints to Adams's privileged position. Adams's modernist critique of modernization invites comparison to the work of T. S. Eliot and William Carlos Williams.

Questions for Class Discussion

1. In his preface to *The Education of Henry Adams*, Adams alludes to the confessional aspirations of most autobiographies. What does Adams "confess" in *Education*?

2. What do the dynamo and the virgin symbolize for Adams? for America?

3. Adams has much to say that's critical about early twentieth-century America. According to Adams, what's wrong with America? What might be changed?

Brief Bibliography

Contosta, David R., and Robert Muccigrosso, eds. *Henry Adams and His World*. Philadelphia: American Philosophical Society, 1993.

Rowe, John Carlos, ed. *New Essays on* The Education of Henry Adams. New York: Cambridge UP, 1996.

Wills, Garry. *Henry Adams and the Making of America*. Boston: Houghton, 2005.

MARY ANTIN   (p. 484)

Approaches to Teaching

The abstract idea "Americanization" dates back to the early nineteenth century, or so the *OED* informs us. Mary Antin, who deploys the word only once in chapter 9 of her autobiography, *The Promised Land*, might well appear next to a dictionary entry for the word, so closely connected is her life with the process of assimilating into an American way of life. (Significantly, *assimilate* appears just once in *The Promised Land*, in an unusual context described by Michael P. Kramer.) In her introduction to *The Promised Land*, Antin admits that her "life has been unusual, but by no means unique" – hers is the immigrant experience par excellence, her entry into American society defines Americanization for the rest of us. The overarching questions raised by Antin's admission – What is unusual and what is unique about her story? – might well frame a discussion of her entry into an American way of life. Of course, the America of Americanization is a constantly moving target; the America that the young immigrant from Polotzk found so bewildering and so beguiling strikes today's students as something of a foreign land. It helps to stress that chronology is to us what geography was to Antin: a distance that requires hard work but that also inspires great wonder.

Classroom Issues and Strategies

In her introduction to *The Promised Land*, Antin admits, "I have not discovered anything, not even by accident, as Columbus discovered America." Even so, the narrative strategy deployed by the chapter is a common one in the literature of "discovery": defamiliarization. We learn how far Antin has come in her journey to an American way of life in this unusual description of ubiquitous food products: "My father produced several kinds of food, ready to eat, without any cooking, from little tin cans that had printing all over them. He attempted to introduce us to a queer, slippery kind of fruit, which he called 'banana,' but had to give it up for the time being." Elsewhere, Antin shares the wonder she felt as she first saw a paved road, a rocking chair, a street lamp, a kitchen stove, a department store, and much more.

The Promised Land reveals significant ambivalence about Antin's eastern European Jewish heritage. She refers to her family's "impossible Hebrew names" and favors all that's modern about America over all that's shopworn about the Old World. Still, Antin chides readers who might harbor negative views about immigrants who don't fully blend in with their American context: "Think, every time you pass the greasy alien on the street, that he was born thousands of years before the oldest native

American; and he may have something to communicate to you, when you two shall have learned a common language." In a fairly backhanded way, Antin rehabilitates the image of the immigrant, suggesting that "greasy" aliens are the backbone of American economy and democracy.

Connections to Other Authors and Texts

The process of Americanization informs a great number of titles collected in *The Bedford Anthology of American Literature*. Generally, Antin's autobiography is held up as an assimilationist yardstick with which to measure more critical figures such as Henry Adams, W. E. B. Du Bois, and Zitkala-Ša.

Questions for Class Discussion

1. Antin describes her initiation into an American way of life as a "second infancy." How are immigration and childhood similar? How are they different?

2. How does Antin utilize the language of religious conversion to describe her assimilation experience?

3. How has America changed since the experience and place described by Antin? What new challenges and opportunities are faced by today's immigrants to the United States?

Brief Bibliography

Kramer, Michael P. "Assimilation in *The Promised Land*: The Jewish Origins of the American Self." *Prooftexts* 18 (1998): 121-48.

Parrish, Timothy. "Whose Americanization?: Self and Other in Mary Antin's *The Promised Land*." *Studies in American Jewish Literature* 13 (1994): 27-38.

Zaborowska, Magdalena J. *How We Found America: Reading Gender through East-European Immigrant Narratives*. Chapel Hill: U of North Carolina P, 1995.

American Literature
1914–1945

THE INTERWAR PERIOD represents the earliest moment in U.S. literary history in which the question "Is there such a thing as an American literature?" was answered by most in the affirmative. In other words, during this time American literature was recognized (belatedly so) as having come of age; it was no longer considered merely an adjunct to British literature. (Difficult as it may be for most students to believe, such monumental figures as Emerson, Dickinson, Melville, and Whitman gained their present-day reputations well into the twentieth century.) Certainly America's geopolitical position following the Great War — a vast and relatively unscathed military; an economy ready to burst at the seams; women and ethnic minorities with hard-won, unprecedented social mobility; a democratic beacon for those displaced by war — furnished its writers with confidence, with subject matter, and with a growing readership. Just as important to the rise of American literary prominence, though, were those emergent cultural institutions described by the anthology's editors: little magazines such as *Poetry, Little Review, Masses, Seven Arts,* and *Crisis*; cultural centers such as Chicago, Greenwich Village, and Harlem; literary movements such as imagism, the little-theater movement, and the Harlem Renaissance; and the risk-taking writers, publishers, booksellers, and readers behind all of them.

Many of the watershed events described in the section introduction — the universal suffrage movement and the eventual ratification of the Nineteenth Amendment; the Great War; anti-immigrant xenophobia and the Red scare; the Jazz Age of the roaring twenties and the Great Depression of the more sober thirties; the rise of Fascism and the Second World War — serve as useful entries into any discussion of "modernization," the rapid change associated with social evolution and technological innovation, and "modernity," the sense of historical belatedness experienced by all historical epochs at least since the Renaissance in Europe. (The illustrations in this section offer visual shorthand for the social and technological change linked to modernization.) More difficult to teach is "modernism," the experimental approach to literary form so often associated with the interwar period. Here Daniel Joseph Singal's outline of American modernism ("Towards a Definition of American Modernism," which is reprinted in the companion volume, *Background Readings for Teachers of American Literature*) offers useful guidance; the essay keeps in view the "full-fledged historical culture" of the period, something on a par with European counterparts such as Victorianism or the Enlightenment. The many clear examples of modernist poetry, prose, and drama collected in this section of *The Bedford Anthology of American Literature* leave no shortage of useful examples of the cultural moment and movement.

Modernisms in American Poetry

As this part of the anthology makes abundantly clear, the world of modern American poetry was remarkably intimate, with a few dozen or so still-remembered poets coming into regular and influential contact with one another: in person, in correspondence, and in the pages of the little magazines that first published much of the modern American poetry canon. And so from a relatively small number of individuals came a multitude of styles (from blank verse to sonnets to free verse) and publications (from *Poetry* to *Others* to *Opportunity*) and movements (from imagism to the Harlem Renaissance). It might be said that the history of modernist poetry is a series of entertaining anecdotes about diverse and lively personalities interacting (for better and for worse) with one another. If the range of poets assembled here recommends any one approach, it would be the biographical case study. For that reason, the editors of the anthology have supplied brief but pertinent biographical sketches of each poet, and in the pages below I recommend additional, usually book-length biographies that might be consulted for more detail. But it would be a shame to limit students' understanding of poetry to the Wordsworthian cliché, a "spontaneous overflow of powerful feelings" later recollected by the tranquil mind. Indeed, modernist poets such as T. S. Eliot insisted on the impersonal in poetry, and for this reason modernist poetry might be accompanied by a quick primer in the basic elements of formal analysis (such as meter and rhyme), particularly in a survey course with a number of undergraduates not well versed in the study of poetry. Rather than strip individual poems of their pleasure, a grounding in poetics reinforces what makes poetry pleasurable to begin with.

AMERICAN CONTEXTS: "Make It New":
Poets on Poetry   (p. 538)

As a number of literary historians have pointed out, modernism is closely associated with the rise of avant-garde dispositions and a proliferation of *-isms*, and the literary manifesto is indispensable to each. This cluster might be assigned at the start of any discussion of literary modernism, particularly one that relies extensively on an examination of modernist poetry. (Some titles here, particularly those by Eliot and Hughes, apply as well to prose.) Even those examples that aren't (strictly speaking) manifestos tend to offer specific advice about how best to write, publish, or read poetry. What's more, such advice is often meant to have a spillover effect upon the wider culture. Several draw explicit connections between modernist poetics and modern American society; when they don't (as in the cases of Eliot, Lowell, and Pound), the absence of social commentary is striking. The notion that an "American language" required a poetry all its own was by no means universal, but it was powerful nonetheless.

Questions for Class Discussion

1. Almost all of the writers in this section are also represented in the anthology's selection of poetry. How does their poetry measure up to the ideas set forth in their prose?

2. Describe the reader implied by each essay. Is he or she a poet? from a particular national or racial group? from a particular moment in history? any intelligent reader from any time in history?

3. Which specific literary models does each poet reference? Are these older or more recent models? Are the models drawn from America, Europe, or elsewhere? Are they examples of "high culture" or "popular culture"?

4. How do the views expressed by male poets differ from those expressed by female poets? How do their views overlap?

JAMES WELDON JOHNSON   (p. 570)

Approaches to Teaching

James Weldon Johnson scholars typically mention that he was the first African American admitted to the Florida Bar, that he was a successful Tin Pan Alley songwriter, that he was a diplomat in Latin America, that he was National Association for the Advancement of Colored People (NAACP) executive secretary, that he was the author of the fictional *The Autobiography of an Ex-Colored Man* (1912), and that he edited the influential *The Book of American Negro Poetry* (1922) – so his remarkable collection of poetry, *God's Trombones: Seven Negro Sermons in Verse* (1927), sometimes falls by the wayside. Such neglect is a shame, because the poems vividly record an important facet of American cultural life (African American preaching in the South) and they put into practice a theory of cultural expression (rendering folk idioms in "literary" language) that, thanks in large measure to Johnson, became central to Harlem Renaissance aesthetics. In his preface to *God's Trombones*, Johnson remarks that the "old-time Negro preacher is rapidly passing. I have here tried sincerely to fix something of him." In so doing, he provided many of his juniors a model to emulate and perhaps transcend, and he offers us an important yardstick with which to measure his and others' work.

Classroom Issues and Strategies

"The Creation," like all of the sermons recorded in *God's Trombones*, purports to be a poetic transcription of an actual sermon delivered by a preacher in the rural South. The poem certainly exhibits many of the hallmarks of a transcribed sermon: close, but not too close, adherence to the Old Testament source; iterative syntactical formations, largely based on the conjunction *and;* and colloquial language rooted in the immediate experience of southern rural life. At the same time, it is important to demonstrate that "The Creation" is a poem, not a sermon, for it departs from African American preaching in key ways: As a print medium, the poem cannot record the musicality and theatricality of African American preaching, which must be heard and seen to be believed; the text is primarily experienced by a solitary reader rather than by a community of worshipers; and although Johnson claims to follow the rhythm of the preachers he listened to, line breaks depend on a visual logic as much as a rhythmic logic. As Johnson admits in his preface, "There is, of course, no way of re-creating the atmosphere" generated by the preacher's performance or by the congregation's response.

Connections to Other Authors and Texts

Dunbar's "An Ante-bellum Sermon" is an important precursor text, and a comparison between the two reveals important differences in the writers' distinct rhetorical strategies for re-creating an African American sermon. Among African American writers, Johnson was arguably the most important poetic influence (in both positive and negative senses) on the younger generation of Harlem Renaissance poets that he championed during the last two decades of his career. These include Sterling Brown, Countee Cullen, Langston Hughes, and Georgia Douglas Johnson.

Questions for Class Discussion

1. In his preface to *God's Trombones*, a collection of poems including "The Creation," Johnson "claim[ed] no more for these poems than that I have written them after the manner of the primitive sermons." How is the poem like a sermon? How does the poem differ from a sermon, that is, what are its "literary" properties? How is a preacher like a poet? How is the God of the poem like a poet?

2. Stage a performance of "The Creation." What vocal elements (tone, tempo, volume) and dramatic elements (gestures, stage blocking, props, lighting) does the poem call for?

3. When "The Creation" was published in *God's Trombones*, the poem appeared alongside a print by Harlem Renaissance artist Aaron Douglas. How does the illustration "interpret" Johnson's poem?

Brief Bibliography

Carroll, Anne. "Art, Literature, and the Harlem Renaissance: The Messages of *God's Trombones*." *College Literature* 29 (2003): 57–82.

Levy, Eugene D. *James Weldon Johnson: Black Leader, Black Voice*. Chicago: U of Chicago P, 1973.

Price, Kenneth M., and Lawrence J. Oliver, eds. *Critical Essays on James Weldon Johnson*. New York: Hall, 1997.

AMY LOWELL   (p. 575)

Approaches to Teaching

Although she did not develop the movement's most often cited dictums (or "don'ts"), Amy Lowell is properly remembered as the most effective spokesperson for imagism, the quintessentially modernist movement in Anglo-American poetry. "Aubade," one of Lowell's early poems, written before she encountered and took up the cause of imagism, captures the movement's spirit in its stripped-down, free-verse form; in its central metaphor, a "smooth and polished kernel" of almond; and in its desire to record "a gem beyond counting." But as Lowell scholars rightly insist, no single movement label, "imagism" or otherwise, captures the full range of her poetic output. Lowell's reintroduction into the canon of American poetry – after a fifty-or-so year absence – has been sustained by a variety of approaches, from the history of Lowell's presence in the literary market-place to the poetics of lesbian eroticism to biographical accounts of the poet and her friends and enemies.

Classroom Issues and Strategies

Because Lowell wrote a number of love poems that might well be called "gushing," this subset of her work makes for an interesting measure of Lowell's imagism. Poems such as "Venus Transiens" and "Madonna of the Evening Flowers," two of Lowell's most popular works, present very memorable images – the poet standing on the shoreline as waves "[r]ipple and stir / [t]he sands," the poet kneeling in prayer before "blue steeples of the larkspur" – but offer virtually nothing concrete about the person who inspires the poem. (The "real" person was Ada Russell, but Lowell offers nothing on which to hang biographical facts.) Rather than give the reader a mental image of the beloved, the poems instead offer visual metaphors for identity.

Lowell's constant return to nature is strikingly complex, if quite traditional. (Many scholars credit Lowell's accessible nature imagery with her popularity during her lifetime.) In most poems, nature serves a strategic purpose (apart from being inherently delightful); that is, the logic of the poem often depends on the logic of nature, whether it is the architecture of a garden in bloom (in "Madonna of the Evening Flowers") or similarities between a garden path and lines of poetry. Unlike the literature of today's ecological movement, Lowell's nature poetry is very much human centered; the poet is always there to exert her will on the natural landscape.

Connections to Other Authors and Texts

Lowell counted herself among the imagist group, which included (thanks to her editorial and publicity work) H.D. and Ezra Pound. It is also worth considering Lowell alongside two poets more closely connected in American literary history with Lowell's native New England: Emily Dickinson (whom Lowell listed among her literary "sisters") and Robert Frost.

Questions for Class Discussion

1. Many of Lowell's poems are inhabited by an "I" (the poet) and a "you" (the beloved). What do we know about each person in Lowell's work? Are they women or men? How old are they? Where do they live? What social identities can we infer?

2. Locate a reprint of Botticelli's *The Birth of Venus*. What features of the painting inspire Lowell's "Venus Transiens"? What does Lowell not borrow from the painting? How is the beloved in the poem like the Venus of the painting? How is the beloved different?

3. How does Lowell locate her poems in physical space? In other words, what clues does she offer about the specific geography and architecture of their setting?

Brief Bibliography

Ambrose, Jane P. "Amy Lowell and the Music of Her Poetry." *New England Quarterly* 62 (1989): 45-62.

Benvenuto, Richard. *Amy Lowell.* Boston: Twayne, 1985.

Munich, Adrienne, and Melissa Bradshaw, eds. *Amy Lowell, American Modern.* New Brunswick: Rutgers UP, 2004.

ROBERT FROST   (p. 581)

Approaches to Teaching

Different student audiences warrant two quite different approaches to Frost. For lower-level college students and high school students, Frost's poetry might be approached by way of our sense of what was once called the "New England character"; after all, the poet scrupulously developed a professional identity largely based on New England cultural myths. Even if most students in a classroom have never been to New England, they likely have a strong sense of the region's past and present associations, some of them deep-seated (Puritan origins; staunch Calvinism; English and later Irish and Italian working-class enclaves), others seemingly more superficial (cranberry harvests; crab cakes; fall foliage; maple syrup). Frost helped to shape our culture's perceptions of New England, in particular its rural landscape and population, at a time when the people and places he describes so memorably were feeling the effects of rapid modernization. For more advanced students, Frost's poetry might be approached by way of its influence in the academy and in the wider culture. The signposts of the Frostian aesthetic – a regionally inflected cultural nationalism and a precise formalism – curried much more favor among a general readership and elicited much more attention among academic critics during the early and mid-twentieth century than they do today. Significantly, Frost's place in American literary history require a many-faceted approach to individual poems. It always helps to ask, What would recommend this poem to a general audience? Why might professional critics like (or dislike) this poem?

Classroom Issues and Strategies

Although experimental personae are more closely identified with self-consciously theoretical modernists (especially Ezra Pound), no discussion of

Frost is complete without a consideration of his diverse personae. Even when Frost seems to be speaking as "Robert Frost, American poet" – as in "Design" and "The Gift Outright" – he still manages to modulate the tone and to preclude any clear autobiographical connections. When the lyric voice takes the shape of pensive New England wanderer – as in "After Apple-Picking" and "Stopping by Woods on a Snowy Evening" – the poems often tease the reader by interweaving folksy certainty and cosmopolitan doubt. And Frost is most obviously experimental with personae in dramatic poems with fully formed characters – as in "Home Burial."

Frost's memorable characters and his homespun lyric voices are considered synonymous with New England regional identity. For better or for worse, the idea of a New England character (however steeped in myth and tourist-industry marketing) is fast fading into the recesses of American cultural history. (Stereotypical New Englanders rarely even find their way onto television and film these days.) Nevertheless, the natural environment of New England, recorded in Frost's many landscape poems, still plays an important role in the American cultural imagination. More than just document the presence of trees and snow, however, Frost ascribes meaning to the landscape in a manner anticipated by the New England transcendentalists and the colonial Puritans.

Many students who encountered Frost at an earlier point in their lives are often startled on more careful consideration to discover how wickedly dark Frost's poetry can be. Poems such as "Mending Wall" and "Home Burial" reveal as much about human depravity by what they don't say as by what they do.

Connections to Other Authors and Texts

The variety and significance of Frost's personae emerge out of a comparison with the personae of Emily Dickinson and Ezra Pound. And Frost's New England merits consideration alongside the landscapes of other so-called regional poets, such as Dickinson, Carl Sandburg, and William Carlos Williams.

Questions for Class Discussion

1. Come up with a dossier for the lyric voice that seems to utter each of Frost's poems. Does the voice belong to a man or a woman? How old is he or she? Where does he or she live? What is the house like? How does the lyric voice spend his or her time? What kinds of things does he or she notice (or fail to notice)?

2. In "Design," Frost obviously suggests a connection between natural processes and poetic creation. What are these processes, and how do the analogies work? In his other work, how does Frost suggest connections between nature and reading or writing?

3. How does Frost come to terms with modernization (the process of becoming "modern") and modernity (the recognition that one occupies the last point at a historical moment)?

Brief Bibliography

Bloom, Harold, ed. *Robert Frost.* Broomall, PA: Chelsea, 1999.

Faggen, Robert. *The Cambridge Companion to Robert Frost.* Cambridge: Cambridge UP, 2001.

Parini, Jay. *Robert Frost: A Life.* New York: Holt, 1999.

Richardson, Mark. *The Ordeal of Robert Frost: The Poet and His Poetics.* Urbana: U of Illinois P, 1997.

GEORGIA DOUGLAS JOHNSON   (p. 595)

Approaches to Teaching

The most famous woman poet of the Harlem Renaissance – with three important volumes of poetry published between 1918 and 1928, and a fourth published in 1962 – Georgia Douglas Johnson was regarded as a historical footnote until quite recently. The neglect is a shame because her fascinating biography reveals that she was an important influence on such younger Harlem Renaissance writers as Langston Hughes and Jean Toomer and the many others who frequented her literary salon in Washington, D.C. (You might encourage students interested in an academic career to consider writing a much-needed, full-length biography of Johnson.) Indeed, Johnson serves as a useful introduction to the movement not only because she proved so influential but also because her work – including the poems anthologized here – captures in miniature the tension between universal themes and racialized identity, a tension that often animates Harlem Renaissance writing.

Classroom Issues and Strategies

An accomplished playwright affiliated with the Krigwa Players (an all-black theater company founded by W. E. B. Du Bois, later known as the Negro Experimental Theatre), Johnson had a well-developed and experimental sense of literary personae. Full appreciation of Johnson's work requires a willingness to separate the poet from her work and to imagine an invented lyric voice uttering the poems. At times the persona is a timeless voice speaking on behalf of all women (as in "The Heart of a Woman" and "Cosmopolite") and at other times the persona is a singular woman inspired by a specific set of circumstances (as in "Black Woman" and "I Want to Die While You Love Me"). These diverse personae explore themes as wide-ranging as romantic love ("The Heart of a Woman" and "I Want to Die While You Love Me") and racial politics ("Black Woman" and "Cosmopolite").

Much of Johnson's verse, and two of four poems anthologized here, takes the shape of quatrains with an obvious and regular rhyme scheme. (Each stanza in "Black Woman" resembles two quatrains yoked together.) Students should understand each stanza both as a discrete unit of thought and as a single link in an interconnected chain of associations.

Connections to Other Authors and Texts

Early in her late-blooming literary career, Johnson sought out two of her wide-ranging influences, Carl Sandburg and Charles W. Chesnutt. Additional comparisons warranted by biographical data include Langston Hughes and Jean Toomer, who attended Johnson's salon, and later Zora Neale Hurston.

Questions for Class Discussion

1. Is "The Heart of a Woman" a feminist poem; that is, does it critique the lot of women in society? Why or why not? Would the poem work if it were about "the heart of a man"?

2. Is it possible to read Johnson's poems about romantic love ("The Heart of a Woman" and "I Want to Die While You Love Me") as racial statements? Is it possible to read her poems about racial politics ("Black Woman" and "Cosmopolite") as feminist statements?

3. Analyze the geographic reach of each stanza in "I Want to Die While You Love Me." That is, where is the lyric voice in physical space? What is the extent of her vision? What senses does she use to perceive the world around her?

Brief Bibliography

Honey, Maureen. "Women's Poetry of the Harlem Renaissance." *Teaching the Harlem Renaissance: Course Design and Classroom Strategies*. Ed. Michael Soto. New York: Lang, forthcoming 2007.

Hull, Gloria T. *Color, Sex, and Poetry: Three Women Writers of the Harlem Renaissance*. Bloomington: Indiana UP, 1987.

Jones, Gwendolyn S. "Georgia Douglas Johnson (1870?–1966)." *African American Authors, 1745–1945: A Bio-bibliographical Critical Sourcebook*. Ed. Emmanuel S. Nelson. Westport, CT: Greenwood, 2000. 284–89.

CARL SANDBURG   (p. 598)

Approaches to Teaching

A case might be made that "Chicago," by far Sandburg's best-known poem, represents the zenith of an American poetry that was simultaneously serious and popular; the so-called high modernism that would follow was deadly serious, but hardly popular. (No one would suggest that all or even most poetry written after 1914 was too difficult for a mass audience; even so, the concept of high modernism is a convenient and useful fiction.) "Chicago" clearly embodies Sandburg's dictum that he wrote "[s]imple poems for simple people." Given the poem's simplicity of diction, it is important to stress its complexities of form: its affinities with ancient and modern verse (the ode and Whitmanesque lines, for example); its odd dramatization of a conversation (beyond the usual apostrophe) with an unstable addressee (a personified city, "those who sneer" at Chicago; the reader; the nation); and its kaleidoscopic inventory of persons and things that evoke myriad senses and emotions. Sandburg's central place among the many writers of the "Chicago Renaissance" says much about Chicago and forces us to rethink the idea that a modern, nationalist rebirth occurs only out of a natural landscape.

Classroom Issues and Strategies

Because so much takes place in the twenty-two lines of "Chicago," it helps to track the poem's constituent parts. For example, simply specifying to whom each pronoun refers ("they," "me," "you," etc.) allows students to untangle the densely packed population of the poem. Similarly, students should be able to account for each verb choice and for the more suggestive modifiers ("wanton," "magnetic"). Only then should they attempt a larger interpretation of the poem.

"Prayers of Steel" offers an excellent opportunity to demonstrate the ambiguous tension that often exists between technological modernity and aesthetic modernism. Sandburg's uneasy juxtaposition of a hypertraditional verse form and a thoroughly modern celebration of steel-frame, high-rise architecture calls into question the antiquity of prayer and the modernity of skyscrapers.

Sandburg's death poems reprinted in the anthology – "Graceland," "Cool Tombs," and "Grass," perhaps also "A Fence" – invite a discussion of sharply different verse forms as well as a discussion of historical context (like most of Sandburg's best-known work, these were published during World War I). In all of Sandburg's work, the dramatic situation, the moment or event or place that occasions a poem, deserves considerable attention.

Connections to Other Authors and Texts

As a poet so closely identified with Chicago, Sandburg invites comparison to other regional poets such as Robert Frost and even local-color writers such as Mark Twain. And the "Chicago Renaissance" designation, although somewhat vague, offers avenues for comparison to later writers affiliated with the Harlem Renaissance or the San Francisco Renaissance.

Questions for Class Discussion

1. The popularity of Sandburg's "Chicago" has eclipsed that of his other work. What features does "Chicago" share with Sandburg's other poetry reprinted in the anthology? How is the poem unique?

2. If you were to update "Chicago" for the twenty-first century, what would you add to its inventories of persons, places, things, and emotions? What parts of your updated inventory are uniquely Chicagoan, and what parts are more universal? What parts of Sandburg's "Chicago" are unique to that city, and what might be associated with any early twentieth-century city?

3. "Graceland," "Cool Tombs," and "Grass" take up the age-old theme that death is the great equalizer. However, the poems utilize radically different personae and assume dramatically different shapes. How would you characterize these differences, and what effects do they create in each poem's coming to terms with death? In other words, how do the poems' different forms create different "meanings"?

Brief Bibliography

Niven, Penelope. *Carl Sandburg: A Biography.* New York: Scribner's, 1991.

Van Wienen, Mark. "Taming the Socialist: Carl Sandburg's *Chicago Poems* and Its Critics." *American Literature* 63 (1991): 89–103.

Yannella, Philip R. *The Other Carl Sandburg.* Jackson: UP of Mississippi, 1996.

WALLACE STEVENS   (p. 605)

Approaches to Teaching

Metaphors describing the mind at work are plenty: to begin with, the mind "at work" or "at rest"; then there are "wheels turning, gears grinding"; the mind can "create" and "invent," it can "weave"; the lively mind can "race," it can be "on fire"; the mind not functioning properly is "off its rocker," it's "lost." Wallace Stevens, in "Of Modern Poetry," proposes that poetry is above all "the act of the mind." Here Stevens famously develops an analogy between poetic invention (the mind at work) and dramatic arts (the actor at work). In much of his poetry, Stevens dramatizes the mind in action, sometimes suggesting strict parallels between mental processes and more tangible phenomena, at other times merely hinting at an ineffable system. Whatever the case, we see thoughts cohere into human consciousness. Such heady poetry can easily put off all but the most gifted and intellectually curious students. It's crucial, therefore, to engage in hand-holding when it comes to the "literal" meaning of Stevens's work, to emphasize his humor and wit, and to insist that admitting defeat can be an appropriate response to poetry, but only after due diligence.

Classroom Issues and Strategies

"The Emperor of Ice-Cream" is short enough and strange enough an example to illustrate the value of hand-holding, humor, and bafflement. The poem has notoriously eluded even professional critics, so Helen Vendler's "*ur*-form" (or "plot") of the poem provides a useful yardstick with which to measure what its form reveals and conceals. Against Vendler's prose backdrop, the unseemliness (and grotesque humor) of the poem registers in memorable phrases such as "roller of big cigars" and "bid him whip / In kitchen cups concupiscent curds" and "If her horny feet protrude." If daring students wish to venture an interpretation of the poem's crux — "Let be be finale of seem" – then encourage them to tease out the distinction between "be" (hard, ugly reality) and "seem" (illusion, hope). If they prefer to enjoy the poem for other reasons, let them have their "ice-cream" and eat it, too.

"Sunday Morning" and "The Idea of Order at Key West" are peopled with characters whose simple outer lives do not betray their remarkable and daring inner lives. Paganism assumes a safely domestic shape in "Sunday Morning," and a woman's voice assumes mythic dimension in "The Idea of Order at Key West." Both poems suggest that inner life might be much more dramatic and unconventional than even the most extreme outward appearances; they also suggest that the poet plays a key role in discovering and revealing the unseen.

"Thirteen Ways of Looking at a Blackbird" may be the quintessential poem of the passing glance or, more precisely, of the central importance of perspective. There are no obvious patterns (of sound, of form) in the poem, but a poem with numbered stanzas, even if quirkily numbered, invites a search for recurring features within the sequence. (Patterns of image and tone are perhaps more easily discerned.) Because the poem can be broken up into discrete parts, it invites small groups of students to look for meaning in repetition.

Connections to Other Authors and Texts

Stevens is loved or loathed because of the sheer originality of his work, a quality that makes comparisons to other poets appear forced at times. Stevens's gift for turning a clever and baffling phrase suggests connections to Gertrude Stein and Hart Crane. And while all poetry represents mental process on some level, Stevens's emphasis on cerebral function is rarely matched; Stein and later Elizabeth Bishop and John Ashbery perhaps come closest.

Questions for Class Discussion

1. Paraphrase in prose the "plot" of one of Stevens's more elusive poems (for example, "The Emperor of Ice-Cream," "Sunday Morning," or "The Idea of Order at Key West"). Compare your paraphrase with that of your classmate(s). How do the paraphrases overlap? How do they differ? What parts of the poem yield the most differences? Why?

2. In "The Idea of Order at Key West," how are the woman and her song described? What can we say about them in a literal sense? (You may wish to compare her song with any well-known song that you know.) What additional senses does the speaker of the poem seem to supply; in other words, what does the song mean to the speaker?

3. How does Christianity traditionally imagine contact with divinity; for example, what do "God" and "heaven" look like? Chart the sense perceptions invoked in "Sunday Morning." What does the religious experience described in "Sunday Morning" look and feel and taste and smell like?

4. The original ordering of stanzas in "Sunday Morning" (in the *Poetry* magazine edition of 1915) was I, VIII, IV, V, and VII. How does this variant differ in tone and meaning from the poem printed in the anthology?

Brief Bibliography

Gelpi, Albert, ed. *Wallace Stevens, the Poetics of Modernism.* Cambridge: Cambridge UP, 1985.

Serio, John N., and B. J. Leggett, eds. *Teaching Wallace Stevens: Practical Essays.* Knoxville: U of Tennessee P, 1994.

Sharpe, Tony. *Wallace Stevens: A Literary Life.* New York: St. Martin's, 2000.

Vendler, Helen Hennessey. *Wallace Stevens: Words Chosen Out of Desire.* Knoxville: U of Tennessee P, 1984.

MINA LOY   (p. 618)

Approaches to Teaching

Judging by the number of recent dissertations exploring Mina Loy's life, cultural context, and poetry, her reputation within the academy rests on rock-solid footing. (At present well over forty dissertations have been written about Loy, and the overwhelming majority of these were completed during the last decade.) The groundswell of scholarly attention parallels in interesting ways the publicity – both positive and negative – that attended Loy's early career, and *Love Songs* helped usher Loy before a public that was partly thrilled, partly bemused, and partly aghast. Setting the context for *Love Songs*, that is, comparing the sequence to more traditional love poetry published at roughly the same time, highlights Loy's bold and quirky eroticism. (*The Bedford Anthology of American Literature* tends not to collect "traditional" love poetry, but Amy Lowell's "Venus Transiens" and Georgia Douglas Johnson's "I Want to Die While You Love Me" are worth a quick glance.) Against the backdrop of convention, a useful way to bring students into dialogue with *Love Songs* is to have them compose an advertisement describing what makes the poem "new and improved" love poetry. Loy's life and work, after all, served as a continuing advertisement for the "modern woman."

Classroom Issues and Strategies

Love Songs virtually screams its modernism. The poem's jaundiced view of traditional romance keeps the physical act of sex at a far remove from the emotional act of love. The language is alternately hypertraditional ("Once upon a time"), blasphemous ("Or broken flesh with one another / At the profane communion table"), grotesque ("wild oats sown in mucous membrane"; "Foetal buffoons"), and playfully sonorous ("braying brassily"; "homophonous hiccoughs"; "flowered flummery"). Individually, the poem's sections challenge the reader with asymmetrical syntax, fragmentation, and unpredictable spacing within and across lines. Taken as a whole, the sections issue a barrage of images and moods, leaving much of the poem's meaning up to individual readers. Like a number of modernism's greatest poems, the poem is as demanding as it is rewarding.

Connections to Other Authors and Texts

Although her work was long ignored, Mina Loy occupied a central place among the avant-garde artists and writers of early twentieth-century Europe and the United States. She was close friends with Gertrude Stein, Ezra Pound, and William Carlos Williams, among many others. The fragmented structure of *Love Songs* suggests comparison with T. S. Eliot's *The Waste Land.*

Questions for Class Discussion

1. Read Loy's manifesto on "Modern Poetry." Does *Love Songs* live up to the aims she identifies in the essay? Why or why not?
2. What unites the thirteen sections of *Love Songs* into a single whole?
3. What body parts does the poem mention? How are they described? How *should* the body figure into love poetry?

Brief Bibliography

Burke, Carolyn. *Becoming Modern: The Life of Mina Loy.* New York: Farrar, 1996.

Goody, Alex. *Modernist Articulations: A Cultural Study of Djuna Barnes, Mina Loy, and Gertrude Stein.* New York: Palgrave Macmillan, 2007.

Miller, Cristanne. *Cultures of Modernism: Marianne Moore, Mina Loy, and Else Lasker-Schüler: Gender and Literary Community in New York and Berlin.* Ann Arbor: U of Michigan P, 2005.

WILLIAM CARLOS WILLIAMS   (p. 626)

Approaches to Teaching

Few poems are simultaneously as memorable and as misunderstood as "The Red Wheelbarrow." Most American students encounter the poem at some point during their primary- or secondary-school careers; few claim to be anything other than befuddled by it. If students find that they can handle "The Red Wheelbarrow," the rest of Williams's corpus suddenly seems much less intimidating. The poem can be approached in terms of its visual patterns (the poem's spacing on the page or its imagery), in terms of sound patterns, in terms of its movement through geography, in terms of its semantics and syntax – and finally in terms of the poem's intrinsic and cultural historical meaning. Ideally, students will emerge with an understanding that the above approaches cannot in the end be separated, but even if students have just one or two ways to appreciate the poem, they might find the confidence to move on. Eventually, "The Red Wheelbarrow" might serve as a touchstone in wider discussions of Williams and his work. The poem allows entry into a number of recurring themes in Williams studies: his search for a vital, nativist idiom; an emphasis on the "thingness" of things; reconsiderations of the individual's place in the natural landscape.

Classroom Issues and Strategies

In "To Elsie," Williams announces in almost celebratory fashion that the "pure products of America / go crazy." Together with such figures as Sherwood Anderson, Willa Cather, Hart Crane, and Amy Lowell, Williams advanced a loosely defined variety of American cultural nationalism; that is, he believed that American writers should concern themselves with expressing the "products of America." Williams found multiple avenues for such expression in his own work: thematically (as in the homespun characters of "To Elsie" or the resurgent grass and leaf of "Spring and All"); rhythmically (as in the aggressive enjambment of the seemingly simple "This Is Just to Say" or the "stepped line" of his later work); and notionally (as in the analogy and parenthetical theorizing in "A Sort of a Song"). Even Williams's more obviously Eurocentric poems (such as "Portrait of a Lady") spring from a wish to remake poetry in an American voice. That "American" is part convention, part invention never much bothered Williams.

Connections to Other Authors and Texts

The Beat generation championed Williams as a useful counterexample to the "stuffy," "high" modernism of T. S. Eliot and Ezra Pound (and indeed *Spring and All* [1923] is widely understood as a kind of anti-*Waste Land*). Like the more programmatic imagists anthologized here (H.D., Amy Lowell, Pound), Williams regularly explores the intrinsic and the cultural value of "things."

Questions for Class Discussion

1. How do typography, line spacing, and line breaks inform the meaning of Williams's poetry (in, for example, "The Young Housewife" or "This Is Just to Say")?

2. Throughout his career, Williams famously advocated for poetry not of "ideas" but of "things." Provide an inventory of things that Williams discusses in his poetry. What ideas does the list of things suggest?

3. Can we describe Williams as a "nature poet"? What constitutes "nature" in his poetry? What parts of the natural environment are left out of his work? Is the nature of Williams's poetry necessarily "American"?

4. In prose and poetry, Williams repeatedly disavowed the "high" modernist project exemplified by T. S. Eliot's *The Waste Land*. How might "Spring and All" be understood as an "anti-*Waste Land*"? How do the two poems seem to overlap?

Brief Bibliography

Bremen, Brian A. *William Carlos Williams and the Diagnostics of Culture.* New York: Oxford UP, 1993.

Mariani, Paul. *William Carlos Williams: A New World Naked*. New York: McGraw-Hill, 1981.

Sayre, Henry M. *The Visual Text of William Carlos Williams*. Urbana: U of Illinois P, 1983.

EZRA POUND   (p. 641)

Approaches to Teaching

Gerald Graff's resonant (and too widely applied) phrase "teach the controversy" certainly pertains to introductory discussions of Ezra Pound, the poet and the personality. Was he a (if not *the*) catalyst for all things "modern" in Europe and the United States, a trailblazing aesthete whose injunction to "make it new" added significantly to the body of great poetry? Or was he a misogynist, racist apologist for Fascism, a traitor to the country he gave up on for much of his adult life? Or was he both? (Humphrey Carter's ample biography suggests that this is the case.) Is it wise or even possible to ignore politics for the sake of poetry? Most scholars have strong opinions about such questions, and there's no reason to discourage students from developing strong and (one hopes) well-substantiated opinions of their own. At the same time, it would be a shame to relinquish the "pleasurable textiness" (to borrow Rachel Blau DuPlessis's wonderful phrase) of Pound's poetry simply because he wouldn't be asked to anyone's hypothetical "if you could invite anyone in history" dinner party. Many are entranced by "In a Station of the Metro" the first time they encounter the poem in high school or college, and they can marvel at its grip on the imagination for years. Watching students make their own pact with Pound is one of the true joys of teaching.

Classroom Issues and Strategies

Although he spent the bulk of his career in a self-imposed exile, Pound contributed greatly to a critique of American social and cultural institutions. To demonstrate the relevance of his ideas to poetic expression, it helps to compare Pound's specifically American poems ("A Pact" and "The Rest") to the remainder of Pound's anthologized work, which is set in Europe or Asia. While Pound has harsh words for his native country, his sharp gaze does not spare other parts of the world. Significantly, what America most sorely lacks, according to Pound, is a literary tradition.

Pound's debt to European and Asian traditions and forms takes a wide array of shapes. His often anthologized "In a Station of the Metro," set in a Paris subway station, was a much longer work until Pound pared down the verse to follow the general pattern (if not the strict verse form) of the haiku.

Elsewhere, Pound evokes Chinese history and culture, but it is a strikingly abstract history and culture. Much of Pound's work purports to be a straightforward translation of Chinese texts. Leaving aside the question of accuracy of translation – Pound scholars differ widely in this respect, and Chinese scholars are generally dismissive of their value as translations – you may wish to point out that the selection of source material is the first among many aesthetic choices that "orientalize" subjects with a long history in Western literature (love, nature, valor, etc.). In "The River Merchant's Wife," for example, each successive stanza isolates specific images (bamboo stilts, blue plums, a wall, dust, swirling eddies) meant to convey the persona's emotional state at specific moments in her courtship and marriage.

Connections to Other Authors and Texts

Pound's influence on American poetry begins with the important imagist movement (and so suggests Amy Lowell and H.D. for comparison), but it extends well beyond there both backward in time (Whitman was an important negative influence, and Dickinson's personae are worth considering) and forward in time (it is difficult to consider T. S. Eliot and William Carlos Williams without taking into account Pound's role in their careers).

Questions for Class Discussion

1. How does Pound's poetry measure up to his call (in "A Retrospect") for "direct treatment of the 'thing,'" for "no word that does not contribute to the presentation," and for the "sequence of the musical phrase, not the sequence of a metronome"? In other words, what seems to count for directness, economy of language, and musicality in Pound's work? Are any of Pound's poems more direct, economical, or musical than others?

2. Compare the different versions of "In a Station of the Metro" (also titled "In a Station"). How do changes in punctuation and in line spacing alter the experience of the poem?

3. Some critics dismiss "Portrait d'une Femme" as an attack on women. Do you agree with such an assessment?

4. What is Pound's vision of China? How does this vision inform an understanding of American cultural life?

Brief Bibliography

Carter, Humphrey. *A Serious Character: The Life of Ezra Pound*. Boston: Houghton, 1988.

DuPlessis, Rachel Blau. "Propounding Modernist Maleness: How Pound Managed a Muse." *Modernism/Modernity* 9 (2002): 389–405.

Nadel, Ira B., ed. *The Cambridge Companion to Ezra Pound.* New York: Cambridge UP, 1999.

Perloff, Marjorie. *The Dance of the Intellect: Studies in the Poetry of the Pound Tradition.* Cambridge: Cambridge UP, 1985.

H.D. (HILDA DOOLITTLE)   (p. 650)

Approaches to Teaching

As H.D. finds an ever wider audience among students and scholars, the range of approaches suggested by academic criticism continues to grow. H.D., a Freudian and a feminist, wrote in such a way as to invite both psychological and historical revisionist readings of her poetry and her still-emergent autobiographical fiction. If you are teaching an introductory course with students who might be overwhelmed by theoretically challenging *-isms*, a more basic, formalist approach may be called for. (Of course the imagist label that attached to H.D. throughout her career almost compels a formalist reading of individual poems.) A very simple series of questions often seamlessly evolves into a more nuanced, theoretically ambitious look at H.D.'s poetry: How would you describe the visual shape of the poetry? What do the poem titles suggest about H.D.'s subject interests and her approach to literary expression? What recurring character types and settings can you discern? What verse forms does H.D. tend to utilize?

Classroom Issues and Strategies

Because H.D.'s work was famously first published (by Ezra Pound's design) as the work of "H.D., Imagiste," her poetry often carried the banner of a movement that was spearheaded by Pound and Amy Lowell. A short lyric such as "Oread" offers a wonderful sense of the economy and fluidity of line associated with the movement, and the poem renders its subject with an unforgettable conflation of sea and land imagery. Indeed, this conflation – Is the sea metaphorical pines, or are the pines a metaphorical sea? – suggests that imagism is often as much about the transformative power of language (the poem bids the sea to "whirl" and "splash" and "hurl" like an incantation) as it is about specific images.

As in "Oread," much of H.D.'s work invokes centuries-old myths to shed light on issues that resonate well into the modernist era. In "Leda" and "Helen," for example, H.D. contemplates the simultaneously dangerous and inspirational force of female beauty in a male-dominated society. The latter poem famously renders Helen as a scapegoat in the production of a Greek cultural nationalism; as Susan Stanford Friedman demonstrates, Greek hatred and revulsion sacrifices the living Helen, who epitomizes the human form, so that she might be reborn as a "still," "cool" statue.

Finally, students would not receive full exposure to H.D. without some consideration of the often eroticized flower imagery so common in her work. Often all that's required is a quick glimpse at a Georgia O'Keeffe floral painting for students to wander into territory quite familiar to H.D. scholars. Rarely will they continue to ask, "Why write a poem about a 'Sheltered Garden'?"

Connections to Other Authors and Texts

For literary historical reasons, H.D. is discussed most often with her fellow imagists Ezra Pound and Amy Lowell and with others in the Eliot-Pound orbit. Her sometimes radical reappraisal of convention perhaps makes her more akin to fellow avant-gardists such as Mina Loy and Gertrude Stein.

Questions for Class Discussion

1. How would you characterize the verbs in "Oread"? Who is speaking the poem? How does the lyric persona's use of language resemble a poet's use of language?

2. Describe the logic of the natural landscape in "Mid-day," "Sheltered Garden," or "Garden." In other words, what might specific literal elements of the natural landscape figuratively represent in each poem?

3. After a consideration of "Leda" and "Helen," what does H.D. seem to be saying about the role or the representation of women in Western culture?

Brief Bibliography

Friedman, Susan Stanford, and Rachel Blau DuPlessis, eds. *Signets: Reading H.D.* Madison: U of Wisconsin P, 1990.

Guest, Barbara. *Herself Defined: The Poet H.D. and Her World.* Garden City: Doubleday, 1984.

King, Michael, ed. *H.D., Woman and Poet.* Orono, ME: National Poetry Foundation, 1986.

Morris, Adalaide Kirby. *How to Live/What to Do: H.D.'s Cultural Poetics.* Urbana: U of Illinois P, 2003.

MARIANNE MOORE   (p. 658)

Approaches to Teaching

Marianne Moore was saddled with the tagline "poet's poet" throughout her career. Her work is notoriously elusive and difficult, which may have gained her admirers among figures as diverse as H.D. and Robert Lowell, but the difficulty can be off-putting to students with little experience handling modernist poetry. For this reason, a poem about poetry – and what could be more about poetry than "Poetry"? – serves as a useful point of entry not only into Moore's work but also into a larger discussion of lyric poetry or literary modernism in general. The poem (at least the first version of it) thematically answers unposed questions that might serve as yardsticks against which all manner of verse and prose might be measured: What is (and isn't) a poem? What is the "raw material of poetry," and what in contrast is "genuine"? How does the poem reinforce or deconstruct the dichotomy? The tell-tale signals of a Moore poem – from her oblique and sometimes absent lyric "I" to her idiosyncratic line and stanza forms, from her quirky use of quotation and footnotes to her radical revisions of the work over time – find their way into "Poetry." When students find themselves with the confidence to have fun with the poem, to speculate (for example) about the meaning of an imaginary garden with a real toad in it, they can proceed with the incaution needed to get through much modernist literature.

Classroom Issues and Strategies

The lofty questions addressed above might easily dominate a discussion of Moore; if not, there is a fun way to explore in Moore's work a feature often viewed as definitively "poetic": rhyme. A poem such as "What Are Years?" may be philosophically and syntactically ambitious, but it offers a subtle and sometimes playful approach to rhyme, one that takes full advantage of unexpected line endings. ("What Are Years?" exemplifies Moore's famously mathematical use of syllables rather than stresses to determine line and stanza shape.) The poem deploys rhyme to underscore continuity among concepts that seem wholly unrelated ("innocence"/"whence," "feels"/"steels") or that appear contradictory on the surface ("surrendering"/"continuing," "mortality"/"eternity"). Ask students to come up with alternative words or syllables that work within the poems' rhyme schemes; the exercise dramatically underscores the difficulty and the exactitude of Moore's aesthetic choices.

Connections to Other Authors and Texts

Moore's connection with H.D., Wallace Stevens, and William Carlos Williams is much more than biographical; all four poets are known for their difficulty (although for remarkably different reasons) and for their enduring influence among twentieth- and now twenty-first-century poets. The poets' differing conceptions of the "thing," to put epistemological and aesthetic controversy too simply, accounts both for their difficulty and for their influence.

Questions for Class Discussion

1. Compare the two versions of "Poetry" anthologized here. What are the most significant differences between them? In what ways do the versions overlap?

2. How does the shape of "The Fish" or "To a Snail" mimic nature? How does the shape of either poem control the poem's rhythm? What do these poems say about poetry?

3. Explain the connection between a Moore poem and its title. Which titles are more obviously connected with the subject of the poems? Which titles require more interpretation?

Brief Bibliography

Erickson, Darlene Williams. *Illusion Is More Precise than Precision: The Poetics of Marianne Moore.* Tuscaloosa: U of Alabama P, 1992.

Molesworth, Charles. *Marianne Moore: A Literary Life.* New York: Atheneum, 1990.

Willis, Patricia, ed. *Marianne Moore: Woman and Poet.* Orono, ME: National Poetry Foundation, 1990.

JUN FUJITA   (p. 666)

Approaches to Teaching

Absolutely central to an understanding of Jun Fujita and his work is an appreciation of the opportunities and limits of the tanka, its form and (perhaps more important) its spirit. Tanka is virtually synonymous with classical Japanese literature; the thirty-one-syllable form is over 1,300 years old and still finds loyal practitioners and readers in the twenty-first century. (The sonnet, in contrast, is roughly 800 years old.) The English tanka is usually divided into five lines of five or seven syllables each: 5-7-5-7-7. Like the haiku, which is probably more familiar to American students, tanka poems tend to offer powerful images drawn from the natural landscape. Fujita's work collected in the anthology is not, strictly speaking, tanka poetry; however, his verse evokes solemn moods and moving images that made Fujita a favorite among the imagist poets associated with *Poetry* magazine. If you ask your students to compose a nature haiku or tanka poem, they might realize that some version of imagism is likely to emerge.

Classroom Issues and Strategies

Fujita's style makes a virtue out of compactness. The longest poem anthologized here has four stanzas and seventeen lines; the longest lines (in "Michigan Boulevard" and "Chicago River") have eleven syllables. In most cases, individual lines reveal a self-contained image and a self-contained sound pattern (usually consonance but sometimes a more intricate alliterative design). Because the units of meaning in a Fujita poem are usually so delicate and small, it is easy to overlook the larger blueprint of a poem. It helps to point out how and suggest why poems are broken up into stanzas, how logical progression and repetition work. For example, the final stanza (the last two lines) of "Chicago River" retreats from the intensely subjective vision of the poet to offer a wider view of the scene. The several stanzas of "My Sister" move in and out of the poet's senses and in and out of his memories of the past.

Connections to Other Authors and Texts

Fujita was closely connected with *Poetry* and the many poets who made the Chicago literary magazine their home: Ezra Pound, Amy Lowell, Carl Sandburg, and others. And like Pound, Fujita strove to update American verse by bringing it into contact with Asian themes and forms.

Questions for Class Discussion

1. In any Fujita poem, which sounds are repeated within a single line? Which sounds are repeated across multiple lines? What is the effect of such repetition?
2. How does Fujita's poetry render the modern (for example, the skyscrapers and streetlamps in "Michigan Boulevard" and the iron bridge in "Chicago River") timeless?

Brief Bibliography

Flanagan, Eileen. "Jun Fujita's Chicago." *Chicago History* 25 (Summer 1996): 34–55.

Joyner, Brian D. *Asian Reflections on the American Landscape: Identifying and Interpreting Asian Heritage.* Washington, DC: National Park Service, U.S. Department of the Interior, 2005.

T. S. ELIOT   (p. 669)

Approaches to Teaching

So much has been said and written about *The Waste Land* that its status in American (and English) cultural history is legendary. A number of prominent writers famously reacted to the poem, either with zeal (Ezra Pound) or with disgust (William Carlos Williams), and fortunately their passionate opinions have been recorded. Because the poem has prompted so many to record their first impressions, students who have never before encountered the poem might be invited simply to write whatever comes to mind for a paragraph or two; then for comparison's sake you might read from contemporaneous reviews of the poem (very handily collected by Jewel Spears Brooker). Not everyone enjoys (or even appreciates) the poem, nor should they necessarily.

A discussion of Eliot's work also provides a useful point of entry into the issues connected with the idea of literary modernism, and Daniel Joseph Singal's discussion of the topic ("Towards a Definition of American Modernism," which is reprinted in the companion volume, *Background Readings for Teachers of American Literature*) provides a useful starting point. As a period marker, modernism is often discussed in relation to the so-called *annus mirabilis* (miracle year) of 1922, the year *The Waste Land, Ulysses,* and *Jacob's Room* first appeared. (The year is singled out by critics Harry Levin and Michael North.) As a reaction to historical and intellectual forces, modernism must be considered in relation to the slaughter of World War I, the consolidation of global empires, the emergence of modern social and physical sciences as academic disciplines, the proliferation of revolutionary ideologies, and the invention of significant new technologies (cameras, steel-frame architecture, automobiles, airplanes, sound recording, film). As a psychological disposition, modernism (and the proliferation of *-isms* that fall under its wide umbrella) suggests the combative spirit (and the letter) of the avant-garde. As a set of formal attributes, modernism might be understood in terms of important aesthetic innovations of the late-nineteenth and early twentieth centuries: free verse and imagist poetry; the arbitrary (or value-neutral) deployment of myth as a structuring device; literary self-reference, which dramatizes the means and conditions of literary expression; and the attempt to reproduce in language the so-called sister arts. Eliot's poetry stands at the center of attempts to define modernism, and it is therefore inevitable that notions of the modern in literature help to define Eliot's poetry.

Classroom Issues and Strategies

As perhaps the paradigmatically difficult poem, *The Waste Land* requires a little demystifying and much hand-holding. Provide an inventory of the poem's basic elements: its geography, its languages, its discourses, and its characters. Because the poem was famously titled "He Do the Police in Different Voices" when it was still a work in progress, it helps to dramatize the many different voices (and perhaps to act out scenes) found in the poem. The exercise not only introduces students to the vast tonal range at play but also lets students relax and enjoy the poem's parts without having to worry about the meaning of the whole.

For decades, Eliot's poetry and criticism exerted a normative – one might even say prescriptive and canon-forming – influence on literary discourse; in effect, he helped institutionalize New Critical formal analysis. But that's not to say that he was silent on issues of history, society, and culture. The fragmented ruins of *The Waste Land* present an obvious example of cultural critique, but a similar notion (if not a similar approach) informs much of Eliot's work, including the other poems anthologized here. Here side-by-side, New Critical analysis of the Eliot oeuvre comes in handy: comparing the personae, tone, and verse structure of "The Love Song of J. Alfred Prufrock," "The Journey of the Magi," and "Burnt Norton" reveals how concrete aesthetic choices create distinct reading experiences and unique manifestations of cultural criticism.

Connections to Other Authors and Texts

Pound's role in giving final shape to *The Waste Land* is well known and well documented, so much so that we might ask questions about the extent of their mutual influence: How Poundian is Eliot? How Eliotic is Pound? Similar questions might be asked in connection to William Carlos Williams, whose distaste for Eliot helped shape Williams's self-conscious Americanism. Because *The Waste Land* and "Burnt Norton" are famous examples of the so-called long poem, they might be discussed alongside other examples of the genre, a few of which (at least in part) find their way into the anthology: Hart Crane's *The Bridge*, Allen Ginsberg's *Howl*, and Robert Hayden's "Middle Passage."

Questions for Class Discussion

1. For each of the five sections in *The Waste Land*, provide a basic census and geography of the poem; in other words, who inhabits the poem,

and where are they located? Keep in mind that a poem's characters and places can be both real and abstract.

2. An early title for sections 1 and 2 of *The Waste Land* was "He Do the Police in Different Voices." Identify where one voice ends in the poem and where another begins. What should each voice sound like? How do we know? Be prepared to provide a list of adjectives describing the tone of each voice or to perform the voice aloud.

3 List all of the specific courses offered by your school that might contribute to an understanding of *The Waste Land*. Be sure to illustrate your ideas with specific lines from the poem.

4. Describe the tone of "The Journey of the Magi." Does this sound like the voice of a man who has come into contact with the infant Jesus? Which details from the encounter "a long time ago" does the lyric voice remember?

5. "Burnt Norton" was ultimately collected in Eliot's *Four Quartets* (1943). How is the poem musical in terms of its theme and form?

6. Taking into account all of Eliot's poems in *The Bedford Anthology of American Literature*, list a few adjectives that describe Eliot's style; in other words, what makes a poem Eliotic?

Brief Bibliography

Ackroyd, Peter. *T. S. Eliot: A Life*. New York: Simon and Schuster, 1984.

Brooker, Jewel Spears, ed. *T. S. Eliot: The Contemporary Reviews*. Cambridge: Cambridge UP, 2004.

Cuddy, Lois A., and David H. Hirsch, eds. *Critical Essays on T. S. Eliot's* The Waste Land. Boston: Hall, 1991.

Moody, A. David. *Cambridge Companion to T. S. Eliot*. Cambridge: Cambridge UP, 1994.

Rainey, Lawrence S. *Revisiting* The Waste Land. New Haven: Yale UP, 2005.

CLAUDE MCKAY   (p. 704)

Approaches to Teaching

Although Claude McKay frequently deployed traditional verse forms (Shakespearean sonnets, for example), he more often than not addressed such "modern" themes as racial alienation and revolutionary political struggle. It is therefore important to extend analysis of McKay's work beyond the "honorary modernism" (Michael North's apt phrase) with which it is often received. Many of the examples located in the anthology allow students to recognize how the conventions of traditional forms might be stretched to their thematic limits. "The Harlem Dancer," to use just one example, updates the Shakespearean form's amorous cynicism by setting "love poetry" (if the phrase still applies) in a seedy Harlem cabaret. Beyond thematic novelty, a poem such as "Outcast" deploys so many metaphors (spatial, temporal, Cartesian) to suggest alienation that the Shakespearean form virtually groans under the weight of its figurative language. The sonnet's awkward attempts to find a suitable language seem wholly in keeping with the lyric speaker's keen sense of racial estrangement: "For I was born, far from my native clime, / Under the white man's menace, out of time." In other words, McKay allows us to see the sonnet in a partly new, wholly modern light.

Classroom Issues and Strategies

There are rare occasions in an American literature course when it is necessary or appropriate to discuss the sonnet form at any length; McKay's poetry is surely one of these. An overview of traditional sonnet themes (foremost among these is unrequited love) and its history in Italy and England are useful but not necessary. More important for an understanding of McKay's work is an appreciation of the sonnet form's strengths and weaknesses. The English sonnet that McKay often deployed allows the poet to address an idea with three variations in the three quatrains and to radically revise the idea in the final couplet. The strict rhyme scheme often suggests unlikely connections. McKay converts the sonnet's sheer weight of tradition, sometimes counted as a liability, into an unlikely and ironic asset.

McKay's longtime and unapologetic connection with the young Soviet Union and with Communist politics deserves some attention, and examples such as "If We Must Die" and "America" readily fit the bill. It helps to remind students that radical, left-leaning political views were hardly uncommon in the early twentieth-century United States; the Socialist magazine the *Liberator*, which McKay helped edit, contributed to mainstream political discussion during the teens and twenties. It is also worth noting that McKay had much closer contact with left-leaning white intellectuals (such as Max Eastman) than with the more moderate black leaders of the Harlem Renaissance (such as W. E. B. Du Bois and Alain Locke) with whom he's more often identified. In fact, McKay, a native of Jamaica, always felt out of place among his younger Harlem counterparts. A poem such as "Outcast" captures something of his outsider's angst.

Connections to Other Authors and Texts

Like McKay, Jean Toomer and Countee Cullen were affiliated with the Harlem Renaissance but never felt at home in the movement; unlike

Toomer and Cullen, McKay had no qualms about the movement's commitment to a racialized identity. McKay's radical politics connect him with fellow travelers such as Charlotte Perkins Gilman, Theodore Dreiser,
Langston Hughes, and John Dos Passos.

Questions for Class Discussion

1. Who is the "we" in "If We Must Die"? Who are the "monsters we defy,"
   the "common foe"? The poem does not make specific reference either
   to racial or class divisions. What language supports a racial interpretation? What language supports a class interpretation?

2. In a Shakespearean sonnet, the "turn" (a dramatic shift in the poem's
   logic) takes shape in a couplet at the end of the poem. In the sonnets
   reprinted in the anthology, where does each poem's logic shift? How do
   the poems' ideas make use of the sonnet form? How do the poems'
   ideas work against the sonnet form?

3. Consider the sonnets "Africa" and "America." How do the poems compare in terms of imagery? tone? What might be considered American
   about "Africa"? What might be considered African about "America"?

Brief Bibliography

Cooper, Wayne F. *Claude McKay: Rebel Sojourner in the Harlem
Renaissance: A Biography*. Baton Rouge: Louisiana State UP, 1987.

Hathaway, Heather. "Exploring 'Something New': The 'Modernism' of
Claude McKay's *Harlem Shadows*." *Race and the Modern Artist*. Eds.
Heather Hathaway et al. Oxford: Oxford UP, 2003. 54–68.

Maxwell, William J. "Introduction: Claude McKay – Lyric Poetry in the Age
of Cataclysm." *Complete Poems of Claude McKay*. Ed. William J.
Maxwell. Urbana: U of Illinois P, 2004. xi–xliv.

EDNA ST. VINCENT MILLAY   (P. 710)

Approaches to Teaching

Students who encounter Edna St. Vincent Millay strictly on the textbook
page are sometimes startled to learn that she was raised in a musical family and known by her contemporaries for her dramatic poetry readings, and
they're downright shocked to learn that she earned (and even cultivated) a
reputation as a bohemian wild child in Greenwich Village. The fusty formalism of much of Millay's verse stands in sharp contrast to her radical life
and the sometimes radical views expressed in her poetry. By all accounts,

had Millay entered any poetry recital contest, she would have won, hands down. To challenge students to find the fire in, say, a Millay sonnet, it is useful to have them compete in a recital contest, with the most appropriately passionate performer winning a token prize. ("I, being born a woman and distressed" is appropriately dramatic and subtly clever.) An exercise like this one is a fun and useful way to approach most poets, but in the case of Millay it allows students to see beyond the surface rigidity of her work and into its fervent and playful depths.

Classroom Issues and Strategies

Perhaps the most obvious and important strategy to deploy is to discuss how Millay rises to the challenge of the sonnet form. Two of her best-known sonnets – "I, being born a woman and distressed" and "Oh, oh, you will be sorry for that word!" – fall squarely in the sonnet tradition by deploying love-sick personae and exploring the theme of unrequited love. In "I, being born a woman and distressed," the poet's almost hackneyed complaint that she is "urged by your propinquity to find / Your person fair, and feel a certain zest / To bear your body's weight upon my breast" is spectacularly and humorously undercut by the sonnet's last two lines: "I find this frenzy insufficient reason / For conversation when we meet again." Similarly, in "Oh, oh, you will be sorry for that word!" the poet imagines a "wife to pattern by" only on the outside; inside, she points out that "Some sane day, not too bright and not too stormy, / I shall be gone, and you may whistle for me."

If Millay is clever and satirical in her approach to domestic politics, her more definitively political poems unite powerful rhetoric with equally powerful imagery. In "Justice Denied in Massachusetts," occasioned by the executions of Sacco and Vanzetti, Millay sharply contrasts the petty decorousness of the "sitting-room" with an external landscape blighted in the jeremiad tradition: "The sun that warmed our stooping backs and withered the weed uprooted – / We shall not feel it again. / We shall die in darkness, and be buried in the rain." The poet prophesies a nation whose children are doomed to inherit a "blighted earth" that they must "till / With a broken hoe."

Connections to Other Authors and Texts

Fellow sonneteer Claude McKay shared Millay's desire to bring the ancient form up-to-date for a twentieth-century audience. And because so much of Millay's work found its way into the pages of *Poetry* magazine, her fairly traditional poetry brings into sharp relief the more avant-garde writers (such as Hart Crane, T. S. Eliot, H.D., Jun Fujita, Marianne Moore, and Ezra Pound) associated with the journal.

Questions for Class Discussion

1. Look up *fig* in the *Oxford English Dictionary*. How do the various meanings (literal and figurative) of the word play out in Millay's two fig poems?

2. How does the stanza form give Millay's sonnets their logical shape? How does her logic defy the sonnet form?

3. Is Millay a feminist poet? Why or why not?

Brief Bibliography

Freedman, Diane P., ed. *Millay at 100: A Critical Reappraisal.* Carbondale: Southern Illinois UP, 1995.

Milford, Nancy. *Savage Beauty: The Life of Edna St. Vincent Millay.* New York: Random, 2001.

Thesing, William B., ed. *Critical Essays on Edna St. Vincent Millay.* New York: Hall, 1993.

E. E. CUMMINGS   (P. 716)

Approaches to Teaching

Rarely does poetry teach itself as obviously as E. E. Cummings's poetry does. His over-the-top poetics announces itself clearly even to the high school student wholly inexperienced in the ways of lyric poetry – students know deep down that Cummings's work is different, that it departs radically from whatever "poetry" is supposed to look and sound like. Assigning Cummings in the middle of a course may make perfect sense chronologically (he falls midway in the 1865-to-the-present chronological scheme that governs most American literary surveys), but it's more difficult to conceive of the iconoclastic Cummings as somehow in the middle of a literary tradition. (For better and for worse, scholars have been more likely to imagine T. S. Eliot and William Carlos Williams as bridging the gap between modernism and postmodernism.) Because of its unconventionality, Cummings's poetry might fit into a course at the beginning of a semester, as an example of what *not* to expect in most verse, or at the end of a semester, as the logical endpoint of a particular kind of modernist experimentation. But wherever Cummings finds himself on a syllabus, allow students playful latitude before setting the record straight on him. (A footnote: Cummings scholars – and Cummings himself – spell his name following convention for capitalization: "E. E. Cummings," not "e. e. cummings.")

Classroom Issues and Strategies

Students immediately recognize the unusual typography of virtually all Cummings' poems, and many quickly name the specific irregularities: unusual capitalization, odd word and line spacing, peculiar punctuation. With gentle prodding, most will quickly offer interpretations of the specific rhetorical effects achieved by Cummings's protoconcrete poetry. "Buffalo Bill 's" and "in Just-" are obvious starting points for a discussion of Cummings's typography, but all of his work deserves this kind of attention.

The memorable diction of Cummings's poetry derives partly from the common, colloquial language he draws upon and partly from the caustic tone he exploits. In "my sweet old etcetera," Cummings juxtaposes the banality of those who rationalize the war from the home front (epitomized by the empty signifier "etcetera") with the grim reality of war (only hinted at as the poet lies "quietly / in the deep mud"). In "next to of course god america i," he strings together patriotic clichés with the unsettling effect of rendering them gibberish (something presumably not lost upon the persona who utters the lines). And the stridently (and vulgarly) pacifist "i sing of Olaf glad and big" mostly speaks for itself.

Connections to Other Authors and Texts

For all of his idiosyncrasies, Cummings fits into a number of American literary traditions: like Dickinson and Robert Frost, he's a New England poet; like Amy Lowell and Robert Lowell, he's an antiwar poet; like H.D. and Wallace Stevens, he's a nature poet. But Cummings handles these and other traditions with a singular, memorable voice. Like Gertrude Stein's poetry and prose, Cummings's work is often considered cubist for its manipulation of physical space to create and complicate meaning.

Questions for Class Discussion

1. Rewrite "in Just-" and "Buffalo Bill 's" with conventional capitalization, spacing, and punctuation. How does your version differ from Cummings's poem?

2. What does it mean (in "the Cambridge ladies who live in furnished souls") to live in a furnished soul? Why does the moon rattle "like a fragment of angry candy"? The poem is fourteen lines, resembles iambic pentameter, and follows a semiregular rhyme scheme. Is it a sonnet? Why or why not?

3. Cummings is obviously an unconventional poet in many ways. But what's traditional (according to your understanding of literary tradition) about his work?

4. If Cummings were alive in the twenty-first century, what current issues and events might his poetry refer to? What might he say about them?

Brief Bibliography

Kennedy, Richard S. *E. E. Cummings Revisited*. New York: Twayne, 1994.

Rotella, Guy, ed. *Critical Essays on E. E. Cummings*. Boston: Hall, 1984.

Sawyer-Lauçanno, Christopher. *E. E. Cummings: A Biography*. Naperville, IL: Sourcebooks, 2004.

CHARLES REZNIKOFF   (p. 726)

Approaches to Teaching

Most American literature courses count among their students a number of future lawyers, and the poetry of Charles Reznikoff (who studied law at New York University and at Columbia University) might give them a unique opportunity to consider literary study in relation to their future professions. Legal proceedings about gruesome human tragedies supply the language of "Testimony," and so the poem offers an intriguing example of how one discourse (legal) can be reshaped into another (literary) with minor but truly significant modifications. It's helpful to discuss with students the similarities and differences between the two types of specialized language and to suggest that the lines separating one discourse from another are blurry and always in flux and mutually constituent.

Classroom Issues and Strategies

The shock effect of "Testimony" stands in sharp contrast to the seeming objectivity of its verse. For this reason, the poem is often considered emblematic of objectivism, a modernist literary movement that emphasized simplicity and clarity in the service of evoking distinct and often powerful emotions. (Reznikoff associated his poetry and the wider movement with T. S. Eliot's notion of an "objective correlative," which identifies "external facts" with an interior emotional state.) Students are usually quite good at specifying the particular emotions inspired by "Testimony," and they will easily recognize concrete language from the poem that elicits the emotions. They may need guidance identifying the specifically literary choices that Reznikoff made to give shape to the poem: lyric voices and dramatic situations, line breaks and stanza form, the inclusion and exclusion of specific narrative details, and the overall four-part design of the poem.

Rather than simply cut and paste language from court proceedings – an important aesthetic choice in its own right – he rearranged the language in compelling ways.

Connections to Other Authors and Texts

Reznikoff worked alongside William Carlos Williams and several others associated with the objectivist movement. His poetry of urban life also resembles (but only in a limited way) the works of Carl Sandburg and Langston Hughes, and Reznikoff was a strong influence on Allen Ginsberg.

Questions for Class Discussion

1. Describe the tone of the poem. How is the tone achieved?
2. Why might Reznikoff begin "Testimony" with a description of a boat launch and a tragedy at sea?
3. Of the many tragic events described in the poem, which is the most horrific? Why?

Brief Bibliography

Fredman, Stephen. *A Menorah for Athena: Charles Reznikoff and the Jewish Dilemmas of Objectivist Poetry*. Chicago: U of Chicago P, 2001.

Hindus, Milton, ed. *Charles Reznikoff: Man and Poet*. Orono, ME: National Poetry Foundation, 1984.

Holsapple, Bruce. "Poetic Design in Reznikoff's 'Testimony.'" *Sagetrieb* 13 (1994): 123-45.

HART CRANE   (p. 734)

Approaches to Teaching

Responding to accusations that his poetry was too difficult, too hard to decipher on a very basic level, Hart Crane famously wrote to *Poetry* magazine in 1926 and demanded that his poetry be understood in terms of its "logic of metaphor." Within poetry's other world (one might even say "heterocosm"), Crane offers, "apparent illogic operates so logically in conjunction with its context in the poem as to establish its claim to another logic, quite independent of the original definition of the word or phrase or image thus employed." Such a view of poetic license is wonderful if you're a poet, but less helpful if you're a teacher. As with any difficult poet, students find that approaching Crane in small, independent groups (rather than individually or with an authority figure looking down on them) helps nudge forward the reading and interpretive acts. Ask multiple groups to paraphrase a poem or even a stanza so that each group arrives at an understanding of the text that's informed (as Crane hoped) by "some event in [its] own history or perceptions – or rejects [the text] altogether" – then suggest how the separate paraphrases overlap and even supply additional layers of meaning to each other. And if ever there was a poet about whom you should say, "Don't worry too much about 'getting it,' just enjoy the music of the language," Crane is probably the one.

Classroom Issues and Strategies

"Voyages," a sequence of six love poems, was inspired by Emil Opffer, a Danish sailor with whom Crane shared an apartment in Brooklyn. The poem explores a long list of nautical metaphors for love in all its traditional manifestations (erotic, platonic, divine, etc.); it is a poem about love for another man and for the sea. The first order of business, perhaps the only task that can be accomplished in a semester-long survey, is to track the shifting moods in the poem within individual stanzas, then throughout a single voyage, and finally across the entire sequence. "Voyages I," for example, begins innocently enough by pointing out the "fresh ruffles of the surf" as children play nearby. Subsequently, the "sun beats lightning on the waves, / The waves fold thunder on the sand," an alarming shift that prefigures the seemingly decisive concluding line, "The bottom of the sea is cruel." This line hovers about the remainder of the sequence, but not always ominously; "Voyages" transports readers to as desolate or as redemptive a region as they may wish to visit.

A relatively simple (but hardly the best) approach to Crane is to locate evidence of literary influence in his work. Numerous critics have explored the influence of Whitman on Crane's poetry, and "To Brooklyn Bridge," for example, is often discussed as an updated version of "Crossing Brooklyn Ferry." Crane's poem develops a more conventional I/thou relationship than Whitman's densely populated lyric – Crane has written an ode, after all – but "To Brooklyn Bridge" is also more radical with its reference to mechanically reproduced mass culture ("I think of cinemas, panoramic sleights / With multitudes bent toward some flashing scene") and its repertoire of homosexual double entendres ("O Sleepless as the river under thee," "dreaming sod").

Connections to Other Authors and Texts

Like so many twentieth-century poets, Crane drew inspiration from Walt Whitman, and a number of critics, for a host of reasons, have dubbed Crane the most Whitmanesque of his heirs. He also obviously took much from

Dickinson. Crane was negatively inspired by T. S. Eliot; Crane hoped to be just as experimental as, but more life-affirming than, Eliot.

Questions for Class Discussion

1. What do bridges typically symbolize? What does the Brooklyn Bridge symbolize in Crane's poem about the structure?

2. Identify sound patterns (especially rhyme and alliteration) in "Voyages" or "The Broken Tower" within and across stanzas. What words sound alike? What do the sound patterns suggest?

3. Is it possible to disentangle Crane's poetry from his homosexuality? Does "Voyages," for example, suffice as a love song about a heterosexual relationship?

Brief Bibliography

Berthoff, Warner. *Hart Crane, A Re-introduction.* Minneapolis: U of Minnesota P, 1988.

Edelman, Lee. *Transmemberment of Song: Hart Crane's Anatomies of Rhetoric and Desire.* Stanford: Stanford UP, 1987.

Fisher, Clive. *Hart Crane: A Life.* New Haven: Yale UP, 2002.

Trachtenberg, Alan, ed. *Hart Crane: A Collection of Critical Essays.* Englewood Cliffs, NJ: Prentice-Hall, 1982.

STERLING A. BROWN   (p. 745)

Approaches to Teaching

Teaching Sterling Brown's poetry can be enormously entertaining for several reasons. His clever handling of dialect, which highlights the performance context of the speech act, gives life to powerful characters and impressive settings. In many cases, his poems draw directly from the rich traditions of jazz and the blues and spirituals. In "Ma Rainey," to take just one example, the poet furnishes us with a front-row seat as the blues pioneer puts on her show. Putting Brown's poetry in its appropriate historical context necessarily dampens the festivities; the racial violence of the Jim Crow South provides the subtext to much of Brown's work as a poet, an educator, and a cultural critic. Students at times resist the grim facts of lynchings, segregation, and disenfranchisement – injustices not of the slave era, but of the 1920s and 1930s, when Brown's pathbreaking *Southern Road* (1932) appeared.

Classroom Issues and Strategies

Taking its leitmotif from Carl Sandburg's "Upstream" – "The strong men keep coming on" – Brown's "Strong Men" folds the whole of African American history and suffering into a few short stanzas. But like Sandburg's short revolutionary poem, "Strong Men" is as much about the present as it is about the past. The poem depicts a timeless, allegorical trinity of characters: "you," "they," and the poet as prophet. The spirituals and work songs to which the poem refers – including "Keep A-Inchin' Along," "Walk Together Children," and "Water Boy" – were sung not only by slaves during the nineteenth century but also by southern chain gangs well into the twentieth century. Similarly, the poem interweaves biblical rhetoric (*"Thou shalt not this"*) with the rhetoric of Jim Crow (*"Reserved for whites only"*).

"Tin Roof Blues" and "Ma Rainey" draw extensively from the verse structure and lyrics of what we now call "classic" blues, but when the poems were written the blues represented the cutting edge of American musical expression. (The earliest blues recording dates to 1920.) Simply taking the blues as an occasion for poetry was a radical act; achieving the results Brown did was revolutionary. As James Weldon Johnson put it in his preface to *Southern Road*, Brown "has actually absorbed the spirit of his material, made it his own; and without diluting its primitive frankness and raciness, truly reexpressed it with artistry and magnified power." Following Johnson's suggestion, ask students to identify the raw "material" in Brown's blues poems and to indicate how Brown makes it "his own."

Connections to Other Authors and Texts

As a key contributor to the Harlem Renaissance and a founding figure in African American studies, Brown had a wide and deep impact on American letters. His dialect verse might be compared with that of his predecessor in the genre, Paul Laurence Dunbar (a personal friend of Brown's father), and against the cultural criticism of James Weldon Johnson (who reevaluated his position on dialect poetry largely at the instigation of Brown's work). Scholars often compare Brown's work with that of Langston Hughes, whose dialect verse created more of a stir than Brown's did. Finally, Amiri Baraka is one of many students of Brown to go on to an important literary career.

Questions for Class Discussion

1. How many voices can you locate in "Strong Men"? Describe the personae behind these voices – who are they and what motivates their expression?

2. The instrumental jazz song "Tin Roof Blues" was written and recorded by the New Orleans Rhythm Kings in the 1920s. If you were to set Brown's poem by the same name to music, what would the music sound like? What instruments would the arrangement include? What style of play fits the poem? What contemporary musician or band would do a good job recording your arrangement?

3. A number of artists have recorded versions of the "Backwater Blues," the song performed by Ma Rainey in the poem of the same name. (The most famous recording of the song is probably Bessie Smith's.) Listen to as many versions of the song as you can. Who performs the song in a manner fitting the context described in "Ma Rainey"? Why?

Brief Bibliography

Rowell, Charles H., and Kendra Hamilton, eds. "Sterling A. Brown: A Special Issue." *Callaloo* 21 (1998): 725-1079.

Sanders, Mark A. *Afro-Modernist Aesthetics and the Poetry of Sterling A. Brown.* Athens: U of Georgia P, 1999.

Smethurst, James. "Teaching Sterling Brown's Poetry." *Teaching the Harlem Renaissance: Course Design and Classroom Strategies.* Ed. Michael Soto. New York: Lang, forthcoming 2007.

LANGSTON HUGHES   (p. 752)

Approaches to Teaching

Because Langston Hughes is rightly known for crafting poetry out of the everyday deeds and language of the African American working classes, it is too easy simply to sit back and watch with a smile as students are moved by his disarmingly straightforward poems. Fortunately, the anthology includes work from over three decades of Hughes's career, and it's possible to enjoy and take pedagogical advantage of in-depth analysis of individual works as well as chart a few trends over time. Some trends worth keeping in mind: the evolving influence of popular music idioms, from the early blues poems to the later free-form jazz poems; the consistent presence of an African American working-class vernacular; the increasingly critical verse influenced by transnational socialist networks; and the ever-present desire to shape the direction of American cultural nationalism. Students very easily fall in love with Hughes's poetry; helping them understand why will likely pose your most difficult challenge.

Classroom Issues and Strategies

Although blues and jazz were considered vulgar forms of expression well into the twentieth century, Hughes unabashedly deployed the musical idioms in his work. These are a modern version of ancient lyricism, as poems such as "The Weary Blues" and "Dream Boogie" suggest. Reviewing the basic shape of the twelve-bar blues format proves especially useful: Most important from a standpoint of understanding Hughes, each verse repeats two lines with a slight variation and provides resolution in the third line, all of which fits into twelve bars of music. Within this loose structure, a musician – or a poet – has much leeway for creativity and idiosyncrasy.

For a poet as popular as he was during his lifetime, Hughes never shied away from strong and sometimes unpopular political stances. He was an avowed Socialist from an early point in his career, and he subsequently emerged as a leading voice of the early civil rights movement. Poems such as "Mulatto," "Christ in Alabama," "Brass Spittoons," and "Harlem" capture the diversity and the stridency of Hughes's political views.

Hughes is easily the most important figure to emerge from the Harlem Renaissance, the most influential (and most often studied) movement in African American cultural history. In this important role, Hughes represents a crucial nexus in American literary history. "I, Too," obviously inspired by Whitman, and "Cross" represent key investigations of the place of African Americans within American society and, by extension, an analysis of the role of African American writing within American letters.

Connections to Other Authors and Texts

Whitman and (to a lesser extent) Ezra Pound were early and important influences on Hughes. Early in his career, Hughes had yet to distinguish himself from several younger poets of the Harlem Renaissance; he was regularly discussed alongside Sterling Brown and Countee Cullen. Hughes would ultimately emerge as one of the most influential American poets of the twentieth century, an influence felt especially prominently by Black Arts Movement poets such as Amiri Baraka and Gwendolyn Brooks.

Questions for Class Discussion

1. How do individual Hughes poems measure up to the ideas he expresses in "The Negro Artist and the Racial Mountain"? Which poem is most consistent with the essay's views? Which poem is least consistent?

2. Who is the "I" in "The Negro Speaks of Rivers"? How should the poem be read aloud? What's an appropriate setting? What's the appropriate tone of voice? Locate a recording of Hughes reading the poem; does he get his own poem right? Why or why not?

3. How does Hughes "signify" (repeat with difference) on Whitman in "The Negro Speaks of Rivers" or in "I, Too"? How does he signify on the blues in "The Weary Blues"?

4. In "The Weary Blues," how does the musician's song overlap with the lyric speaker's voice semantically and thematically? What does the lyric speaker add that's not present in the song?

5. Discuss the symbolic importance of specific geographic markers (e.g., places in Harlem, the South, Africa) in individual Hughes poems.

Brief Bibliography

Gates, Henry Louis, Jr., and K. A. Appiah, eds. *Langston Hughes: Critical Perspectives Past and Present*. New York: Amistad, 1993.

Patterson, Anita. "Teaching Langston Hughes's Poetry." *Teaching the Harlem Renaissance: Course Design and Classroom Strategies*. Ed. Michael Soto. New York: Lang, forthcoming 2007.

Rampersad, Arnold. *The Life of Langston Hughes*. 2nd ed. New York: Oxford UP, 2002.

Tracy, Steven C., ed. *A Historical Guide to Langston Hughes*. New York: Oxford UP, 2004.

COUNTEE CULLEN   (P. 765)

Approaches to Teaching

If anyone represented the best hopes of the Harlem Renaissance during its heyday, it was Countee Cullen. For much of the 1920s, he was known as the "Negro Poet Laureate" and with good reason: his well-received *Color* (1925) appeared even before he finished college; his next two books would follow within just two years; and his edited collection, *Caroling Dusk* (1927), gave added dimension to the idea that African American poetry had come of age. Cullen's verse and his critical essays were read by African Americans far and wide and celebrated by the leading African American intellectuals of the period. Why, then, is Cullen so little read today? No doubt Cullen's standing in comparison to more popular Harlem Renaissance figures such as Langston Hughes and Zora Neale Hurston derives from issues intrinsic to his work (see below), but it is worth asking students how they might answer the question; after all, Cullen's reputation is now in their hands.

Classroom Issues and Strategies

Today's readers sometimes find difficulty in the convoluted logic and archaic diction of a poem such as Cullen's sonnet, "Yet Do I Marvel." A brief outline of the poem's structure unlocks its basic meaning and illustrates Cullen's cunning: The first eight lines offer two quatrains exploring the paradox of a just God who nevertheless allows injustice (blindness, mortality, the eternal fates of Tantalus and Sisyphus) to occur. Unlike most sonnets, the syntax of the quatrain is rendered more difficult (and arguably more interesting) by enjambment, and the God is not necessarily Christian. The last six lines offer three couplets, including a dramatic turn in the last couplet, exposing the final, inscrutable paradox: a kind God who nevertheless allows a black poet. The poem meets expectations of form and logic here but skillfully disregards them there.

All of Cullen's best-known poems, including those anthologized here, reflect the profound irony of a poet who wanted to transcend racial themes but who is best known for his "racial" poetry. The tension of Cullen's career finds a fruitful outlet in poetry such as "Heritage": The poem, which was reprinted alongside photographs of African statues and masks in a famous *Survey Graphic* magazine issue about Harlem, never directly answers its rhetorical question, "What is Africa to me?" Even so, the poem's strident beat and fanciful imagery reveal that even heavy-handed grotesqueries might form the basis of poetry that combines power and thoughtfulness.

Although "Heritage" shows some traces of decadence, the homosexuality for which Cullen was known even early in his career does not explicitly reveal itself in the poems anthologized here. But in a clever and convincing reading of the poem's variant printings, James Kelley argues that Cullen's poem, and the illustrations that accompany it in *Color*, insist on same-sex innuendo.

Connections to Other Authors and Texts

Throughout his short career, Cullen repeatedly invoked the name of the great Romantic poet John Keats as a source of inspiration; even so, Cullen was (and still is) more often compared with Langston Hughes and the other poets of the Harlem Renaissance. A great irony of Cullen's career is that (as James Weldon Johnson and others have pointed out) his best work explores racial themes even though he never wished to be known simply as a "Negro" poet.

Questions for Class Discussion

1. In "Yet Do I Marvel," how does Cullen use the Shakespearean sonnet form to arrange an array of references – from Christianity to Greek myth to modern America? What is ironic about this logical structure?

2. Where does Cullen derive his African imagery in "Heritage"? How real is Africa? How imaginary is it?

3. "Heritage" is written in trochaic tetrameter (a sequence of four strong and soft beats: ´ ◡ ´ ◡ ´ ◡ ´ ◡). How does this rhythm inform the meaning of the poem?

Brief Bibliography

Bernard, Patrick. "Teaching Countee Cullen's Poetry." *Teaching the Harlem Renaissance: Course Design and Classroom Strategies.* Ed. Michael Soto. New York: Lang, forthcoming 2007.

Kelley, James. "Blossoming in Strange New Forms: Male Homosexuality and the Harlem Renaissance." *Soundings* 80 (1997): 498-517.

Shucard, Alan R. *Countee Cullen.* Boston: Twayne, 1984.

The Emergence of Modern American Drama

This section of *The Bedford Anthology of American Literature* introduces students to modern American drama by way of two playwrights who defined the movement. Susan Glaspell and Eugene O'Neill were part of a discrete group, the Provincetown Players, that wielded a profound and long-lasting force on literary culture; the small theater troupe was arguably the most influential of the many modernist literary movements in U.S. cultural history. What is important to emphasize – and here the editors' section introduction succeeds admirably – is that Glaspell and O'Neill were reacting (in positive and negative ways) against the pressures exerted on them by the mass-entertainment industry, especially the dominant role of Broadway in American theater and the world-transformative rise of "talking pictures."

The ongoing influence of modern American dramatists such as Glaspell and O'Neill can still be felt on college campuses throughout the nation, many of which boast of performance spaces that are large and relatively showy (in a way that's analogous to Broadway theaters) alongside spaces that are small and intimate (in a way that's analogous to off-Broadway theaters). Even campuses lacking an obviously dichotomous approach to dramatic performance still have locations that might be suitable for larger or smaller performances (say, gymnasiums versus classrooms). Bringing issues of performance space to a local level allows students to envision concretely the challenges posed by bringing a play's text to life in performance.

SUSAN GLASPELL   (p. 780)

Approaches to Teaching

At first glance, Susan Glaspell's important and entertaining *Trifles* seems
to require very little attention to politics. Students very quickly emerge
from the text with a good understanding of the play's feminist analysis of
discourse-specific, context-driven, and gendered versions of the truth. But
textual analysis only goes so far in the case of a work written for the stage.
Because the play is so short, *Trifles* presents a rare opportunity to stage a
reading or a full-fledged production in the classroom setting. And because
the character list is fairly short, you might consider staging multiple productions within a single class. Some students will find a *Trifles* performance contest a new and engaging way to take on literary analysis.
Importantly, strict fidelity to Glaspell's text is no longer faithful to the
play's politics – these days, a "woman's place" is no longer in the kitchen –
so student performers must choose between either a textually accurate or
a politically relevant approach to the play. Setting the play at the present
moment raises an important question: In which contexts are men and
women still expected to view the world differently? In what ways does the
"truth" depend on whether you are a man or a woman?

Classroom Issues and Strategies

Trifles effectively juxtaposes two radically different modes of truth telling.
On the one hand, the play is a murder mystery, with easily recognized characters drawn from the law-enforcement community. On the other hand, the
play is set in a home, and primarily in the kitchen, a setting with its own
unique expectations. Women are excluded from the first mode of truth
telling, and men exclude themselves from the second. Glaspell's attention
to the details of homemaking and to the details of crime solving generates
a unique and unexpected tension along gender lines.

Significantly, not all of the characters in the play are aware of the gendered tension. You may wish to identify the first time women gain knowledge that's overlooked by their male counterparts (when Mrs. Hale realizes
that it was likely the deputy sheriff who sullied the kitchen towel) and ask
students to keep track of the remaining such moments. Then, discuss the
subtleties of voice, facial expression, and body movement that are required
to convey the delicacy of each occasion.

The play's stage directions and dialogue often supply blunt symbols: a
disheveled kitchen, a songbird with a wrung neck, and so on. Other symbols are less obvious and many possess unclear or debatable meaning: the
cold weather, the burst jars of jam, the knotted quilt. A useful way to
address the play's symbolism is to transfer ownership of meaning to stu-

dents: Ask them how they would design the set or provide direction to actors so that the symbols are properly rendered for an audience.

Connections to Other Authors and Texts

Although *Trifles* might be considered alongside all of the plays collected in the anthology, Glaspell's closest literary historical cousin is fellow Provincetown Players member Eugene O'Neill. The politics of domestic performance are also taken up in Abraham Cahan's "A Ghetto Wedding" and Edith Wharton's "The Other Two."

Questions for Class Discussion

1. Look up the word *trifle* in the *Oxford English Dictionary*. Which definition entries relate to the play's title? How do they relate?
2. In the twenty-first century, female county attorneys and sheriffs are fairly common, as are male homemakers. If you wanted to retain the play's gender politics (however you understand them) into our own era, which characters would you include? Where would you set the play?
3. How do the play's male characters perform their authority over other men? over women? How do less powerful characters (male or female) resist?
4. If Mrs. Hale and Mrs. Peters were to try Mrs. Wright for murder knowing all the details that they're privy to, how might they present their case? How does their case differ from the county attorney's?

Brief Bibliography

Ben-Zvi, Linda, ed. *Susan Glaspell: Essays on Her Theater and Fiction*. Ann Arbor: U of Michigan P, 1995.

———. *Susan Glaspell: Her Life and Times*. New York: Oxford UP, 2005.

Gainor, J. Ellen. *Susan Glaspell in Context: American Theater, Culture, and Politics, 1915–48*. Ann Arbor: U of Michigan P, 2001.

Papke, Mary E. *Susan Glaspell: A Research and Production Sourcebook*. Westport, CT: Greenwood, 1993.

EUGENE O'NEILL   (p. 792)

Approaches to Teaching

There exists no single candidate for the title of "America's greatest poet," and perhaps a dozen or more candidates have been assigned the mantle of "America's greatest novelist." Even so, most critics agree that the title of "America's greatest playwright" belongs to Eugene O'Neill. And perhaps more than any other single play in his extensive repertoire, *The Emperor Jones* stands at a crossroads in O'Neill's career, and more generally in American theater: The play marks the beginning of O'Neill's experimental 1920s, during which he also wrote *Anna Christie, All God's Chillun Got Wings,* and *Strange Interlude;* the play serves as an important junction between the avant-garde little-theater movement and the more mainstream Broadway stage; finally, the play helped bring together (in cooperation and conflict) white Greenwich Village and black Harlem. And so while *The Emperor Jones* may not be the greatest American playwright's single greatest play — most assign that role to the posthumously produced *Long Day's Journey into Night* (1956) — *The Emperor Jones* certainly shaped the relationships, dispositions, and approaches to language and culture that would forever change American drama.

Classroom Issues and Strategies

The plot of *The Emperor Jones,* which follows the title character deep into a tropical woods peopled with the ghosts of his troubled past, thematically dovetails discourses of historical and psychological regression. In other words, the play underscores the troubled past of Africans and African Americans who encountered first slavery, then Jim Crow segregation, followed by negatively stacked odds in the American economy. The play also dramatizes Brutus Jones's personal inner demons, the individual choices that dictate his life options. As a consideration of historical forces, the play explores racial specificity; as a consideration of psychology, the play explores human universals.

Students not well versed in twentieth-century drama sometimes have trouble making sense of the play's novelistic stage directions. Some of the directions appear to be little more than hyperprecise descriptions of the set or the costumes, a challenge to a "faithful" production, but not beyond the realm of possibility. Other directions — as at the start of scene 1, which mentions that "*there is an oppressive burden of exhausting heat in the air*" — suggest a mood that could never be realized fully on stage, at least not in the manner required by the text. The effect, of course, is for the reader rather than for the viewer of the play. The implied audience of the written text is not simply the director and the actors but rather a wider reading public.

The film version of *The Emperor Jones* (1933), directed by Dudley Murphy and with a screenplay by Dubose Heyward, was perhaps as important in American cultural history as the play itself. A screening of the film highlights both the limits and the possibilities of staged drama. The film's first forty-five minutes are given over to dramatizing in a fairly conventional way Brutus Jones's life before his ascendancy to emperor. O'Neill's play manages to incorporate the same information in the radically different context of a play that unfolds during a single day and night.

Connections to Other Authors and Texts

The Emperor Jones was one of the Provincetown Players' better known productions, so it merits consideration alongside Susan Glaspell's *Trifles*. The play was equally (if not more) important to Harlem Renaissance intellectuals, who took its initial production in 1920 as an occasion to celebrate and to ponder the appropriate representation of African Americans on the stage. The play's mythic dimensions anticipate the avant-garde theatrics of Amiri Baraka's *Dutchman.*

Questions for Class Discussion

1. When *The Emperor Jones* had its Broadway premiere in December 1920, critics hailed the play as a model for the artistic portrayal of African American life, or they excoriated the play for trafficking in stereotype and white supremacy. Find textual evidence from the play itself on behalf of both sides of the argument. Based on the evidence, which case is more convincing?

2. From a production standpoint, what are the major problems presented by the play? In other words, what difficulties arise when it comes to selecting a cast, constructing a set, or directing the action?

3. View the 1933 film adaptation of *The Emperor Jones.* How does the film depart from the text of the play? What effects do the departures impart on the viewing experience?

Brief Bibliography

Emperor Jones. Dir. Dudley Murphy. Perf. Paul Robeson and Dudley Digges. 1933. DVD. Image Entertainment, 2003.

Gelb, Arthur, and Barbara Gelb. *O'Neill: Life with Monte Cristo.* New York: Applause, 2000.

Manheim, Michael, ed. *The Cambridge Companion to Eugene O'Neill.* New York: Cambridge UP, 1998.

Manuel, Carme. "A Ghost in the Expressionist Jungle of O'Neill's *The Emperor Jones.*" *African American Review* 39 (2005): 67-85.

At Home and Abroad: American Fiction between the Wars

Before the early part of the twentieth century, prose fiction ranked third or at best a distant second in the English hierarchy of literary genres (behind poetry and sometimes oratory and nonfiction prose). For a number of reasons, including those outlined in the editors' introduction to this section of the anthology, prose fiction emerged at this time as the central thrust of the American literary marketplace, and in the minds of many writers and critics it eclipsed rival genres in prestige. Because most of the short stories collected in the anthology originally found a wide and receptive audience, taken individually they virtually teach themselves. (Even so, you will find plenty of practical suggestions for teaching them in the following pages.) Taken as a whole, they reveal much about American society and history and literary art during the era, including a profound concern with the many varieties of regional identity and expression that inform American modernism. If you assign several of the short stories, it helps to locate the setting of individual titles on a U.S. map; as the days and weeks of the semester progress, students will find that they've traveled not only back in time, but also across the continent.

*AMERICAN CONTEXTS: From the Great War
to the Great Depression: American Writers and
the Challenges of Modernity*   (p. 826)

The title of this cluster suggests that fiction writers during the interwar period were more interested in sociohistorical questions than in aesthetic ones. Although the science is hardly precise, even a quick examination of the essay titles located here suggests that the cluster title is indeed accurate. Just as it is impossible to separate altogether issues of literary content and form, so too is it impossible to separate social history and aesthetics. Each essay suggests something about the connection between art and life, between form and subject matter. Students might be asked to envision the society that would occasion individual essays: What are ordinary people like? How does the essay suggest that they come into contact with literature? What kind of reader does the essay imagine? Is the reader representative of an ordinary person, or is he or she somehow different? Does the writer see herself or himself as an ordinary person or somehow different? If a writer betrays an obvious concern about social issues (as do Davidson and Gold), it helps to emphasize the aesthetic import of the essay; if a writer is an obvious aesthete (as Stein is), it helps to emphasize the essay's social ramifications.

Questions for Class Discussion

1. Compare the essays collected here with the American poetry manifestos found elsewhere in the anthology ("'Make It New': Poets on Poetry"). What concerns do the fiction writers and poets share? In what ways do they differ?

2. According to the writers in this section, what seems to be wrong with American literature in the twentieth century? What seems right about American literature? What can be salvaged, and what must be jettisoned altogether?

3. On a progressive scale, determine which authors are more interested in aesthetic change and which are more interested in social change.

4. Almost all of the writers in this section are also represented in the anthology's selection of prose fiction. How does their fiction measure up to the ideas set forth in their nonfiction prose?

GERTRUDE STEIN   (p. 847)

Approaches to Teaching

Few writers intimidate students as thoroughly as Gertrude Stein – for that matter, her work can intimidate even the most seasoned scholars of American literature. For that reason you will find below recommendations of not only book-length studies of Stein's life and work, but also thoughtful and useful essays about individual texts in the anthology: "Ada" (see Burke), "Miss Furr and Miss Skeene" (see Behling), and "Picasso" (see Haselstein). Each essay takes up Stein's work in rich and fascinating detail. Fortunately, the anthology collects work that is enjoyable on a very basic, rhythmic level, and getting students to read Stein's prose out loud is a challenge that's easily overcome and that often leads to fruitful discussions about repetitive visual and sound patterns. Picasso's famous portrait of Stein, widely considered a protocubist work, is also helpful in underscoring the similarities and (more importantly) the differences between his painting and her prose.

Classroom Issues and Strategies

The most obvious element in virtually all of Stein's prose is repetition, and an example such as "Ada" reveals the richness and inventiveness of using the same or nearly the same words in slightly modified contexts. Take the example of these four sentences from the portrait's final paragraph:

> Some one who was living was almost always listening.
> Some one who was loving was almost always listening.
> That one who was loving was almost always listening.
> That one who was loving was telling about being one then listening.

Writing each sentence on a separate line (as one might transcribe poetry) reveals how repetition with subtle differences transforms the meaning of individual words (as in the difference between "that *one*" and "some *one*") and suggests as well connections where none exist in any obvious way (as in the connection between "living" and "loving"). In contrast, "Miss Furr and Miss Skeene" repeats the word *gay* so often that its range of associations arguably extends well beyond the widely recognized senses of "happy" and "homosexual" (particularly when she pairs "gay" with "regular"). A useful exercise in handling the repetition of a single word across several sentences and paragraphs is to replace the word with blank lines (_____) and to ask students to fill in the blanks, using alternate words in a way that makes syntactical and logical sense. The exercise reveals the malleability of Stein's language and at least part of the rationale for her use of repetition.

Stein scholars routinely refer to her prose as cubist, and her "Picasso" portrait usually figures into the discussion. Her work has been read as cubist in a number of ways: Stein uses repetition to suggest the simultaneity of multiple visual planes; Stein's prose rubs up against the limits of verbal representation and thus suggests a visual dimension just beyond the horizon of language; Stein profoundly trusts in the reader to invest the work of art with meaning by drawing logical associations across time and space and by working through the contingencies of linguistic context. Beyond thinking about the portrait's connection to cubism, it is useful to consider "Picasso" against the tradition of literary portraiture (which, as Ulla Haselstein points out, must always be considered alongside visual portraiture). The portrait of the famous artist shows us not his iconic visual figure but instead draws us into his magnetic personality and portends his unmatched importance in twentieth-century visual art.

Connections to Other Authors and Texts

Because she occupied the center of what was arguably modernism's most important salon, Stein influenced and was influenced by many of the leading writers and artists of her time, including Sherwood Anderson, Ernest Hemingway, F. Scott Fitzgerald, Mina Loy, and Ezra Pound. A similarly cubist aesthetic has also been identified in the work of E. E. Cummings and Jean Toomer.

Questions for Class Discussion

1. Type one of Stein's paragraphs into a word-processing program that has grammar-checking tool. What grammatical "mistakes" does the program highlight? Why do you think that Stein commits the specific "errors"?

2. "Miss Furr and Miss Skeene" reached its largest audience when it was published in *Vanity Fair*, perhaps the most important "society magazine" of the early twentieth century. How might the sketch's original readership reconcile its avant-garde style with nearby celebrity gossip? In other words, how might reading "Miss Furr and Miss Skeene" make one fashionable?

3. How is Stein's "Picasso" a cubist work?

4. List the ways in which reading Stein's work is enjoyable. List the ways in which reading her work is frustrating.

Brief Bibliography

Behling, Laura. "'More Regularly Gay and in a *Wholly New Way*': Marketing a Heterosexual Cure to Gertrude Stein in *Vanity Fair*." *Journal of Modern Literature* 21 (1997): 151-54.

Burke, Carolyn. "Gertrude Stein, the Cone Sisters, and the Puzzle of Female Friendship." *Critical Inquiry* 8 (1982): 543-64.

Dydo, Ulla E. *Gertrude Stein: The Language That Rises: 1923-1934.* Evanston: Northwestern UP, 2003.

Haselstein, Ulla. "Gertrude Stein's Portraits of Matisse and Picasso." *New Literary History* 34 (2003): 723-43.

Malcolm, Janet. *Two Lives: Gertrude and Alice.* New Haven: Yale UP, 2007.

SHERWOOD ANDERSON   (p. 857)

Approaches to Teaching

Today's students tend not to know much (if anything at all) about Sherwood Anderson, which is remarkable and unfortunate given his still-lingering influence on American fiction. Any discussion of Anderson and his work would be incomplete without addressing the issues and themes that routinely enter into Anderson criticism: his reaction to realism and naturalism; his modernist version of local-color fiction; his attention to the hidden drives, especially sexual, that occasionally rise to the surface of an individual's behavior. But of course Anderson's work transcends any reductive attempt to place it in a simple category. His wit and humor and caring attention to details that are routinely overlooked explain why he continues to be read by writers if not by many students.

Classroom Issues and Strategies

"The Book of the Grotesque" is a fascinating and entertaining short story in its own right. The coy narrator, who obviously identifies with (but is not the same person as) the old writer, develops a voice that is memorable as much for what he conceals as for what he reveals. The narrator's reticence makes the strange, almost allegorical waking dream of the old writer doubly suggestive. We are left with more questions than answers: In what ways are the figures on parade "grotesque"? What is the distinction between "thoughts" and "truths"? What does the narrator understand now that he has seen "The Book of the Grotesque"? The short story's self-referentiality is a quintessentially modernist gesture, but one that's homespun and hospitable.

In addition to the remarkable and unprecedented portrayals of small-town characters – Wing Biddlebaum is among the most memorable in American literature – the narrator of *Winesburg, Ohio* deploys an impressionistic style to delve into the characters' hidden lives both past and present. At one point in "Hands" the narrator concedes that Biddlebaum's distressing youth "needs the poet" to do it justice, but there's much poetry in

Anderson's deceptively simple prose. In "Paper Pills," for example, a host of overlapping symbols – Doctor Reefy's knotted hands, the "gnarled, twisted apples," and the paper wads stuffed into the doctor's pockets – lend resonance and depth to a life whose unremarkable surface masks the character's true self.

Connections to Other Authors and Texts

Anderson was moved to approach prose form as an experiment by Gertrude Stein, who remained a close friend for much of Anderson's career. Ernest Hemingway and Jean Toomer were also close associates during the early parts of their careers in the 1920s, and their work during that period displays Anderson's obvious influence.

Questions for Class Discussion

1. What seems to be the point of "The Book of the Grotesque"? How does this introductory short story relate to those that follow? Is there anything grotesque about Anderson's style of fiction?
2. What do we know about the narrator? How old is he (or is it possibly a she)? Is he rich or poor or in-between? How well does he seem to know the short stories' characters? Which characters does he seem closest to?
3. The narrator often looks back in time, into an eventful moment in a character's past. What prompts the backward glance? How does a character's past determine his future?

Brief Bibliography

Bloom, Harold, ed. *Sherwood Anderson*. Philadelphia: Chelsea House, 2003.

Crowley, John W. *New Essays on* Winesburg, Ohio. Cambridge: Cambridge UP, 1990.

Rideout, Walter B. *Sherwood Anderson: A Writer in America*. Madison: U of Wisconsin P, 2006.

KATHERINE ANNE PORTER   (p. 869)

Approaches to Teaching

A short story as densely woven together as "Flowering Judas" can be off-putting to many students. Where to begin to make sense of its multilayered symbols; its distinct, present-tense narration; or its idiosyncratic characters? The ending in particular frustrates some readers: The narrative's lapse into free, indirect discourse ("1-2-3-4-5 – it is monstrous to confuse love with revolution, night with day, life with death – ah, Eugenio!") and the hazy line between hard reality and dreamscape confound those with little experience negotiating the formal challenges of modernism. Reassurance demands a careful explanation of the short story's basic elements (point-of-view, focus, tense) so that students can confidently engage its more open-ended features (symbols, themes, "meaning"). With careful study, the narrator might be seen as Laura's alter ego. This realization helps explain the vexing ending: How else, we might conclude, should a guilty conscience be narrated?

Classroom Issues and Strategies

"Flowering Judas" is narrated in the present tense, suggesting an eternal present throughout the short story – that is, with a key exception at the center of the narrative. In the middle of paragraph fifteen, the narration shifts to the past tense: "No dancer dances more beautifully than Laura walks, and she inspires some amusing, unexpected ardors, which cause little gossip, because nothing comes of them. A young captain who had been a soldier in Zapata's army attempted, during a horseback ride near Cuernavaca, to express his desire for her. . . ." We quickly come to realize that Laura's interaction with a procession of suitors may elicit little gossip, but they're centrally important to the short story. The shift in tense is one small register that the men represent competing versions of romantic love and distinct possible futures for Laura. If we read the possibility of romantic union allegorically, as a commentary on ancient chivalry or the modern art of publishing or revolutionary politics (as a number of critics have), then the narrative's backward glance is more than incidental. The striking, animalistic characterization of Braggioni at the start of the short story (the language points to his subhuman qualities: "heaped," "furry," "surly," "snarling") suggests that even characters deserve symbolic interpretation.

The short story's symbols may be easy to identify, but their larger importance is shifting and opaque. Rather than suggest specific readings of individual symbols – at least initially – it is often useful to prod students by asking them about how a symbol's meaning would be shifted with only slight modification: What if Braggioni had eagle's eyes instead of "cat's eyes"? What if Braggioni's wife washed his face instead of his feet? What if a cock crowed at midnight instead of the bell tolling? What if Laura dreamt about a palm tree instead of a Judas tree?

Connections to Other Authors and Texts

Like María Cristina Mena, Porter's fiction helped shape American views of Mexico (and in particular revolutionary Mexico). Her example would

inspire generations of writers, perhaps none more directly than Eudora
Welty.

Questions for Class Discussion

1. How would you characterize the language used to describe Braggioni?
2. Where is "Flowering Judas" narrated in the present tense? Where is the
   short story narrated in the past tense? How does the past inform the
   present (and vice versa)?
3. Where is the narrator's voice overtaken by the thoughts or words of
   specific characters? What is the function of such "free, indirect discourse" in the short story's telling?
4. List the images that appear to function as Christian symbols. How do
   individual characters relate to Christian symbolism?

Brief Bibliography

Carr, Virginia Spencer, ed. *"Flowering Judas": Katherine Anne Porter.* New
    Brunswick: Rutgers UP, 1993.

Givner, Joan. *Katherine Anne Porter: A Life.* Rev. ed. Athens: U of Georgia P,
    1991.

Titus, Mary. *The Ambivalent Art of Katherine Anne Porter.* Athens: U of
    Georgia P, 2005.

Unrue, Darlene Harbour, ed. *Critical Essays on Katherine Anne Porter.* New
    York: Hall, 1997.

ZORA NEALE HURSTON   (p. 880)

Approaches to Teaching

Because *Their Eyes Were Watching God* (1937) is one of the most frequently
assigned novels in American high schools and colleges, a large percentage
of students will have already come into contact with Hurston's work;
indeed, many students will already have strong opinions about Hurston,
usually (but not always) quite positive. "The Gilded Six-Bits," one of
Hurston's best-known short stories, develops some of the themes and formal approaches found in the more famous novel – including modern challenges to romantic fidelity and the prominent use of dialect to spur on and
give shape to the narrative – but the short story is more deceptively simple
than *Their Eyes.* Unlike the novel, "The Gilded Six-Bits" does not offer a
protagonist whose storytelling obviously mirrors the author's craft, but it
does deploy a stunning literary artistry.

Classroom Issues and Strategies

A central question occupies most students: Why does Joe forgive Missie May at the end of the short story? It's worthwhile to allow students to speculate about the possible motives behind his gesture of forgiveness, or her act of betrayal, and usually students will invent a suitable history for the two fictional characters. In other words, they will provide the characters with depth, seeing in their humble devotion to each other a redemptive alternative to the slickness of Otis D. Slemmons and finding in their dialect speech patterns a simple eloquence. Hurston's revolutionary contribution to American fiction is what allows for speculation: She gives nuance and insight to characters who, like Joe and Missie May, speak dialect, a form previously associated with two-dimensional simpletons.

Hurston's politics – if one delves into the subject – are also complicated by the short story. Although many Hurston scholars regard her views, especially during and after World War II, as an apology for American imperialism, they ran a wide gamut of opinion. As Hildegard Hoeller demonstrates in a fascinating interpretation of the short story, Hurston's politics when it came to monetary policy tended toward populism, and "The Gilded Six-Bits" might be understood as a subtle exploration of issues of monetary exchange and racial identity. In a more obvious sense, the short story takes aim at fast-talking urbanites who hoodwink the laboring class.

Connections to Other Authors and Texts

Although Hurston has obvious forerunners when it comes to the use of dialect – including Paul Laurence Dunbar and James Weldon Johnson – she broke new ground with the form. Her work is regularly cited as a major force in the Harlem Renaissance, and she directly inspired Alice Walker's career.

Questions for Class Discussion

1. The first three paragraphs of the short story carefully describe its setting. What is the significance of the description?
2. Explain the symbolic meaning of the iconic, rich white men (Rockefeller, Ford, Packard, Cadillac) who are mentioned in "The Gilded Six-Bits."
3. Joe and Missie May are compared with well-known biblical figures. How do the references operate in the short story?

Brief Bibliography

Bloom, Harold, ed. *Zora Neale Hurston*. New York: Chelsea House, 1986.

Boyd, Valerie. *Wrapped in Rainbows: The Life of Zora Neale Hurston*. New York: Scribner, 2003.

Hoeller, Hildegard. "Racial Currency: Zora Neale Hurston's 'The Gilded Six-Bits' and the Gold-Standard Debate." *American Literature* 77 (2005): 761-85.

NELLA LARSEN   (p. 891)

Approaches to Teaching

Whenever one teaches Nella Larsen's "Sanctuary," the elephant in the room is the charge of plagiarism that, according to most Larsen biographers, brought her red-hot literary career to a halt. (George Hutchinson's new biography of Larsen complicates received wisdom about the subject.) Just after the short story was published in the *Forum* in 1930, a reader notified the magazine's editors that Larsen's work bore an uncanny resemblance to Sheila Kaye-Smith's "Mrs. Adis," first published eight years before in the *Century*. (The looming literary scandal was the talk of the town well before it broke publicly.) Although the *Forum*'s editors agreed with Larsen's explanation – that the resemblance was an extraordinary coincidence, based probably on a shared folkloric source – Larsen never published fiction again and settled into professional life as a nurse. Even Larsen's most ardent supporters tend to agree that she was at best an unintentional plagiarist, that she was the victim of an unconscious desire to rewrite the work of a successful white writer or that she was betrayed by a near photographic memory. Virtually all commentators find that her explanation of the resemblances, published in a subsequent issue of the *Forum*, remains unconvincing. Rather than shy away from a discussion of the plagiarism charge, the similarities between "Sanctuary" and "Mrs. Adis" might form the basis of several thoughtful approaches to the work.

Classroom Issues and Strategies

A side-by-side examination of the text of "Sanctuary" and the text of "Mrs. Adis" reveals resemblances too striking to dismiss. The basic plot of the short stories, as well as specific physical descriptions and several examples of dialogue, are virtually identical. Whenever I ask students to compare the two short stories and to adjudge Larsen based on the same honor code to which the students are bound, they almost always find her guilty of plagiarism. But then I ask them to decide which short story they find more successful. Again there is almost unanimous agreement, this time in Larsen's favor. Her handling of character is more nuanced than Kaye-Smith's, and Larsen's modulation of the narrative's pace is effective without the melodrama of "Mrs. Adis." Even Larsen's use of dialect – a feature of her work found only in "Sanctuary" – lends realism to the characters' speech without a heavy hand. Even though "Sanctuary" may be derivative, it is nevertheless a gripping short story.

But perhaps charges of "derivativeness" begin with the wrong premise. In a recent and provocative analysis of the short story, Hildegard Hoeller makes the case that rather than view "Sanctuary" as a plagiarized version of an authentic source, we see Larsen's fiction instead as a "racialized masquerade," a primitivist-modernist appropriation and updating of a stale European form: "Even if we assume that Larsen indeed had Kaye-Smith's text in front of her, it is hard to consider her revisions 'plagiarism.' They come closer to an experiment in literary voice and form." Seen in its appropriate cultural historical context, Hoeller offers, "Sanctuary" is best understood as a critique of the prevailing discourse of modernism, which views as perfectly acceptable the appropriation and repackaging of so-called primitive forms.

Connections to Other Authors and Texts

Whether or not Larsen plagiarized from Sheila Kaye-Smith, a writer known for depicting the regional culture of Sussex, in England, Larsen's "Sanctuary" certainly follows in the regionalist tradition exemplified by a number of writers in the anthology: Mark Twain, Charles Chesnutt, and Kate Chopin (to name just three). She was also among the most celebrated fiction writers of the Harlem Renaissance.

Questions for Class Discussion

1. Identify the most suspenseful moment in "Sanctuary." How does the short story build suspense? How is the suspense resolved?

2. Explain the significance of the "snowy sheets" and the "freshly laundered linen" in which Jim hides.

3. Compare the text of Larsen's short story with that of Sheila Kaye-Smith's "Mrs. Adis" (1922). Do you think Larsen plagiarized Kaye-Smith's text? Why or why not?

Brief Bibliography

Hoeller, Hildegard. "Race, Modernism, and Plagiarism: The Case of Nella Larsen's 'Sanctuary.'" *African American Review* 40 (2006): 421-37.

Hutchinson, George. *In Search of Nella Larsen: A Biography of the Color Line.* Cambridge: Harvard UP, 2006.

Kaye-Smith, Sheila. "Mrs. Adis." *Century* 103 (January 1922): 320-26.

MARÍA CRISTINA MENA   (p. 898)

Approaches to Teaching

With the possible exception of living writers, María Cristina Mena is the newest addition to the American literary canon among all the writers represented in *The Bedford Anthology of American Literature*. Her short stories were difficult to find before they were collected (by Amy Doherty) in 1997 as part of Arte Público Press's Recovering the U.S. Literary Heritage Project, which republishes out-of-print work by Latino writers. Scholars usually address two important features of Mena's life and work: first, the unlikely circumstance of a Mexican American woman writer who published in mainstream U.S. journals at a time of extreme xenophobia; and second, her opposition to the negative cultural stereotypes that regularly sustain the rhetoric of manifest destiny. "The Vine-Leaf" allows for such discussion, at least provisionally, and the issues should unquestionably contribute to any discussion of Mena. Still, it would be unfortunate to restrict the conversation to literary history and cultural critique; indeed, Mena belongs in the American canon because of her clever and compelling approach to narrative form.

Classroom Issues and Strategies

The scenario set in motion in "The Vine-Leaf" — a male doctor shares a tale so that he might assuage a female patient's reluctance to confide in him — seems reminiscent of a folksy but contrived vehicle for generating fiction. (Even the opening phrase of the short story, "It is a saying in the capital of Mexico . . . ," imposes the tone of homespun narrative.) At the same time, Mena's short story achieves a formal unity and coherence, without a detail out of place, resembling the works of Hawthorne and Henry James. The narrator's attenuated asides — "I've forgotten which one" and "but that has nothing to do with this story," for instance — might be considered evidence of the artistic placement of seemingly artless expression.

Nowhere is Mena defter than in her handling of the relationship between the third-person narrator and the principal character, Dr. Malsufrido. (The English translation of *malsufrido* is "impatient.") Because a conversation between Malsufrido and an unnamed female patient comprises much of the narrative, the doctor in effect serves as the short story's narrator; Malsufrido even refers to himself in the third person. The arrangement suggests an analogy between the doctor and the narrator, and by extension between medicine and writing. One might extend the analogy further by considering the connection between being a patient and reading fiction.

Connections to Other Authors and Texts

It is tempting to discuss Mena alongside other writers who inhabit the margins of American literary culture, but the facts of her early life (she was a well-educated member of the Mexican elite who published in mainstream U.S. journals) warrant some caution. "The Vine-Leaf" most closely resembles the work of writers interested in playful and clever narration, including Edith Wharton and Willa Cather. The short story is probably closest in spirit to "Flowering Judas," by Mena's fellow recorder of Mexican social life, Katherine Anne Porter.

Questions for Class Discussion

1. Compare the narrator and Dr. Malsufrido. In what ways do their voices overlap? In what ways do their voices diverge?

2. "The Vine-Leaf" is technically a murder mystery, but it isn't very mysterious. If issues of guilt and innocence are of secondary importance to the short story, what issues come first?

3. Although the narrator makes light of his religious views, Dr. Malsufrido considers himself a confessor. What ethical or moral standards does Dr. Malsufrido adhere to?

Brief Bibliography

Doherty, Amy. "Redefining the Borders of Local Color Fiction: María Cristina Mena's Short Stories in the *Century Magazine*." *"The Only Efficient Instrument": American Women Writers and the Periodical, 1837–1916*. Eds. Aleta Feinsod Cane and Susan Alves. Iowa City: U of Iowa P, 2001. 165–78.

Garza-Falcón, Leticia. *Gente Decente: A Borderlands Response to the Rhetoric of Dominance*. Austin: U of Texas P, 1998.

Leal, Luis. "María Cristina Mena (María Cristina Chambers)." *Chicano Writers: Third Series*. Eds. Francisco A. Lomelí and Carl R. Shirley. Detroit: Gale, 1999. 150–54.

JEAN TOOMER   (p. 905)

Approaches to Teaching

With the publication of *Cane* in 1923, the Harlem Renaissance intelligentsia unanimously celebrated Jean Toomer as the movement's rising star and the book as a harbinger of many similar great works to come. Then as now, critics regard the singular book as significantly modern and modernist, a far cry from the "plantation darkie" stereotypes of the unreconstructed South. Students familiar with the various –isms of modernism – including imagism, futurism, and surrealism – will have at their disposal the same building blocks that Toomer worked with in assembling *Cane,* a unique assortment of poems and prose sketches set in the Deep South and in Washington, D.C., and Chicago. Students not familiar with modernist movements will find surer footing approaching *Cane* with more traditional literary themes – including tragic love triangles and the literary strategy of the blazon – in mind. Interestingly, Toomer is also the only figure who has been identified as a member of both the Harlem Renaissance and the Lost Generation – a literary historical stand-in for the question, Was he black or white? The productive tensions between convention and innovation, between black and white, are among the best ways to approach Toomer and his work.

Classroom Issues and Strategies

"Blood-Burning Moon" is one of the more conventional prose sketches in *Cane:* It has a stable, third-person narrator who relays events in the past tense; it has an easily recognizable cast of a few characters; it occupies a short and one-directional time span; and it relays a tragic occurrence (an interracial love triangle that results in a brutal lynching) that's eerily familiar in American literature. Even so, the narrative demonstrates Toomer's experimental streak on occasion: The narrative focus switches between Louisa, Bob, Tom, and the town folk, at times external to their consciousnesses, at times residing deep within their inner thoughts; the narrative also incorporates a poetic refrain ("Red nigger moon. Sinner! / Blood-burning moon. Sinner! / Come out that fact'ry door") that anticipates the narrative's violent conclusion and that is alternately sung by individuals and by the entire community. "Blood-Burning Moon" is a gripping tale in its own right; highlighting the intricate narrative design adds further dimension to students' understanding of the work.

"Portrait in Georgia" and "Seventh Street" depart fairly sharply from "Blood-Burning Moon" in terms of their radically experimental forms. ("Portrait in Georgia" immediately precedes "Blood-Burning Moon" at the conclusion of part 1 of *Cane,* and "Seventh Street" opens part 2.) "Portrait in Georgia" anticipates the prose sketch by invoking the theme of interracial sexual desire and a violent lynching, but its grotesque use of the blazon – comparing hair to a lyncher's rope, eyes to burning fagots, lips to scars, and skin to white ash – updates the literary convention in a brutal and disturbing way. "Seventh Street" occupies a blurry space between poetry and prose. Its jazz-inflected rhythms evoke African American street life in Prohibition-era Washington, D.C., but the effect is produced entirely impressionistically. No time transpires during the sketch, and although the geography is fairly discrete, no characters inhabit its space. Not even the narrator can be pinned down to a recognizable figure.

Connections to Other Authors and Texts

Toomer was a good friend and admirer of Sherwood Anderson and Hart Crane, and his prose and poetry bears traces of their respective influences. Toomer also admired and studied T. S. Eliot and the imagists. But Toomer is most often discussed as a member of the Harlem Renaissance, and indeed his novel approach to representing southern folklife helped inspire writers such as Sterling Brown, Langston Hughes, and Zora Neale Hurston. And much of Toomer's work contributes to the literature of lynching, a tradition that also includes contributions from Pauline Hopkins, Sterling Brown, and James Baldwin.

Questions for Class Discussion

1. Follow the narrative's focus in "Blood-Burning Moon." At a given moment in the sketch, which character does the narrator seem to be hovering around? Is the narrator describing the situation external to the character, or is the narrator privy to the character's hidden thoughts?

2. Who utters the refrain of "Blood-Burning Moon" ("Red nigger moon. Sinner! . . .")?

3. What seems conventional (in terms of form or theme) in "Portrait in Georgia"? What seems innovative or experimental about the poem?

4. List the ways in which Toomer personifies the urban geography described in "Seventh Street." What is the rhetorical effect of such personification? In other words, what seems to be the point?

Brief Bibliography

Fabre, Geneviève and Michel Feith, eds. *Jean Toomer and the Harlem Renaissance.* New Brunswick: Rutgers UP, 2001.

Kerman, Cynthia Earl, and Richard Eldridge. *The Lives of Jean Toomer: A Hunger for Wholeness.* Baton Rouge: Louisiana State UP, 1987.

Thompson Cager, Chezia. *Teaching Jean Toomer's 1923* Cane. New York: Lang, 2006.

F. SCOTT FITZGERALD   (p. 915)

Approaches to Teaching

As David W. Ullrich points out, F. Scott Fitzgerald's reputation has always suffered from a perceived lack of gravitas. Unfortunately, the titles of the publications in which "The Ice Palace" originally appeared – *Saturday Evening Post* (May 1920) and *Flappers and Philosophers* (1920) – reinforce the image of a naive but lucky genius, as do the Jazz Age symbols that lend their allure to many high school prom themes. Fortunately, many if not most students will already have read *The Great Gatsby* (1925), and so instructors can take full advantage of a comparison between the short story and Fitzgerald's best-known novel. Among the points of comparison are clever and absolutely memorable phrases, an obviously (but subtly) symbolic landscape, a focus on the social habits and mores of the upper classes, an examination of regional differences (and similarities), and an implicit critique of U.S. society. And although the narrator of "The Ice Palace" is nowhere near as memorable as Nick Carraway, the short story's narration still clings to a single character (Sally Carrol Happer) and is obviously influenced by her worldview.

Classroom Issues and Strategies

The major source of critical controversy surrounding "The Ice Palace" is the extent to which Fitzgerald reinforces or undermines regional stereotypes; the controversy suggests that regional identity in the short story provides fertile ground for discussion. Regional difference takes shape in numerous and sometimes conflicted ways in "The Ice Palace": southern dialect versus standard written (and spoken) English; southern versus northern landscape and architecture; "Scandinavian" versus "American" phenotype and state of mind; attitudes about the past, present, and future U.S. economy and society; and of course the southern cemetery versus the northern ice palace. The indolent, bob-haired Sally Carrol and the peppy, socially conscious Harry complicate any simplistic North-South binaries, as does the judgmental and arguably racist narrator. Sally Carrol and Harry's romance suggests the possibility – ultimately frustrated – of sectional reconciliation and national transcendence.

   It would be a shame for students to encounter "The Ice Palace" without gaining a sense of what's Fitzgeraldian about it. Fortunately, there is no shortage of memorably Fitzgeraldian phrases in the short story, even in the opening paragraphs: "bobbed corn-colored hair with a rose-littered sunbonnet" (to describe Sally Carrol's appearance); "this languid paradise of dreamy skies and firefly evenings and noisy street fairs" (to describe the appearance and especially the mood of the city of Tarleton); "brought up on memories instead of money" (to describe how southern girls are raised).

Connections to Other Authors and Texts

As a central figure of the so-called Lost Generation, there are many other writers in the anthology who share chronology and social space (if not writing style) with Fitzgerald, including Ernest Hemingway, Gertrude Stein, and John Dos Passos. Texts that share a similar interest in exploring sectional differences in narrative form include Willa Cather's "A Wagner Matinée" and Katherine Anne Porter's "Flowering Judas."

Questions for Class Discussion

1. What is southern about Sally Carrol? What is northern about Harry? What *should* the characters learn about themselves and about others by the short story's end? Based solely on the evidence supplied by the text, what *do* they learn?

2. Fitzgerald implies a strong connection between a cemetery and the South and between the ice palace and the North. What does each site represent about the respective U.S. regions? How do each site's physical properties contribute to your interpretation?

3. How does phenotype represent an individual's character traits according to the short story's logic? In other words, what does the way a character looks reveal about her or his personality?

4. Locate phrases that seem unique to Fitzgerald's writing. What makes them "Fitzgeraldian"?

Brief Bibliography

Hook, Andrew. *F. Scott Fitzgerald: A Literary Life.* New York: Palgrave Macmillan, 2002.

Kuehl, John. *F. Scott Fitzgerald: A Study of the Short Fiction.* Boston: Twayne, 1991.

Petry, Alice Hall. *Fitzgerald's Craft of Short Fiction: The Collected Stories, 1920–1935.* Tuscaloosa: U of Alabama P, 1989.

Ullrich, David W. "Memorials and Monuments: Historical Method and the (Re)construction of Memory in F. Scott Fitzgerald's 'The Ice Palace.'" *Studies in Short Fiction* 36 (1999): 417–36.

JOHN DOS PASSOS   (p. 937)

Approaches to Teaching

Perhaps the most difficult part of teaching John Dos Passos and representing faithfully his legacy for today's students is contextualizing the political
climate that gave rise to his views and career. The post-World War I era was
a time of almost millennial hope and fear throughout the globe, and the
future shape of U.S. society and government were considered entirely up
for grabs in many circles. Radical views were part of mainstream political
discussion and found their way into the venues that published Dos Passos's
work. But Dos Passos was a literary artist, not a propagandist. This aspect
of his work is fairly self-evident, but it becomes even more so when his
work is contrasted against, for example, the preamble to the constitution of
the Industrial Workers of the World (available online at www.iww.org/
culture/official/preamble.shtm). The unique shape and structure of "1919 –
Two Portraits" and the lyricism of "Vag" – not their politics – explain their
inclusion in the anthology.

Classroom Issues and Strategies

The portraits found in "1919 – Two Portraits" descend from ancient cultural
traditions, literary portraiture and elegy, but their distinct shape and tone
render them utterly modern and modernist. Whether or not students are
familiar with Morgan (a likely bet) or Bourne (doubtful), they will undoubtedly have some familiarity with the conventions associated with descriptions of the dearly departed. It is helpful to ask students to comment on (or
to point out to them directly) how Dos Passos's language either honors or
disparages the memories of the two men who died during the 1910s.

The prose of "Vag" is written primarily in the third person, but Dos
Passos experiments with narrative focus and with point of view to offer a
multidimensional understanding of the title figure, a young vagrant who
wanders the American road. At times the description is external to the character and fairly objective, at other times we are given access to his innermost
feelings and distant memories. A long (ten paragraph) parenthetical aside
then lifts us into an airplane and we see the American continent through the
eyes and ears of well-to-do airplane passengers. The effect is dizzying and
remarkable: In the space of a few hundred words we are introduced to the
wide variety of American society members and American landscapes.

Connections to Other Authors and Texts

The politics if not the styles of Theodore Dreiser and Frank Norris suggest
one way of locating Dos Passos in American literary history. During World

War I, Dos Passos grew to know and admire E. E. Cummings, and subsequently Ernest Hemingway was an important figure in Dos Passos's career.

Questions for Class Discussion

1. How do the idiosyncratic grammar and formatting of "1919 – Two Portraits" influence the reading experience?

2. How would you contrast the tone of the two parts of "1919 – Two Portraits"? How is the difference achieved?

3. "Vag" was also published as the concluding vignette of Dos Passos's epic trilogy, *U.S.A.* In what ways is the vignette appropriate as an ending to a much longer work? In what ways does the sketch stand alone as a discrete form of literary expression?

Brief Bibliography

Carr, Virginia Spencer. *Dos Passos: A Life.* Evanston: Northwestern UP, 2004.

Nanney, Lisa. *John Dos Passos.* New York: Twayne, 1998.

WILLIAM FAULKNER   (p. 948)

Approaches to Teaching

The public persona that William Faulkner cultivated for most of his career – that of a wayward Southern genius with bottle in hand – sometimes comes between students and a full appreciation of his work. That so much of it takes place in the fictional and now-legendary Yoknapatawpha County does little to separate the fiction from the mythical fiction writer. This is not to suggest that students can't enjoy Faulkner partly based on his reputation; rather, it's to offer a way beyond the reputation. Students with an active interest in creative writing will be especially drawn to Faulkner's short stories and with good reason: His unique brand of storytelling is considered the epitome of American literary modernism and he has inspired generations of the world's greatest writers.

Classroom Issues and Strategies

"That Evening Sun" records a moment in the young life of its narrator, Quentin Compson, a central character in Faulkner's fiction whose intelligence and introspection, qualities that ultimately lead to his suicide, distinguish him from other characters in *The Sound and the Fury* (1929) and

Absalom, Absalom! (1936). In "That Evening Sun," Quentin's adult self, the self that presumably looks back on events from fifteen years earlier, is quickly submerged in the naive and confused memories of the nine-year-old boy. The children are only dimly aware of the sexual indiscretion, class and race inequality, and danger that inform the adults' understanding of events. The short story's narrative approach to naivete is a clever (and potentially confusing) distillation of partially overheard conversations and incomplete descriptions of characters and places.

"Barn Burning" is similarly confusing even though the short story is told by a third-person narrator. The modernist confusion – perhaps better understood as modernist insight – derives from the narrative's focus around Sarty Snopes, a character whose sense of family loyalty comes into sharp conflict with a more universal understanding of social responsibility and justice. Descriptions of petty thievery take on a healthy dose of irony when the narrator juxtaposes the young boy's ignorance and the lessons that he will learn later in life: "The nights were still cool and they had a fire against it, of a rail lifted from a nearby fence and cut into lengths – a small fire, neat, niggard almost, a shrewd fire; such fires were his father's habit and custom always, even in freezing weather. Older, the boy might have remarked this and wondered why not a big one; why should not a man who had not only seen the waste and extravagance of war, but who had in his blood an inherent voracious prodigality with material that was not his own, have burned everything in sight?" An example such as this highlights in miniature the elegance of Faulkner's prose and the keenness of his insight. The gap between a character's innocence and his subsequent experience is a major theme of Faulkner's work.

Connections to Other Authors and Texts

Faulkner is one of the quintessential modernists, whose experimentation with narrative form makes his fiction as difficult and rewarding as that written by such figures as Gertrude Stein, Katherine Anne Porter, and Jean Toomer. Like his fellow Mississippi writers Richard Wright and Eudora Welty, Faulkner's fiction is both local in scope and universal in theme.

Questions for Class Discussion

1. "That Evening Sun" is narrated fifteen years after the events it describes. At what point in the short story is the narration fully immersed in the past? What distinguishes the adult Quentin's narration from the child Quentin's recollections?

2. How many separate characters inhabit "Barn Burning"? How many separate dialects inhabit the story? List the characters and dialects in order of social standing.

3. Other than spoken language use (i.e., dialect), how does Faulkner introduce social difference in "Barn Burning"? In other words, how do people look and act in ways that suggest their social positions?

4. Because Sarty Snopes is the story's narrative focus (i.e., the center of
   consciousness who informs the narrator's storytelling), the narrative
   at times appears confused and confusing. What moments in the story
   are most confused? What is Sarty's state of mind at these moments?
   What does the narrator's perspective add that Sarty seems incapable
   of understanding; in other words, how does the narrator interpret the
   "facts" of the story?

Brief Bibliography

Jones, Diane Brown. *A Reader's Guide to the Short Stories of William
   Faulkner.* New York: Hall, 1994.

Porter, Carolyn. *William Faulkner.* Oxford: Oxford UP, 2007.

Skei, Hans H. *Reading Faulkner's Best Short Stories.* Columbia: U of South
   Carolina P, 1999.

ERNEST HEMINGWAY   (p. 976)

Approaches to Teaching

Feminist scholars have been razing the myth of "Papa" – the notion that
Hemingway embodied a hard-working, hard-playing, booze-fueled, woman-
izing machismo; that he drank and fished and hunted and loved and fought
as well as he wrote – for longer than most college students have been alive.
In fact, "Big Two-Hearted River" has been the regular subject of feminist
reappraisal. For these reasons, it may be necessary to summarize the
Hemingway myth and, more important, to describe how "Big Two-Hearted
River" conforms to or departs from those features we expect in
"Hemingwayesque" prose. The short story certainly meets several of the
myth's demands: Characterization is stripped down ("hard-boiled") to its
barest essentials, with little or no moralizing and only subtle clues about
what motivates Nick; the setting and plot might be understood as masculinist disavowals of the trappings of civilization; the Great War looms
ominously in the background; and the plot revolves around the basics of
hiking, camping, and fishing. But if students are to appreciate
Hemingway's most important contributions to American literature – say,
A Farewell to Arms or *For Whom the Bell Tolls* – they should leave behind
any preconceptions that might be suggested by the short story and especially any preconceptions based on the myth of Papa. In the end, close

scrutiny of the short story's formal dynamics proves much more rewarding than adherence to a ham-fisted myth.

Classroom Issues and Strategies

The narrator of "Big Two-Hearted River," about whom we know next to nothing, tells us surprisingly little about its protagonist, Nick Adams. Nevertheless, we can supply considerable character traits on top of what's sometimes (but not always) explicitly stated. Be sure to highlight – or ask students to identify – portions of the narrative that reveal Nick's emotional state and generosity (or parsimony) of feeling. You may wish to mention that Nick is a recurring character in Hemingway's short fiction and that they can discover more about Nick for themselves in *In Our Time* (1925) and especially *The Nick Adams Stories* (1972). Even so, "Big Two-Hearted River" was published separately in *This Quarter* and stands alone very well.

The short story's famous silence about the war is practically deafening. The burnt-out ruins of Seney, seen fleetingly, perhaps reluctantly, through Nick's eyes, resemble a postapocalyptic battlefield. Nick's obsessive attention to detail is often interpreted as a sign that he suffers from post-traumatic stress disorder (or "shell-shock" as it was known at the time). His journey farther and farther into the wilderness is a means of escape, a return to simpler, happier routines and memories. And as Paul Civello suggests, the grasshoppers and trout killed by Nick might be understood as a sacrifice meant to purge chaotic wartime violence with ritualistic and redemptive violence.

Connections to Other Authors and Texts

As the most famous member of the Lost Generation that he helped to mythologize, Hemingway should be considered alongside the group's elder statespersons such as Sherwood Anderson and Gertrude Stein as well as its younger stars such as E. E. Cummings, John Dos Passos, and F. Scott Fitzgerald. Hemingway's subtle treatment of the Great War is strikingly muted in contrast to obvious antiwar fiction by Mark Twain (Hemingway's hero) and Ambrose Bierce.

Questions for Class Discussion

1. Select any paragraph from the short story. Count the number of words in the paragraph, then divide by the number of syllables in the paragraph. How many syllables per word does the paragraph contain? Provide a list of themes that the paragraph explores. For example, paragraph 1 has 111 words and 121 syllables, or an average of 1.09 syllables per word. In addition to introducing the short story's only charac-

ter, the paragraph explores themes of human versus mechanized travel, the violent force of nature, and individual isolation in the wake of social destruction.

2. Locate the rare moments when the narrator directly reports something that Nick says aloud. How does the narrator qualify Nick's spoken utterances? How does the narrator reveal Nick's inner thoughts?

3. What "writerly" qualities does Nick possess? How are hiking, camping, and fishing like writing?

Brief Bibliography

Baker, Carlos. *Ernest Hemingway: A Life Story.* New York: Collier, 1988.

Bloom, Harold, ed. *Nick Adams.* Philadelphia: Chelsea House, 2004.

Civello, Paul. "Hemingway's 'Primitivism': Archetypal Patterns in 'Big Two-Hearted River.'" *Hemingway Review* 13 (1993): 1-16.

Wagner-Martin, Linda. *A Historical Guide to Ernest Hemingway.* New York: Oxford UP, 2000.

JOHN STEINBECK   (p. 993)

Approaches to Teaching

John Steinbeck's approach to narrative form at the macro level varies so greatly that it would be misleading to suggest that "Flight" is representative of his fiction style. Throughout his career, Steinbeck sought to match narrative form with subject matter: picaresque for *Tortilla Flat* (1935), social realism for *In Dubious Battle* (1936) and *The Grapes of Wrath* (1939), and psychological (perhaps autobiographical) introspection in his late novels. Still, there are important ways in which "Flight" evokes recurring themes in the whole of Steinbeck's work: a narrative focus around a plain-spoken individual from a simple rural society; the all-important factor of intense biological drives, especially the will to survive; and a richly drawn landscape, with flora and fauna that serve important roles in the narrative's plot and symbolism. But "Flight" is a riveting short story in its own right; Pepé Torres's harrowing travels across the California landscape provide ample material for lively classroom discussion.

Classroom Issues and Strategies

A central theme addressed in "Flight" and somewhat common in Steinbeck's work (and modernist literature more generally) is the emergence, often painful, from childhood into adulthood. Pepé's wish to be a man, and more important to be recognized as a man by others, at first assumes a comic aspect (a hatband and a green handkerchief do the trick), only to take a tragic turn by the short story's end. Steinbeck deploys a number of symbols to explore the theme of a tragic route to manhood: The landscape is increasingly rugged and dry and deadly; Pepé is virtually integrated into the mountain pass's animal society, suggesting that manhood requires a radical departure from feminized society (a ubiquitous theme in literary westerns); and Pepé's nameless, faceless pursuer takes on an otherworldly, sinister aspect.

Steinbeck's representation of Mexican American characters has drawn criticism since the publication of *Tortilla Flat* – they tend to be demeaning, rustic character types rather than fully formed individuals, some contend – and the Torres family in "Flight" warrants some attention in this respect. The characters' physical descriptions – Mama Torres is a "lean, dry woman with ancient eyes," her youngest children are "two undersized black ones," and Pepé has "sharp Indian cheek bones and an eagle nose" – set the stage for their narrow (for better and for worse) range of responses to trouble. The Torres family also speaks a colloquial Spanish, often translated into an archaic English abundant in *thees* and *thous* (meant to signify the familiar Spanish second-person pronoun).

Connections to Other Authors and Texts

The naturalism of Stephen Crane and Jack London anticipates Steinbeck's approach in "Flight." Although he had precursors (such as Mary Austin), Steinbeck would help define the California experience in American literature.

Questions for Class Discussion

1. How does Pepé "perform" his childhood or manhood? How does he act and dress and speak and otherwise look the part?

2. How does Pepé's flight render him more and more animal-like? To what extent does he retain his humanity despite increasingly difficult circumstances?

3. Feel free to speculate as you answer these questions: Who are the "dark watchers" inhabiting the California foothills? Who is pursuing Pepé? What does the pursuit represent (beyond the literal flight from justice)?

Brief Bibliography

Hughes, R. S. *John Steinbeck: A Study of the Short Fiction.* New York: Twayne, 1989.

Parini, Jay. *John Steinbeck: A Biography*. New York: Holt, 1995.

Timmerman, John H. *The Dramatic Landscape of Steinbeck's Short Stories*. Norman: U of Oklahoma P, 1990.

RICHARD WRIGHT   (p. 1008)

Approaches to Teaching

Richard Wright's short story first appeared as "Almos' a Man" in 1939, when Wright was at the height of his fame and powers as a writer. (He had recently brought out *Uncle Tom's Children* [1938], and would soon publish *Native Son* [1940] and *Black Boy* [1945].) It would be republished as "The Man Who Was Almost a Man" in 1961. The title shift is certainly worth some attention in class. Although the short story lacks the venom of his better-known book-length works, there is still much about "Almos' a Man" that might serve as a general introduction to Wright and his aesthetics: a setting in the unreconstructed South; the dangerous violence of American racism; characters whose destiny seems governed by powerful external forces beyond individual control; the real-life speech patterns of the working classes; and a narrator who gives readers access to lives that appear quite simple on the surface. The short story's central character, Dave, may be similar in age to many of your students (he is seventeen), but they likely won't identify too closely with his excessively childish behavior. They may, however, wish to identify with Wright's skillful execution as a storyteller.

Classroom Issues and Strategies

The short story strikes a playful attitude toward racial division and the stereotypes on which it is built, and the reader is immediately drawn into the language games. Dave uses the racial epithet *nigger* to describe his fellow laborers, for example, and we do not learn that he is African American until well into the narrative. Dave's mother, an upwardly mobile member of the working class, remains scrupulously conscious of the outward signs of racialized class stereotyping – through her, Wright gives the lie to a simple conflation of race and class. (Her wish to use the Sears catalog in the outhouse – although common in the era before indoor plumbing–is a lighthearted stab at middle-class aspirations.) The climax of the short story – Dave's accidental shooting of the mule – provides more farce than drama. Still, the specter of a deep racial divide looms over the text. Dave's mother reasons that her husband needs a gun in a racially conflicted society, and one's social status in the short story coincides exactly with one's racial identity.

Normally, the use of free indirect discourse generates a strong resemblance between a character and the narrator, implying that the character is an artist figure, someone who narrates his own story. In this case, though, nothing could be further from the truth. Any suggestion that Dave is an artist figure is quickly frustrated by the wide gap between Dave's simpleminded stubbornness and the narrator's more thoughtful reflection on events. The gap is evident as quickly as the short story's opening sentences: "Dave struck out across the fields, looking homeward through paling light. Whuts the usa talkin wid em niggers in the field?" The distance between narrator and character is underscored by the side-by-side use of standard English and southern dialect.

Connections to Other Authors and Texts

Wright's connection with literary naturalism suggests comparison to earlier practitioners of the genre, including Stephen Crane, Frank Norris, and Theodore Dreiser. Wright also falls squarely into a tradition of southern fiction, such as that written by Jean Toomer, or more specifically Mississippi fiction, such as that written by William Faulkner and Eudora Welty.

Questions for Class Discussion

1. At what point in the short story did you realize Dave's racial identity? What evidence provides the answer? How does the first paragraph confuse the issue?

2. How does the meaning of *nigger* depend on its use in context? Who uses the racial epithet? To whom does it apply? What occasions the word's use?

3. What does it mean to "be a man" according to Dave? according to the townspeople? according to you?

4. Why does Wright give the mule's death so much attention? What does the mule symbolize? What does the mule's death symbolize?

Brief Bibliography

Gates, Henry Louis, Jr., and K. A. Appiah, eds. *Richard Wright: Critical Perspectives Past and Present*. New York: Amistad, 1993.

Loftis, John E. "Domestic Prey: Richard Wright's Parody of the Hunt Tradition in 'The Man Who Was Almost a Man.'" *Studies in Short Fiction* 23 (1986): 437–42.

Rowley, Hazel. *Richard Wright: The Life and Times*. New York: Henry Holt, 2001.

EUDORA WELTY   (p. 1021)

Approaches to Teaching

When Eudora Welty died in 2001, one of her obituary headlines read, "Eudora Welty, Voice of Southern Simplicity, Dies." Like the fictional Phoenix Jackson, the fiction of Eudora Welty often disarms readers with its apparent simplicity, but "simple" characters should not be confused with simplicity of narrative form. (And as the quotation marks imply, even "simple" characters are rarely quite so simple in Welty's fiction.) The difficult obscurity in the work of William Faulkner, another Mississippi fiction writer, places "A Worn Path" into sharp relief, but it helps to underscore the ways in which Welty's work overlaps with the more obviously experimental modernism of Faulkner. Welty's short story gives us a central character who is at once inscrutable and entirely sympathetic; the narrator hovers around the likeable old Phoenix, showing us her every move and utterance, but forcing us for much of the short story to guess at her inner thoughts and motives. Among the many morals of the tale are these: Appearances can be deceiving, and a careful eye (and careful reading) often yields great rewards. In addition to her career as a writer, Welty was an accomplished photographer whose work lent dignity and grace to her subjects, including many Southerners. A quick look at Welty's widely available photographs is a wonderful way to introduce her work.

Classroom Issues and Strategies

The short story's two opening paragraphs are remarkable feats of characterization: We encounter Phoenix first from a slight distance (ample enough to see her full form and her immediate surroundings), then from no more than a few inches (close enough to see the "numberless branching wrinkles" of her forehead and the "yellow burning under the dark" of her cheeks). Because narrative occupies space in time, the effect is more cinematic than photographic. The short story's opening instructs readers that they must pay close, careful attention to all details — nothing is irrelevant.

If we regard all details with the care that they deserve, then we quickly realize that Phoenix emerges as a Christ figure. Although Welty scholars quibble about their larger significance, they tend to agree on what counts as a Christian reference: the marble-cake hallucination, which resembles the sacrament of Holy Communion; the difficult climb up the hill, which resembles the stations of the cross on the road to Calvary; Phoenix's fall and the aid of a kind stranger, which also resembles specific stations of the cross; the presence of mistletoe, widely associated with Christmas pageantry and with the renowned wood of the holy cross; and of course the legendary rebirth of the Phoenix, which is closely connected with the Resurrection.

Phoenix's various interactions with white characters also serves as an object lesson in how to act kindly toward strangers, even in a not-fully-reconstructed South. It was not uncommon for white Southerners to regard elderly former slaves with respect; doing so even fit into the mythology of a pre–Civil War chivalric code of southern gentility. But considered carefully, Phoenix's verbal and nonverbal interaction with the young hunter, the perfumed lady, and the clinic attendant and nurse reveals a cagey and dignified sense of social awareness and self-worth. At the health clinic, for instance, Phoenix does not speak (perhaps refuses to speak?) until she's given the recognition that she deserves. On all occasions, she seems to get exactly what she wants from a given situation.

Connections to Other Authors and Texts

Katherine Anne Porter was one of Welty's greatest boosters and a major influence. Her contemporaries and fellow Mississippians William Faulkner and Richard Wright also did much to bring acclaim to the short story as an important genre.

Questions for Class Discussion

1. Many scholars have discussed the Christian imagery in "A Worn Path," but the imagery seems to extend beyond recognizable religious influences. What other symbols can you identify in the short story? What might they represent?

2. Examine Phoenix Jackson's interactions with various white characters (the hunter, the "lady," and the clinic attendant and nurse). How does she relate to each of these characters? How does the social context (an elderly African American woman in the early twentieth-century South) determine her words and her behavior?

3. Many critics have speculated about whether Phoenix's grandson is alive or dead. (Welty herself chimed in on the issue in 1974.) What do you think? Which character in the short story asks whether or not the boy is alive or dead?

Brief Bibliography

Johnston, Carol Ann. *Eudora Welty: A Study of the Short Fiction*. New York: Twayne, 1997.

Marrs, Suzanne. *Eudora Welty: A Biography*. Orlando: Harcourt, 2005.

Orr, Elaine. "'Unsettling Every Definition of Otherness': Another Reading of Welty's 'A Worn Path.'" *South Atlantic Quarterly* 57.2 (1992): 57–72.

CARLOS BULOSAN   (p. 1029)

Approaches to Teaching

The phrase *Asian American* is a relatively recent addition to the English lex-icon – it was popularized during the 1970s as an antidote to borderline slurs such as "Oriental" or outright slurs that need no repeating here – and Carlos Bulosan's short story dramatizes the diversity and even the tension that exists within the pan-ethnic identity label. The Filipino American sol-diers in "The End of the War" have even taken up the anti-Japanese stereo-types that circulated freely and widely in the wartime United States. Mess Sergeant Ponso goes so far as to blame the Japanese emperor (the "Son of Heaven") for disrupting his American dream of owning a Ford car and hav-ing money in the bank. To be an American in this milieu is to be anti-Japanese. In many respects "The End of the War" is the classic immigrant tale, but its historical context during World War II and its setting in a mili-tary camp raise the stakes of Americanization for its several characters.

Classroom Issues and Strategies

The tone of "The End of the War" can be described as a comic lightheart-edness, which means that it is easy to overlook the more serious issues that it takes up. Most obviously, the short story offers an account of Filipino Americans' contributions to the war effort; specifically, the char-acters carry out the unsung duties – cooking and cleaning – that support combat troops. And it also suggests that the army is a meritocracy in which one's rank depends on effort, not on social status: "But it had been hard on Private Fidel when, some months after their enlistment, his cousin Pitong was promoted. Pitong had always been his inferior in civilian life, espe-cially when they were working on the farm." The irony, of course, is that the Filipino American soldiers serve in a segregated unit because U.S. society hadn't yet extended them the full rights and benefits of citizenship.

Connections to Other Authors and Texts

"The End of the War" might be considered against more obviously antiwar titles (such as William Dean Howells's "Editha" and Ambrose Bierce's "Chickamauga") if only to underscore that Bulosan's short story is not, strictly speaking, pacifist. It also offers a vision of California social life that's a far cry from the California of Mary Austin or John Steinbeck.

Questions for Class Discussion

1. The song "Amor" – which begins "Amor, amor, amor / The word is so sweet that I repeat / Means I adore you" – was a hit for Bing Crosby

during the summer of 1944. Why do you think that the short story begins and ends with Pascual Fidel picking up his harmonica and playing the song?

2. Bulosan was a tireless advocate for Filipino American civil rights. How might "The End of the War" contribute to the cause?

Brief Bibliography

Evangelista, Susan. "Carlos Bulosan." *Asian American Writers*. Ed. Deborah L. Madsen. Detroit: Gale, 2005. 10-18.

Lee, Rachel C. *The Americas of Asian American Literature: Gendered Fictions of Nation and Transnation*. Princeton: Princeton UP, 1999.

American Literature
Since 1945

W_E HAVE COME TO KNOW the period in literary history following World War II as the "postmodern era," the "contemporary era," or both. One thing is certain: Most students will likely find both labels puzzling, and the period introduction will help clear up much of their confusion. The editors of *The Bedford Anthology of American Literature* historicize the period in ways that are useful and relevant to students, with special emphases on the rise of suburbia, the emergence of modern higher education, the civil rights and women's movements, Vietnam War-era protest, and the role of mass culture in shaping literary production. As teachers of students who were born in the 1980s (or even the 1990s), it is important to keep in mind that to them cable television is an outmoded technology, the women's movement is known as much by media clichés as by lived experience, suburban sprawl is a natural part of the American landscape, and (except for conspiracy theorists among them) Elvis has always been dead. In other words, what's "contemporary" to some is "history" to others.

The notion of the "postmodern" is fairly new to literary studies (even if the term is a century old). Still, a number of the definitively postmodern writers anthologized here (such as John Berryman and Sylvia Plath) were long dead when most of today's students were born. The editors' very brief and clear definition of *postmodernism* is a valuable teaching resource, one that will help organize courses loosely arranged around an evolution from modernism in the early twentieth century to postmodernism in the late twentieth century. The lens of ethnic studies provides another useful way to organize this part of a survey: Writers such as Toni Morrison and Sandra Cisneros and Sherman Alexie have redefined American literature, and in so doing they have redefined the African American, Latina, and Native American experience.

From Modernism to Postmodernism

This final section of *The Bedford Anthology of American Literature* embodies in its design a key concept affiliated with postmodernism: poetry, fiction, nonfiction prose, and drama are reproduced side by side, with no separation of writers and their texts according to genre. In their period introduction, the editors point out additional boundaries that postmodernism calls into question: "high" and "low" cultural forms, representation and reality, and the signifier and the signified. Most important of all, though, the editors rightly point out that hard-and-fast categories such as "postmodernism" do an injustice to the multiplicity of voices and forms that emerged in the aftermath of World War II. The rise of a truly multicultural literary environment — in which *culture* stands for social class, race, ethnicity, gender, and sexuality — is perhaps the hallmark of American writing and literary study up to the present moment.

There are, in fact, a number of discrete movements that fall under the rubric of postmodernism, and the examples anthologized here represent some of the key literary movements of the late twentieth and early twenty-first centuries. The movements represented by this part of *The Bedford Anthology of American Literature* include (in alphabetical order) the Beat generation, the Black Arts Movement, the Chicana/o Renaissance and the "Latin Boom," confessional poetry, feminism, the Native American Renaissance, the New York school, and the Queer Renaissance. Considering individual writers as representatives of a movement, or as representatives of tendencies within postmodernism, highlights the social role (or absence thereof) of concrete literary expression.

THEODORE ROETHKE   (p. 000)

Approaches to Teaching

If the climate allows for it, bring a few fresh-cut stems in a jar of water to class, place the jar on a table or desk, and ask students to point out what they see that Roethke also sees in his two "Cuttings" poems. Where is the poet located in physical space to see and record what he does? How far away is he from the cuttings? From what angle does he see them? Roethke's vividly alive attention to detail, not just here but in all his work, asks readers to see the universe in a fresh light and to rethink their place in the world: his light and his world. Encourage students to come up with a new terminology for their own encounters with cuttings, and then have them investigate Roethke's word choices with a good dictionary. (A similar exercise works well for most poems, not just his.) The double and triple entendres built into such words as *sheath* and *horn* reveal the poems to be quite traditional in their equation of vegetable and animal procreation (including human sexuality) and uniquely modern in their scientific objectivity.

Classroom Issues and Strategies

Roethke's attention to detail exerts a powerful influence on each poem's tone, and a short poem – "My Papa's Waltz" – offers a useful place to investigate tone in his work. The simple (even simplistic) meter of "My Papa's Waltz," a steady iambic trimeter, does not often find its way into English verse because it so thoroughly confines the poet. When asked to describe the meter, students sometimes offer that it sounds "singsongy," like a nursery rhyme. A close look at the poem reveals that Roethke modulates the poem's rhythm with the careful use of enjambment and punctuation and by departing from strict iambs just often enough to give each of the four sentences a unique metrical shape. The rhythmic subtlety contributes to the tonal subtlety, as does the evolving description of human body parts: from a mother's "countenance" that "[c]ould not unfrown itself" to a father's "battered . . . knuckle" and palm that "beat time" on the boy's head.

Because Roethke experimented with such a wide range of verse forms – from the hypertraditional villanelle to ultramodern free verse – the shape of his poetry varies widely. Accounting for the shape of his poems is an important exercise: Why does each "Cuttings" poem occupy two stanzas, and why does the second stanza differ in shape from one version to the next? Why does "The Far Field" occupy four sections, and why is section two so much longer than the others? There is of course no single answer to any of these questions, but acknowledging their importance to an understanding of Roethke's poetry is a useful point of entry.

Connections to Other Authors and Texts

Roethke is a nature poet whose unique take on the "natural" emerges from a comparison with Amy Lowell, Robert Frost, William Carlos Williams, and H. D. His understanding of the "thing" is also worth considering alongside the work of an imagist such as T. S. Eliot or an objectivist such as Charles Reznikoff.

Questions for Class Discussion

1. How does punctuation contribute to the rhythm and meaning(s) of "Cuttings" and "Cuttings (later)"? How is the poet able to see and hear what he describes?

2. How does the rhythm of "My Papa's Waltz" complicate the tone of the poem? How do individual words take on double and triple meanings that further complicate the tone?

3. In "I Knew a Woman," what does the poet know about the woman? What does he not know about her?

Brief Bibliography

Bloom, Harold, ed. *Theodore Roethke*. New York: Chelsea House, 1988.

Bogen, Don. *Theodore Roethke and the Writing Process*. Athens: Ohio UP, 1991.

Seager, Allan. *Glass House: The Life of Theodore Roethke*. Ann Arbor: U of Michigan P, 1991.

ELIZABETH BISHOP   (p. 000)

Approaches to Teaching

Just as Robert Lowell's "Skunk Hour" (1959) says as much (if not more) about Lowell than about Elizabeth Bishop, to whom the poem is dedicated, so too does Bishop's "The Armadillo" (1957) say more about Bishop than about Lowell, to whom it is dedicated. It helps to read the poems in tandem and to ask what we can glean about each poet from their descriptions of Nautilus Island eccentrics and South American wildlife: How is this poem about Bishop or Lowell? In the specific case of "The Armadillo," what does Bishop suggest by connecting radiant beauty (the fire balloons) and horrific tragedy (the scorched earth)? What does it mean that the armadillo asserts "*a weak mailed fist / clenched ignorant against the sky*"? All of Bishop's poetry derives at least in part from early childhood tragedy, but more important than the biographical underpinnings of her poetry is her commitment to the transformative power of beauty. The final injunction to "(*Write* it!)" found in her "One Art" makes a virtue of even the most horrific disaster.

Classroom Issues and Strategies

Bishop produced a very small body of poems in her long and eminent career, and her work exhibits the formal intricacy that might be expected of a poet who regularly spent months or even years revising a single poem. Bishop was hardly the only twentieth-century poet to handle the so-called fixed forms, but thanks to such sparkling examples as "Sestina" and "One Art" she is perhaps more closely connected with fixed poetic structures than most. Each poem stands as an example of an emotionally rich dramatic situation tempered by a rigorous formal restraint. The namesake verse form of "Sestina," for example, dramatizes simultaneously a cozy domesticity and a more troubling range of feelings partly hidden from view. "One Art," a villanelle, plays a notion of formal exactitude ("master") against the brutal reality ("disaster") that's only temporarily held at bay.

Although Bishop's work can be emotionally wrenching – Susan McCabe calls hers a "poetics of loss" – we see quite little of her biography in her best-known poems, including those anthologized here. We see the places (as in "Brazil, January 1, 1502") and the people (as in "In the Waiting Room") that she loved dearly, but "Elizabeth Bishop, Poet" rarely makes an appearance. (Certainly, "Elizabeth Bishop, Lesbian Poet" does not announce herself in this sample of her work.) "In the Waiting Room" delivers us an "I" who calls herself "Elizabeth," but the persona's ("I's") detachment from the poem's character ("Elizabeth") represents a continuation of modernism's impersonal poetry rather than a precursor to postmodernism's confessional poetry.

Connections to Other Authors and Texts

Beginning with their encounter at Vassar, Marianne Moore exerted an important influence on Bishop. Her contemporary Robert Lowell was also a lifelong influence and close friend.

Questions for Class Discussion

1. Consider the six recurring end words in "Sestina": *house, grandmother, child, stove, almanac,* and *tears.* Write a sentence that incorporates all six words. Describe the emotional range of each word. Which emotions dominate the tone of the poem?

2. How does the poet regard the Brazilian landscape in "Brazil, January 1, 1502"? How do the Christian colonists regard the landscape?

3. If it's available at your library, examine the February 1918 issue of *National Geographic* (specifically, the article titled "The Valley of Ten Thousand Smokes") that's referenced by "In the Waiting Room." What does the poet remember from her girlhood encounter with the magazine? How does the visual imagery suggested by the magazine correspond with the self-discovery recorded in the poem?

4. In "One Art," the words *master* and *disaster* appear four times each (thus completing the intricate form known as villanelle). Which of the two words exerts more force in the poem; in other words, which word wins?

Brief Bibliography

McCabe, Susan. *Elizabeth Bishop: Her Poetics of Loss.* University Park: Pennsylvania State UP, 1994.

Millier, Brett Candlish. *Elizabeth Bishop: Life and the Memory of It.* Berkeley: U of California P, 1993.

Zona, Kirstin Hotelling. *Marianne Moore, Elizabeth Bishop, and May Swenson: The Feminist Poetics of Self-Restraint.* Ann Arbor: U of Michigan P, 2002.

TENNESSEE WILLIAMS   (p. 000)

Approaches to Teaching

The brevity of *Portrait of a Madonna* (1945) allows a hands-on dramatic experience: Students might be asked to stage a reading or a full-fledged production in the classroom setting. At the very least, Lucretia's "dreamy" reminiscence of a traumatic childhood experience (beginning "I used to think I'd never get to the end of that last block") might form the basis of comparative performance analysis. Some students might even find a *Portrait* performance contest a new and appealing way to take on literary analysis. Depending on your students' backgrounds, you may need to rehearse for them the ideology of southern gentility and maidenhood that is so central to an understanding of the play (indeed, to an understanding of many of Williams's plays).

Classroom Issues and Strategies

There exist dozens (if not hundreds) of iconic visual images of the Madonna, from Michelangelo's *Pietà* to Dalí's *Madonna of Port Lligat*; in the overwhelming majority of these, she offers comfort or consolation; she is an image of chastity and strength. Ask students how the play's title conditions their expectations for Lucretia Collins, and how she lives up to or departs from the title. You might then point out the several direct and indirect religious references in the play, including the numerous mentions of Sunday school and the gossip-hungry churchgoers, Lucretia's church-pageant costume work, visits to the children's hospital at Christmas and Easter, and the possibility of an immaculate conception (at an advanced age, no less).

Lucretia's predicament – her mental instability and her profound isolation – derives at least in part from the expectations for a southern belle in a society that has no place for her. Her character is fully developed in spite of her delusions, and the role, made famous by Jessica Tandy, demands much from the actor who portrays her. Although Lucretia occupies center stage, the play's minor characters, especially the Porter and the Elevator Boy, fulfill important duties. The Porter is a dutiful, working-class figure who sympathizes with the distressed Lucretia (even if he cannot fully understand her); the Elevator Boy is a young wiseacre whose brash sense of humor fits Lucretia into a series of demeaning stereotypes. Together they represent a wide spectrum of social commentary about Lucretia and others like her.

Connections to Other Authors and Texts

Charlotte Perkins Gilman's "The Yellow Wall-Paper" (p. 000) offers a radically different literary representation of a character's descent into delusion. Susan Glaspell's one-act *Trifles* (p. 000) is short enough to compare with Williams's *Portrait* in a single class period; both plays investigate a woman's identity that is defined by more and less sympathetic spectators.

Questions for Class Discussion

1. Explain the title of Williams's play. Why "portrait"? Why "Madonna"?

2. Provide a list of contemporary actors who might round out the cast of a new production of *Portrait of a Madonna*. Explain the character traits that each actor must be prepared to embody.

3. Lucretia represents what is sometimes called a "faded southern belle." How does the play suggest that she perform her southern identity?

Brief Bibliography

Bloom, Harold, ed. *Tennessee Williams*. New York: Bloom's Literary Criticism, 2007.

Roudané, Matthew C., ed. *The Cambridge Companion to Tennessee Williams*. Cambridge: Cambridge UP, 1997.

Spoto, Donald. *Kindness of Strangers: The Life of Tennessee Williams*. New York: Da Capo, 1997.

ROBERT HAYDEN   (p. 000)

Approaches to Teaching

The fascinating tale of the mutiny aboard the slave-trading vessel the *Amistad* is the stuff of legend, not to mention poetry, fiction, and film. (Students already familiar with the tale will likely have gleaned their information from the 1997 Steven Spielberg film.) The historical background for Robert Hayden's account of the uprising, "Middle Passage," is quickly and clearly recounted in the editors' headnote to the poem. Students might be asked to read the headnote aloud before reading the poem aloud to gain a sharper understanding of how Hayden transformed historical events – indeed, written history itself – into poetic art. The poem assumes a narrative shape out of disjointed elements, a narrative that serves as a myth of origins for the African American experience. Hayden rescues heroism and hope out of a dehumanizing tragedy; in this respect, the poet encounters perhaps the key challenge facing all writers who have struggled with forging an "American literature."

Classroom Issues and Strategies

An important lesson to impart to students of "Middle Passage" is a sense of how Hayden manages the multiple and disparate voices that inhabit the poem, including history, church hymns, captain's logs, Shakespearean cadences, and legal depositions. At the simplest level, visual cues indicate where one voice ends and another begins: Hayden deploys italics, strategic indentation and line spacing, quotation marks, and stanza breaks to keep the multiple voices separate in visual space. At a more complex level, linguistic cues signify the shift from voice to voice: national language (English with some Spanish and the occasional African name), point of view and tone, and other discourse markers reveal the source material. Hovering above all of these voices is the prophetic voice of the poet, whose redemptive refrain ("Voyage through death / to life upon these shores") yokes together the poem's disparate elements and places its contents within the narrative arc of the African diaspora.

The Afro-diasporic leanings of "Middle Passage" might serve as an interesting point of entry into the Black Arts Movement that would take shape in the 1960s, some two decades after Hayden first published his remarkable poem. Although the relatively older and less radical Hayden was an outsider to the movement, his work nevertheless influenced (mostly negatively) the young writers who took part in the first Black Writers' Conference, held in 1966 at Hayden's academic home, Fisk University.

Connections to Other Authors and Texts

T. S. Eliot's *The Waste Land* (p. 000) offers an earlier (and more experimental) version of a poem that incorporates a multiplicity of voices into its pages. Hayden always acknowledged the influence of Harlem Renaissance poets such as Countee Cullen and Langston Hughes, and his work left its mark on subsequent Black Arts Movement poets such as Gwendolyn Brooks (who attended the second Black Writers' Conference at Fisk University).

Questions for Class Discussion

1. How do some of the signposts of "epic" poetry function in "Middle Passage"? (These include a vast geographic scale, catalogs, a figure [or figures] of great importance to a people, incredible [even superhuman] deeds, and an active presence of the gods.) Where is the poem set geographically? What gets cataloged, and how? Is Cinquez a "hero," and if so, to whom? What deeds are recorded, how are they recorded, and who records them? What is the role of Christianity (and the Christian God) in the poem?

2. How many voices can you identify in "Middle Passage"? From what sources are these voices derived? Are some voices more "authentic" than others?

Brief Bibliography

Goldstein, Laurence, and Robert Chrisman, eds. *Robert Hayden: Essays on the Poetry*. Ann Arbor: U of Michigan P, 2001.

Kutzinski, Vera M. "Changing Permanences: Historical and Literary Revisionism in Robert Hayden's 'Middle Passage.'" *Callaloo* 9 (1986): 171-83.

Williams, Pontheolla. *Robert Hayden: A Critical Analysis of His Poetry*. Urbana: U of Illinois P, 1987.

TILLIE OLSEN   (p. 000)

Approaches to Teaching

"I Stand Here Ironing" might be approached in so many ways that the variety of options is almost dizzying. The abundance of approaches opens up the opportunity in a one- or two-semester survey to review important tendencies in American literary history: The concern with opportunities open to women in a less-than-supportive society; the emergence of working-class characters as an object of legitimate concern for fiction writers; the modernist experimentation with form, in particular the connection between a narrator's subjectivity and the unfolding of narrative time. Students might be asked to describe for themselves how the short story fits into these wider issues in American cultural history. Because most students are roughly the age of Emily at the short story's narrating instance (the same age as the narrator herself when she was a new mother), they will have no shortage of interest in the two central characters.

Classroom Issues and Strategies

The narrator's evolving relationship with her daughter, and the profound sense of guilt that the relationship generates, is the short story's central concern, and it is therefore no surprise that much of the commentary about "I Stand Here Ironing" borrows more or less from the language of psychology and psychoanalysis. As one might expect in a counseling or psychotherapy session, the narrative is inspired and propelled along by open-ended questions. The short story begins with a vague reference to one such question: "I stand here ironing, and *what you asked me* moves tormented back and forth with the iron" (my emphasis). At key points the narrator asks herself questions that are partly asked in earnest, partly rhetorical: "In this and other ways she leaves her seal, I say aloud. And startle at my saying it. What do I mean? What did I start to gather together, to try and make coherent?" When seen in light of a therapeutic impulse, the narrator emerges as both therapist and patient; the analogy raises important questions about the role of writing and reading in twentieth- and twenty-first-century society.

On a global level, the narrative structure of "I Stand Here Ironing" is fairly simple to describe: As a woman irons a dress, she recalls several troubling moments in her nineteen-year-old daughter's life. The narrative is mostly retrospective, but it is occasionally punctuated by a return to the narrating instance (as when the narrator notes, "I put the iron down"). The short story is thus profoundly concerned with the role of subjective memory in knowledge and understanding, and with the connection between a narrator's subjectivity and her narrative's form. At the same time, the short story investigates how domestic work and the art of fiction overlap or compete for a writer's time and energy.

Connections to Other Authors and Texts

Like Olsen, Charlotte Perkins Gilman and Edith Wharton explore (although from dramatically different perspectives) the link between domesticity and storytelling. Olsen also updates from a feminist outlook the tradition of working-class fiction that first appears in the work of naturalists such as Frank Norris and Theodore Dreiser.

Questions for Class Discussion

1. Discuss the symbolic importance of ironing in the short story. How would the short story be different if the narrator had been cooking or mopping the floor?

2. Identify the verbs that the narrator uses to describe her own efforts at remembering and storytelling. (For example, she asks early on, "Why do I *put* that first? I do not even know if it *matters,* or if it *explains* anything.") What do these verb choices say about the art of fiction writing? about the act of reading?

3. On its surface, "I Stand Here Ironing" concerns the shifting and sometimes troubled relationship between a mother and her daughter. How might the short story also be understood as an indictment of America's class structure and social support system?

Brief Bibliography

Coiner, Constance. *Better Red: The Writing and Resistance of Tillie Olsen and Meridel Le Sueur.* New York: Oxford UP, 1995.

Frye, Joanne S. *Tillie Olsen: A Study of the Short Fiction.* New York: Twayne, 1995.

Nelson, Kay Hoyle, and Nancy Huse, eds. *The Critical Response to Tillie Olsen.* Westport, CT: Greenwood, 1994.

JOHN BERRYMAN   (p. 000)

Approaches to Teaching

Given their importance in his career (not to mention their prominence in this anthology), some background to and explanation of Berryman's *Dream Songs* provide a fitting introduction to the poet. First, the poems came about long after Berryman established his reputation as a poet (most notably for his ambitious *Homage to Mistress Bradstreet* [1953]), after he had divorced twice (and married a third time), and after he had been hospitalized for alcoholism and mental breakdowns – all the while proceeding with a stellar career as a poet and an academic. Second, the title suggests a paradoxical public rendering of the intimately private. Or as one critic aptly puts it, "Blurring the boundaries between poetry and hype, between confession and publicity, [Berryman] presents himself as a literary *personality*, a figure whose individuality appears as a general reflection of public life" (Blake). Third, the poems insist on a tension between individual and collective attention and interpretation. In other words, each separately numbered song requires understanding as a discrete unit of expression; at the same time, the whole deserves appreciation as a collection gathered together at a variety of points in Berryman's later poetic career. In this respect, the *Dream Songs* resemble Ezra Pound's *Cantos* or Walt Whitman's *Leaves of Grass* (both of which Berryman no doubt had in mind).

Classroom Issues and Strategies

Robert Lowell famously commented that the *Dream Songs* "are much too difficult, packed, and wrenched to be sung." Although Lowell later recanted, his willingness to take the sequence title seriously highlights an important way to regard the poems: as an exploration of tone. (At least initially, Lowell undervalued the poems' use of rhyme and their semiregular four-beat rhythm.) The humor and absurdity of *Dream Songs* – embodied in such playful lines as "Filling her compact & delicious body / with chicken páprika, she glanced at me" – do little to mask the more serious undertones of the sequence. Students may not be familiar with such dissonance in poetry, but they are no doubt familiar with music whose lyrics eerily mismatch the tune (as in the work of Kurt Weill or Aimee Mann).

The variety of voices emanating from a single "self" in the poems contributes greatly to their tonal instability. The single persona of the *Dream Songs* multiplies into an array of characters and character types from the start: *Dream Song* 1 introduces readers to "Huffy Henry," to "unappeasable Henry," to a first-person "I" (who is in fact Henry), and so on. In a sense, the poem gives order (or records the chaos) of a "self" beset by what was once called "multiple personality disorder."

Connections to Other Authors and Texts

The confessional poetry of Robert Lowell and Sylvia Plath probably come closest in spirit to the inimitable work of Berryman; however, a poet who experiments with personae (such as Emily Dickinson or Ezra Pound) might offer a source for comparison.

Questions for Class Discussion

1. How would you set individual songs in Dream Songs to music? Provide concrete examples of musical styles suggested by the poems.
2. Describe the evolution of Henry across a single song and across multiple songs.

Brief Bibliography

Blake, David Haven. "Public Dreams: Berryman, Celebrity, and the Culture of Confession." *American Literary History* 13 (2001): 716-36.

Kelley, Richard J., and Alan K. Lathrop, eds. *Recovering Berryman: Essays on a Poet.* Ann Arbor: U of Michigan P, 1993.

Mariani, Paul. *Dream Song: The Life of John Berryman.* New York: W. Morrow, 1990.

RALPH ELLISON   (p. 000)

Approaches to Teaching

After the publication of his *Invisible Man* in 1952, Ralph Ellison suffered perhaps the most famous writer's block in American literary history. Arnold Rampersad's new biography of Ellison explores the topic from a host of angles – psychological, sociological, historical – but the topic might also be mentioned as a way to introduce the novel's significance to twentieth-century American literature (that is, we consider Ellison a great writer in spite of the problem) and to raise a dilemma that often faces student writers (not to mention their teachers). Throughout his career, Ellison struggled with the burden of living up to the promise of a novel that speaks for the entire African American experience, a pseudo-universalist notion rightly critiqued by feminist critics. The opening chapter anthologized here invites a part-for-whole analysis that sees the invisible narrator as a spokesperson for an entire race: "I am not a freak of nature, nor of history," he declares. The narrator's family background connects him with the slave experience; the references to Booker T. Washington connect the narrator's ambitions with post-Reconstruction politics; and the chapter's symbolism – heavy-handed and elusive at the same time – requires sociohistorical and psychological interpretation that transcends an individual life.

Classroom Issues and Strategies

Ellison's invisible narrator comments from a perspective that is twenty years removed from the days of his youth. The narrator seemingly offers a critical, objective analysis of his early naivete, and yet he is hardly a sympathetic figure. Unlike most putatively autobiographical narratives, even works of fiction that pose as autobiography, *The Invisible Man* is narrated from a "privileged" perspective of cynical insight. Whereas Frederick Douglass tells of "how a slave became a man," Ellison's novel tells of how an ambitious boy became an "invisible man." It is difficult to sympathize with a life whose ultimate meaning is alienation and estrangement, but there is no difficulty finding meaning and even aesthetic pleasure in the work.

The chapter's key symbols are fairly easy to identify: the young blonde woman, the electrified rug, the trophy briefcase, and of course the battle royal itself. Each of these symbols might serve as the focus of attention in class. The elaborate description of the young blonde woman, for example, descends from multiple and sometimes overlapping discourses: the allegorical traditions of New World and Orientalist and African travel writing; stereotypes about African American male sexuality; and pornographic fantasy. The "Battle Royal" fight reveals more about the town's white elite who watch on drunkenly than about the young African American boxers who fight "hysterically." The description, which humorously and disturbingly mingles sports writing with the absurd, owes much to folktales that propose social analysis: "It was complete anarchy. Everybody fought everybody else. No group fought together for long. Two, three, four fought one, then turned to fight each other, were themselves attacked."

Connections to Other Authors and Texts

Ellison owes much to the rich tradition of African American autobiography, and the chapter explicitly refers to the work of Booker T. Washington. W. E. B. Du Bois's autobiographical *The Souls of Black Folk* (p. 466) and Richard Wright's third-person "Almos' a Man" (p. 1011) offer additional counterpoints to the invisible narrator's coming-of-age story.

Questions for Class Discussion

1. This selection represents the first chapter of Ellison's landmark novel, *The Invisible Man.* Based on this chapter, what would you expect from the rest of the novel?

2. The short story juxtaposes the narrator's observations with language from Booker T. Washington's famous "Atlanta Exposition Address." What is the rhetorical effect of the juxtaposition?

3. If "Battle Royal" functions as an implicit critique of Booker T. Washingtonian accommodation, does it resemble in any obvious way W. E. B. Du Bois's more explicit critique of Washington? Does it embody the ideals discussed elsewhere in Du Bois's *The Souls of Black Folk* (p. 466)?

Brief Bibliography

Callahan, John F., ed. *Ralph Ellison's* Invisible Man: *A Casebook.* New York: Oxford UP, 2004.

Posnock, Ross, ed. *The Cambridge Companion to Ralph Ellison*. Cambridge: Cambridge UP, 2005.

Rampersad, Arnold. *Ralph Ellison: A Biography*. New York: Knopf, 2007.

BERNARD MALAMUD   (p. 000)

Approaches to Teaching

The historical, geographic, and ultimately cultural specificity of "The First Seven Years" obscures the universality of its central conflict between materialism and idealism (or as Miriam phrases it, between "things" and "soul"). Put another way: between the immigrant characters' practicality and romanticism. Very plainly the conflict takes the shape of Miriam's two suitors, the acquisitive Max and the bookish Sobel. But the choice is not entirely Miriam's, and the suitors are hardly fetching in any obvious sense, so students will have to consider mating rituals that seem historically remote, and they will have to delve deeply into Malamud's clever narrative structure. The short story relinquishes important character details only gradually, and what the narrator reveals depends greatly upon its central focus, the well-meaning but close-minded Feld. "The First Seven Years" is thus a remarkable study of how characterization and narrative focus go hand in hand.

Classroom Issues and Strategies

Looking through Feld's eyes, the narrator describes Max as "tall and grotesquely thin, with sharply cut features, particularly a beak-like nose." He wears "a loose, long slushy overcoat draped over his bony shoulders, and a soggy, old brown hat." The narrator describes Sobel as a "stocky man, poorly dressed, with a bald head that had once been blond, a severely plain face and soft blue eyes prone to tears"; he is "a young man but old." We thus see the two as Feld does, and by the end of the short story we realize that we must put more stock in how they behave than in how they look or what they say. Sobel's insistent hammering mirrors his jealousy when Max enters the shoe-repair shop; his clenched fists and sobbing confirm the depth of his feelings. Miriam's noncommittal attitude toward Max and her fondness for Sobel's books reveal her true feelings. Max, meanwhile, is always cloaked in ill-fitting clothes that mask his nonverbal gestures. Like Feld, readers must reevaluate their earliest impressions of all three youngsters.

Because we know the other characters as Feld knows them, our understanding of them evolves as Feld's understanding of them evolves (indeed, as Feld evolves as a character). Our opinion of Max, never too sympathetic to begin with, takes a turn for the worse as we learn about his petty materialism. Our opinion of Sobel, in contrast, takes a turn for the better because we can appreciate his bookishness and because we see his asceticism as a form of romantic devotion. By the time Feld allows Sobel to court his daughter, our opinion of the shoemaker is vastly improved.

Connections to Other Authors and Texts

Those who wish to find additional examinations of the Jewish ghetto might look to Abraham Cahan and Mary Antin. The tension between immigrant values and romantic freedom is also explored by Theodore Dreiser and Hisaye Yamamoto.

Questions for Class Discussion

1. Compare the physical descriptions of Max and Sobel. Based on their physical appearances alone, is it possible to tell which of the two is a better match for Miriam? Why or why not?

2. How do Max, Sobel, and Miriam express their emotions without using words? How does Feld interpret their nonverbal communication?

3. Which details from the short story place it in the mid-twentieth century? Which details seem more remote in time?

Brief Bibliography

Brown, Peter C. "Negative Capability and the Mystery of Hope in Malamud's 'The First Seven Years.'" *Religion and Literature* 29 (1997): 63–94.

Davis, Philip. *Bernard Malamud: A Writer's Life*. Oxford: Oxford UP, 2007.

Solotaroff, Robert. *Bernard Malamud: A Study of the Short Fiction*. Boston: Twayne, 1989.

SAUL BELLOW   (p. 000)

Approaches to Teaching

With its reference to Augustine's "fallen world of appearances," it would be easy to place "Looking for Mr. Green" in that rarefied and sometimes off-putting category, the "literature of ideas." Although Bellow pays much attention to the philosophical distinction between the "real" and the "ideal," no worries about esotericism or abstruseness need hinder a discussion of "Looking for Mr. Green," for its characters and settings are drawn from the hardscrabble world of inner-city Chicago. The short story's occasions for philosophy are revealing: A conversation between Grebe and Raynor that's peppered with bureaucratic pettiness; Grebe's conversation with a cynical Italian grocer; Grebe's pondering the utility of Mr. Field's millionaire-a-month scheme; the seeming incongruity between a real government check and the elusive Mr. Green.

Classroom Issues and Strategies

The narrator of "Looking for Mr. Green" exists in an odd and shifting relationship with the short story's protagonist, Grebe. Although the narrative focus and even some of the narrator's language rely on Grebe, our sense of Grebe is often achieved in terms of negation, in terms of what Grebe doesn't do or think or feel. In the short story's first paragraph, for example, we learn that Grebe "wasn't used to walking and stair-climbing," and so he must now be doing much walking and stair-climbing; we learn that his new job delivering relief checks "wasn't literally hard work," so it must be difficult in some other way; we learn that "he didn't look much like a hunter," so he presumably looks at home in the city. The narrator routinely measures Grebe by what he is not, because this is precisely how Grebe views himself. We can trust the narrator only as far as we can trust Grebe, and as the consummate outsider in the slums of the Chicago South Side, our knowledge of the setting and characters is provisional at best.

We might find in "Looking for Mr. Green" important and memorable sociohistorical traces of the Great Depression. For example, in a state of extreme privation, class and ethnic boundaries are rubbed raw and interaction across class and ethnic lines is fraught with a dangerous tension. Three characters in particular – Raynor, the Italian grocer, and Grebe – express attitudes toward African Americans that range from condescension to racist paranoia to speechlessness. Bellow's minute attention to the grimmest details underscores the precariousness of Depression-era existence, even in one of America's great cities.

Connections to Other Authors and Texts

Like Bellow, Bernard Malamud and Arthur Miller impart a measure of lyricism onto the stark realities of postwar American life. Although they are poets, Claude McKay, Langston Hughes, and Gwendolyn Brooks share Bellow's interest in inner-city African American life.

Questions for Class Discussion

1. Discuss the significance of the names "Mr. Green" and "Grebe." (Note: A "grebe" is a type of swimming and diving bird, similar to a loon or a duck.)

2. Although Grebe never actually finds Mr. Green, what does he find – literally and figuratively – along the way? If (as some critics suggest) the story can be taken as a symbolic quest, what is the object of discovery? If the story can be taken as a parable, what lessons are learned (by George Grebe or by the reader)?

3. How does the Great Depression exert an influence on the story's setting? On the story's characters? On the storytelling itself (narrative voice)?

4. Is your education preparing you for a job like George Grebe's? If so, how?

Brief Bibliography

Atlas, James. *Bellow: A Biography.* New York: Random, 2000.

Bach, Gerhard, and Gloria L. Cronin, eds. *Small Planets: Saul Bellow and the Art of Short Fiction.* East Lansing: Michigan State UP, 2000.

Friedrich, Marianne M. *Character and Narration in the Short Fiction of Saul Bellow.* New York: Peter Lang, 1995.

ARTHUR MILLER   (p. 000)

Approaches to Teaching

Given its original production and publication date, *Death of a Salesman* (1949) will likely find a place near the front of the latter half of an American literature syllabus, just after the midterm period in a semester-long course. For this reason it is useful to discuss Arthur Miller's play as a test case in the analysis of literary postmodernism. If postmodernism is taken as a post-World War II period marker, then the play is avowedly postwar. If postmodernism is concerned with the changing face of technology and the global economy, then the play embodies the theme of the postindustrial shift from a manufacturing to a sales economy and it looks nostalgically at an outmoded form of technology (broadcast radio, which threatens to be overtaken by Howard's wire recorder). But the play cannot necessarily be identified with postmodernism's nihilism; Willy's famous diatribe ("a man is not a piece of fruit!") echoes an earlier era's tendency toward realist social criticism. In some respects, *Death of a Salesman* keeps one foot on the side of modernism, one on the side of postmodernism. The play resembles a tragedy, but Willy is no conventional "hero." There are no recognizable scene breaks – chronological time itself is upended – but many critics recognize the play's three-part structure as a nod to convention. Finally, a number of characters float on and off the stage; their spectral presence might be conceived as traditional ghosts or as character types robbed of any deeper human significance.

Classroom Issues and Strategies

Because *Death of a Salesman* tracks Willy's consciousness from present to past and back again, staging a production of the play, even in the minds of students, poses unique and intriguing difficulties. The stage directions provide some guidance, but students should be asked to consider some of the potential pitfalls that lie in wait for the play's cast and crew. For instance, when Willy addresses an offstage Biff as he polishes the car, Biff responds with "Whatta ya got, Dad?" Biff's tone of voice at this crucial juncture – it is where the play adopts Willy's delusional perspective for the first time – makes all the difference in whether or not the audience is appropriately jolted back in time. His voice (and costume and stage presence) should capture the innocence and youth of an earlier era. In other words, if the performance works – if the voice and lighting and blocking and costumes perform as expected – then the audience will agree to the illusion of time travel; if not, then the audience will feel trapped in a gimmick. The distinction (convincing illusion versus lackluster gimmick) is crucial to the play's indictment of the American dream.

Although *Salesman* is a staple of American theater companies, many students will be more familiar with the 1985 film version directed by Volker Schlondorff and starring Dustin Hoffman. A comparison of the film and the text of the play reveals many of the challenges facing the producer and director of a live-action play: The film makes constant use of techniques – such as shifting camera angles and film splicing – that are not available in a live-action play.

Connections to Other Authors and Texts

Saul Bellow's "Looking for Mr. Green" (p. 000) offers an indictment of the American dream that is set in a slightly earlier era. *Salesman* was a Broadway success; an Off-Broadway success such as Amiri Baraka's *Dutchman* (p. 000) puts the on/off distinction into sharp focus.

Questions for Class Discussion

1. Identify moments in the play in which Willy's delusions govern the action on stage. How would you direct such moments; what instructions would you give to the actors about how to perform specific lines?

2. Describe the role of modern technology (such as cars, radios, and wire recorders) in the play.

3. Cast your own version of *Death of a Salesman* using contemporary actors. Be prepared to defend your casting choices.

Brief Bibliography

Bloom, Harold, ed. *Arthur Miller's* Death of a Salesman. New York: Chelsea House, 2007.

Death of a Salesman. Dir. Volker Schlondorff. Perf. Dustin Hoffman, Charles Durning, Kate Reid, Stephen Lang, and John Malkovich. 1985. DVD. Image Entertainment, 2003.

Gottfried, Martin. *Arthur Miller: His Life and Work.* Cambridge: Da Capo, 2003.

Roudané, Matthew C. *Approaches to Teaching Miller's* Death of a Salesman. New York: Modern Language Association, 1995.

ROBERT LOWELL   (P. 000)

Approaches to Teaching

The idea of confession in poetry implies a lack of subtlety and restraint. Indeed, much of the bad adolescent poetry written these days – uncontrolled wailings from an immature mind and voice – probably descends directly from the confessional mode with which Robert Lowell is closely connected. For this reason, it helps when discussing Lowell to emphasize that "confessional" does not mean the same thing as "unrestrained" and it certainly should not impute "rushed." Even a quintessentially confessional moment in a Lowell poem – say, the second stanza of "Memories of West Street and Lepke" (1959), with its reference to psychopharmacology ("the tranquillized *Fifties*"), its rapid-fire list of social identities ("fire-breathing Catholic C.O."), and its self-analysis ("manic") – evinces a tempered cadence, regular line lengths (if unpredictable line breaks), and the occasional rhyme. As all of his work attests, Lowell was above all else patient and diligent in his craft, willing to revise a poem multiple times over the course of his career.

Classroom Issues and Strategies

Lowell was as famous for his political as for his poetic views, and it is impossible to avoid politics in work such as "Memories of West Street and Lepke," "Waking Early Sunday Morning," and "For the Union Dead." The latter poem, ostensibly an elegy for long-departed Civil War soldiers, participates in the jeremiad tradition that was so important to Lowell's Puritan forebears. Like Saint-Gaudens's famous statue of Colonel Shaw and his African American regiment (which "sticks like a fishbone / in the city's throat"), the poem indicts Boston and the nation and an age capable of little more than nuclear annihilation or petty consumerism. The poem's prophecy may be oblique, but its indictment of American society – a "savage servility" – could not be more clear.

Much has been made of the weight of the Puritan past that rested uneasily on Lowell's shoulders, and rightly so. His "Waking Early Sunday Morning" might obviously be read as an antiwar poem, one that links tragic foreign-policy blunders with government callousness, but the poem goes further than that: It links earthly troubles with spiritual shallowness, a common theme in Puritan writing.

Connections to Other Authors and Texts

A case might be made on biographical grounds that Amy Lowell exerted an influence on Robert Lowell, but an even stronger case might be made about the role of Elizabeth Bishop in his life and career. Robert Lowell's impact on confessional poetry links him directly or indirectly with Sylvia Plath and John Berryman.

Questions for Class Discussion

1. What is wrong with the society depicted in "Skunk Hour"? How is poetry (or at least this poem) complicit with social ills?

2. "For the Union Dead" suggests a comparison between the Civil War era and the turbulent present (the 1960s). How does present-day Boston fare in this comparison? What does the Boston of the past represent? What does the Boston of the present represent?

3. Compare and contrast the ideas and rhetorical strategies of Lowell's "Waking Early Sunday Morning" (p. 1262) and Wallace Stevens's "Sunday Morning" (p. 607).

Brief Bibliography

Axelrod, Steven Gould, ed. *The Critical Response to Robert Lowell*. Westport, CT: Greenwood, 1999.

Mariani, Paul. *Lost Puritan: A Life of Robert Lowell*. New York: Norton, 1994.

Vendler, Helen. *The Given and the Made: Strategies of Poetic Definition*. Cambridge: Harvard UP, 1995.

GWENDOLYN BROOKS   (p. 000)

Approaches to Teaching

Rarely does a writer so radically and so effectively redefine an already-successful career as Gwendolyn Brooks did when she encountered the burgeoning Black Arts Movement at the second Black Writers' Conference at Fisk University in 1967. This is not to suggest that Brooks had little interest in black life earlier in her career; *A Street in Bronzeville* (1945) is such a revolutionary work because it delves into African American life as no one had before. Indeed, most of the poems collected here were published long before the Black Arts Movement came into existence, and their unique and memorable take on African American life suggests that the building blocks of a Black Arts aesthetic, if not its final shape, were already in place at midcentury.

Classroom Issues and Strategies

Brooks's use of multiple and varied personae rivals other poets widely known for experimenting with a range of voices (such as Emily Dickinson and Ezra Pound). A useful classroom strategy is simply to ask students to account for the character behind each voice. Who is she? What is she like? What motivates her speaking; that is, what is the poem's dramatic situation? With little effort students find themselves reconstructing Brooks's memorable characters: The disconsolate mother in "the mother"; the seven defiant pool players in "We Real Cool"; the collective African American consciousness in "Malcolm X."

All poems derive their meaning from the logic of their form, and Brooks's work offers ample evidence of the connection between meaning and form. The tightly closed rhyme scheme of "kitchenette building," for example, mimics the claustrophobic architecture and the dream-stifling reality described in the poem. The short lines and distinctive line breaks (and the resulting combination of end rhyme and internal rhyme) found in "We Real Cool" aggressively highlight the collective lyric voice ("we") at the end of each line. (An Academy of American Poets recording of Brooks reading the poem underscores the significance of the line breaks; the recording can be found at www.poets.org.) In a 1966 broadside printing of the poem, Brooks makes even more assertive use of visual space: The large, all-capital white lettering against a black background looks like a message scrawled on a chalkboard. (The broadside image can be found at the Library of Congress American Memory site: www.memory.loc.gov.)

Connections to Other Authors and Texts

Although she was inspired by Harlem Renaissance poet Countee Cullen, Brooks's work more closely resembles the experimental verse of Ezra

Pound and E. E. Cummings. Her contemporary Robert Hayden offers an interesting example of a poet's vastly different representation of the African American experience.

Questions for Class Discussion

1. How do Brooks's pre-Black Arts Movement poems (before 1967) antici- pate her later poem ("Malcolm X" [1968]) informed by the Black Arts Movement?

2. List the sense perceptions that inform "kitchenette building." Which perceptions are charged positively? which negatively? which neutrally? Which perception has the strongest presence in the poem?

3. Are the seven young pool players in "We Real Cool" sympathetic char- acters in the poem that they give voice to? Why or why not? What about the "old yellow pair" in "The Bean Eaters"? What is the poet's attitude toward the couple?

Brief Bibliography

Kent, George E. *A Life of Gwendolyn Brooks.* Lexington: UP of Kentucky,1990.

Mootry, Maria K., and Gary Smith, eds. *A Life Distilled: Gwendolyn Brooks. Her Poetry and Fiction.* Urbana: U of Illinois P, 1987.

Wright, Stephen Caldwell, ed. *On Gwendolyn Brooks: Reliant Contemplation.* Ann Arbor: U of Michigan P, 1996.

HISAYE YAMAMOTO   (p. 000)

Approaches to Teaching

Virtually no Hisaye Yamamoto critic fails to bring up in some way the haiku form when discussing "Seventeen Syllables" (1949). The act of writing haiku stands at the center of Tomé Hayashi's "rebellious" act as a Japanese American wife and mother. The narrator incorporates a bilingual (English and French) haiku at an early moment in the short story. And the narrator paraphrases Tomé's definition of the verse form for her daughter, Rosie: "See, Rosie, she said, it was a *haiku*, a poem in which she must pack all her meaning into seventeen syllables only, which were divided into three lines of five, seven, and five syllables." And yet this sentence from the short story – a full forty-nine syllables long – highlights the sharp disjunction between the haiku form and Yamamoto's narrative: Haiku are lyric poems that occupy no space in time, whereas the short story elapses over a meas-

urable length of time; haiku offer a fleeting glimpse of the natural landscape, whereas the short story offers multiple perspectives and yields
information about characters' inner lives; and the haiku form is centuries
old and firmly rooted in Japanese culture, whereas the short story is a
much more recent invention and its modern form emerged as much in the
United States as anywhere else.

Classroom Issues and Strategies

Rosie's romantic dalliance with the symbolically named Jesús and Tomé's
youthful love affair in Japan highlight a recurring theme in American literature, particularly in ethnic American literature: Americanization is rendered in terms of romantic independence, in terms of the freedom to
choose one's romantic partner. The stifling Old World values that lead to
tragedy for Tomé are mirrored by the more open New World values that suggest a hopeful future for Rosie. Significantly, Yamamoto complicates the
overly simple analogy (Tomé is to Rosie as Old World is to New World) by
interweaving varieties of freedom and restraint in both women's lives.

On multiple occasions, "Seventeen Syllables" dramatizes literary creation: We gain access to how poetry is both written and published. We learn
that Rosie's "mother was writing the haiku for a daily newspaper, the
Mainichi Shinbun, that was published in San Francisco. . . . Once a week, the
Mainichi would have a section devoted to *haiku,* and her mother became an
extravagant contributor, taking for herself the blossoming pen name, Umé
Hanazono." Discussions of haiku are important to the social lives of Tomé
and Mr. Hayano; when a fellow writer drops by, she compares "ecstatic
notes with the visiting poet." Details such as these add an important backdrop against which we view the short story's shocking climax – Tomé's tale
about how she met Rosie's father, "like a story out of the magazines, illustrated in sepia" – but on their own they suggest that Yamamoto is deeply
concerned with the means by and conditions in which literature emerges.

Connections to Other Authors and Texts

Jun Fujita is best known for his tanka verse, an ancient Japanese form that
shares important characteristics with the haiku (although his poems collected in the anthology are not strictly speaking tanka). Several writers,
including Sarah Orne Jewett and Kate Chopin, explore a woman's sexual
coming-of-age.

Questions for Class Discussion

1. Early in the short story, the narrator quotes from a haiku that Rosie
   appreciates but that her mother does not. What does the haiku (includ-

ing the languages and idiolects that it incorporates) say about Rosie and Tomé (Rosie's mother)?

2. How do the life options, choices, and outcomes of Rosie and Tomé resemble each other? How are they different?

3. Rosie serves as the focus of the short story that's relayed by a third-person narrator. To what extent does the narrator rely on Rosie's sense perceptions for narrative details? What does the narrator describe that is beyond Rosie's understanding?

Brief Bibliography

Cheung, King-Kok. *Articulate Silences : Hisaye Yamamoto, Maxine Hong Kingston, Joy Kogawa*. Ithaca: Cornell UP, 1993.

–––. "Reading between the Syllables: Hisaye Yamamoto's *Seventeen Syllables and Other Stories*." *Teaching American Ethnic Literatures: Nineteen Essays*. Eds. John R. Maitino and David R. Peck. Albuquerque: U of New Mexico P, 1996. 313-25.

Davis, Rocío G. "Yamamoto, Hisaye (1921-)." *The Greenwood Encyclopedia of Multiethnic American Literature*. Ed. Emmanuel S. Nelson. Westport, CT: Greenwood, 2005. 2330-33.

JAMES BALDWIN   (p. 000)

Approaches to Teaching

From the opening lines of "Notes of a Native Son," one gains the sense that James Baldwin views his family history as a part-for-whole version of the wider African American experience and that the trauma and dislocations faced by the Baldwins reenact in miniature the social chaos and violence of the modern American ghetto. As the family waits for Baldwin's father to die and for his brother to be born, "there had been, in Detroit, one of the bloodiest race riots of the century." And the family transports his father's coffin for burial "through a wilderness of smashed plate glass," the aftermath of yet another race riot in Harlem. There are many similar moments that students will likely identify, moments in which Baldwin family strife echoes the strife visiting African Americans throughout the nation. And yet "Notes of a Native Son" forces readers to reconsider traditional notions of national unity during World War II (when the memoir is set) and during the cold war 1950s (when the memoir was written).

Classroom Issues and Strategies

Baldwin wrote the memoir in Europe, where he established himself for most of his professional career as an expatriate with a keen understanding of the American scene. By writing as the consummate outsider, Baldwin allows himself inside the places and debates at the intersection of black and white America: Not only is "Notes of a Native Son" brimming with vivid detail about life in Harlem and elsewhere but also the memoir holds American society to task for its many shortcomings. Baldwin's ultimate philosophical resolution of the dilemmas facing him as an individual, facing his family, facing African Americans, and facing the United States – accepting "life as it is," including life's many injustices, and fighting injustices "with all one's strength" – reads like a sober-minded prescription for social activism.

The emotional climax of "Notes of a Native Son" is probably found in Baldwin's description of a near-fatal scene in a New Jersey restaurant, when he explodes at a waitress who refuses him service. Baldwin highlights the degree to which each character in this scene is acting out familiar (and very likely often rehearsed) social roles: "She did not ask me what I wanted, but repeated, as though she had learned it somewhere, 'We don't serve Negroes here.' She did not say it with the blunt, derisive hostility to which I had grown so accustomed, but, rather, with a note of apology in her voice, and fear. This made me colder and more murderous than ever. I felt I had to do something with my hands. I wanted her to come close enough for me to get her neck between my hands." The scene derives its power from Baldwin's manipulation of our expectations: We know what usually happens in such a situation, and his behavior plays out the tension to an absurd and disturbing end. Here and elsewhere in "Notes of a Native Son," Baldwin exposes the hollowness of society by demonstrating how familiar social roles border on the extremes of violence and vapidity.

Connections to Other Authors and Texts

It is worthwhile to consider "Notes of a Native Son" as an extension of the social analysis that W. E. B. Du Bois performs in his explanation of "double-consciousness." Baldwin was inspired (positively and negatively) by Richard Wright, from whom he borrows the title of the memoir. Allen Ginsberg offers a similar outsider perspective of American social life during the immediate postwar period, and Amiri Baraka explores similarly explosive racial tension in his *Dutchman* (p. 1400).

Questions for Class Discussion

1. At the end of "Notes of a Native Son," Baldwin stresses that "one . . . must fight [injustices] with all one's strength." How might one fight the injustices to which Baldwin refers? In other words, what kinds of social change does he seem to be calling for?

2. At one point Baldwin describes his father's voice as "harsh and vindictively polite" to visiting welfare workers and bill collectors. How might

such a voice be performed? Where else does Baldwin suggest the social performance of a specific form of identity?

3. Discuss a scene in which Baldwin deploys the tools of fiction (narrative time, characterization, dialogue) to enhance the reading experience.

Brief Bibliography

Bloom, Harold, ed. *James Baldwin*. New York: Chelsea House, 2007.

Campbell, James. *Talking at the Gates: A Life of James Baldwin: With a New Afterword*. Berkeley: U of California P, 2002.

Rusk, Lauren. *The Life Writing of Otherness: Woolf, Baldwin, Kingston, and Winterson*. New York: Routledge, 2002.

FLANNERY O'CONNOR   (p. 000)

Approaches to Teaching

A tale such as "A Good Man Is Hard to Find" (1955) provides a refreshing reminder that it is still possible to shock today's students. Flanner O'Connor's famous short story offers ample opportunity for students to locate shocking material, and it is a useful exercise to ask them what they find shocking about it. The list of unexpected and disturbing elements that they provide usually includes the following: a sense of unease at finding humor in accounts of gruesome violence; the violence itself, especially the mother's quick acceptance of her own and her daughter's murder; the fact that none of the characters in the short story are even remotely likeable; and the Misfit's twisted theology, a misshapen version of Pascal's wager (unable to accept probability theory like that offered by Pascal, the Misfit decides that no conclusive evidence of God's existence requires a life of "?killing somebody or burning down his house'") and his spot-on analysis of the grandmother's character ("?She would of been a good woman,'" he decides, "?if it had been somebody there to shoot her every minute of her life'"). What is important to demonstrate about a list such as this is that the short story's shock value derives from O'Connor's skillful manipulation of characterization and plot.

Classroom Issues and Strategies

Perhaps the most remarkable feature of "A Good Man Is Hard to Find" is that it contains an abundance of straightforward and dark humor in its pages. Beginning with the title, we might find humor in the extent to which O'Connor twists our expectations; light romantic comedy is nowhere to be found. Characters are wonderfully drawn in all their hypocritical glory: The pig-headed, racist, sanctimonious grandmother, for instance, wears a "straw sailor hat with a bunch of white violets on the brim and a navy blue dress with a small white dot in the print" so that, in the event of a car accident, "anyone seeing her dead on the highway would know at once that she was a lady." (The narrator never says so, but we just know that that's how the grandmother explains her attire to others.) The multiple, interconnecting plot twists that result in a gruesome mass murder are also darkly humorous for their heavy-handed absurdity: The grandmother's paranoid ramblings turn out to be true; the family just happens not only to travel the precise same road as the Misfit but also to wreck the car there; and the characters are killed at least in part for their character flaws (the grandmother for her stubborn self-importance, which leads to a ridiculous car accident; Bailey for his sheer inability to recognize the real predicament that he faces; the children for their belligerent rudeness). O'Connor seems to challenge us to read beyond the absurdity and humor to find a more lasting message, to find a moral amid all the immorality.

Connections to Other Authors and Texts

Like Jean Toomer and William Faulkner, O'Connor suggests that southern history and society yield a peculiarly southern violence. O'Connor's linking of violence and absurdity presages the postmodernism of Don DeLillo and Donald Barthelme.

Questions for Class Discussion

1. What should one expect from a short story titled "A Good Man Is Hard to Find"? How does O'Connor live up to or subvert our expectations?

2. Which characters are the most sympathetic in the short story? Which are the least sympathetic? Why do you like or dislike individual characters?

3. Isolate humorous moments in the short story. How does the humor work? How does the humor contribute to your understanding of the short story's themes?

4. Discuss the logic of the Misfit's theological musings. What does he enlist as evidence? How does he ponder the evidence? What conclusions does he reach? Where is his logic sound? Where is it flawed?

Brief Bibliography

Asals, Frederick, ed. *A Good Man Is Hard to Find*. New Brunswick: Rutgers UP, 1993.

Darretta, John Lawrence. *Before the Sun Has Set: Retribution in the Fiction of Flannery O'Connor.* New York: Peter Lang, 2006.

Simpson, Melissa. *Flannery O'Connor: A Biography.* Westport, CT: Greenwood, 2005.

ALLEN GINSBERG   (p. 000)

Approaches to Teaching

Howl may well be the most influential American poem since T. S. Eliot's *The Waste Land.* Ginsberg's jeremiad has in the last half century directly influenced virtually every major U.S. poet, many of whom have recorded Ginsberg's influence in poetry and prose. It is useful to share passages reflecting on *Howl* by such writers as Jack Kerouac (in *Dharma Bums*), Diane di Prima (in *Memoirs of a Beatnik*), and Ed Sanders (in *Tales of Beatnik Glory*). Before doing so, however, ask students to share their so-called gut reactions to *Howl,* because there already exists a long and important tradition of recording first encounters with the poem, a tradition rivaled only by accounts of first encounters with Whitman. Poems are first and foremost locations for aesthetic pleasure or displeasure, and all other concerns (identity, history, politics) flow from there. Readers have for decades loved and hated *Howl,* and they will no doubt continue to do so for many decades to come. Asking students to isolate elements in *Howl* that are loveable or hateable furnishes a steady supply of points of entry into the poem.

Classroom Issues and Strategies

It would be too easy, given the poem's title and subject matter, to dismiss *Howl* as the formless effusions of an inspired maniac. And yet the poem's form might be identified in terms of local features (biblical syntax, punctuation, word choices, associative logic) that cohere into global trends. If students provide a list of the geography, characters and character types, and tone for each of the poem's three sections, they gain a sense of the poem's direction and overall shape. In section 1, the poem traverses the whole of the United States and the rest of the globe with a wayward group of social misfits. In section 2, the poem lands readers in a mythical space that might also be any modern industrial city; the primary character here is a mythical creature that obviously represents contemporary social ills. In section 3, the poem is confined to a specific mental institution (and at one point in a single bed there) and it is peopled by two named individuals. In other words, the poem evolves from the global to the mythic to the local, and generally speaking the poem's tone evolves from ecstatic despondency to moral outrage to compassion.

Howl was the subject of a famous 1957 obscenity trial, an event that propelled Ginsberg and City Lights Books onto the national stage. (Thanks to a widely reported reading of *Howl* at the Six Gallery in San Francisco, the poem was already the talk of poetry circles from coast-to-coast even before its publication.) Because legal institutions play an important role in defining what counts as literature and in determining how literature is disseminated, it is a useful and entertaining exercise to place *Howl* on trial for obscenity. (In *Miller v. California* [1973], the U.S. Supreme Court defined obscene materials as those that [1] "'the average person, applying contemporary community standards'" finds, "taken as a whole, appeals to the prurient interest"; [2] "depicts or describes, in a patently offensive way, sexual conduct"; and [3] "taken as a whole, lacks serious literary, artistic, political, or scientific value.") The exercise will force students to ponder a readership beyond the classroom environment, the social effects of literary expression, and the literary value of controversial poetry.

Connections to Other Authors and Texts

Ginsberg drew inspiration and support from William Carlos Williams, although ironically *Howl* owes at least as much to T. S. Eliot's *The Waste Land*. Ginsberg belongs to the group of confessional poets (such as John Berryman and Sylvia Plath) who came of age in post-World War II society, and *Howl* compares in intriguing ways with the work of fellow Beat poet Gary Snyder.

Questions for Class Discussion

1. When *Howl* was first published, it was hailed (and derided) as revolutionary. What seems wholly new in *Howl?* In what ways is *Howl* a traditional poem?

2. Chart the following in each of the three sections of *Howl:* characters and character types; literal and figurative geography; punctuation; tone. What directional trends can you identify from section to section?

3. Research your state's statutory definition of *obscenity*, then hold a mock trial in which Ginsberg is charged with the crime. Is *Howl* obscene? Why or why not?

Brief Bibliography

Ginsberg, Allen. *Howl: Original Draft Facsimile, Transcript, and Variant Versions, Fully Annotated by Author, with Contemporaneous Correspondence, Account of First Public Reading, Legal Skirmishes, Precursor Texts, and Bibliography.* Ed. Barry Miles. New York: Harper, 1986.

310 Volume Two: 1865 to the Present

Morgan, Bill, and Nancy J. Peters, eds. Howl *on Trial: The Battle for Free Expression*. San Francisco: City Lights, 2006.

Raskin, Jonah. *American Scream: Allen Ginsberg's* Howl *and the Making of the Beat Generation*. Berkeley: U of California P, 2004.

Schumacher, Michael. *Dharma Lion: A Biography of Allen Ginsberg*. New York: St. Martin's, 1992.

JOHN ASHBERY   (p. 000)

Approaches to Teaching

If John Ashbery finds his way into an American literature course – and, as a figure universally regarded as among the most important contemporary poets, he should – then he will likely find a space at or near the end of a syllabus. This presents an opportunity to use Ashbery's poetry as an occasion to revisit some of the major themes of twentieth-century American verse: The status of the "thing" and the connection between the signified and the signifier in language; the relative importance of the natural landscape and human society; the opacity of identity grounded in language; the need to find new words and new forms to capture the American experience. Handling Ashbery's poetry in this manner may take some of the pressure off of instructors and their students, who may find the difficulty of Ashbery's work overwhelming. Plus, considering Ashbery's place at the terminus of American literary history highlights what makes him so utterly unique.

Classroom Issues and Strategies

Many critics have labeled Ashbery's work "occasional poetry" because he is profoundly concerned with how the intellect responds to and reshapes in language everyday occurrences, the occasions that occupy our lives. Making meaning out of an Ashbery poem, therefore, requires surrendering to the mind's (his mind's) tendency to wander without aim, to take comfort in aimlessness, and subsequently to assert one's authority as a reader, to wrest meaning from language. One of the best ways to approach an Ashbery poem is to ask a simple question of it: What might occasion a poet to notice and record this particular set of details? When and where is the poem being spoken? What literally is he seeing and feeling and thinking? What is his emotional state? We might notice a trend in the dramatic situations of Ashbery's poems: They tend to take place in a present moment that is very localized and very concrete, but from the local details we are asked to derive a larger significance.

Connections to Other Authors and Texts

Like the work of Gertrude Stein and Wallace Stevens, Ashbery's is a poetry of mental processes. His concern about the status of the linguistic sign often aligns him with postmodernists such as Don DeLillo.

Questions for Class Discussion

1. What seems to occasion "The One Thing That Can Save America"? What is the poet's state of mind in the poem?

2. Who is the "you" in "Paradoxes and Oxymorons"? Why does "you" interrupt the poet to ask questions in stanza 2? Do you think that "you" is satisfied with the answers?

3. Identify the commonly used phrases in "One Coat of Paint." What about the poem rescues these phrases from being cliché?

Brief Bibliography

Bloom, Harold, ed. *John Ashbery: Comprehensive Research and Study Guide*. Philadelphia: Chelsea House, 2004.

Du Bois, Andrew. *Ashbery's Forms of Attention*. Tuscaloosa: U of Alabama P, 2006.

Vendler, Helen Hennessy. *Invisible Listeners: Lyric Intimacy in Herbert, Whitman, and Ashbery*. Princeton: Princeton UP, 2005.

EDWARD ALBEE　　(p. 000)

Approaches to Teaching

The brevity and simple structure of Edward Albee's *The Sandbox* (1960) suggests that a classroom staging of the play might be easily handled; after all, the play lasts but a few minutes, it requires a cast of just five actors, and the stage directions call for the bare minimum in set design and props. Be forewarned, however: *The Sandbox* is decidedly not a play that teaches itself in performance. A classroom production will not necessarily clear up student confusion, nor will it inevitably lead student discussion along interesting paths. In fact, there is the distinct possibility that the play's quirks will lead students to dismiss it from serious consideration. It makes sense to lay the groundwork for a classroom production with a brief discussion of the theater of the absurd, in particular the mode's flouting of dramatic conventions. Albee is arguably America's foremost absurdist playwright, and in that role he has done much to bring existentialist alienation to the American stage. The play's meaninglessness acquires a significance – a meaning – when considered in such light.

Classroom Issues and Strategies

The theater of the absurd is affiliated with seemingly directionless plots that bear little resemblance to quotidian reality; their guiding principle is a sharp and irreverent departure from reality. In *The Sandbox*, the ham-fisted characters bear little resemblance to the social roles for which they're named. Even the allegorically identified Young Man bears more resemblance to a bumbling lifeguard wannabe actor than to the "Angel of Death" that he claims to be. The plot (if it can be called that) revolves around what appears to be the ritual abandonment of an elderly woman (Grandma) at what might represent a beach (but then again, the titular sandbox might represent a sandbox). And the characters regularly address each other as actors in a play or they speak to the audience directly, shattering any possibility for a "fourth wall" illusion.

The Sandbox deconstructs the conventions of theater, and from the rubble we must reconstruct its larger meaning. It would be a shame to sell the play short by insisting on any single meaning behind its meaninglessness. True, *The Sandbox* is a humorous indictment of crass "family" values, but it might also be understood as an existentialist inquiry into transcendent intergenerational communication – or it might be a night out's entertainment at the local theater.

Connections to Other Authors and Texts

Amiri Baraka, Donald Barthelme, and Ursula K. Le Guin share Albee's penchant for the absurd, but each one approaches absurdity with unique social and political commentary.

Questions for Class Discussion

1. If we take for granted that *The Sandbox* is in many ways meaningless, what does it mean to express meaninglessness on the stage? What role might "meaningless" theater play in our culture and society?

2. What kind of music should the Musician play when he's ordered to do so by Mommy? Explain your choice.

3. Cast your own version of *The Sandbox* with well-known contemporary actors. What do your choices suggest about the effect(s) that you wish to achieve?

Brief Bibliography

Bottoms, Stephen. *Cambridge Companion to Edward Albee*. Cambridge: Cambridge UP, 2005.

Gussow, Mel. *Edward Albee: A Singular Journey: A Biography.* New York: Simon and Schuster, 1999.

ADRIENNE RICH　　　(p. 000)

Approaches to Teaching

Based on the strength of her nonfiction prose alone, one might make the case that Adrienne Rich deserves a place among a handful of the most important feminist voices of our time; add her poetry to the equation, and one might well say that Rich is the single most important feminist voice of the last generation. In the event that a student arrives at class with a notion of feminism informed by little more than talk radio, it helps to keep handy a simple definition of the term. This one from *Webster's* is useful for its simplicity: "1: the theory of the political, economic, and social equality of the sexes; 2: organized activity on behalf of women's rights and interests." Building from a simple foundation such as this may save some time and prevent unnecessary headache; and if the definition disabuses a student of a stereotyped image of feminists, all the better. But of course the feminism to be found in Rich's poetry offers far greater variety and subtlety than any dictionary definition might suggest. Even if feminism achieves its goal as an emancipatory discourse (and thus obviates its mission), Rich's poetry will live on as a testament to the power of poetry that emerges from and transforms a major social movement. We might approach her work by anticipating how readers in a politically, economically, and socially equal society will look back on individual poems.

Classroom Issues and Strategies

Throughout her career, Rich has been fascinated by the need to renew language in the furtherance of a feminist vision. At times this requires a quintessentially modernist gesture, writing poems about poetry: "Diving into the Wreck" and "Power" imaginatively reconceive language and poetry as something else (undersea archaeology, nuclear physics). At other times this requires taking up and radically transforming the ancient tradition of love poetry: "A Valediction Forbidding Mourning" and "Trying to Talk with a Man" displace the language of love and desire from its standard heterosexual context.

　　It is important to keep the poems' formal design in view when discussing Rich's feminism – too often it is easy to lose sight of how she connects literary and political identity with a poem's arrangement. Although the title lacks the colon found in John Donne's version, Rich's "A Valediction Forbidding Mourning" is a poem of colons and the forced equivalencies that they impose. The visual shape of "Diving into the Wreck," with its short, semiregular lines, hints at depth and tentative exploration. "Power" is a free-verse poem with a structure – jagged line breaks and wide gaps within lines – that mimics the crumbling earth and decomposing elements; the poem's fragmentation allows for visual and semantic associations within and across lines.

Connections to Other Authors and Texts

Like Robert Lowell and (mostly) unlike Sylvia Plath, Rich put confessional poetry to work for political ends. Her wish to imagine a postgender world aligns Rich's work with that of Ursula K. Le Guin.

Questions for Class Discussion

1. Compare and contrast Rich's "A Valediction Forbidding Mourning" with John Donne's "A Valediction: Forbidding Mourning." In what ways does Rich seem to be commenting on the work of her predecessor?

2. What might the wreck (in "Diving into the Wreck") symbolize? What details from the poem support specific symbolic interpretations of the wreck? What might the "book of myths" represent?

3. The literal source of power referred to in "Power" is radium (or a similarly dangerous element). How might the source of power be understood figuratively; that is, what do Marie Curie's life and death represent?

Brief Bibliography

Dickie, Margaret. *Stein, Bishop and Rich: Lyrics of Love, War and Place.* Chapel Hill: U of North Carolina P, 1997.

Sheridan, Susan. "Adrienne Rich and the Women's Liberation Movement: A Politics of Reception." *Women's Studies* 35 (2006): 17-45.

Sickels, Amy. *Adrienne Rich.* Philadelphia: Chelsea House, 2005.

Templeton, Alice. *The Dream and the Dialogue: Adrienne Rich's Feminist Poetics.* Knoxville: U of Tennessee P, 1994.

URSULA K. LE GUIN   (p. 1349)

Approaches to Teaching

Many discussions of postmodernism in literature reside somewhere between the stratosphere and the ionosphere. Ursula K. Le Guin's "She

Unnames Them" (1985) offers firm ground from which to launch a discussion of literary postmodernism, and it has the added bonuses of being short enough to handle in its entirety and of finding a popular place among student readers. Whereas modernism routinely deploys mythic patterns that have been stripped free of moral commentary, postmodernism deploys mythic patterns to absurdist ends. Le Guin's radical and humorously irreverent reformulation of the creation myth in Genesis reverses the moral poles of its source. Whereas modernism questions the foundations of realism, postmodernism often commits to magic realism and fabulism. Le Guin goes a step further: "She Unnames Them" creates a logic in which fable and science and myth exist side by side, on roughly equal terms. Whereas modernism underscores the disjuncture between lived experience and narrative time, postmodernism sometimes rejects the very premise of linear time. "She Unnames Them" collapses biblical time onto modern time and allows them to flow in reverse. And whereas modernist experimentation often derives from a perceived crisis of language, postmodernist experimentation tends to see language simply as a game with arbitrary (and easily broken) rules. Here Le Guin doesn't fit so neatly into a strict postmodernist camp: Her commitment to social change is too earnest to dismiss as a mere game.

Classroom Issues and Strategies

Le Guin alludes to Jonathan Swift and T. S. Eliot in her short story, but the key source is obviously the book of Genesis (Gen. 1–3). Both the source text and "She Unnames Them" are short enough to compare side by side in class. Le Guin insists on unpacking the gender politics of the Bible, so it is helpful to be prepared with an interpretation of gendered (and postgendered) language in both texts. For convenience's sake, here is the relevant passage from the New International Version:

> Now the Lord God had formed out of the ground all the beasts of the field and all the birds of the air. He brought them to the man to see what he would name them; and whatever the man called each living creature, that was its name. So the man gave names to all the livestock, the birds of the air and all the beasts of the field. But for Adam no suitable helper was found. So the Lord God caused the man to fall into a deep sleep; and while he was sleeping, he took one of the man's ribs and closed up the place with flesh. Then the Lord God made a woman from the rib he had taken out of the man, and he brought her to the man. (Gen. 2:19-22)

I won't presume to suggest a particular biblical interpretation here. In the short story, Eve sums up her interpretation as follows: "You and your father lent me this [name] — gave it to me, actually. It's been really useful, but it doesn't exactly seem to fit very well lately."

Much of the short story's humor derives from the personification of animals; each species takes on a unique and quirkily human personality. Some of these personality traits are part of our cultural repertoire (the cats and dogs behave especially predictably), others take on a new role (the yaks observe a matrilineal politics). The ultimate effect of Le Guin's humor is the decentering of a human perspective; as Eve points out, cats and dogs and yaks exist as our equals in the short story's postname, postspecies society.

Connections to Other Authors and Texts

Le Guin's playful suggestion that animals are like humans (and vice versa) places her in an ecocentric lineage that descends from Henry David Thoreau through Sarah Orne Jewett, Gary Snyder, and Leslie Marmon Silko. Her consideration of a postgender world connects her with Adrienne Rich.

Questions for Class Discussion

1. Identify language in "She Unnames Them" that sounds biblical. How does "She Unnames Them" borrow from the story of creation as told in Genesis? In what ways does she depart from her source? What elements of the short story rely on scientific fact? What elements seem closer in spirit to fable?

2. How would you describe the personalities of the diverse species mentioned in "She Unnames Them"? Which human foibles does Le Guin satirize in the guise of animals? According to the logic of the short story, how are animals like humans, and how are humans like animals?

3. How is the narrator (Eve) like Adam or God? How is she different?

Brief Bibliography

Bernardo, Susan M. *Ursula K. Le Guin: A Critical Companion.* Westport, CT: Greenwood, 2006.

Reid, Suzanne Elizabeth. *Presenting Ursula K. Le Guin.* New York: Twayne, 1997.

Wheat, Jennifer C. "Mindless Fools and Leaves That Run: Subjectivity, Politics, and Myth in Scientific Nomenclature." *Coming into Contact: Explorations in Ecocritical Theory and Practice.* Eds. Annie Merrill Ingram et al. Athens: U of Georgia P, 2007. 209-20.

GARY SNYDER   (p. 000)

Approaches to Teaching

It might be said that all poets are philosophers of language; the statement certainly rings true in the case of Gary Snyder. Of the many positions occupied by Snyder in American cultural history – Zen icon of the Beat generation, seminal figure in the ongoing ecocritical movement – his role as language philosopher may offer the most lasting presence. Among the poems collected in *The Bedford Anthology of American Literature,* we see a glimpse of key notions informing Snyder's aesthetic. First, we encounter (in "Riprap") a hard analogy between language and a discrete presence in the physical world (in this case, words are "like rocks"). Second, we are given to understand that human language offers but transient meaning in the eternal conversation of the universe. Nature, we learn in "Ripples on the Surface," is "not a book, but a *performance,* a / high old culture" that rewrites itself in ways that outlast a human lifetime (indeed, human existence). Third, even though Snyder decenters human consciousness in a manner consistent with today's ecocritical movement, he still insists on the primal, transformative power of poetry. Poets, as he remarks in "Axe Handles," model for us "[h]ow we go on."

Classroom Issues and Strategies

In "Ripples on the Surface," Snyder describes nature not as "a book, but a *performance,* a / high old culture." This gesture would seem to anthropomorphize nature, to understand it primarily (and perhaps dangerously) in human terms. And yet in calling attention to the human dimensions of the natural landscape, he repeatedly stresses that human activity finds a place—neither central nor in the margins – in nature's order. He continues: "The vast wild / the house, alone. / The little house in the wild, / the wild in the house." Snyder emphasizes not only that the boundary between the human and the natural is hazy, but also that the boundary is a human invention – one that can be unmade. Seen in this light, the granite of "Riprap" reveals a natural vocabulary, and in "Beneath My Hand and Eye the Distant Hills, Your Body," the human body is transfigured into nature just as much as the opposite is true.

Snyder's incorporation of Asian cultural history into his American poetry deserves some attention, and a comparison with the Orientalist work of Ezra Pound yields interesting results. Viewed against Pound, Snyder appears less aggressive, more tentative in his incorporation of Asian themes and idioms. Whereas Pound purports to translate directly ancient Chinese texts, for example, Snyder deploys quotatives and similes to stress that Asian references are rhetorical figures: "The worlds" are "*like* an endless / four-dimensional / Game of *Go*" in "Riprap" (my emphasis on like); Lu Ji's *Wê Fu* is a text, a source to be mined, not re-created, in "Axe Handles."

Connections to Other Authors and Texts

Ezra Pound's appropriation of Asian forms, themes, and texts serves as an obvious influence in Snyder's career. And though his fellow Beat poet Allen Ginsberg shared a number of relationships and experiences with Snyder, the two found remarkably different voices to record them.

Questions for Class Discussion

1. How does the physical shape of "Riprap" enact the poem's message? How does the poem's rhythm underscore the connection in the poem between language and laying down rocks?

2. Where is the speaker situated in physical space in the various lines of "Beneath My Hand and Eye the Distant Hills, Your Body"? How do the "I" and the "eye" of the poem produce each other? What is the effect of the quotation marks in the poem?

3. In "Axe Handles," how are poets like axes? If Pound (for example) is an axe, what is the poem's speaker?

Brief Bibliography

Gray, Timothy. *Gary Snyder and the Pacific Rim: Creating Countercultural Community.* Iowa City: U of Iowa P, 2006.

Halper, Jon, ed. *Gary Snyder: Dimensions of a Life.* San Francisco: Sierra Club, 1991.

Murphy, Patrick D., ed. *Critical Essays on Gary Snyder.* Boston: Hall, 1991.

Murphy, Patrick D. *A Place for Wayfaring: The Poetry and Prose of Gary Snyder.* Corvallis: Oregon State UP, 2000.

DONALD BARTHELME   (p. 000)

Approaches to Teaching

Schools, and especially public schools, represent the best in human potential. They embody a society's choice to invest valuable resources in human capital. They are (or should be at least) refuges from violence; they are (or should be) a place where the human capacity for wonder receives its due attention. Schools are institutions that Americanize in all the best ways.

But such is not the case in Donald Barthelme's "The School" (1974). (Several details, including the polyethnic roster of students and the school's location next to a federal building, suggest that it is an inner-city public school.) Coming to terms with the setting (what do schools represent in our culture?) and its characters (what do schoolchildren and teachers represent in our culture?) provides an important backdrop for Barthelme's postmodernist formal choices and the social critique ultimately served by literary form.

Classroom Issues and Strategies

The narrator begins the short story simply enough – with the near-universal conversation starter, "Well . . ." – and in a simple tone implying that an easygoing conversation is about to follow: "Well, we had all these children out planting trees, see, because we figured that ... that was part of their education, to see how, you know, the root systems . . ." You might ask one group of students to point out this and similar language in which the short story proceeds conversationally. The conversational tics diminish in number as "The School" proceeds, but it never departs from the understated, deadpan voice, even when bizarre tragedy is heaped upon bizarre tragedy. You might ask a second group of students to highlight moments in the short story that are bizarrely shocking. These increase in number as the short story proceeds. At key moments, the two lists will no doubt overlap; the convergence provides a useful occasion for talking about tone, the attitude that the writer takes toward the audience and the subject.

When the *how* of tone is clear, the more important and more difficult question of *why* remains: What is the larger point of Barthelme's poker-faced gallows humor? The answer largely depends on the point that you wish to make about Barthelme's career (such absurdly humorous short stories were his meal ticket for decades), about the postmodernist "literature of exhaustion" (to borrow John Barth's phrase), or about the value of satire as a form of cultural critique.

Connections to Other Authors and Texts

Barthelme's use of an incongruously deadpan narrative voice has predecessors in the work of Mark Twain and Ambrose Bierce. Vastly different representations of American education can be found in the work of Zitkala-?a and Toni Morrison.

Questions for Class Discussion

1. Locate unexpected or even shocking moments in the short story. Why are they unexpected? How do Barthelme's language choices increase their shock value?

2. Paraphrase the children's precocious question – "isn't death the fundamental datum, the means by which the taken-for-granted mundanity of the everyday may be transcended" – into your own terms. Is this the message of the short story? Why or why not?

3. Does "The School" have a happy ending? Why or why not?

Brief Bibliography

Barthelme, Helen Moore. *Donald Barthelme: The Genesis of a Cool Sound.* College Station: Texas A&M UP, 2001.

Patteson, Richard F., ed. *Critical Essays on Donald Barthelme.* New York: Hall, 1992.

Roe, Barbara L. *Donald Barthelme: A Study of the Short Fiction.* New York: Twayne, 1992.

Trachtenberg, Stanley. *Understanding Donald Barthelme.* Columbia: U of South Carolina P, 1990.

TONI MORRISON   (p. 000)

Approaches to Teaching

Although there are certainly other candidates for the distinction, one could make a strong case that Toni Morrison is the single most important American fiction writer of the late twentieth and early twenty-first centuries, a position achieved on the basis of her many groundbreaking novels. "Recitatif" is therefore a handy gateway into Morrison's longer fiction, and it is important to stress how the short story reflects her wider interests. To begin with, the short story is profoundly concerned with the weight of a troubled American history in the present-day arena of race relations. The short story also calls attention to the special role of subjective memory (the narrator's unique take on the world) in reconstituting the textures of the past. The short story is also a significant meditation on the bonds that occur between women because of (or in spite of) the social pressures that they encounter. Finally, the short story offers numerous opportunities to highlight the elegance of the narrative's larger structure and the eloquence of Morrison's prose at the level of individual sentences.

Classroom Issues and Strategies

The unavoidable question posed by "Recitatif" (1983) concerns the racial identities of its primary characters, Twyla (the narrator) and Roberta. One is obviously black, the other is obviously white – the question remains,

though: Which is which? Morrison embeds a long supply of racial stereotypes in the narrative – stereotypes about clothing and hair and body odor
and musical preferences and political attitudes and social class – but the
stereotypes adhere willy-nilly to the individual characters, with no obvious
pattern revealing a character's blackness or whiteness. Why the instability? Why doesn't Morrison let blackness or whiteness emerge clearly so
that she can move on to the social concerns (educational opportunity and
school desegregation, the economic stresses facing working mothers) in
the short story's margins? Late in the short story, Twyla observes of her
protest placard that "my sign didn't make sense without Roberta's." On a
literal level, Twyla means that "AND SO DO CHILDREN****" makes no sense
unless it's held up alongside "MOTHERS HAVE RIGHTS TOO!"; seen as a statement
about racial coding, however, Twyla's relativist observation is a homespun
version of what social theorists call "differential identity," identity formations that achieve meaning only in contrast to alternative formations.

Many of the cultural signposts found in "Recitatif" – attending a Jimi
Hendrix concert, school busing controversies, *The Brady Bunch* –occupy a
readily identifiable moment in our cultural history. Morrison appears to
indicate that the language of racial controversy and understanding evolves
over time, but the basic shape of the issue continues unchanged. The
anthology supplies useful footnotes that allude to the cultural significance
of the references, but additional guidance and detail may be required.

Connections to Other Authors and Texts

"Recitatif" ponders the question of interracial communication (and mis-
communication) and hints at the possibility of racial transcendence; these
features of the short story place it in a direct line from the work of W. E. B.
Du Bois, Zora Neale Hurston, and Jean Toomer.

Questions for Class Discussion

1. On several occasions the story refers to the principle characters' racial
   identity without specifying who is black and who is white. How does
   the story pique the reader's interest in solving the puzzle of race? Who
   do you think is black or white? What "evidence" is there to support
   your view?

2. *Webster's* defines *recitative* (the Anglicization of *recitatif*) as "a rhythmically free vocal style that imitates the natural inflections of speech
   and that is used for dialogue and narrative in operas and oratorios;
   also: a passage to be delivered in this style." How does the short-story
   title relate to its contents?

3. The short story is narrated in the 1980s, but also set in the 1960s and
'70s. How does each decade exert unique pressures on the interracial
relationship between Twyla and Roberta? If the short story was continued into this century, what cultural signposts might Morrison refer to?

Brief Bibliography

Abel, Elizabeth. "Black Writing, White Reading." *Critical Inquiry* 19 (1993):
470-98.

Beaulieu, Elizabeth Ann, ed. *The Toni Morrison Encyclopedia*. Westport, CT:
Greenwood, 2003.

Goldstein-Shirley, David. "Race and Response: Toni Morrison's 'Recitatif.'"
Short Story 5 (1997): 77-86.

Kubitschek, Missy Dehn, ed. *Toni Morrison: A Critical Companion*. Westport,
CT: Greenwood, 1998.

SYLVIA PLATH   (p. 000)

Approaches to Teaching

Sylvia Plath's work challenges the notion that confessional poetry gives us
accurate access to the innermost drives and hidden thoughts of an individual writer. Many students will have a sense of the legend that Plath constructed around the basic framework of her biography, but as her biographers insist, the legend found in her poetry bears only a tenuous
relationship to the writer who imagined a poetic career from an early age.
(The recent film *Sylvia* [2003], starring Gwyneth Paltrow in the title role,
may be the source of the legend for many students.) An example such as
"Lady Lazarus" provides a useful tool for prying students away from the
legend so that they can focus instead on the intricacies of Plath's poetry.
The poem relates in some indirect way to the suicide attempts that punctuated Plath's life – most students have at least heard of Plath's final, successful attempt – but it more clearly creates a phoenixlike fictional persona, or more accurately personae (because the Lazarus figure speaks in a
multiplicity of voices: helpless victim, blasphemous exhibitionist, vindic-
tive femme fatale). The title of the poem alone reveals that Plath is more
interested in reconfiguring our culture's organizing mythologies than in
faithfully rendering the facts of her life.

Classroom Issues and Strategies

As with all confessional poetry, it is important when discussing Plath's
work to stress the care with which it rearranges intimate human experi-

ence into the stuff of literature. The basic questions of prosody – Does the poem rhyme, and if so, how? What kind of rhythm or recognizable meter does the poem exhibit? What organizing principles govern the length and shape of individual stanzas? – are the first questions to ask of a Plath poem. It is also useful to investigate the personae who utter individual poems, beginning with those examples that are most obviously fictional (such as "Mirror") and advancing to those that are seemingly autobiographical (such as "Daddy" and "Lady Lazarus"). The more enterprising students will likely recognize a close connection between prosody and persona; in "Daddy," for example, the uncanny voice of the poem emerges out of the odd juxtapositions of baby talk, strident meter (many students correctly compare the poem's rhythm with the rhythm of nursery rhymes), and horrific imagery.

Connections to Other Authors and Texts

Plath helped advance and popularize the confessional mode that had already been identified with Robert Lowell. Her construction of legendary female personae invites comparison with the work of Mina Loy and Adrienne Rich.

Questions for Class Discussion

1. Recite "Morning Song," "Daddy," and "Lady Lazarus." What kind of voice or voices do the poems call for in performance? Why?
2. Identify details in Plath's poetry that might be autobiographical and those that are obviously fabricated. How do we know the difference?
3. Plath's father was not a Nazi, and her mother was not Jewish. Why would Plath invent such a past for herself in "Daddy"? What are the rhetorical effects of the invented biographical references?

Brief Bibliography

Bassnett, Susan. *Sylvia Plath: An Introduction to the Poetry*. New York: Palgrave Macmillan, 2005.

Bloom, Harold, ed. *Sylvia Plath*. New York: Bloom's Literary Criticism, 2007.

Gill, Jo, ed. *The Cambridge Companion to Sylvia Plath*. Cambridge: Cambridge UP, 2006.

Wagner-Martin, Linda. *Sylvia Plath: A Literary Life*. 2nd ed. New York: Palgrave, 2003.

JOHN UPDIKE   (p. 000)

Approaches to Teaching

Because John Updike's "A & P" (1961) recalls the experiences of a working-class nineteen-year-old youth, the short story is instantly accessible to students and it is deceptively simple in its form. It is possible to step back from "A & P" and allow students to explain what they like or dislike about the short story. Odds are that most of the discussion will center on the memorable narrator, Sammy: on his unique and quirky voice and on his objectifying obsession with the female body. Be sure to set aside ample time to address the intricacies of narrative time and the short story's observations about the performance of social class. A careful consideration of "A & P" allows readers to complicate the pigeonhole (masculinist fiction of Waspy suburbs) into which Updike's work is sometimes placed.

Classroom Issues and Strategies

From the opening sentence, Sammy emerges as a narrator who speaks with absolute authenticity, even when he traffics in clichés. (Indeed, his heavy reliance on clichés may be one of the important markers of his authenticity.) If you ask students to highlight words and phrases that seem unique to Sammy, they will produce a long and idiosyncratic list of Sammyisms. Those familiar enough with 1950s American cultural history will even be able to speculate about the kinds of music or movies that Sammy enjoys when he isn't working. They should be cautioned, though, to identify the nineteen-year-old Sammy of the short story with the Sammy who narrates the short story. Sammy reveals that the episode at the A & P will have a dramatic (but never revealed) impact on his adult life: "my stomach kind of fell as I felt how hard the world was going to be to me hereafter." The moment has instantly aged him, although to what extent isn't wholly clear. Updike further complicates the picture with a dynamic mixture of present-tense ("In walks these three girls . . .") and past-tense ("The one that caught my eye first was...") narration.

At one point in the short story, Sammy nonchalantly mentions that his fellow A & P employee Stokesie "thinks he's going to be manager some sunny day, maybe in 1990 when it's called the Great Alexandrov and Petrooshki Tea Company or something." The reference reminds us of the cold war geopolitical context in which the short story is set; it also alerts us to be mindful of a world struggle between capitalism and communism. Sammy imagines the struggle in terms of the parties thrown by Queenie's parents and those thrown by his own parents. The wealthier set serves "herring snacks on toothpicks off a big glass plate" along with "drinks the color of water with olives and sprigs of mint in them"; Sammy's parents, on the other hand, serve lemonade or "Schlitz in tall glasses with 'They'll Do It Every Time' cartoons stencilled on." (*They'll Do It Every Time* is a comic strip that has been in syndication since 1929.) Rather than put off Sammy, Queenie's social status adds to her allure. Given the symbolism of its geography and its inventory of supermarket goods, the short story takes an even more critical stance toward the American social structure than Sammy does.

Connections to Other Authors and Texts

It is interesting to consider how Updike and Sherwood Anderson pinpoint the spiritual center of American identity in vastly different geographic locations. Like Arthur Miller, Updike explores the troubling underside of the American dream.

Questions for Class Discussion

1. What do supermarkets symbolize in the American cultural landscape? What supermarket details does Updike record in "A & P"? How might these details be understood symbolically?

2. Sammy is nineteen when the incident that he describes takes place. How old is he when he narrates the short story? How can you tell?

3. Does Sammy learn any important life lessons during the short story? What might these be?

Brief Bibliography

Bloom, Harold, ed. *John Updike*. Broomall, PA: Chelsea House, 2001.

Luscher, Robert M. *John Updike: A Study of the Short Fiction*. New York: Twayne, 1993.

Olster, Stacy, ed. *Cambridge Companion to John Updike*. Cambridge: Cambridge UP, 2006.

Saldívar, Toni. "The Art of John Updike's 'A & P.'" *Studies in Short Fiction* 34 (1997): 215-25.

AMIRI BARAKA (LEROI JONES)   (p. 1397)

Approaches to Teaching

In the mid-1960s, Amiri Baraka changed his name, left his white wife for a black woman, and moved from Greenwich Village to Harlem; Baraka's life at this momentous time represents in miniature the black nationalism that would later come to be known as the Black Arts Movement. Clay's memorable invective near the end of *Dutchman* (1964) might be seen as a kind of proto-Black Arts Movement manifesto; the notion that Bessie Smith and Charlie Parker share one message with white fans and another message with black fans, that Clay's "bastard literature" only needs "a simple knife thrust," anticipates important strains of the Black Arts aesthetic: black writing for black readers and the inseparability of art and politics. From its initial performance, audiences and reviewers recognized that Clay's outburst represented the crux of the play, but only with the dawn of the Black Arts Movement did they have a clear framework in which to understand the violent language. For this reason, *Dutchman* is a key text of the movement and a useful way to introduce its aims.

Classroom Issues and Strategies

In 1964, *Dutchman* won the Obie Award, presented by the *Village Voice* to Off-Broadway productions, for Best American Play. (That same year Samuel Beckett's *Play* won the Obie for Best Play.) Baraka's play presents a clear opportunity to address the distinction between a Broadway production and an Off-Broadway production – not just in terms of the obvious geographical distinction, but also in terms of aesthetics. The play's departure from realism in favor of a ritualistic savagery is perhaps its most obvious Off-Broadway feature. The play's cast list, unusual stage directions, and vulgar language are additional textual traces.

Among the list of characters, only Clay and Lula are given names, and they're described specifically in terms of their race, gender, and age. The Riders of Coach are described simply as "white and black"; another character is listed as a Young Negro, with no further details; and the Conductor is described as an "old Negro" at the end of the play. The characters obviously serve as social types whose identity and behavior is strictly limited. They evolve by the play's end into mythic figures; Lula's ritualized murder of Clay, the play implies, will be repeated again and again because the characters are locked into social roles that depend entirely on their race, gender, and age. *Dutchman* is thus an inquiry into the social behavior and identity options available within black manhood and white womanhood – and by extension, the options available to all Americans.

Connections to Other Authors and Texts

Dutchman is preoccupied with the public performance of race, as are Eugene O'Neill's *The Emperor Jones* (p. 000) and Toni Morrison's "Recitatif" (p. 000). *Dutchman* was written at the end of Baraka's association with Beat writers such as Allen Ginsberg. Like Baraka, Gwendolyn Brooks and Audre Lorde were closely identified with the Black Arts

Movement.

Questions for Class Discussion

1. The *Oxford English Dictionary* defines *Off-Broadway* as an adjective "designating a class of theaters in New York City that are smaller than and at a remove from those in the Broadway theater district and typically mount less expensive, often less conventional productions." How does the text of *Dutchman* signal its Off-Broadway origins?

2. If you were the set designer for a production of *Dutchman*, how would you interpret the stage direction that "*[t]he subway [is] heaped in modern myth*"? What would that look like in a practical way?

3. Are there moments in the play when interracial romance might allow Clay and Lula to transcend their differences?

4. What does the play's ending suggest about the future of American race relations?

Brief Bibliography

Rebhord, Matthew. "Flaying Dutchman: Masochism, Minstrelsy, and the Gender Politics of Amiri Baraka's *Dutchman*." *Callaloo* 26 (2003): 796–812.

Watts, Jerry Gafio. *Amiri Baraka: The Politics and Art of a Black Intellectual.* New York: New York UP, 2001.

Woodard, K. Komozi. *A Nation within a Nation: Amiri Baraka (LeRoi Jones) and Black Power Politics.* Chapel Hill: U of North Carolina P, 1999.

AUDRE LORDE   (p. 000)

Approaches to Teaching

In her study of Audre Lorde's work, Cassie Premo Steele makes an astute case that the poet's personal trauma echoes and stands for the pain experienced by African Americans at all points in their history. (Goethe remarked that "true symbolism" can be found "where the particular represents the universal.") Seen in this light, the burden carried by the lyric "I" is indeed great. What is useful to keep in mind is that this lyric "I" always assumes a strategic shape in Lorde's poetry: The first-person-singular pronoun can be found in three of the four poems anthologized here. "I" certainly matters in Lorde's work, but the "I" might be understood as representing unique periods in the poet's life or a difficult to pin down perspective or a wholly fictional persona. Comparing Lorde's first-person poems and coming to terms with her shifting "I" provide multiple paths into the particular and the universal.

Classroom Issues and Strategies

The opening stanza of "Coal" might be understood as emblematic of an important feature of Lorde's work: The emergence of form out of seeming formlessness. The poem begins:

I   is the total black
being spoken
from the earth's inside.

Lorde departs from conventional syntax and line spacing to destabilize fixed meaning. "I" might be understood as a human lyric voice, as the anthropomorphized coal, as a linguistic abstraction (English-language first-person-singular pronoun), or as the ink pressed onto the page in the printing process. Each shifting, contingent interpretation of "I" requires an equally unstable reading of the rest of the sentence. (Thus, "total black / being" might be understood as a geological formation or as a human figure; "being" functions either as the present participle of *be* or as a noun signifying "person" or "essence.") Encourage students to recognize the plasticity of language so that they might appreciate the range of expression to be found in "black lesbian feminist" poetry.

Connections to Other Authors and Texts

Lorde was influenced by and in turn influenced both Adrienne Rich and Gloria Anzaldúa. Their work yields useful nodes of comparison not only because they helped shape a lesbian American literary tradition but also because they strove for an organic relationship between political conviction and literary form.

Questions for Class Discussion

1. Locate a sentence in "Coal" that appears to lack proper punctuation. How does the absence of punctuation allow for multiple interpretations of the sentence?

2. What is the "woman thing" that the poet speaks of in "The Woman Thing"?

3. What sounds autobiographical in "Black Mother Woman"? How much biographical information does the poem divulge?

Brief Bibliography

Burr, Zofia. *Of Women, Poetry, and Power: Strategies of Address in Dickinson, Miles, Brooks, Lorde, and Angelou.* Urbana: U of Illinois P, 2002.

De Veaux, Alexis. *Warrior Poet: A Biography of Audre Lorde*. New York: Norton, 2004.

Steele, Cassie Premo. *We Heal from Memory: Sexton, Lorde, Anzaldu?a, and the Poetry of Witness*. New York: Palgrave, 2000.

DON DELILLO   (p. 000)

Approaches to Teaching

Regularly featured in discussions of literary postmodernism, Don DeLillo has forged a central place in ongoing debates about the function (and even the possibility) of serious literature in contemporary culture. A short story such as "Videotape" (1994) obviously participates in such debates by asserting the hypnotic role of television and by re-creating to the extent possible in fiction the act of watching, over and over again, a short but disturbing video clip. (In so doing, DeLillo highlights the extent to which prose fiction cannot re-create the television-watching experience and the extent to which television falls short of the reading experience.) The short story's narrator reflects on how "[t]here's something about the nature of the tape, the grain of the image, the sputtering black-and-white tones, the starkness – you think this is more real, truer-to-life than anything around you. The things around you have a rehearsed and layered and cosmetic look." Passages such as this one invite discussions of postmodern "hyperreality" along the lines proffered by Jean Baudrillard (most famously in *Simulacra and Simulation* [1994]). But the short story may be more easily approached in terms of literary authenticity and even in terms of realist theory that emerged fully a century before. The narrator's favored word to describe the reality effect of videotape – it is "superreal," he says – might also be considered an Anglicization of the better-known term coined by French modernists, *surrealism*.

Classroom Issues and Strategies

The first order of business when discussing "Videotape" is handling its forceful use of second-person narration. By the end of the short story, the reader ("you") is defined in the following ways: male, U.S. citizen, middle class, married (to Janet), aggressive (toward Janet), and obsessive (about the videotaped murder and about mortality). There are at least two overlapping ways to discuss the short story's use of the second person: in terms of tone and in terms of the implied reader. Both of these issues inform a prominent theme in DeLillo's work that finds its way into "Videotape": a fear of death bordering on paranoia. By the end of the short story, the narrator reflects that the videotaped murder "demonstrates an elemental truth, that every breath you take has two possible endings." The narrator attempts to locate black humor in a morbid (and arguably not at all funny) situation. Here as in much of his work, DeLillo suggests that a paranoid fear of death is symptomatic of a pervasive cultural malady.

Connections to Other Authors and Texts

The tone of "Videotape" resembles in many ways that found in Donald Barthelme's "The School" (p. 000). As in DeLillo's short story, Tim O'Brien's "The Things They Carried" (p. 000) retells on multiple occasions the events surrounding a single death.

Questions for Class Discussion

1. Describe the effect on the reading experience of the narrator's use of the second person ("you").

2. The narrator of "Videotape" argues that the recording's amateurish qualities lend it a "truer-to-life" authenticity. Is it possible for film-makers to re-create fictionally the "superreal" effect described in the short story? If so, how do they accomplish superrealism?

3. How have present-day video-capture technologies altered the mechanics of "chance" video recordings? Has this technological shift also changed the logic of videotape described in the short story?

Brief Bibliography

Bloom, Harold, ed. *Don DeLillo*. Philadelphia: Chelsea House, 2003.

Boxall, Peter. *Don DeLillo: The Possibility of Fiction*. London: Routledge, 2006.

MICHAEL S. HARPER   (p. 000)

Approaches to Teaching

It would seem ill-advised to begin a discussion of Michael S. Harper's poetry without some basic understanding of the folk-music idioms, especially jazz and the blues, on which much of it is founded. Jazz and blues music might be understood in terms of the sound patterns (or impro-visatory patternlessness) that organize the music itself. They might be understood in terms of a range of working-class, African American speech, often taking the shape of dialect, that's infused with an antiestablishment outlook and a predilection for sexual double entendre. And because jazz and blues performers regularly return to a staple of standards – and because no matter how often a standard is played, no two performances will ever sound exactly alike -- the music encodes a cyclic vision of history: In the past lies the future and in the future, the past.

Classroom Issues and Strategies

As important as jazz and blues are to Harper in terms of the poems' forms and themes, individual poems only loosely follow the musical blueprint on which they're based. For instance, "Dear John, Dear Coltrane," for all its improvisatory looseness, exhibits a much tighter structure (visually and rhythmically) than John Coltrane's free-jazz classic *A Love Supreme*. "Martin's Blues," one of a growing number of jazz and blues elegies, departs significantly from the twelve-bar blues format followed more closely by Sterling Brown or Langston Hughes. And "'Bird Lives': Charles Parker in St. Louis," borrows from the vocabulary of jazz aficionados but bears only a passing resemblance to any of the monumental recorded performances listed in the poem.

Connections to Other Authors and Texts

Harper's career was shaped in important ways by his mentors, Sterling Brown and Robert Hayden. Harper's jazz and blues poems also invite comparison with the work of Langston Hughes.

Questions for Class Discussion

1. Three of the four poems anthologized here refer specifically to jazz or blues music. How do the poems approach the musical form on which they are based? How do they depart from the examples of jazz or the blues?

2. Listen to a recording of John Coltrane's *A Love Supreme*. What from Coltrane's performance finds its way into Harper's "Dear John, Dear Coltrane"? What does the poem leave out?

Brief Bibliography

Lenz, Günter H. "Black Poetry and Black Music: History and Tradition: Michael S. Harper and John Coltrane." *History and Tradition in Afro-American Culture*. Ed. Günter H. Lenz. Frankfurt: Campus, 1984. 277-319.

"Michael S. Harper, American Poet: A Special Section." *Callaloo* 13 (1990): 749-829.

Stepto, Robert B. "Michael Harper's Extended Tree: John Coltrane and Sterling Brown." *Twayne Companion to Literature in English*. Eds. R. H. W. Dillard and Amanda Cockrell. New York: Twayne, 2002. 423-37.

RAYMOND CARVER   (p. 000)

Approaches to Teaching

Bill Mullen makes a useful point about the twin traditions, minimalism and social realism, in which Raymond Carver's work is traditionally read: "The appreciation of 'two Carvers,' one prized primarily as a formal innovator, the other as a social-realist, suggests a false but ongoing separation in criticism of form and content." As Mullen goes on to point out, minimalism might be seen as the objective correlative of a gritty, working-class existence, and Carver's application of a subtle narrative art to unglamorous characters and settings is a major accomplishment. Taken individually, the details located in "Are These Actual Miles?" register as indices of a bleak existence; taken as a whole, they advance the projects of both late-nineteenth-century realism and early twentieth-century modernism.

Classroom Issues and Strategies

For Carver, minimalism does not rule out the possibility of fixation on relevant details. The focus of Carver's narrative, the hapless and largely helpless Leo, provides the short story with its spare but memorable features. The third-person narrator seems surprised to learn (but not too surprised) that Leo's hand trembles as he pours yet another glass of Scotch. The narrator records every painful nuance of a telephone conversation between Leo and Toni. The narrator fixates on Toni's makeup before her trip to the used-car lot and on her skin and clothes after her night out with a used-car dealer, all in an effort to confirm the sordid details that are Leo's painful obsession.

Because Leo is a man obsessed, and because he attempts unsuccessfully to drown his thoughts in alcohol, the narrative lurches forward sporadically or grinds to a halt depending on what occupies his mind at a given moment. The narrative's haphazard progression through the difficult night captures the torment of a man falling apart.

Connections to Other Authors and Texts

Carver's minimalism is best understood against a wide range of precursors, from the realism of Frank Norris to the lyricism of Willa Cather. The representation of life's mundane struggles recommends comparison with Abraham Cahan.

Questions for Class Discussion

1. What details about Toni's appearance does the narrator observe in the greatest detail? Why are these important?

2. What does Leo's external appearance reveal about his state of mind?

Brief Bibliography

Bethea, Arthur F. *Technique and Sensibility in the Fiction and Poetry of Raymond Carver.* New York: Routledge, 2001.

Mullen, Bill. "A Subtle Spectacle: Televisual Culture in the Short Stories of Raymond Carver." *Critique* 39 (1998): 99–114.

Stull, William L., and Maureen P. Carroll, eds. *Remembering Ray: A Composite Biography of Raymond Carver.* Santa Barbara: Capra, 1993.

GLORIA ANZALDÚA   (p. ooo)

Approaches to Teaching

Gloria Anzaldúa's notion of a cultural borderlands reaches far and wide, and her influence extends equally across the landscape of American poetry and American critical theory. Central to Anzaldúa's theory and practice is the concept of *mestizaje,* which the *Oxford English Dictionary* defines as "[i]nterbreeding and cultural intermixing of Spanish and American Indian people (originally in Mexico, and subsequently also in other parts of Latin America); miscegenation, racial and cultural intermixing; (also) an instance of this." It is thus possible to connect Anzaldúa's project with a long tradition of "mulatto" prose and poetry and with postmodern concerns with the fragmentation and reassembly of language and individual identity.

Classroom Issues and Strategies

Beginning with its title, a transliteration of "son of a bitch," "El sonavabitche" records intense anger born of almost unspeakable indignity and injustice. Students might recoil from the poem's harsh tone; even if they do, they might be asked to specify what in Anzaldúa's choices of words and imagery creates the poem's tone. By describing (for example) farmworkers in terms of "that wide cavernous look of the hunted / the look of hares," the poet gives metaphorical shape and a literal voice to the voiceless. More than that, though, the poem, twelve years after the fact, dramatizes a vivid and conflicted moment in an Indiana migrant-labor camp. It gives poetic shape to events that twelve years before inspired righteous indignation and a demand for justice.

Connections to Other Authors and Texts

Like Adrienne Rich and Audre Lorde, Anzaldúa is known for writing poetry and prose that fuses the personal and the political.

Questions for Class Discussion

1. What do we know about the voice of the poem? What do we know about the title character (*el sonavabitche*)? How does the poem introduce the character details to us?

2. Explain the logic guiding individual line and stanza breaks. What is the rhetorical effect of the poem's shape?

Brief Bibliography

Keating, AnaLouise, ed. Entre mundos/*Among Worlds: New Perspectives on Gloria E. Anzaldúa*. New York: Palgrave Macmillan, 2005.

Steele, Cassie Premo. *We Heal from Memory: Sexton, Lorde, Anzaldu?a, and the Poetry of Witness*. New York: Palgrave, 2000.

ALICE WALKER   (p. 000)

Approaches to Teaching

Alice Walker's "Everyday Use" (1973) elicits simple questions that might serve as an intriguing introduction to key issues embedded in the short story: If your mother narrated a short story about you, what would she say? More important, how would she say it? What would both (the what and the how) reveal about your mother? Much of the short story's charm and bitter sweetness stems from the singular voice that serves as its narrator. Mama describes her physical appearance very quickly: "I am a large, big-boned woman with rough, man-working hands." But her emotional state, her ambivalence toward her daughter Wangero and her fierce loyalty to her daughter Maggie emerge in much more subtle ways. Although Mama does not explicitly voice her feelings, readers know how she feels—and by extension how readers feel—about the two young women.

Classroom Issues and Strategies

Spaces in "Everyday Use" take on a symbolic importance both in terms of their traditional architectural symbolism (for instance, the front yard is often considered "an extended living room," as Mama describes it) and in terms of their artistic refashioning (Mama and Maggie make the yard "clean and wavy"). The implements of everyday life take on an even more important symbolism in the short story: Different characters value the dining-room benches, the butter churn, the dasher, and the quilts for different properties, either functional or aesthetic or both. How these items are viewed provides not only the short story's title but also an ethical yardstick against which to measure each character.

"Everyday Use" explores a deep generational divide born of the Black Arts Movement of the 1960s. This divide can be measured culturally, in terms of the touchstones (such as the quilts) that fill the family home, and linguistically, in terms of names that assume significance because of their family history (such as "Dee") or their Afrocentrism (such as "Wangero"). Walker even manages some humor when Mama mistakenly assumes that "Asalamalakim" is a proper name.

Connections to Other Authors and Texts

Walker publicly acknowledged the influence of Zora Neale Hurston and Nella Larsen on her writing and career, but her interest in African American life in the rural South was shared with a much larger group of writers.

Questions for Class Discussion

1. What objects do Mama and Wangero (Dee) identify as important in their cultural and family heritage? In what ways are these things important to each character?

2. List the possible reasons that Dee changes her name to Wangero Leewanika Kemanjo. What does the name change reveal about the character?

3. Does the narrator learn a significant life lesson during the course of the short story? Does Maggie or Wangero (Dee)?

Brief Bibliography

Dieke, Ikenna, ed. *Critical Essays on Alice Walker*. Westport, CT: Greenwood, 1999.

Gates, Henry Louis, Jr. and K. A. Appiah, eds. *Alice Walker: Critical Perspectives Past and Present*. New York: Amistad, 1993.

Noe, Marcia. "Teaching Alice Walker's 'Everyday Use': Employing Race, Class, and Gender, with an Annotated Bibliography." *Eureka Studies in Teaching Short Fiction* 5 (2004): 123-36.

White, Evelyn C. *Alice Walker: A Life*. New York: Norton, 2004.

TIM O'BRIEN   (p. 000)

Approaches to Teaching

For many college and even high school teachers, the Vietnam War served as a defining moment on the path from youth to adulthood, from innocence to experience. For most college and presumably all high school students, the Vietnam War is the stuff of history textbooks; it can be found just after World War II and the Korean War, and well before the wars in Iraq. Even so, the place name *Vietnam* conjures a discrete list of associations, mostly negative, and many strictly about U.S. history and culture rather than Vietnamese history and culture. Discussing our culture's use of "Vietnam" as a touchstone is a constructive way to consider how "The Things They Carried" makes the actual place vivid in our imaginations once again and how the short story bears the burden of American cultural history. ("The Things They Carried" first appeared in 1986, eight years after *The Deer Hunter* and four years after *First Blood* gave American cinema two unforgettable versions of the war and its toll on the human psyche.) The short story, like all Vietnam War fiction and film, faced the daunting tasks of representing the "reality" of the experience on the ground and speaking to an American public that rendered experience secondary to political and cultural concerns.

Classroom Issues and Strategies

The short story's narrator deserves some attention, particularly when considered in the context of *The Things They Carried* (1990), the collection in which the work appeared alongside additional Vietnam War fiction. (The short-story cycle's narrator is identified as "Tim O'Brien," not to be confused with the author necessarily, but certainly closely connected with him.) The narrative of "The Things They Carried" is focused externally around the character Jimmy Cross, but on occasion readers are allowed glimpses of his hidden thoughts and emotions.

The brilliance of the short story is its use of lists to achieve multiple, overlapping, and sometimes conflicting effects. The listing of items exposes the mundanity and mendacity of the war and it records the eccentricity or humanity of individuals caught up in the war. Because they are used and reused so often and in different ways, specific items achieve a distinct significance depending on the context. Similarly, the words *things* and *carry/carried* in particular achieve an elasticity of meaning by the end of the short story; the words are asked to perform heavy lifting (so to speak) and their ability to signify greatly increases over time.

Connections to Other Authors and Texts

O'Brien defamiliarizes and deromanticizes war, much as Mark Twain and Ambrose Bierce did a century earlier. It is worth considering "The Things They Carried" a meditation on war trauma and its lingering aftereffects, thus connecting the short story with Ernest Hemingway's "Big Two-Hearted River" (p. 000).

Questions for Class Discussion

1. In general, how does the listing of "things" set the tone for the narrative?

2. Examine any one list in the short story. What does this list say about the individual to whom it applies? Does the order in which items appear follow a particular logic?

3. Jimmy Cross's name implies that his character should be understood as a Christ figure. Is this a fitting interpretation of the character? Why or why not?

4. Compile a list of words from the short story that appear to be army slang. Which of these words' meanings is clear from the context? How does the context reveal a word's meaning?

5. If you were a soldier in Lieutenant Jimmy Cross's unit, what would you carry? Why?

Brief Bibliography

Bloom, Harold, ed. *Tim O'Brien's* The Things They Carried. Philadelphia: Chelsea House, 2005.

Herzog, Tobey C. *Tim O'Brien.* New York: Twayne, 1997.

Smith, Patrick A. *Tim O'Brien: A Critical Companion.* Westport, CT: Greenwood, 2005.

LESLIE MARMON SILKO   (p. 000)

Approaches to Teaching

The earliest discussions of literary postmodernism tended to focus on writers who were fully ensconced within the European and American cultural mainstream but before long theories of postmodern literature were forced to contend with postcolonial voices and voices from the cultural margins of Europe and the United States. One such voice was that of Leslie Marmon

Silko, whose self-professed multicultural background and innovative approach to representation interrogate the easy divisions ("low"/"high"; tradition/innovation; written/oral; fantasy/reality; nature/civilization) that postmodernism was said to muddle. "Yellow Woman" (1974), written and published just as literary postmodernism and literary multicultural-ism were gaining traction in the U.S. academy, raises important questions: Which is more "traditional," the short story's borrowing from orally trans-mitted folklore or its exploitation of modernist narrative conventions? How ironic or earnest is the narrator's identification with the Yellow Woman myth? Can we reconcile the concerns of postmodernism with multicultur-alism's interest in affirming identity?

Classroom Issues and Strategies

Most students will be unfamiliar with the Yellow Woman myth of the Pueblo peoples, and Silko's short story may not be the most reliable source for those interested in pursuing study of the figure. According to Silko scholar Louise Barnett, "Yellow Woman in old Pueblo tales is both heroic and sexual, that is, she protects the Pueblos with her heroism and also with her uninhibited sexuality, which affirms the life force of nature. . . . The Yellow Women tales, which generally have these two components, are female fantasies in which the wider sphere of male activity and the admired qualities related to it are appropriated by the woman and her desire for sexual freedom given voice." As Barnett later adds, the "Yellow Woman" narrative realizes the Yellow Woman legend only incompletely; the character seems to lack the heroic power and self-determination required of the mythical figure. Silko's storytelling calls into question the possibility of mythical identity not just in the modern world, but at any moment in time: "I was wondering if Yellow Woman had known who she was — if she knew that she would become part of the stories."

Connections to Other Authors and Texts

Like Zora Neale Hurston, Silko updates oral tales in modern literary forms. A comparison of "Yellow Woman" with the work of Sarah Winnemucca Hopkins and Sherman Alexie reveals the rich diversity of American Indian narrative.

Questions for Class Discussion

1. The narrator describes how she listened to Yellow Woman stories told by her grandfather. Imagine the conditions in which such storytelling might occur. How are the conditions similar to your own encounter with the legend in reading the short story? How are the conditions different?

2. Is the Yellow Woman a sympathetic figure? Is Silva? Why or why not?

3. Identify those passages that represent modern "reality" and those that represent timeless "legend." How do you know the difference? Do the two modes of representation ever overlap?

Brief Bibliography

Barnett, Louise. "Yellow Woman and Leslie Marmon Silko's Feminism." *Studies in American Indian Literatures* 17 (2005): 18-31.

Barnett, Louise K., and James L. Thorson, eds. *Leslie Marmon Silko: A Collection of Critical Essays.* Albuquerque: U of New Mexico P, 1999.

Jaskoski, Helen. *Leslie Marmon Silko: A Study of the Short Fiction.* New York: Twayne, 1988.

JOY HARJO   (p. 000)

Approaches to Teaching

Because most of the poets anthologized in *The Bedford Anthology of American Literature* are no longer with us, we can only historically reconstruct their careers. In sharp contrast, Joy Harjo, in her regularly updated Web site (www.joyharjo.com), gives us a unique glimpse into an active and lively poetic career. The Web site is useful because it provides a sense of how a contemporary poet's life revolves around public readings, teaching, and (especially in Harjo's case) multimedia merchandising. In addition, the Web site reveals that Harjo's poetic concerns – such as American Indian history and the transformation of environmental awareness – animate the whole of her career.

Classroom Issues and Strategies

An irony of Harjo's poetry, of all truly committed ecocritical writing, is that it decenters human consciousness and identity in the medium most often connected with humanity: language. Poems such as "If You Look with the Mind of the Swirling Earth" and "This Land Is a Poem" quite obviously call attention to the paradox of writing about the submersion of human identity into the natural landscape. (She pointedly asks, "does anything written ever matter to the earth, wind, and sky?") But the other poems located here similarly measure human civilization and human history against the much vaster reaches of earth geography and earth history. It is possible to address Harjo's ecocritical stance in terms of her Creek identity, but the poetry speaks not just to her fellow Creeks but to us all.

Connections to Other Authors and Texts

Like Marianne Moore, Harjo incorporates footnotes that are central to a poem's literal meaning and to its tone. Gary Snyder is another poet who is important to the contemporary environmental movement.

Questions for Class Discussion

1. In any Harjo poem, identify the traces of civilization and the traces of the natural landscape that she records. Where do humans fit into the setting that she describes; that is, how do humans relate to civilization or to the natural landscape?

2. What do Harjo's footnotes add to her poems? Would the poems be the same without the notes?

Brief Bibliography

Bryson, J. Scott. *The West Side of Any Mountain: Place, Space, and Ecopoetry.* Iowa City: U of Iowa P, 2005.

Coltelli, Laura. "Joy Harjo's Poetry." *The Cambridge Companion to Native American Literature.* Eds. Joy Porter and Kenneth M. Roemer. Cambridge: Cambridge UP, 2005. 283-95.

RITA DOVE   (p. 000)

Approaches to Teaching

When the librarian of Congress appointed Rita Dove the seventh U.S. poet laureate, he described her as a poet of "distinction and versatility," a "representative of a new and richly variegated generation of American poets." It is worth considering what raises a poet to the stature required for appointment to the position, especially at Dove's remarkably young age (forty-one) when she received the honor. Four of the five poems collected here were written before she served as poet laureate, and so the discussion might progress from the abstract to the particular, from the post to the poetry. These examples certainly testify to Dove's versatility: her formal range (everything from the sonnet to the prose poem), her geographic range (from Deep South to New England), and her temporal range (from the distant past to the timeless present). It is worth pointing out that Dove is also an accomplished fiction writer, dramatist, teacher, and singer – a modern-day renaissance woman.

Classroom Issues and Strategies

Dove's work helps to remind students that each poem requires individual consideration based on the internal logic unique to its form. For example, the three-line stanzas of "The House Slave," not quite terza rima but close at times, represent one kind of formal logic. In contrast, the prose poem "Kentucky, 1833" represents another kind of formal logic that's consistent with a wholly different lyric voice. "History," a sonnet, follows its own unique pattern and thus represents a third formal logic. The connection between form and idea emerges naturally, perhaps inevitably, from an analysis of Dove's work; finding common threads, thematically or otherwise, is a more difficult proposition. Small groups of students might be asked to consider the formal logic of individual poems; the entire class might then reconvene to address the larger issues that emerge from the study of Dove's poetry.

Connections to Other Authors and Texts

Dove is the youngest of the many U.S. poets laureate (or consultant in poetry to the Library of Congress as the post was known before 1986) collected in the anthology: Robert Lowell, Elizabeth Bishop, William Carlos Williams, Robert Frost, Robert Hayden, and Gwendolyn Brooks. It is worth considering what, if anything, the poets share in common.

Questions for Class Discussion

1. In "David Walker (1785-1830)," describe the relationship between the voice of the poet and the passages excerpted from Walker's *Appeal.* What prompts the poet to quote from Walker? Does she integrate his words seamlessly, or is there some dissonance between the two voices?

2. Compare the lyric voices found in "The House Slave" and "Kentucky, 1833." Why does each poem take the shape that it does?

3. What does Dove celebrate about Billie Holiday in "Canary"? What does she mourn?

Brief Bibliography

Pereira, Malin. *Rita Dove's Cosmopolitanism.* Urbana: U of Illinois P, 2003.

Righelato, Pat. *Understanding Rita Dove.* Columbia: U of South Carolina P, 2006.

SANDRA CISNEROS   (p. 000)

Approaches to Teaching

Much of Sandra Cisneros's fiction, including "Mericans" (1991), is narrated by or filtered through the consciousness of an observant young girl. The effect is sometimes disarming and cute, sometimes jarring and perverse. This particular short story is narrated by Micaela, a young girl who is more interested in candy and games with her brothers than in recording the intricacies of worship in a Mexican church or the idiosyncrasies of her extended family – and yet she records both. She is precociously attentive to the details that surround her and fill her life with a meaning that she doesn't yet fully appreciate; one might make the case that she is a literary artist in the making. And like Micaela, the American reading public may not in the past have appreciated her gift for observation nor the details that she records, but the reading public of the present has made the adult Cisneros a vital part of the American literary mainstream.

Classroom Issues and Strategies

Although Micaela admits to understanding Spanish only when she pays attention, Cisneros's prose moves effortlessly between a colloquial and for-mal English and Spanish. Even without the explanatory notes, most of the Spanish phrases can be deciphered by non-Spanish speakers thanks to the context in which they appear: "'¿Quieres chicle?' the lady asks in a Spanish too big for her mouth," Micaela reports at one point, followed by a description of how the woman gives Micaela's brother a handful of chewing gum (*chicle*). Elsewhere, Cisneros transliterates idiomatic Spanish into strik-ingly unusual English: For example, "awful grandmother" is the English equivalent of the melodious Spanish phrase *abuela tremenda* and "Auntie Light-skin" is the equivalent of the Spanish nickname *tía güera* that she's probably known by. In other words, Micaela's status as an English-speak-ing Latina in Mexico expands the English language even as she introduces readers to a "foreign" experience.

Connections to Other Authors and Texts

Cisneros offers a vastly different portrait of the American in Mexico than the one drawn by Katherine Anne Porter. Like Gloria Anzaldúa, Cisneros routinely crosses literal and linguistic borders in her work.

Questions for Class Discussion

1. What do we know about the narrator? How old is she? What details reveal her age? Is she rich or poor or in-between? What details reveal

her ethnic identity? Does she learn a significant life lesson as the short story evolves?

2. What does it mean to be "Merican" in the context of the short story? Is this the same thing as being "American"? Why or why not?

Brief Bibliography

Doyle, Jacqueline. "Faces of the Virgin in Sandra Cisneros's *Woman Hollering Creek.*" *Things of the Spirit: Women Writers Constructing Spirituality.* Ed. Kristina K. Groover. Notre Dame: U of Notre Dame P, 2004. 256–83.

Mirriam-Goldberg, Caryn. *Sandra Cisneros: Latina Writer and Activist.* Springfield, NJ: Enslow, 1998.

MARTÍN ESPADA   (p. 000)

Approaches to Teaching

Several years after the tragic events of September 11, 2001, we are still awash in controversy over what is and isn't appropriate in efforts to memorialize those who lost their lives that day in New York, Pennsylvania, and Washington, D.C. The issue is too important to our culture not to bring up, and there is no shortage of concrete examples in film and television, in architecture and urban design, and in literary expression. Martín Espada's "Alabanza: In Praise of Local 100" (2003) was instantly recognized as a classic expression of profound grief and international unity; not only is it the most important poem to commemorate September 11th, it also may be the single greatest elegy of the twenty-first century thus far.

Classroom Issues and Strategies

Much as we see in the poetry of Walt Whitman, "Alabanza: In Praise of Local 100" elevates the humdrum routine of working-class characters to heroic status. The poem's use of hortatory religious language ("*Alabanza,*" "Praise") in connection with those who normally remain hidden in plain sight (cooks, busboys, dishwashers) allows their lives to represent a host of meanings: the American dream, ethnic pride, and human joy. The poem's iterative form and incantatory list of details illustrate the magic of language.

All of Espada's poetry synthesizes language (primarily English with some Spanish) and cultural references to craft a vision of Pan-American identity. Perhaps Espada's greatest gift to American culture is an awareness that our greatest strength, culturally and politically, is our diversity.

Connections to Other Authors and Texts

Allen Ginsberg was one of Espada's early literary heroes. A century before Espada, José Martí advanced a Pan-American political and cultural vision. Espada, along with Gloria Anzaldúa and Sandra Cisneros, refreshes the English language with a strategic dose of multilingualism and translingualism.

Questions for Class Discussion

1. According to "Bully," what is Theodore Roosevelt's vision for American society and culture? How does the poem resist Roosevelt's vision?
2. What is appropriate or inappropriate in reference to September 11, 2001? What does "Alabanza: In Praise of Local 100" add to our culture's depiction of events on that momentous day?

Brief Bibliography

Salgado, César A. "About Martín Espada." *Ploughshares* 31.1 (2005): 203-8.

———. "Martín Espada (1957-)." *Latino and Latina Writers.* Eds. Alan West-Durán et al. New York: Scribners, 2004. 851-72.

SHERMAN ALEXIE   (p. 1502)

Approaches to Teaching

Sherman Alexie's shining multimedia career is emblematic of a profound shift in our literary culture, which today makes ample room for a self-described "kid from the rez" and the notion that a down-and-out, homeless, alcoholic Spokane Indian might serve as a short story's narrator. That such a narrator might offer a measure of wisdom and even profundity – all without a whiff of irony – further illustrates how far American literature has come by the twenty-first century. A discussion of "What You Pawn I Will Redeem" (2003) allows for a review of key issues in twentieth- and twenty-first-century American literature: the emergence of working-class and ethnic individuals as central characters and narrators; the romanticization of socially marginalized figures; and a foregrounding of the link between subjective consciousness and narrative form. But the short story should also be considered in terms of what is wholly new about it, including its role in redefining what counts as "American" and what counts as "literature."

Classroom Issues and Strategies

Jackson Jackson, the short story's narrator, acknowledges that he is on a quest, and his challenge, as a man and as a narrator, is to live up to the audacity of that idea, to elevate his actions and his language in an appropriate manner. At times he takes refuge in euphemism; for instance, he describes three bottles of cheap liquor as "three bottles of imagination." More important, though, Jackson represents his actions as a race against the clock; time is the figurative dragon that he must slay.

Just as Jackson foregrounds the quest motif, so too does he highlight the cultural stereotypes with which American Indians have been saddled for centuries. Rather than dismiss the stereotypes outright, however, the short story reveals that beneath living examples of racist stereotypes — Indians as convenience-store drunks, Indians as impetuous risk takers — exist multifaceted characters with complex thoughts and noble aspirations. The short story's plot rewards Jackson not because of who he appears to be but because of who he is at the core of his being.

Connections to Other Authors and Texts

As we see in Alexie's short story, John Dos Passos's "Vag" makes a down-and-out character the central figure of the narrative. Leslie Marmon Silko and N. Scott Momaday are important precursors in American Indian prose writing.

Questions for Class Discussion

1. What is the rhetorical effect of dividing the narrative according to specific times of the day and night?

2. At several early points in the short story, the narrator, Jackson Jackson, directly addresses the reader ("you"). What is his attitude toward the reader? What does he assume to be the reader's attitude toward him?

3. How does Alexie complicate stereotypical notions about American Indians?

Brief Bibliography

Grassian, Daniel. *Understanding Sherman Alexie*. Columbia: U of South Carolina P, 2005.

Moore, David L. "Sherman Alexie: Irony, Intimacy, and Agency." *The Cambridge Companion to Native American Literature*. Eds. Joy Porter and Kenneth M. Roemer. Cambridge: Cambridge UP, 2005. 297-310.

AMERICAN CONTEXTS: "Inventing the Truth":
The Contemporary Memoir   (p. 1521)

In early 2006, James Frey's *A Million Little Pieces* (2003), billed by its author
and publisher as a memoir, was revealed to contain numerous fictional elements. (The Library of Congress catalog contains a publisher's description
declaring the book "an uncommonly genuine account of a life destroyed
and a life reconstructed." *A Million Little Pieces* is still cataloged under the
Library of Congress subject heading, "Drug addicts – Minnesota –
Biography.") The ensuing firestorm involved everyone from Frey, who publicly apologized for the deception, to Oprah Winfrey, who withdrew her
lucrative book club endorsement of the title. (Oprah's endorsement had previously sent the book to the top of the best-seller list.) The well-publicized
episode marks not only a rare moment when literary history and celebrity-
TV culture converge but also an important index of the magnitude of the literary memoir in contemporary cultural life. As the editors point out in their
introduction to this cluster of readings, the memoir as distinct from the
autobiography has reached unprecedented levels of appeal and importance.

This unit might serve multiple roles in a syllabus, each depending on
the particular emphases of a course. The memoirs might be considered
late-twentieth-century versions of the autobiographical tradition, a positioning that rewards reflection on the distinction between *autobiography*
and *memoir* discussed by the editors' introduction to the material. The
memoirs might also be considered alongside post–World War II poetry as a
version of postmodern confession, one that dismisses conventional
notions of "truth" (as factual, reality-based, prosaic) in favor of the multiple
and contingent "truths" to be gleaned from the play of language.

Questions for Class Discussion

1. How would an external observer (a third-person narrator) portray the
   moments recorded in any of the memoirs collected here?

2. Although the details of each life described in these memoirs are
   unique, what are some of the universal themes that the writers address
   in common?

3. Think about an ordinary moment in your life that you recall in extraordinary detail. Why is this moment etched in your memory? What lesson lies embedded in the moment?

Sample Syllabus 3: Historical Survey Course

INTRODUCTION TO AMERICAN LITERATURE: FROM 1865 TO THE PRESENT
(15-WEEK COURSE, ADAPTABLE TO A 12-WEEK COURSE)

NOTE TO INSTRUCTORS: *According to instructors, the chronological historical survey is the most commonly taught course in American literature. The challenges of this course include the decision about how much material to cover and how much students will be able to read and absorb. We have provided a sample syllabus below that includes most of the options in The Bedford Anthology of American Literature. Naturally, instructors will want to alter the length and number of readings and, of course, omit writers and works, according to their own priorities and interests. Instructors may also wish alter the chronological ordering of writers in The Bedford Anthology of American Literature and group writers according to thematic preferences, such as "Realism and Naturalism," "Regionalism," "The Harlem Renaissance," "American Drama," "Modernist Poetry," and/or "Postmodern Fiction." Finally instructors will want to decide how much time they wish to devote to contemporary authors and works. Most instructors do not choose to include all of the works in the anthology on a course syllabus, but in the sample writing and group assignments following the sample calendar, we have indicated ways in which instructors might use writers and texts as the basis for other assignments in the course.*

Course Description

This course is a chronological survey of American literature that begins with the literature of realism and naturalism written after 1865 and concludes with a sampler of the contemporary memoir. The intention is to provide a broad overview of what constitutes American literature from the Civil War to the present. We will read and study works of poetry, fiction, and nonfiction prose, including autobiography, by a range of writers, men and women of diverse backgrounds and interests. Our object will be to study some of the many voices that constitute what we call American literature, addressing questions such as: How do the gender, race, and class of writers and readers affect the creation and reception of a literary text? What constitutes a literary canon? What does *American* mean? What role has literature played in the ongoing story of culture and history of the United States? How are the broad cultural movements of realism, naturalism, modernism, and postmodernism reflected in literary works and how do those movements shape the writing and reception of literature? What is the place of literature in the United States in the twenty-first century?

Required Texts

The Bedford Anthology of American Literature, Volume Two

NOTE TO INSTRUCTORS: *Instructors who wish to use one of the Bedford College Editions designed for the second half of the American literature survey,* Adventures of Huckleberry Finn *or* The Awakening, *might substitute one or both of these texts for other works given on the syllabus below.*

Calendar

NOTE TO INSTRUCTORS: *More writers and texts are included here for each week than most instructors would wish to include. The selections given here are merely examples. Many instructors choose to incorporate works not covered on the syllabus in writing or group assignments, given below. Further, many instructors may choose to include thematic units within the chronological divisions.*

American Literature, 1865-1914

WEEK 1:   Realism, Regionalism, and Naturalism; American Contexts: "The America of the Mind": Critics, Writers, and the Representation of Reality; Twain, Howells, Bierce

WEEK 2:   James, Jewett, Chopin, Chesnutt

WEEK 3:   Hopkins, Gilman, Cahan, Wharton, Sui Sin Far, Austin

WEEK 4:   Norris, Crane, Dreiser, Dunbar, Cather; Writing "American" Lives

American Literature, 1914-1945

WEEK 5:   Modernisms in American Poetry; American Contexts: 'Make it New': Poets on Poetry; J. W. Johnson, Lowell, Frost, G. D. Johnson, Sandburg

WEEK 6:   Stevens, Loy, Williams, Pound, H.D., Moore, Fujita

WEEK 7:   Eliot, McKay, Millay, Cummings, Crane, Brown, Hughes, Cullen

WEEK 8:   The Emergence of American Drama; O'Neill and Glaspell

WEEK 9:   At Home and Abroad: American Fiction between the Wars; Ameri-can Contexts: From the Great War to the Great Depression: American Writers and the Challenges of Modernity; Stein, Anderson, Porter, Hurston

WEEK 10: Larsen, Mena, Toomer, Fitzgerald, Dos Passos, Faulkner

WEEK 11: Hemingway, Steinbeck, Wright, Welty, Bulosan

American Literature since 1945

WEEK 12: From Modernism to Postmodernism; Roethke, Bishop, Williams, Hayden, Olsen, Ellison

WEEK 13: Miller, Lowell, Brooks, Yamamoto

WEEK 14: O'Connor, Ginsberg, Rich, Morrison, Plath, Baraka

WEEK 15: Anzaldúa, Walker, O'Brien, Alexie; American Contexts: "Inventing the Truth": The Contemporary Memoir

Course Requirements

NOTE TO INSTRUCTORS: *The requirements listed below are examples of a variety of activities for use in courses and may be readily adapted to particular institutional contexts:*

Periodic Response Papers, Quizzes, and Class Participation

Several times during the semester, students will write brief responses in class to questions about topics in the course or a response to a short reading quiz of several questions. These will be unannounced. All students are expected to come to class meetings prepared to discuss reading assignments and to interact with members of the class. Learning how to speak on one's feet is an important aspect of education, and students will be asked to give opinions, respond to questions, and make assessments of what they are reading and learning.

Writing Assignment(s)

NOTE TO INSTRUCTORS: *The following assignments could be adapted for use in courses requiring either one or multiple writing assignments. As noted in the sample calendar section, we have emphasized using works that instructors have not included on their course syllabus so that students have easy access to other texts and can expand their understanding of American literature through additional reading and study.*

Example Assignment for Using Only Works Not Included on the Syllabus

1. Choose a work (or selection of poems) from the Anthology that is NOT on the syllabus for this course. Read the selections carefully and write an essay in which you argue for the inclusion of this work on a syllabus that surveys American literature. Some questions to consider are: What is the nature of the work? What strikes you as important about this work? This writer? How is the work different or similar to others we have read? How would this work relate to others we have read in the class?

Example Assignment for Using "American Contexts" (One Not Included on the Syllabus)

2. Using the cluster of texts in "American Contexts: From the Great War to the Great Depression: American Writers and the Challenges of Modernity," write an essay in which you explore the topics and themes of one or two of the works in this collection. What are some of the similarities in these writings? The differences? What conclusions can you draw about the emerging notion of modernism in these texts? How do the ideas in these works connect to writers we have read?

Example Assignments for Comparative Essays

3. A number of writers on the syllabus take up the notion of "American" and what that means. Compare and contrast the idea of "American" in the works of Mary Antin, Henry Adams, W. E. B. Du Bois, and/or Zitkala-Ša.

4. Ezra Pound called on writers to "make it new" in the years following World War I, and a host of writers sought to do just that. These writers, generally called modernists, ushered in innovations in poetry and prose. Consider two writers from this period and discuss how their works differ one of the writers in the section, American Literature, 1865-1914.

5. Several writers in this course are often considered a part of a literary movement known as the Harlem Renaissance, often regarded as the most influential movement in African American literary history. The writers include Georgia Douglas Johnson, Claude McKay, Sterling Brown, Langston Hughes, Countee Cullen, Zora Neale Hurston, Nella Larsen, and Jean Toomer. Choose two or three of these writers and compare and contrast their thematic concerns and stylistic innovations, especially their use of language or dialect.

6. Using the definition of "postmodernism" that the editors provide in the introduction (pp. 1067-1078), choose two fiction writers, such as Don DeLillo, Ursula K. Le Guin, Donald Barthelme, Toni Morrison, Tim O'Brien, or Sherman Alexie, and discuss what makes these writers' works "postmodern."

7. One of the hallmarks of contemporary literature is the ethnic and racial diversity of writers in the United States today. Many scholars feel that writers such as Toni Morrison, Sandra Cisneros, Sherman Alexie, Leslie Marmon Silko, Martín Espada, and Hisaye Yamamoto have profoundly altered the idea of what constitutes an American literature. Choose two of these writers and compare and contrast the ways in which they have redefined "American" literature.

Example Assignment for Using a Longer Literary Work in Comparison with Others

8. In *Death of a Salesman*, Arthur Miller takes up a number of issues treated by many writers in the post-war era: the idea of the "American dream," the effects of new technologies, consumerism, and the place of the individual in an urban, industrialized society. Read works that are not included on the syllabus from this period and choose one (examples might include Saul Bellow's "Looking for Mr. Green" or Alice Walker's "Everyday Use" if they are not on the instructor's course syllabus) and consider how writers treat one or more of these issues similarly and differently.

Group Presentation

INTRODUCTION TO A WRITER, WORK, OR GROUP OF WORKS

Each student will be assigned to a small group to work on a twenty-minute introductory presentation on one of the authors and his or her works in *The Bedford Anthology of American Literature*. In addition to the historical, social, or cultural context, groups are encouraged to consider a variety of topics concerning the work(s), for example, initial reception and / or controversies generated. Groups should also connect the work of this writer or group of texts to others studied in the course. Multimedia presentations are strongly encouraged — our classroom is fully equipped to handle various kinds of presentations. The first task of each group will be to select a chairperson, who will be responsible for coordinating the group's activities and for communicating with me. The second task will be to read the work well in advance and to decide on the major topic(s) of the presentation, in consultation with the instructor. Groups will be responsible for notifying the class in advance about any additional works we are to read (and how to find them), making the presentation, and leading a discussion based on questions that the group will distribute to the class.

Midterm Exam

Comprehensive Final Exam

Index of Authors

All page numbers in boldface indicate the main discussions of the authors.